Satisfied *Do What You Are* readers respond:

•

"*Do What You Are* is the *best* career-help book that is on the market today! I have read quite a few books on choosing a career, but yours is the most helpful."

—Kathy Hance, Deaver, Wyoming

•

"*Do What You Are* is a marvelous book. I not only found appealing career suggestions but was able to put my finger on characteristics that would be necessary for a job to make me happy. Thank you. Thank you. Thank you."

—Serena Mitchell, Don Mills, Ontario

•

"*Do What You Are* is very useful and has provided me with some new insights into myself and what I should be doing. I would highly recommend your book to anyone wondering, 'What do I want to be when I grow up.'"

—Kathy Hence, Groveland, California

•

"This book has changed my life! *Do What You Are* helped me find a whole new career in the personnel and recruiting field. And not only did it help me make a great career change, but now I use it daily to help other people find work that lets them 'do what they are.' Thanks!"

—Gary Gardner, President,
M&M Personnel and Pro Placement, Cleveland, Ohio

•

"*Do What You Are* has unlocked a door to which I wasn't sure I would ever find the key. It is the last (and perhaps most important) piece of a puzzle that I need to complete to find career happiness."

—Don Ghostlaw, Windsor, Connecticut

•

"In reading *Do What You Are* I found tremendous satisfaction and insights."

—Susan Nickbarg, Madison, New Jersey

•

"Your book helps people use Type effectively in making career choices and conducting job searches. The information is presented in a very positive, empowering way so that people can be proud of their strengths and think of creative ways to deal with possible pitfalls. Thank you for this excellent book."

—Frieda Flint, The Private Industry Council,
Portland, Oregon

•

"*Do What You Are* is an invaluable tool for anyone seriously interested in exploring career options. I have recommended it to many friends and coworkers. My copy is dog-eared from multiple readings."

—Paul Faulkner, Windsor Locks, Connecticut

Do What
You Are

Other Books by Paul D. Tieger and Barbara Barron

Nurture by Nature
The Art of SpeedReading People
Just Your Type

Do What You Are

Fifth Edition

Discover the Perfect Career for You Through the Secrets of Personality Type

Paul D. Tieger, Barbara Barron, and Kelly Tieger

Little, Brown and Company

New York   Boston   London

Little, Brown and Company
Hachette Book Group
1290 Avenue of the Americas, New York, NY 10104
littlebrown.com

Fifth Edition: April 2014

Little, Brown and Company is a division of Hachette Book Group, Inc.
The Little, Brown name and logo are trademarks of Hachette Book Group, Inc.

The publisher is not responsible for websites (or their content) that are not owned by the publisher.

ISBN 978-0-316-23673-7 (5th ed.)
Library of Congress Control Number 2014930598

10 9 8 7 6 5

RRD-C

Printed in the United States of America

Dedicated to Herb, Evelyn, Richard, and Helen

Contents

❙ Read This First

How This Book Will Change Your Life

Since its first publication in 1992, *Do What You Are* has helped over a million people find satisfying careers and conduct more successful job searches. We've heard from hundreds of people who report that by helping them discover the kind of work they were meant to do, *Do What You Are* forever changed their lives and made them feel more productive, more appreciated, and more satisfied.

In the seven years since the fourth edition of *Do What You Are* was released, the world has changed in profound and myriad ways. We experienced the Great Recession, and its historic impact continues to be felt in almost every aspect of American life. High unemployment rates and a slow economic recovery have given many Americans a sobering reality check. Millennials graduating college and baby boomers alike—and everyone in between—are trying to find stable yet satisfying work in a very unstable world. And perhaps it may seem like a luxury to try to find a career that allows you to "do what you are" when so many people are struggling just to put bread on the table.

The good news is, this book can help.

You hold in your hands a tool that can set you apart in an increasingly competitive market. This book can help you to identify work that is satisfying and that you can excel at, even in a changing world. We can point you toward industries that remain resilient in the face of an economic downturn and jobs that are evolving to become indispensible in the coming years.

Dozens of books have been written to help people make good career decisions. But *Do What You Are* is different from every other guide in a fundamental way. It does not offer generic, one-size-fits-all advice. For as certainly as people are different from each other, advice that's right for one person often is completely wrong for another. Our expertise in the well-respected, scientifically validated system called Personality Type enables us to truly *individualize* the career discovery process—to give you invaluable insights about yourself, and to enable you to find a career that makes the best use of your natural talents.

Technology has continued to influence—and even define—the means by which people identify and procure employment. Increasingly, the job search has moved online, with social and professional networking sites, job postings, and career websites becoming the primary ways people find employment. However, technology has had surprisingly little effect on the equally important need for people to find work that is intrinsically satisfying—work they are naturally designed to do. So the primary goal of *Do What You Are*—to help you find the most satisfying career—remains decidedly low tech. In fact, the only tool required is the book you are now holding in your hands!

Yes, We're Talking to You

We're assuming that you picked up this book because you're at a turning point in your work. Maybe you're a student just about to choose that first important job, or perhaps you're re-entering the workplace after some time off and are considering all your options. Maybe you're dissatisfied with your job and believe there must be a better alternative. Or perhaps you're finishing up one career and thinking about starting on another. Congratulations—you've come to the right book!

Some special encouragement is in order for job changers. If you're wondering about the wisdom of trying to change horses in midstream, you should know that millions of people change jobs every year. In fact, it is estimated that most people will have five to seven different careers in their lifetime. These statistics don't provide much solace, however, if you find yourself stuck in an unfulfilling job that you feel you can't quit.

There are some very practical reasons why people can't just impulsively leave their jobs and strike out in a new direction. You have bills to pay, maybe a family to support. It takes a lot of courage to give up a steady paycheck, even when it comes from an unsatisfying job. It's difficult to look for a new job while you're still at an old one—anyone who has tried it can tell you it's like having a job on top of a job—and yet the idea of actually being out of work while you conduct a job search can be terrifying. Most of us don't have the financial resources to carry us over a period of unemployment, especially when there's no guarantee that we'll be successful in finding a new job quickly.

It can also be extremely difficult to go against what others expect of you. Even if you're unhappy in your job, you may feel pressure from others to stay right where you are. During a career change, support and encouragement from family and friends is an important resource. If those close to you disapprove of your making a change, you're more likely to keep doing what you're doing.

It's also true that once you've established a particular lifestyle, it's difficult to imagine a different way of life. The longer you've been living a certain way, the more invested you become in keeping your life the way it is. If you've attained a certain level of success and are accustomed to being regarded as successful, starting all over can seem unimaginable.

To make matters worse, most of us don't really know what we need to satisfy us. We know what we *don't* like—that much we've learned from experience—but we don't know how to think up, much less find, a fulfilling alternative.

Changing careers can be extremely stressful, and it's not uncommon for the process to take several months. Many people compare the experience of changing careers to a very scary roller-coaster ride. There are plenty of ups and downs, and even though you know a steep drop lies ahead, your heart still pounds when you start to descend. We've been through this process with hundreds of clients, and we know how hard it can be. However, we also know how wonderful the rewards can be.

Here's the "good news." By unlocking the secrets of your personality type, you *can* find a truly fulfilling job that enhances the quality of your life. Even though changing jobs is frightening, and even though it's easier to keep doing what you're doing, we hope you'll use this book to discover exactly what you need to be satisfied in your work and how to find the right work for you. It can be done, and it's well worth the effort—we promise!

How This Book Will Help You

Do What You Are is designed to help you make better career choices, conduct a successful job search campaign, and be most effective in *any* job. We're excited about what we've learned about the relationship between Personality Type and career satisfaction, and we want to share our most important discoveries with you. Please know, however, that we aren't going to rehash a lot of information you can get elsewhere, such as how to write a résumé or dress for success. Our main interest is in helping you figure out what career satisfaction is for you and in helping you go about finding work you'll love.

Since a full career spans many years, you'll want to use *Do What You Are* to make sure you and your career continue to grow together instead of apart. We hope you'll revisit this book periodically to reevaluate where you are, how you've changed, and where you want to be. We think you'll find this book a valuable ongoing resource, one you will refer to often and will want to share with family and friends.

As you read *Do What You Are,* you'll start to enjoy many of the "fringe benefits" that come with an understanding of Personality Type. Recognizing and understanding your personality type can change the way you see yourself—which in turn affects everything you do and every aspect of your life. Personality Type is so well respected that the majority of *Fortune* 500 companies use it daily. Over the past twenty years, we've used Personality Type to help managers motivate and communicate with their employees; teachers to reach very different types of students; work teams to understand their strengths and weaknesses and to communicate more productively; and, of course, we've used it to train thousands of career counselors and outplacement consultants to help their clients make the best career choices. If you are a parent, Type will give you a whole new perspective on your family dynamics and help you understand and communicate better with your children. If you are part of a couple, Type will help you understand, accept, and appreciate the similarities and differences between you and your partner. In short, we're confident that the knowledge you gain from this book will forever change the way you look at yourself and others.

How to Use This Book

Reading *Do What You Are* requires some active participation on your part. No, nothing painful! But we do hope you'll read this book during quiet moments when you can pause to think. The fact is, we aren't interested in telling you what to do. Instead, we want to introduce you to a process that works and that will be useful to you all your life. So although we ask you all the right questions and provide you with as much information and as many examples as we can, ultimately the answers must come from you because you know you best. We see this as a collaborative effort: we supply the expertise and experience, and you supply the essential information about yourself. Together we'll be successful in finding the best possible career match for you.

We've divided *Do What You Are* into three parts. Part 1, Unlocking the Secrets of Personality Type, will take you step by step through the discovery and understanding of your own personality type. Part 2, The "Fourmula" for Career Satisfaction, will introduce you to the four ingredients you must have in your work if it is to be truly fulfilling. In Part 3, Getting to Work, we'll show you how to put to good use all that you've learned about yourself. This part of the book is divided according to personality type. In your section you'll meet other people of your type and will learn what kinds of jobs they find fulfilling. Reading about their experiences, likes and dislikes, joys and frustrations will help you clarify what you need in a job for it to be really satisfying. To assist you further, we provide a type-specific list of key ingredients for career satisfaction, suggestions for your ideal work environment, a rundown of your work-related strengths, some exercises to highlight your basic values, and a list of potentially satisfying career options. Finally, we provide you with job search strategies that are designed specifically to be effective for *you* and people like you. We will show you how to make the most of your natural strengths and how to minimize your innate weaknesses as you engage in information gathering, personal marketing, interviewing with prospective employers, following up, and decision making. And finally—should you choose to stay in your current job—we will outline specific things you can do to be happier and more successful.

A Glimpse into the Future…Where the Jobs and Careers Will Be

Some people's choice of a career is dictated by their passions. They simply *have* to create art, or make music, or seek the cure for cancer. And certainly we are all better off for their efforts. Other people are more pragmatic and give more weight to practical concerns when making career decisions. Regardless of what camp you fall into, all career seekers can benefit from looking down the road at the careers the experts predict will be most in demand in the future. With this in mind, we share some new information about a few important trends.

According to the latest edition of the *Occupational Outlook Handbook* (published by the Bureau of Labor Statistics), employment growth from 2010 to 2020 is projected to be highly concentrated in the health care and social services industries. In fact, it is projected that by 2020 nearly one in nine jobs in the United States will be in the health sector. The technology industry is also on the rise, with mobile application technologies leading the way and changing paradigms within the field of technology and in almost every other field as well. Franchising offers many opportunities for success and growth for people with an entrepreneurial spirit looking to minimize their risk. And jobs in construction are expected to grow as the housing market recovers and energy-conscious technologies continue to rise in demand. The green construction industry is estimated to reach $122 billion in 2015!

THE TEN OCCUPATIONS PROJECTED TO GROW
THE FASTEST

Personal care aides	70.5%
Home health aides	69.4%
Biomedical engineers	61.7%
Veterinary technologists and technicians	52.0%
Physical therapy assistants	45.7%
Meeting, convention, and event planners	43.7%
Occupational therapy assistants	43.3%
Interpreters and translators	42.2%
Market research analysts and marketing specialists	41.2%
Marriage and family therapists	41.2%

Other occupations expected to grow at a rapid rate include physical therapists (39.0%), dental hygienists (37.7%), audiologists (36.8%), health educators (36.5%), medical scientists (36.4%), cost estimators (36.4%), mental health counselors (36.3%), and veterinarians (35.9%).

Mobile Technologies … the Wave of the Future

If you're reading this, chances are that you own a cell phone. And whether you upgrade once a month or once a decade, it's clear that the mobile technology economy is growing fast, driven by a pervasive "upgrade culture" that makes many technologies obsolete in a matter of months. The field of mobile technology includes both the hardware for cell phones, tablets, and laptops as well as the extensive software design of operating systems, applications, and network systems. Whereas once a cell phone had exactly one function, the phones of today and tomorrow are sophisticated handheld computers, replete with GPS navigation, web browsers, state-of-the-art cameras and video recorders, and much more.

The good news is that opportunities in this trillion-dollar industry are growing as fast as the new product lines. For instance, the demand for mobile application developers is still far greater than the supply, and the industries calling for them range far and wide, including video game studios, advertising and marketing firms, media firms looking to distribute content via mobile apps, and government agencies and financial institutions that want to adapt their services to mobile users. Not to mention actual software development firms!

Jobs in the field of mobile applications are expected to skyrocket by 32 percent from 2010 to 2020 — an increase that ranks among the highest for any occupation. Close to 300,000 new jobs are expected to be created, the majority of these in application development for Android and iOS, which account for almost 90 percent of all smartphones in the United States. And with an exploding market expected to reach seven billion people in the next five years, it's easy to see that mobile technologies are not going anywhere soon.

Franchising . . . Not Just Burgers and Fries!

There's a huge difference in the success rates between people who start a new business and those who buy a franchise. Why the disparity? One of the biggest issues revolves around uncertainty. New businesses — almost by definition — are fraught with uncertainty, while established franchises leave very little to chance. For starters, they have a systemized way of doing business that ensures quality, uniformity, consistency, and a well-known brand. In addition, franchisees receive a tremendous amount of support and advice from people who have a long history of success, and they save significantly by sharing marketing and material expenses.

No wonder more and more people are trading traditional work arrangements for the chance to take charge of their own destiny. For the business-minded among them, franchising is a popular and profitable alternative. According to the International Franchise Association (IFA), there are more than 785,000 franchise units in the United States, which generate over $782 billion annually — that's about 4 percent of the U.S. gross domestic product!

Most of us are familiar with the most common form of franchise — the ubiquitous fast-food restaurant — but there is so much more to the franchise picture than burgers and fries. In fact, there are dozens of *categories* of opportunities, including pet day care centers, estate planning firms, tanning salons, and assisted living centers. Although franchising is not the right career option for everyone, there are many reasons why it is attractive to a wide array of people, especially baby boomers who have the resources to make the required financial investment. For instance, many people already possess the skills and temperament necessary to be successful franchisees, and there are no specific educational requirements or specialized training for most opportunities. While many personality types can and do thrive on owning a franchise, there are three central qualities that most successful franchisees have in common: they are enthusiastic, hardworking, and able to follow an established system and set of procedures.

Construction . . . Building a Bright Future

Another of the fastest-growing industries for the coming decade is construction. Population growth, deteriorating infrastructures, and aging buildings are estimated to cause the construction industry to grow by 19 percent through the year 2018, compared with 11 percent for all industries combined. As the housing market recovers from the early 2000s and the oldest children of the baby boomers reach their peak house-buying years in the coming decade, jobs in specialty trade contracting, subcontracting, and construction labor will flourish. Other related professions, such as electricians, plumbers, pipe fitters, and steamfitters, can also expect a higher demand, as can remodeling specialists like carpenters, brickmasons, and blockmasons.

Nonresidential construction is also predicted to grow, and civil engineers and urban planners will see a bump in demand as development spreads, especially in the South and West, with new highways, bridges, and streets to be constructed. And with an aging population, the need for medical treatment facilities will continue to grow as well. In fact, the large number of workers anticipated to leave positions in the construction industry will add more jobs than economic growth will as replacement needs skyrocket.

This boom in construction has a huge impact on jobs in related fields. For instance, architects who design these many buildings and structures can expect to enjoy job growth of 24 percent. Transportation is also expected to see a bump, with jobs for heavy and tractor-trailer truck drivers as well as hazardous material movers growing by 21 percent. So if one of these hands-on, action-packed jobs sounds good to you, the odds are in your favor!

The Doctor Is In . . . Health Care Is King!

There's no doubt about it: if you plan to pursue work in the health care industry, the opportunities are both varied and plentiful. And as the fastest-growing sector of the American economy, health care is the most stable bet for the next decade. The health care industry is projected to grow by 30 percent between 2010 and 2020, compared with only 13 percent growth for jobs in all other employment sectors.

Increased demand for health care services is being driven by an upswing in both the volume and quality of medical technologies, paired with an aging baby boomer population. In short, as boomers age and life expectancies get longer, health services will continue to provide many of the job opportunities in this country, outstripping even the computer industry—and occupation growth projections—since the last revision of this book! In fact, health care was the only industry to grow during the recession.

In such a vast industry, there are many different types of positions and work environments. For example, of the 4.2 million jobs in health care expected to be added by 2020, 63 percent are outside of hospitals—whether in offices of practitioners, nursing homes, or people's residences. As increasing numbers of aging baby boomers wish to live in their own homes, the personal care services sector is exploding, with occupations as home health and personal care aides growing the fastest and adding the greatest number of new jobs. And as baby boomer practitioners retire, their jobs will need to be filled. In fact, seven hundred thousand positions for registered nurses, home health aides, and personal care aides are expected to open up because of attrition alone. It's easy to see that the health care industry has something for everyone. Variety and opportunity are the name of the game, and the impact will reach far into the next decade.

Education and Training…Finding the Right Fit

In an age of escalating costs for higher education, the degree and training requirements for a chosen occupation are no small consideration. Even people who pursue a degree full-time often need to earn an income simultaneously, making short or flexible programs a necessity. Add to the mix the increasing prevalence of career changers—those of us who have the need or desire to pursue a different field of interest—and you have a whole population balancing new schooling and professional transitions with responsibilities to life partners and kids! Luckily, the way we pursue education is changing, too. Options like accredited online universities can offer a cost-effective and flexible path to the degree of your choice.

The following table from the Bureau of Labor Statistics sheds some light on the education and training levels required for occupations growing the fastest through the next seven years. As you begin to identify the type of work that

Education or training level	Fastest-growing occupations	Occupations having the largest numerical job growth
Master's degree or higher	Physical therapists Medical scientists Marriage and family therapists	Physician's assistants Postsecondary teachers Physicians and surgeons
Bachelor's degree	Biomedical engineers Interpreters and translators Market research analysts and marketing specialists	Accountants and auditors Civil engineers Network and communication system administrators
Associate's degree	Veterinary technologists and technicians Physical therapy Dental hygienists/ assistants Diagnostic medical sonographers	Registered nurses Paralegals
Short-term on-the-job training	Home health aides Personal care aides Construction laborers and helpers	Retail salespeople Child care provider Customer service representatives

suits your personality type, this table may prove a helpful reference about how you might get there from here. In fact, if you find yourself interested in education and training itself, you can choose to pursue one of the 1.7 million projected job openings in the education, training, or library occupations!

A New Edition

The Kids Are All Right

You've probably heard a lot lately about the demographic group know as generation Y, or more commonly, millennials. Demographers dispute the exact dates, but this generation is generally agreed to include people born between the early 1980s and late 1990s. Millennials can sometimes get a bad rap. They've been called entitled, narcissistic, and easily distracted—criticized for their obsessive self-documentation on social media and apparent lack of concern for matters of privacy. But this characterization may be unfair, and is certainly not the whole picture. Millennials have also been shown to be innovative boundary breakers: leaders in the start-up revolution, global thinkers who challenge the status quo. Millennials were raised in a radically different world than the generation before and thus have a fluency in the languages of technology, social media, and interconnectivity that can be a huge asset to companies trying to adapt to the twenty-first century. In fact, this generation can adapt to new things nimbly and quickly, a by-product of growing up in a time when technologies become obsolete in months rather than years, and news can travel at the speed of Wi-Fi.

We believe that, while cohort traits can be instructive, there is no one millennial personality. There are, however, common experiences and capabilities that can set millennials apart and help make them attractive job candidates, and ultimately employees. Millennials are entering the workforce in droves, estimated to comprise 36 percent of the U.S. workforce by 2014, and by 2020 that number will rocket to 50 percent. The trick for millennials is to carve out a niche that makes use of both their cohort abilities, like a greater ease and familiarity with technology, and their individual personality type.

In this edition, we've included in each type chapter a profile of a successful millennial who has found satisfying work that makes use of the natural gifts and talents inherent in his or her personality type. You'll see some common themes: technology frequently plays a key role, and their career path is generally much less straightforward than for previous generations. It is often a path that relies on the interplay of education, networking, and chance. While the economic climate and consequent lack of job security have shaken up the traditional job trajectory for millennials, many of the people we interviewed have found opportunity and liberation in charting the road less traveled.

What's Next for Baby Boomers?

Ten thousand baby boomers reach the age of sixty-five every day. And while the average retirement age is sixty-seven, many will be leaving their jobs at much earlier ages—often in their mid to late fifties—because of the economic climate, changing values in the workplace, and job elimination due to technology. But in reality, a relatively small percentage of retirement-aged boomers either are financially able or want to completely retire. It is estimated that 70 percent will work in some capacity during retirement; of these, about 30 percent will continue because they have to. And according to an AARP survey, 40 percent plan to work "until they drop."

At the same time, the average life expectancy in the United States has increased to 78.5 years. As a result, a significant percentage of boomers leaving the workforce will have between ten and twenty years to do…something! So if you're a boomer, your working life may be far from over—and this time, there's a good chance that you may find work that is considerably more satisfying than your first career!

For this edition, we've added an entirely new chapter especially for boomers. In Chapter 25, Encore! Encore!, you'll discover the recipe for a fulfilling postretirement career. You can also read about boomers who are similar to you, and learn how their choices and experiences helped them to find the most satisfying "encore" career.

The Story of *Do What You Are*

When we began studying Personality Type over thirty years ago, we were extremely fortunate to be trained by some of the world's best-respected experts. We went on to discover how powerful this tool actually was by working with individual clients seeking career guidance. Then we designed and conducted the first workshops ever to provide specialized training for career professionals. Over the years we have trained thousands of career counselors, human resources specialists, and outplacement consultants. In 1986 we created the Personality Type Tool Kit, a resource that was highly regarded by career counselors. In writing *Do What You Are,* we have drawn not only on our experience with our clients and the counselors we have trained, but also on *their* experience with *their* clients.

As our expertise with Type grew and we had children, we began to appreciate how much Type could help parents truly understand and connect with their children. Using our own experience and extensive research with hundreds of parents, we wrote *Nurture by Nature: Understand Your Child's Personality Type—And Become a Better Parent,* which was published in 1997. In the book you can discover your child's Type and learn the most effective strategies for nurturing him or her.

While we were researching and writing, we were also consulting—with organizations to train their managers and help them develop productive teams, and with trial lawyers to help them select jurors and present their cases most effectively. As a result of our work with attorneys, we developed a shorthand system for quickly identifying others' personality types and communicating with them in their language. The result was our third book, *The Art of SpeedReading People: How to Size People Up and Speak Their Language,* a tool for salespeople, managers, human resources professionals, and others, published in 1998. *The Art of SpeedReading People* has turned out to be a powerful tool for job seekers as well, as it enables them to quickly "read" job interviewers and present themselves in the way most likely to impress each individual interviewer.

As we traveled around the country talking about Personality Type, we found people were extremely interested in using Type to better understand their partners and to improve their personal relationships. And while we had plenty of anecdotal evidence that Type can provide rich insights into romantic relationships, there had been no serious scientific study to date on the subject. This prompted us to undertake extensive research—including an online survey filled out by more than twenty-five hundred people and interviews with hundreds of couples. Our findings became the basis for our fourth book, *Just Your Type: Create the Relationship You've Always Wanted Using the Secrets of Personality Type,* published in 2000.

In the following pages, you will begin—or continue—an incredible journey of self-discovery. While the goal of this book is to offer practical and prescriptive advice about your career, it will also provide you with some extraordinary insights into other aspects of your life. We would love to hear your comments and suggestions for future editions of *Do What You Are* and will try to respond to your questions. You can reach us via e-mail at www.PersonalityType.com. We wish you the greatest success!

Paul D. Tieger, Barbara Barron, and Kelly Tieger

Part One | UNLOCKING THE SECRETS OF PERSONALITY TYPE

1 | SUIT YOURSELF

The Secret of Career Satisfaction

It's important to find the right job. Despite the universal fantasies of winning the lottery, buying expensive cars and homes, and doing fascinating work with interesting people in exotic places, the sober reality is that most of us have to work, hard, for a long time. If you spend forty to fifty years—not an unlikely scenario—working at jobs you'd rather not be doing, you are in truth throwing away a large part of your life. This is unnecessary and sad, especially since a career you can love is within your reach.

What Is the Ideal Job, Anyway?

The right job enhances your life. It is personally fulfilling because it nourishes the most important aspects of your personality. It suits the way you like to do things and reflects who you are. It lets you use your innate strengths in ways that come naturally to you, and it doesn't force you to do things you don't do well (at least, not often!).

How can you tell if you're in the right job? Here are some general guidelines. If you're not employed, keep them in mind as you search for your ideal job. If you are employed, see how your present job measures up.

If you're in the right job, you should:

- Look forward to going to work
- Feel energized (most of the time) by what you do
- Feel your contribution is respected and appreciated
- Feel proud when describing your work to others
- Enjoy and respect the people you work with
- Feel optimistic about your future

We'd like to make something clear right away. It's important to recognize that there are as many different paths to career satisfaction as there are happily employed people. There is no one "ideal job" to which everyone should aspire. But there is an ideal job *for you.*

There are an infinite number of variables in the workplace. To achieve career satisfaction, you need to figure out what your preferences are and then find a job that accommodates them. Some jobs provide warmth and stability; some are risky and challenging. Some are structured, some aren't. One job may require a lot of socializing, while another may require quiet concentration. Do you know exactly what kind of job suits you best? Have you ever even stopped to think about it?

It's a good thing there are so many different kinds of jobs available, since people are so different in their abilities and priorities. Some people enjoy making high-level management decisions; others simply aren't suited to making these kinds of choices. For some people, money is a top priority. They want to make lots of it! Others, however, want most to make a contribution to society; the money is less important. Some people are perfectly comfortable with facts and details and statistics, while others get a headache just trying to read a profit-and-loss statement. And so on, and so on!

When we were hired to conduct a series of personal effectiveness training workshops for job placement professionals (also known as executive recruiters or headhunters), we came face-to-face with a dramatic example of how a job that is perfect for one person can be perfectly wrong for another.

We were training several headhunters who worked for the same recruiting firm. Their job was to find applicants to fill positions at a variety of companies by calling people who were already employed and convincing them to apply for these positions. If an applicant successfully switched jobs and stayed with the new company for at least three months, the placement counselor received a generous commission. It was a highly competitive, results-oriented job that required excellent communication skills and the ability to fill as many positions as possible as quickly as possible.

One of the placement counselors we trained, Arthur, couldn't have been happier. He loved the fast pace of the job. Arthur was a high-energy person, a great talker who enjoyed meeting lots of people over the phone. He used his excellent reasoning skills to persuade other people to make a move to a new opportunity, and he got a lot of satisfaction out of meeting his goal and then some. Arthur knew and understood the formula: for every fifty calls he made, he'd get ten people who were interested, and out of these ten, he might make two or three placements. Arthur's "thick skin" helped him in the job because he often heard "no" during the day, but he never took the rejection personally. What Arthur found really energizing was closing the sale and moving on to the next challenge. He worked hard all day long and made a lot of money.

For Julie, it was a totally different story. Like Arthur, Julie enjoyed talking to lots of people all day and establishing relationships with them. However, unlike

Arthur, Julie wanted to help each person find the job that would be really right for him or her. She liked to look for opportunities that would enable her applicants to grow and experience personal success and satisfaction. Julie had been cautioned repeatedly by her supervisor about spending too much time on the phone with each individual rather than quickly determining whether or not someone was interested in a position and then moving on to the next prospect. Rather than filling jobs, Julie was counseling clients. The fact that she could make a great deal of money did not motivate her. She found little reward in simply filling a job opening with a person who probably wasn't right for the position but whom she had successfully pressured into giving it a try.

When we returned six weeks later for a follow-up training session, we weren't surprised to learn that Julie had quit.

People are different in their needs, desires, interests, skills, values, and personalities. Unless you and I have similar personality types, work that you find intrinsically enjoyable is likely to have a different, even opposite, effect on me. Different jobs and even different aspects of jobs satisfy different types of people, a fundamental truth which has, in our view, not been fully appreciated by career advisers or career manuals—until now.

To Suit Yourself, You Must Know Yourself

As we said earlier, the secret of career satisfaction lies in doing what you enjoy most. A few lucky people discover this secret early in life, but most of us are caught in a kind of psychological wrestling match, torn between what we think we *can* do, what we (or others) feel we *ought* to do, and what we think we *want* to do. Our advice? Concentrate instead on *who you are,* and the rest will fall into place.

Not long ago, a friend called us. She calls all the time—there's a phone in practically every room of her home—but this was more than a social call. Ellen was mad. A co-worker of hers whom she regarded as "more boring than a turnip" had been given a prime assignment designing a complex computer system for a growing retail chain. Ellen, who had been hired just six months before to do exactly this kind of work, was stunned. Obviously something was wrong—but what?

Ellen had evaluated her new job with the utmost care before accepting it. She had both the analytical ability and the background experience the job required. She was well liked and found the technical aspects of the job challenging. She'd had a series of unsatisfying jobs before, but this one was going to be different. So why was her golden opportunity turning to brass? Worse...why was the turnip doing better than she?

We thought we knew the answer. Ellen's co-worker, as she described him, was absolutely content to work long hours in relative isolation, quietly but steadily getting the job done. He wasn't a lot of fun around the office, but he was intelligent and dependable, and he never made waves. He was, in fact, the perfect person for the job—and he was happy doing it.

Ellen, on the other hand, loved the stimulation of rallying her staff for an urgent deadline and enjoyed talking to clients about their needs. She was terrific at explaining the intricacies of computer systems and could charm people into doing remarkable things. She liked going to industry conferences, and she didn't mind spending all day in meetings. Unfortunately, none of these activities were a significant part of her new position.

It was clear to us that even though Ellen could handle her responsibilities adequately, the job required more solitude, concentration, and what we call "task focus" than she liked. As she talked things through (and some people are like that—they like to think out loud), she began to recognize that in all her careful planning she had overlooked just one thing…her own personality!

At this point in our conversation, Ellen panicked. She was afraid she had spent eight years in the wrong career. No wonder she'd found her previous jobs less than thrilling! However, she wasn't actually in the wrong field—she was just working in the wrong end of it. Ellen moved over into the sales division of the same company, and today she is thriving in her new position.

Perhaps a little experiment will clarify what we're talking about. On a piece of paper, or even in the margin, write your signature. Done? OK. Now do the same thing, using your opposite hand. (If you just groaned, you are not alone; most people have a similar reaction.) How did it feel when you used your preferred hand? Most people use words like "natural," "easy," "quick," "effortless." How did it feel when you used the opposite hand? Some typical responses: "slow," "awkward," "hard," "draining," "tiring," "it took much longer," "it required more energy and concentration."

We think that handedness is a good way to think about using your natural strengths in your work. The use of your preferred hand is comfortable and assured. If you were forced to use your other hand, you could no doubt develop your abilities—but using that hand would never be as effortless as using your preferred hand, and the finished product would never be as skillfully executed.

The Traditional Approach—and Why It Doesn't Work

Career professionals have long been aware that certain kinds of people are better at certain types of jobs, and that it's important to find as good a match as possible between the person you are and the kind of job you choose. The problem is that the traditional approach doesn't take enough considerations into account. The conventional analysis looks at only the "big three": your abilities, interests, and values.

As career counselors ourselves, we recognize the importance of these factors. Certainly you need the right skills to perform a job well. It also helps if you're interested in your work. And it's important to feel good about what you do. But this is far from the whole picture! Your personality has additional dimensions that also need to be recognized. As a general rule, the more aspects of your personality you match to your work, the more satisfied you'll be on the job.

As we saw with Ellen, a vital consideration—often overlooked—is how much stimulation from other people you need in your work. Are you more energized by being around lots of people most of the time, or are you more comfortable in small groups, talking one-on-one, or maybe working alone? You can see what a profound impact this preference can have upon your choice of a job. Other important factors include the kind of information you naturally notice, the way you make decisions, and whether you prefer to live in a more structured or a more spontaneous way. These preferences reflect mental processes that are basic to every human being but that clearly differ from one personality type to another. Trying to find the best job for you without taking these preferences into account is like trying to find a tiny island in the vast ocean without a chart. With luck, you might get there—but you might not!

Joanne was a client of ours who came to us in a career crisis. At the age of thirty, she was at the end of her rope. After seven years of teaching math at the elementary school level she was completely burned out and was wondering if she was in the right career.

Being a teacher had seemed the most natural thing in the world for Joanne. The eldest of four, she had grown up taking care of children. She had excelled in math throughout school and was interested in education. Joanne had received some career counseling early on, and all the signs had seemed to point in the same direction. In high school, and again in college, Joanne had taken the standard career aptitude tests and assessment instruments to determine her skills, her interests, and her values. Each time, career counselors had encouraged her to obtain a teaching degree and to teach math to young kids. Everything seemed perfect.

After her first challenging year, Joanne became increasingly frustrated with the rigid structure of the public elementary school setting. She disliked the endless rules both she and the students had to live by as well as many of the rules she had to enforce. She hated having to prepare lesson plans six weeks in advance that left her unable to respond to the interests of the children and to her own creative inspirations. She found the standard workbooks inane, and the busywork that both she and her students were required to do left her drained and irritated. Joanne felt very isolated because her colleagues all seemed to have interests and values that were not like hers, and she began to discover that she missed the intellectual stimulation of working on challenging projects with her intellectual equals. She had tried switching grades and even changing schools, but nothing seemed to help.

After talking with us, Joanne was relieved to discover that she wasn't crazy; she was just in the wrong career. As her early counselors had determined, Joanne had many of the right qualifications for teaching. However, the things she found most stimulating—intellectual challenge, opportunities to raise her level of competence, and creative innovation—were totally lacking in her job. Moreover, the public school setting forced her to work in a highly structured and detailed way, which was not at all the way she liked to operate.

Luckily, the solution quickly became clear. We suggested that Joanne return to school and obtain a master's degree in order to teach math—still a thriving interest of hers—in higher education. In a college setting, she would be able to enjoy much more flexibility in her work schedule and obligations, teach more complicated courses, and be part of an intellectual environment.

Joanne did get a master's degree, and shortly thereafter she accepted a position in the math department of a small college. Today she teaches graduate-level math courses while continuing her studies toward obtaining a Ph.D.

There's also another reason why the traditional approach to career counseling is inadequate. The "big three"—your abilities, interests, and values—all change with age. As you gain work experience, you gain new skills. As you live longer, you may pick up new interests and discard old ones. And often your goals are different later in life than they were earlier. You can keep changing your career according to where you find yourself at a particular point in time, or you can base your choice from the beginning on a deeper understanding of who you are (and who you'll always be!).

Alex is a thirty-nine-year-old internist with a successful practice in a Chicago suburb. While he was growing up it was always assumed that he would follow in the family tradition and become a doctor. Through twelve years of college, medical school, internship, and residency, he never allowed himself to question his decision. After practicing medicine for five years, he has come to a painful conclusion with far-reaching implications for himself and his family: he doesn't want to be a doctor any more. What's more, he realizes he probably never did.

Alex's predicament is not unusual. If you doubt this, pick any ten people you know and ask them, "If you could have any job you wanted, what would it be?" Our experience as career counselors suggests that at least *half* would rather be doing something else.

Most of us make our most important career decisions when we are least prepared to do so. The decisions we make early in life set into motion a chain of events that will influence our entire lives. Yet when we're young we have little or no experience making job choices, and we tend to have an overabundance of idealistic enthusiasm, plus a reckless lack of concern for future consequences. We haven't lived long enough to see ourselves tested in a variety of situations, and we're highly susceptible to bad advice from well-intentioned parents, teachers, counselors, or friends. No wonder so many people get off to a poor start.

The solution? To achieve as great a degree of self-awareness as you can before making any decision with long-lasting career consequences. Happily, "finding yourself" does not require a guru, a lot of money, or any period of experimentation.

You Can't Help It—You Were Born That Way!

Since the right job flows directly out of all the elements of your personality type, you need to spend some time figuring out what makes you tick. By making a conscious effort to discover the "real you," you can learn how to focus your natural strengths and inclinations into a career you can love for as long as you choose to work. This is where Type is so helpful. It provides a systematic, effective way to evaluate both your strong points and your probable weaknesses or blind spots. Once you have these figured out, you'll know how to make sure you are always operating from a position of strength.

Each one of us has a distinct personality, like an innate blueprint that stays with us for life. We are born with a personality type, we go through life with that type, and when we are laid to rest (hopefully at the end of a long and fruitful life), it is with the same type.

Now you are probably wondering, "Wait a minute. I might be one way sometimes, but at other times I'm a very different person. Doesn't the situation influence my personality type?"

The answer is no, it doesn't. Do we change our behavior in certain situations? Certainly! Most human beings have a tremendous repertoire of behaviors available to them. We couldn't function very successfully if we didn't. Sure, we act differently at work than we do at home, and it makes a difference whether we're with strangers, close friends, at a ball park, or at a funeral. But people don't change their basic personalities with every new door they walk through.

All this is not to say that environmental factors are not extremely important; they are. Parents, siblings, teachers, and economic, social, and political circumstances all can play a role in determining what directions our lives take. Some people are forced by circumstances to act in a certain way until they are literally "not themselves" (more about this later). But we all start off with a particular personality type that predisposes us to behave in certain ways for our entire lives.

If you are skeptical about the idea that personality type is inborn, take a look at different children from the same family. These could be your own children, your siblings, or even children from a family you know. Do they have different personalities? You bet they do, and often the differences are apparent from birth (or even in utero).

The concept of "personality type" is not new. People have always been aware of the similarities and differences between individuals, and over the centuries many systems and models for understanding or categorizing these differences have been developed. Today, our understanding of human behavior has been expanded to such a degree that we are now able to accurately identify sixteen distinctly different personality types.

Finding the right job for each of these distinct personalities may seem like an awesome task. However, all sixteen personality types do function in the world. As we will see, it is possible to identify your own personality type, and the types of others, to understand why certain types flourish in certain kinds of jobs, and to clarify why people find career satisfaction in different ways.

2 | JUST WHO DO YOU THINK YOU ARE?

Discovering Your Personality Type

In this chapter you'll learn how Type works, and, even better, you'll discover your own personality type. But before we assist you in identifying your type, we think it would be helpful for you to know something about how Type has come to be used by so many people in so many different ways.

A Brief History of Type

The concept of Personality Type owes its existence to the work of Swiss psychologist Carl Jung and two American women, Katharine Briggs and her daughter, Isabel Briggs Myers. Jung, an eclectic psychoanalyst and disciple of Sigmund Freud, realized that behavior that seemed unpredictable could in fact be anticipated if one understood the underlying mental functions and attitudes people preferred.

While Jung was making his discoveries, Katharine Briggs, who had long been intrigued with similarities and differences between human personalities, began to develop her own system for "typing" people. In 1921, Jung's theory of personality was published in a book called *Psychological Types*. When Katharine read the English translation published in 1923, she realized that Jung had already discovered what she had been looking for, so she adopted his model and began a serious study of his work. Fortunately for us, she interested her young daughter Isabel in her pursuit.

The study of Personality Type, and the discussion of the subject in this book, owe a substantial debt to the pioneering research and writing of Katharine Briggs and her daughter, Isabel Briggs Myers.* Myers and Briggs built upon the theoretical work related to type done by Carl Jung, and both expanded it and gave it a practical application. Jung posited that there existed three personality preference scales and eight personality types; Katharine Briggs and Isabel Briggs Myers determined, based on their many years of study, that there were four personality preference scales and sixteen distinct personality types. These are the sixteen personality types which we discuss in this book. Much of our discussion derives from the writings of Isabel Briggs Myers and other authors, who, like her, are published by Consulting Psychologists Press, Inc. Certain material and quotations contained in this book are published with the permission of Consulting Psychologists Press, Inc.

Starting in the 1940s, Katharine Briggs and Isabel Briggs Myers began developing the MBTI® test instrument,† a detailed test to measure psychological type, which has been refined and improved over the years. Moreover, data from the MBTI® test has been collected and analyzed from the time the test was first given, providing scientific validation for the MBTI® test and the results it yields.

As Isabel Briggs Myers determined, and as our experience has verified over and over again, there are sixteen different personality types, and every person fits into one of them. This is not to say that people are not all unique, for they certainly are. One hundred people of the same personality type in a room would all be different because they have different parents, genes, experiences, interests, and so on. But they would also have a tremendous amount in common. Identifying your personality type helps you discover and learn how to take advantage of that commonality.

As you become more familiar with Type, you'll see that all personality types are equally valuable, with inherent strengths and blind spots. There are no better or worse, smarter or duller, healthier or sicker types. Type does *not* determine intelligence or predict success, nor does it indicate how well adjusted anyone will be. It *does,* however, help us discover what best motivates and energizes each of us as individuals, and this in turn empowers us to seek these elements in the work we choose to do.

How to Determine Your Personality Type

As we discussed earlier, one way to determine your personality type is to complete the Myers-Briggs Type Indicator (MBTI®) instrument and have the results interpreted by a trained professional. However, since that is not practical for the purposes of this book, we offer another method that we have used to successfully help hundreds of clients discover their true types.

The first of this two-step process begins with reading the following section in which we describe each of the four dimensions of Personality Type.

---

*If you are interested in learning more about these remarkable women's lives, we suggest you read *Katharine & Isabel*, by Frances W. Saunders.

†Myers-Briggs Type Indicator and MBTI are registered trademarks of Consulting Psychologists Press.

As you read about each type dimension, think about which preference sounds more like you. Most of what you read about your preference will ring true for you, but remember, the preferences are generalities and represent the extremes. Try to focus not on isolated examples of each preference, but rather on a pattern of behavior that is more consistently like you than its opposite. Even if one example sounds just like you, see how you feel about all the others before making up your mind.

At the end of the discussion of each dimension you'll find a continuum (or scale). Please place a check mark along the continuum at the point which you think most accurately reflects how strong your preference is. The closer your mark is to the center of the scale (on either side), the less clear your preference is; the farther away your mark is, the stronger your preference is. Even if you are not certain of your preference, try to indicate if you can which side of the midpoint you *probably* fall on, because what is most helpful in determining your type is which *side* of each scale you prefer, *not* how clear or unclear your preference is.

By "estimating" your type preference for each of the four type dimensions in this way, you will end up with a four-letter code. For most of you, that code will represent your personality type, or one that is very close to it. Toward the end of this chapter, we will provide a space for you to record the letters of your type code.

The second step in identifying your type comes after you've read the descriptions of the preferences and made your estimates. But that happens just a little later on. Now it's time to learn about Personality Type.

The Four Dimensions of Personality Type

The Type system of personality assessment is based on four basic aspects of human personality: how we interact with the world and where we direct our energy; the kind of information we naturally notice; how we make decisions; and whether we prefer to live in a more structured way (making decisions) or in a more spontaneous way (taking in information). We call these aspects of human personality **dimensions** because each one can be pictured as a continuum between opposite extremes, like this:

How we interact with the world and where we direct our energy	(E) Extraversion —+—	Introversion (I)
The kind of information we naturally notice	(S) Sensing —+—	Intuition (N)
How we make decisions	(T) Thinking —+—	Feeling (F)
Whether we prefer to live in a more structured way (making decisions) or in a more spontaneous way (taking in information)	(J) Judging —+—	Perceiving (P)

Everyone's personality falls onto one side of the midpoint or the other on each of these four scales. We call the opposite ends of the scales **preferences**. If you fall on the extraverted side, for example, then you are said to have a preference for Extraversion. If you fall on the introverted side, your preference is for Introversion.

In reality, you use both sides of each scale in daily life, but you also have an innate preference for one side or the other. Remember the exercise in which you used each hand to write your name? Your preference is generally more comfortable, automatic, and trustworthy; for these reasons, you are most successful while using it. If you don't have a particularly pronounced preference on one continuum, you may be just slightly to one side of the midpoint. If you have an extreme preference, you'll find yourself at one end or the other. People with strong preferences who find themselves at the opposite ends of a scale are very different from each other.

For the time being, don't worry too much about the terms used to describe the four dimensions (for example, "Sensing" versus "Intuition"). In some cases, these terms don't mean exactly what you think they do. Although they are words you know, they mean something different in this context. We'll explain them in detail shortly.

You'll notice that since each continuum has opposite preferences at either end, there are eight preferences in all, each represented by a particular letter. These letters are used in combination to designate the sixteen personality types. Your particular combination of preferences is more meaningful than any one preference by itself.

By now you may be wondering what is magical about sixteen. Why aren't there twelve personality types? Or twenty? Or two hundred? The answer lies in simple mathematics. If you calculate all the possible combinations of the eight letters (preferences), you end up with sixteen possible types. It's easier to visualize them when organized in a chart, like the one originally suggested by Isabel Briggs Myers.

ISTJ	ISFJ	INFJ	INTJ
ISTP	ISFP	INFP	INTP
ESTP	ESFP	ENFP	ENTP
ESTJ	ESFJ	ENFJ	ENTJ

Everyone fits into one of these sixteen categories. Although Type is systematic, it is also flexible; it is limited enough to be useful, but accommodating enough to fit everyone.

(E) Extraversion / Introversion (I)

The first dimension of Personality Type concerns how we prefer to interact with the world and where we direct our energy. Carl Jung originated the concepts of "extraversion" and "introversion" to describe how we live in the world outside ourselves and the world inside ourselves. Each of us has a natural preference for either the outer or inner world, although by necessity we all function in both. Functioning in our preferred world energizes us; functioning in the opposite world is more difficult and can be tiring. We call those who prefer the outer world **Extraverts** and those who prefer the inner world **Introverts**.

Most people think that extraverted means "talkative" and introverted means "shy." This is a good example of how the terms used to describe the Type preferences can be somewhat misleading. There is far more to extraversion and introversion than talkativeness.

Because they focus their energy in opposite directions, there are clear, distinct, and profound differences between Extraverts and Introverts. Extraverts focus their attention and energy on the world outside of themselves. They seek out other people and enjoy lots of interaction, whether one-on-one or in groups. They are constantly (and naturally) pulled to the outer world of people and things. Because Extraverts need to experience the world to understand it, they tend to like a lot of activity. Extraverts get their "batteries charged up" by being with others and usually know a lot of people. Because they like to be at the center of the action and are approachable, they tend to meet new people frequently and with ease. Extraverts look at a situation and ask themselves, "How do I affect this?"

Introverts focus their attention and energy on the world inside of themselves. They enjoy spending time alone and need this time to "recharge their batteries." Introverts try to understand the world before they experience it, which means a lot of their activity is mental. They prefer social interaction on a smaller scale — one-on-one or in small groups. Introverts avoid being the center of attention and are generally more reserved than Extraverts. They prefer to get to know new people slowly. Introverts look at a situation and ask themselves, "How does this affect me?"

Peter, a true Extravert, puts it this way: "When I return from a trip to the supermarket, my wife always asks me, 'Well, was it a success?' You might assume that she's checking to see if I got everything I needed, but in fact, knowing how Extraverted I am, what she really means is, 'How many people did you see whom you know?' To me, interacting with people, especially friends, is fun and energizing. I love the fact that no matter where I go, I'll almost always run into someone I know."

Brent, who is quite Introverted, feels just the opposite. "I like people," he explains, "but I don't care for quick, superficial exchanges. My wife loves parties, but I just find them exhausting. To me, it's draining and unsatisfying to have to meet all those people whose names I can't remember and whom I'll probably never see again. What's the point?"

Someone's preference for Extraversion or Introversion can be seen in practically everything he or she does. For example, take the study habits of Jill, a college sophomore. As Jill explains it, "I always prefer to study with friends. In one class we have a study group which really works out well. If no one is around, I'll go to the library. I find it much less boring than sitting alone in my dorm room reading by myself. At the library I can always find somebody I know to take a break with."

We think it's safe to say that usually most Extraverts don't *really* go to the library to study. They go there to be with other people.

If you don't know what an Extravert is thinking...you haven't been listening, because he or she will tell you. If you don't know what an Introvert is thinking...you haven't asked, or, in some cases, you haven't waited long enough for an answer. Asked a question, an Extravert will usually start talking, because Extraverts are most comfortable doing their thinking out loud (in the outer world). In fact, Extraverts often need to talk to think. On the other hand, there will often be a pause before an Introvert answers a question, because Introverts are more comfortable thinking silently (in the inner world). Introverts "bake" their ideas inside, much as cake is cooked in the oven and presented to the outside world only after it is finished. Extraverts only partially "bake" their ideas inside, preferring to finish them out in the world (which, of course, occasionally results in "half-baked" ideas!). However, Extraverts *do* finish their ideas eventually.

Shawn, another Extravert, recalls, "When I was in elementary school, I used to get all excited when I wanted the teacher to call on me. I would wave my whole arm so vigorously I had to hold it up with my other hand to keep from getting tired! But when the teacher finally did call on me, I often didn't know the answer. Naturally she would say something very sensitive and understanding, like, 'If you don't know the answer, then why did you raise your hand?' I didn't know then, but I know now: I needed to talk the answer out. I just couldn't think it through quietly in my head."

Unlike Shawn, Introverted students need time to form their answers in their minds before they can respond to a teacher's question. Since most elementary school teachers are Extraverts, they tend to move quickly from one child to the next. In our workshops, we have trained teachers to wait just a few seconds after asking an Introverted child a question—and we hear from these teachers that their class participation rates have tripled!

Many Extraverts find that their preference helps them at work because they generally can think quickly on their feet. When asked a question, they just start talking. Eventually they come up with an answer, and usually they can persuade others that it makes sense.

Leslie, like most Introverts, had a different experience. "I'll never forget how frustrating my first job was for me," she told us. "It seemed as if everybody in the company, including my boss, was a huge Extravert. For one thing, I was always being forced to do group activities, like attending brainstorming sessions and sales conferences—and we were *always* having meetings! But even worse, my boss wouldn't give me enough time to answer his questions. I guess he thought I was stupid, or else he figured I was taking so long because I didn't know the answer."

Extraverts tend to be much more public than Introverts and share personal information freely. Introverts are more private, as is demonstrated by a situation that Gerry, an Introvert, experienced. "A new co-worker in our department had heard that I was a good cook," reported Gerry, "so she kept badgering me to invite her over for dinner. Finally I did, and the meal went fine. But the next day, she began telling everyone at our weekly staff meeting about the great meal I'd made. Her effusive compliments were bad enough, but then she went on to describe, in great detail, the contents of my entire house! She talked all about the personal treasures I've been collecting for the past thirty years. I was furious. If I'd wanted all my co-workers to know that much about me, I'd have invited them over myself and conducted a tour!"

The Extraverted co-worker, incidentally, was mortified to learn that she had violated Gerry's privacy. She'd had the best of intentions and thought she'd only been sincerely complimenting Gerry's good taste.

It's important to recognize that the gift of Extraversion is breadth, and the gift of Introversion is depth. Usually Extraverts are interested in many things, but not necessarily at a very deep level. Introverts have fewer interests, but they pursue them in much greater depth. Once you get an Introvert talking about his or her interest, he may go on forever.

Despite their best efforts to get out of it, Larry and Mark found themselves at the annual holiday party given by the company where both their wives worked. Since both men are Introverts, you can imagine the joy each felt as he anticipated spending the next four hours with 120 total strangers. Fortunately for both, they met early on while ordering drinks at the bar. After some uncomfortable small talk, they learned (by accident) that each was an avid sailor. They spent the entire party talking boats, equipment, and cruising spots, and telling near-disaster stories.

Bill, whose wife works for the same company, couldn't wait to get to the party. He'd met many of the employees' spouses last year and he was eager to rekindle these acquaintances. As soon as they arrived, Bill and his wife—who was also an Extravert—went their separate ways, and by the end of the evening Bill had talked with a dozen and a half people, covering about twice as many topics. He and his wife were so "charged up" by all the stimulation that they moved the party down to the hotel lounge with another group of late-nighters (more Extraverts) after everyone else left.

Although there is some controversy as to how many Extraverts and Introverts there are in the world, the latest research suggests that the American population is about equally divided between Extraverts and Introverts. However, because Extraverts tend to talk more and louder than Introverts, there seems to be a fairly strong bias toward Extraverts in our culture.

Extraverts	**Introverts**
Are energized by being with other people	Are energized by spending time alone
Like being the center of attention	Avoid being the center of attention
Act, then think	Think, then act
Tend to think out loud	Think things through inside their heads
Are easier to "read" and know; share personal information freely	Are more private; prefer to share personal information with a select few
Talk more than listen	Listen more than talk
Communicate with enthusiasm	Keep their enthusiasm to themselves
Respond quickly; enjoy a fast pace	Respond after taking the time to think things through; enjoy a slower pace
Prefer breadth to depth	Prefer depth to breadth

Now that you've read about Extraverts and Introverts, can you guess which one you are? Sometimes it's hard to decide between these two preferences because of the way we change with age (for example, you may be more interested in your inner world now than you once were) or because of the demands made upon us by our jobs (for example, you may have learned how to function well in the outer world because that's what your job requires of you). If you are still undecided between Extraversion and Introversion, ask yourself this question: "If I had to be one way or the other for the rest of my life, which would I choose?" A thoughtful answer will often nudge the most ambivalent person in the direction of his or her true preference.

Please indicate your preference on the continuum below.

(E) Extraversion ——————————————————— Introversion (I)

(S) Sensing / Intuition (N)

The second dimension of Personality Type concerns the kind of information we naturally notice. Some people focus on "what is," while others focus on "what could be." These approaches—both valid—are fundamentally different.

Again, some definitions are in order. We use the term "Sensing" to describe the process of gathering data by means of the five senses. People who prefer Sensing—we call them **Sensors**—concentrate on what can be seen, heard, felt, smelled, or tasted. They trust whatever can be measured or documented and focus on what is real and concrete. Sensors trust their five senses to give them accurate information about the world, and they also trust their own personal experience. They are oriented to the present and concentrate on whatever is happening at the moment. A Sensor will look at a situation and want to determine exactly what is going on.

While it's obvious that we all use our five senses to take in information, some people are more interested in meanings, relationships, and possibilities based on facts than in the facts themselves. You could say these people trust their "sixth sense" (Intuition) more than their other five. Those who prefer Intuition—we call them **Intuitives**—naturally read between the lines and look for meaning in all things. (Intuition is abbreviated by the letter *N*.) Intuitives focus on implications and inferences. Unlike Sensors, they value imagination and trust their inspirations and hunches. Intuitives are oriented toward the future; they tend to anticipate events and generally try to make things different rather than maintaining them the way they are. An Intuitive will look at a situation and want to know what it means and what its consequences might be.

Everyone uses both Sensing and Intuition in daily life. Intuitives are well aware of the data their five senses bring in, and Sensors can interpret the meaning of someone's words, figure out a new way to handle a problem, or guess "who done it." Even so, everyone has a preference for either Sensing or Intuition. We all use one process more naturally, more often, and with more success than the other.

Sensors are especially good at noticing and remembering a great many facts, and Intuitives are best at interpreting facts or gleaning insights, as the following story illustrates.

Elizabeth, a Sensor, and Jim, an Intuitive, work together at a cosmetics-manufacturing company. One day the president hastily called all department heads together for a rather tense meeting. He proceeded to run through some figures that painted a grim economic picture for the company. If things didn't improve, he said, employees would have to be laid off and other cost-cutting measures taken.

The meeting ended abruptly, and the department heads left in some confusion. Jim and Elizabeth immediately went behind closed doors to compare notes. Elizabeth recognized that the company was truly in financial trouble because she understood the figures the president had quoted. As Elizabeth made additional calculations on a memo pad, her results—clear as could be in black and white—alarmed her even more than the meeting had.

Although Jim didn't have a "head for numbers," he, too, was quite alarmed. He had known something was wrong as soon as he'd walked into the meeting, and he now had a sense that there was more going on than the president had indicated. Jim had noticed immediately that their usually easygoing president was agitated, and he'd also seen several department heads exchange furtive looks. He now remarked to Elizabeth that relations seemed particularly strained between the president and the vice president for research and development. Although nothing had been said about it at the meeting, Jim wondered if the company's greatly anticipated new skin-care line that was still being developed might be in trouble, which would have a drastic effect on the bottom line.

As it turned out, both Jim and Elizabeth were correct. A few days later the president broke the bad news—and for completely different reasons, as we've seen, neither Jim nor Elizabeth was surprised. Although they each had focused on different kinds of data, they both had arrived at the same conclusion.

While Sensors like details and see clearly what is actually before them, Intuitives have little interest in details and tend to look for underlying patterns or go for the "big picture." A Sensor and an Intuitive can see exactly the same situation very differently, which means they'll recollect things differently, too.

Steve and Karen were standing near a busy intersection when they witnessed a car accident. Shortly after the incident, the police interviewed each of them.

"I saw a late-model blue Chevrolet station wagon approach the intersection while the light was green," reported Karen, a Sensor. "I also noticed an old red Mustang coming out of a side street much too fast—I'd say at least fifty miles per hour. I heard the screech of the Mustang's brakes, then a loud bang as the Mustang struck the driver's side of the station wagon. The impact made the wagon spin around two complete times before it smashed into a street sign on the opposite corner."

Steve, an Intuitive, told the police that he, too, had seen and heard the two cars collide. He *thought* the Mustang might have gone through a red light, but everything had happened so quickly he really couldn't be sure. Actually, Steve could offer the police few details about what had occurred. He remembered wondering where the red Mustang was going in such a hurry—he knew it was a Mustang because he used to have a car like it—and he remembered thinking that someone should call an ambulance quickly. He hoped everybody had insurance, and he was concerned about the driver, who looked a little like someone he knew.

Intuitives approach tasks very differently from Sensors. For example, an Intuitive would rather rely on his or her sense of direction than use a map, or might try to figure out how to operate a new air conditioner without reading the manual. A Sensor would almost certainly take a more practical approach.

For their first anniversary, Sharon gave George a gas barbecue grill. It had to be assembled and came with ten pages of detailed instructions and diagrams. Being the clear Intuitive that he is, George started to assemble his grill based upon "which parts seemed like they should go together." When he had finished two hours later, what he'd made looked more like a bicycle than a gas grill. Plus, he had a handful of parts left over, and he frankly had *no* idea where they belonged! It took Sharon, a Sensor, one hour to disassemble George's work and reassemble the grill correctly. "Naturally," she followed the directions. She wouldn't consider doing it any other way!

Sensors have a great capacity for enjoying the here and now. Often they are content to let things be. Intuitives, on the other hand, anticipate the future and tend to agitate for change.

Phil, a Sensor, and Jessie, an Intuitive, frequently take long walks near the town reservoir. Phil loves these walks because they put him back in touch with nature. He loves the smell of the woods, the feel of the breeze on his face, the deep blue of the sky in contrast to the multicolored leaves on the trees. Plus, he just likes exercise. Jessie likes being outdoors, too, but during their walks she spends so much of her time thinking or talking about new ideas for her current project that often she'll reach the end of the walk without ever really stopping to notice where she's been.

Both Intuitives and Sensors have important roles to play in organizations. Intuitives naturally focus on possibilities; Sensors naturally focus on realities. Variations on the same scenario are played out thousands of times daily across the country whenever the two types meet. Sensors and Intuitives see the world in fundamentally different ways and often fail to appreciate the value of each other's perspective.

As James, an Intuitive, expresses it, "I'm an idea man. Nothing feels better to me than to take a troublesome situation and figure out a new approach that will make it work better. The problem with this company is that no one has any vision—especially my boss, Warren. He can't see beyond the end of his desk. I come to him with a terrific idea that can have a significant impact on the future of this company, and all he wants to know is, 'What will it cost? How much time will it take? Who's going to do your job while you're out doing this new "job du jour"?'"

Now Warren, a Sensor, sees things differently, as you might expect. "Maybe it's because Jim is a more creative guy than I am, but frankly, I don't know where he comes up with half of his ideas. It's not that they're *bad* ideas, it's just that most of them are totally unrealistic. Jim doesn't understand what it takes to get things done around here. This place runs on the bottom line. To recommend a plan to *my* boss, I have to present a well-thought-out cost/benefit analysis, which means I need to have realistic data concerning expenses, time frames, and the anticipated impact on the company. This all takes the kind of careful, methodical research that Jim doesn't seem to be interested in doing."

Like Extraverts, Sensors have something of an advantage in our society because there are more of them. About 65 percent of the American population are Sensors, which puts Intuitives clearly in the minority.

Sensors	*Intuitives*
Trust what is certain and concrete	Trust inspiration and inference
Like new ideas only if they have practical applications	Like new ideas and concepts for their own sake
Value realism and common sense	Value imagination and innovation

Sensors	**Intuitives**
Like to use and hone established skills	Like to learn new skills; get bored easily after mastering skills
Tend to be specific and literal; give detailed descriptions	Tend to be general and figurative; use metaphors and analogies
Present information in a step-by-step manner	Present information through leaps, in a roundabout manner
Are oriented to the present	Are oriented toward the future

By now it should be clear that people really do take in information in two very different ways. Please indicate your preference on the continuum below.

(S) Sensing ————————————————— Intuition (N)

(T) Thinking / Feeling (F)

The third dimension of Personality Type concerns the way in which we make decisions and come to conclusions. Just as there are two different ways of interacting with the world and two different ways of taking in information, so are there two different ways of making decisions: by means of Thinking or Feeling.

In the context of Type, Thinking refers to making decisions impersonally, and Feeling refers to making decisions based on personal values. Although emotions can play a part in decision making, Feeling here simply means making decisions based upon what is important to you and others.

Thinkers prefer decisions that make sense logically. They pride themselves on their ability to be objective and analytical in the decision-making process. They make decisions by analyzing and weighing the evidence, even if that means coming to unpleasant conclusions. **Feelers** make decisions based on how much they care or what they feel is right. They pride themselves on their ability to be empathetic and compassionate. Obviously, Thinkers and Feelers have very different priorities.

Some people find it especially difficult to decide between Thinking and Feeling. Sometimes the terms carry certain connotations that may make one choice seem less desirable than the other. Also, in our culture there is a very strong gender bias regarding certain kinds of behavior. Different sex role expectations can cause some people to "falsify" their preference. A woman who is naturally a Thinker may be socialized to behave more like a Feeler (the life-giver, the mother, and the nurturer, ever sympathetic and supportive), and a man who is naturally a Feeler may be socialized to behave more like a Thinker (the hunter, the competitor, cool-headed, detached, and unemotional). When you read the following paragraphs, think about which preference suits the *real* you, not necessarily how you were raised or encouraged to be. For people who have been acting "out of type" for a long time, clarifying this preference can be an especially enlightening and liberating experience.

As we have said before (and will no doubt say again, because it is so important), everyone uses both preferences. Thinkers do have emotions and personal values, and Feelers can be perfectly logical. However, each of us uses one process more naturally, more often, and more successfully than the other.

Thinking is usually considered a rational way of making decisions, while a Feeling approach is considered irrational. This is not the case. Thinking and Feeling are both rational methods; they just use different criteria in the decision-making process.

Take the example of Robert, a Feeler, who is the assistant dean of students at a small liberal arts college. Robert is responsible for conducting disciplinary hearings for students accused of violating the college's rules. He also decides the appropriate punishments as needed. A student, Henry, was caught smoking marijuana in his dormitory, a violation that usually carries a penalty of suspension for one semester, followed by two semesters of probation. Looking into the case, Robert discovered that Henry, a freshman, had been assigned to a room with two upperclassmen who had both been in and out of trouble. Robert also learned that Henry had an excellent academic record, and he had never been in any trouble before. Henry appeared to be genuinely contrite, and he was terrified about how his parents might react if he were suspended, since they had made real sacrifices to send him to school. Taking all these things into consideration, Robert fixed Henry's punishment at mandatory attendance in a six-week campus drug awareness program, followed by one semester of probation.

The dean, a Thinker, thought this punishment was too lenient and made no sense. She thought that failing to hold all students to the same standard set a dangerous precedent, and she asked Robert to justify his decision.

As Robert put it, "I know I could have suspended Henry. But I looked at the situation this way: We never should have assigned him the roommates we did, especially knowing how eager freshmen are to be accepted. As far as I'm concerned, we created the problem. Henry is a good kid, a good student, and an asset to the school. And after all, we are first and foremost an educational institution. I feel Henry has learned a valuable lesson from this experience, and I see no need to punish him for a relatively minor offense in a way which could affect his whole life."

Although Robert's decision was based on his own personal values and interpretation of the situation, you can see that he certainly did not make his decision irrationally.

Lauren, a Feeler, and Bert, a Thinker, are a good example of how people who are different on this preference can provide important balance for one another. They work together in the editorial department of a health and fitness magazine, and they have come to appreciate each other's values. "Lauren is very perceptive about people," explains Bert. "When I have trouble with a particular writer, or when I can't understand why someone is acting a certain way, I'll discuss it with

Lauren. She's always able to see why the person is feeling the way he or she is — and sometimes how I've been responsible. Lauren's insights and suggestions about how to handle specific situations have bailed me out on many occasions."

For her part, Lauren says, "Bert is probably the most honest person I know. Not always the most tactful or diplomatic...but the most honest. I always go to him when I want to know what the logical thing to do is, instead of just going with what feels right to me. I don't always like what Bert has to say, or the blunt way he says it, but I know I'll always get a truly objective view — something I need and appreciate!"

Thinkers can be analytical to the point of seeming cold, and Feelers can be personally involved to the point of seeming overemotional. When Thinkers and Feelers clash, more often than not the Feeler ends up hurt and angry, while the Thinker is confused about what went wrong.

Tony, a Feeler, is a salesman for a large office-furniture manufacturer. He booked a morning flight to Chicago to attend a lunch meeting with some representatives from a company that was refurbishing its offices. Tony's boss had flown in the night before in order to wine and dine these important prospective clients.

When Tony arrived an hour and a half late to the important ten o'clock meeting, his boss was clearly irritated. Tony explained that one of the engines on his first flight had burst into flames en route, necessitating an emergency landing — complete with waiting firetrucks — in Detroit. After he'd waited for two hours, the airline finally found Tony a seat in the first-class section of another flight so he could complete his trip.

When his boss's first question was how much the extra first-class accommodation had cost the firm, Tony stared at his boss with astonishment, hurt at his apparent lack of appreciation for what Tony had just been through.

Tony's boss was baffled and said, "I don't understand why you're upset with me. It's not that I don't care about your safety. But it's obvious that you're all right so now I'm simply curious about the added cost."

To help you decide which preference suits you, see which side you would take in the following disagreement.

Tom, a Feeler, has a tough decision to make. Because of a restructuring of his company, he is being forced to lay off one employee from the marketing department. The choice has come down to Ted, a fifty-seven-year-old with twenty-two years at the company, or Alan, thirty-six, who joined the firm two years ago. Both men have similar job descriptions and satisfactory performance.

At a meeting with his boss, Ernie, Tom explained why he would like to keep Ted and let Alan go. "Ted has been a loyal employee, and I appreciate the fact that he is always willing to go the extra mile to get a job done right and to help others succeed. As far as his personal situation is concerned, Ted has one son in college and another starting next fall. His wife, Mary, is in poor health. I'm concerned that a man his age who has worked exclusively for one company this long would have a hard time finding a comparable job. Alan is young, ambitious, and mobile; he'll have no trouble finding a good job. Besides, I feel that by rewarding loyalty and hard work, we make all of our employees feel better about working here."

Ernie, a Thinker, sees the situation differently. "No one's saying that Ted isn't a great guy and a good employee. Personally, I've always liked him. But this decision has to be based on what's best for the *company,* not what's best for one individual. Ted's best years are behind him, and it's unlikely that he will ever move up. Alan's best years are ahead of him. He is senior management material; with proper grooming, he could become a very important asset to the company. Also, because of his seniority, we pay Ted twenty thousand dollars more than we pay Alan, and there is a greater likelihood of significant health care costs down the road for Ted than there is for Alan. It's an unfortunate situation, but it just doesn't make sense to keep Ted and let Alan go."

If you vote to keep Ted, chances are you're a Feeler. If you vote to keep Alan, you're probably a Thinker.

The American population is evenly split between Thinkers and Feelers. However, this is the only type dimension in which clear gender differences show up. About two-thirds of men prefer Thinking, and about two-thirds of women prefer Feeling. We aren't sure to what extent these results are due to socialization.

Thinkers	*Feelers*
Step back; apply impersonal analysis to problems	Step forward; consider effect of actions on others
Value logic, justice, and fairness; one standard for all	Value empathy and harmony; see the exception to the rule
Naturally see flaws and tend to be critical	Naturally like to please others; show appreciation easily
May be seen as heartless, insensitive, and uncaring	May be seen as overemotional, illogical, and weak
Consider it more important to be truthful than tactful	Consider it important to be tactful as well as truthful
Believe feelings are valid only if they are logical	Believe any feeling is valid, whether it makes sense or not
Are motivated by a desire for achievement and accomplishment	Are motivated by a desire to be appreciated

Once again we'd like you to estimate where you think you belong on the continuum below.

(T) Thinking ——————————|—————————— Feeling (F)

(J) Judging / Perceiving (P)

The fourth dimension of Personality Type concerns whether we prefer to live in a more structured way (making decisions) or in a more spontaneous way (taking in information). Again, there is a range between opposite extremes of behavior.

People with a preference for Judging—we call them **Judgers**—tend to live in an orderly way and are happiest when their lives are structured and matters are settled. They have a judging attitude and like to make decisions. Judgers seek to regulate and control life. People with a preference for Perceiving—we call them **Perceivers**—like to live in a spontaneous way and are happiest when their lives are flexible. They have a perceiving attitude and like to stay open to all kinds of possibilities. Perceivers seek to understand life rather than control it.

Judgers are *not* necessarily judgmental (opinionated); they just like to have issues resolved. Perceivers are *not* necessarily perceptive (astute about seeing things accurately); they simply like perceiving options.

An important distinction between Judgers and Perceivers is the issue of closure. Judgers experience tension until closure is reached and are constantly drawn toward making a decision. Perceivers, on the other hand, experience tension when they are forced to make a decision; they avoid closure and prefer to keep their options open.

Everyone uses both Judging and Perceiving in daily life. As with the other preferences, no one behaves strictly one way or the other. It's good to seek a balance of Judging and Perceiving, since Judgers run the risk of becoming rigid, dogmatic, and inflexible, and Perceivers run the risk of leaving things open-ended to the point that they procrastinate their lives away.

When Cynthia, a Perceiver, volunteered to put together a monthly newsletter for a local bookstore, the other employees were enthusiastic. Cynthia seemed natural for the job: she was easygoing and well known in the community; she also was artistically talented and had done newsletters before. Cynthia set about gathering articles and important dates, but the first of the month came and went and no newsletter appeared. When pressed for an explanation, Cynthia was unperturbed. She explained that her mother had come to visit, one of her children had gotten sick, plus she and her husband had gone skiing one weekend and she hadn't gotten as much done as she'd hoped. In addition, she was having trouble gathering some of the facts she needed, and she hadn't yet been able to reach a few people by phone. Eventually Cynthia assembled a nice little newsletter, and the process began all over again. In six months the bookstore published two entertaining, informal newsletters of which Cynthia was very proud.

This all drove Betsy, a manager at the bookstore, absolutely wild. Betsy, a Judger, expected a newsletter to appear on the first of every month, and she expected it to include a calendar of all the important dates for that month. Betsy was so irritated by Cynthia's performance that she eventually took over the newsletter herself. She had no trouble whatsoever gathering the information she needed, and if for some reason an article was missing, she simply published the newsletter without it. Betsy turned out professional, succinct, occasionally dry newsletters, and they were *always* on time.

Judgers prefer a planned and orderly world, living with structure that has a beginning, middle, and end. They like to be in control of what is happening and they like to make decisions. Judgers tend to see things in black and white and like to come down on one side or the other of an issue. They are more comfortable when issues are settled rather than being left up in the air—even if they aren't the ones making the decision! Judgers may not be particularly adaptable, and they generally don't like surprises.

Perceivers like their world to be flexible, allowing for lots of opportunities for spontaneity. They feel constrained by structure, and prefer things to be free-flowing. Perceivers enjoy adapting to new and changing situations and tend to delay making decisions. They leave things open-ended whenever they can, wanting to suspend judgment as long as possible. Perceivers see issues in shades of gray and enjoy the unexpected in nearly all areas of their lives.

Jeff and Amy decided it was time to finally get in shape, so they went together to the sporting goods store to buy bicycles. Jeff, a Perceiver, found a salesman, and over the next half hour asked him about a hundred questions. He wasn't sure which bike was best for him, and he was troubled by the store's returns policy (you could return a bike, but only for store credit). Jeff finally left, saying he'd have to think over his decision. On the way home, he stopped at two other sporting goods stores to "get a little more information."

Amy, a Judger, looked over all the bikes on display for a few minutes, then found a salesman and asked, "Which bike do you recommend?" When the salesman showed her the store's top-selling bike, she said, "Fine. I'll take it."

In the work world, these two different styles can create conflicts, especially when Judgers and Perceivers are under pressure together. As is always the case, it helps to be aware of other people's preferences. Knowing that people naturally behave differently can make irritating behavior not only easier to tolerate but also easier to anticipate.

Irene and Suzanne, both employees of a corporate training department, were assigned to co-train a one-day management development program. Each of them had conducted this program individually many times before, but this was the first time they had worked together. They divided up the portions of the program each would be responsible for: Irene, a Perceiver, was to start the program at 8:00 and conduct a thirty-minute introduction; then Suzanne, a Judger, would present the first section, which would last one and a half hours until the morning break at 10:00.

At 8:00, seven of the twenty-five participants had not arrived. Suzanne wanted to get started anyway, but Irene opted to wait until all were present, which took about fifteen minutes. During Irene's introduction, several people had questions about the program. Suzanne diplomatically tried to interject that many of the questions would be answered as the day progressed, but Irene decided it was important to address them at that moment. By the time Irene finished, it was 9:00, which meant that Suzanne had only one hour in which to make her ninety-minute presentation. She raced through her presentation, barely covering all the necessary information, and ended the segment feeling disorganized and very stressed.

At the ten o'clock break, Suzanne was furious and confronted Irene. They soon found themselves in a heated conflict. Suzanne accused Irene of having poor time-management skills and said she'd acted irresponsibly. She pointed out that Irene's mismanagement of the morning had put her in the position of having to scramble through her presentation. Suzanne felt that it had been ridiculous to make eighteen people who had come on time wait for seven who hadn't, and she said that rushing through her notes had made her look ridiculous. She felt that she had not had enough time to present her part of the program effectively, and she resented the fact that all of her careful planning had been ruined for no good reason.

Irene felt that Suzanne was overreacting and was being too rigid. She thought it was entirely appropriate to wait for the missing third of the participants. Moreover, she regarded interruptions as a typical and often necessary part of the program. She felt it was important to address questions early on in order to set the right tone for the day and knew they could make up the rest of the program later. Irene didn't appreciate the fact that Suzanne had tried to cut her answers short, and said she felt that Suzanne had undercut her authority in front of the group.

Since the two women still had a full day's program remaining, they ultimately realized that they had better figure out how to work together more smoothly. Irene promised to watch the clock more carefully, but was still committed to keeping the lines of communication open between herself and the program participants. Suzanne promised to try to be more flexible about what was discussed when, but she reserved the right to remind Irene of their schedule in front of the group. Fortunately the rest of the program went without incident.

One indication of your preference between Judging and Perceiving may be the condition of your desk. Typically *(but not always)*, a Judger's desk is fairly neat. It is well organized. There are spots for pencils, pads, paperweights, and so forth, and these items can usually be found—at least at the beginning and end of the day—in their proper places. The IN basket contains information to be reviewed, and the OUT basket is reserved for completed work. Important information is filed away in a manner that allows for easy retrieval. It is not unusual to see on a Judger's desk a list of "things to do" with a line drawn through most, if not all, the items on the list at the end of the day.

A Perceiver's desk, on the other hand, is often *(but not always)* considerably less organized. It might contain several "works in progress," messages that need to be answered, toys, malfunctioning ball-point pens, and perhaps the best indicator of all...the "just for now" pile (or piles). When put on the defensive, Perceivers will always claim that they can find anything they need in their office. (They just don't admit how much time it will take to do it!)

The condition of your desk (and possibly the inside of your closet, purse, or car) reflects how your mind works. Let's say a Judger and a Perceiver both receive a brochure announcing an upcoming conference that is to take place in four months. The Judger is likely to do one of the following: 1) Throw the brochure away because she went last year or already has a prior commitment; 2) Fill out the application, write out the check to cover the registration fee, and send them in; or 3) Pass the brochure along to someone else who might be interested. The Judger makes a decision and gets the brochure off her desk.

The Perceiver in the same situation is likely to behave differently. First of all, four months into the future is a long time from now. Recognizing that a lot could happen between now and then (and that maybe something better will come along), the Perceiver believes it's too soon to make a decision. She realizes she should file the brochure someplace, but if she does, she'll probably forget all about it, so instead she adds it to her substantial "just for now" stack of papers and folders already occupying space on her desk. Unless it is truly important, the brochure is apt to get lost in the pile, only to be discovered after the deadline for registration (or even the conference itself) has come and gone. The Perceiver doesn't make a decision, so the brochure hangs around on her desk until the time for decision making has passed.

Everyone has a "to do" list or a "just for now" pile. That's not unusual. But Perceivers are likely to have all kinds of items in their "think about" pile, and they can probably recall several opportunities they missed because they procrastinated too long.

In the American population, about 60 percent are Judgers and 40 percent are Perceivers. There are no gender differences.

Judgers	*Perceivers*
Are happiest after decisions have been made	Are happiest leaving their options open
Have a "work ethic": work first, play later (if there's time)	Have a "play ethic": enjoy now, finish the job later (if there's time)
Set goals and work toward achieving them on time	Change goals as new information becomes available
Prefer knowing what they are getting into	Like adapting to new situations
Are product oriented (emphasis is on completing the task)	Are process oriented (emphasis is on how the task is completed)
Derive satisfaction from finishing projects	Derive satisfaction from starting projects
See time as a finite resource and take deadlines seriously	See time as a renewable resource and see deadlines as elastic

As you think about which preference suits you, keep in mind that circumstances often force us to behave in certain ways that don't necessarily reflect our true selves. Most of us have to behave like Judgers at least part of the time, particularly at work. If you have a demanding job, you have to get there on time, meet deadlines, and make lots of decisions. To complicate things further, as your personal and work lives get more and more intertwined, it may become increasingly difficult to tell which is the "real you." In this case, try to step back and see which preference would give you the most satisfaction if you could behave any way you wished.

It's time again to estimate your preference on the continuum below.

(J) Judging ——————————————|—————————————— Perceiving (P)

Now that you have estimated your preference for all four type dimensions, please write those letters in the spaces below.

_____	_____	_____	_____
E or I	S or N	T or F	J or P

KEY

E = Extraverted   I   = Introverted
S = Sensing   N = Intuitive
T = Thinking   F = Feeling
J = Judging   P = Perceiving

Congratulations! By going through this exercise, you have more than likely identified your personality type. However, the process of *making sure* that you have identified your type correctly requires one more step, which we call "verification."

Verifying Your Type

Chapter 3 contains "Verifying Type Profiles" for each of the sixteen types. After reading the brief introduction to the chapter, we will ask you to find the profile for the type that you feel reflects the code you came up with in step one.

For example, suppose you estimated your type preferences to be: Extravert, Sensing, Thinking, and Judging (or ESTJ in Type language). You would first find and read the ESTJ profile.

If ESTJ is really your personality type, then you will probably think that it describes you very well. In fact, most people are taken aback at just how well their type profile describes them! If you feel this way, then you have very probably verified your type. We say "very probably" only to discourage those of you with the tendency to make quick decisions (and you know who you are!) from foreclosing any other possibilities which *might* be better fits. So until you have read several other chapters which describe Type more thoroughly, we suggest you think of the type you come up with by doing this exercise as a sort of "working hypothesis."

On the other hand, if you read ESTJ and you think it sounds *somewhat* like you, but not *very much* like you, then you probably haven't yet identified your one "true" type.

If you find yourself in that situation, here's what to do. Go back to the continuums (scales) for each of the preferences. Note which ones you marked closer to the center line (in other words, the less clear preferences). Then see which ones you marked farther away from the center lines (the ones that seemed clearer to you).

Using the ESTJ again for an example, suppose that by going back you discover that you felt pretty clear about your preferences for Extraversion (E), Sensing (S), and Thinking (T), but less clear about your preference for Judging (J). Well, it's possible that you may really be an ESTP rather than an ESTJ. As you will learn shortly, these two types, while identical on three letters, are *very* different from each other in many ways. Therefore, you will want to read the ESTP profile as well.

If it turns out that your preference really is for *Perceiving* rather than Judging, then the ESTP profile should fit you much better. Thus you may have to go through this process of examining a few (and in rare instances, several) types to find your true type.

You may ask: "But shouldn't I be able to identify my type right away?" Not necessarily. Often circumstances just don't permit people to "be themselves." For example, you may have had parents who encouraged only certain kinds of behavior, or you may have been obliged to do what was expected of you (say, run the family business) instead of what interested you (studying architecture). Some people who experienced very difficult childhoods were forced to adopt certain kinds of behavior as a form of self-defense. This, too, can affect how you see yourself and can place a barrier between the "you" who survived and the "you" you were meant to be. This is the time to try to determine who you really are deep down.

It is important to carefully pin down all four of your preferences because your personality is in large part determined by the unique way in which your preferences interact with each other. Perhaps you're familiar with the concept of "synergism." Basically, synergy occurs when the whole of something is greater than the sum of its individual parts. This is certainly true of Type. And as useful as it is for people to know that they prefer Sensing to Intuition, for example, no one is *just* a Sensor. People who prefer Sensing come in eight different varieties, depending upon their other preferences—and it is the *combination* of preferences (indicated by letters) that results in such useful information.

Although you don't *have* to know your personality type in order to benefit from the rest of this book, you'll certainly get more out of *Do What You Are* if you can successfully identify your personality type before going on to Part 2. As you review this chapter and read the next one, please keep in mind that there is *no time limit* for discovering your true type. The Type Police will not come crashing through your door if you haven't verified your type after finishing Part 1. In this fast-paced world of ours we often feel pressured to decide everything quickly. We don't believe in "McTyping," so take your time and review this material as much as you need. Keep refining your working hypothesis until you have identified the personality type that most accurately reflects you. Then have a little celebration—you've found the real you!

Descriptions of the sixteen personality types in the next chapter draw substantially upon the following works: *Introduction to Type: A Description of the Theory and Application of the Myers-Briggs Type Indicator,* by Isabel Briggs Myers (1987); *Introduction to Type in Organizations,* by Sandra Krebs Hirsh and Jean M. Kummerow (1990); *Manual: A Guide to the Development and Use of the Myers-Briggs Type Indicator,* by Isabel Briggs Myers and Mary McCaulley (1985); and *Gifts Differing,* by Isabel Briggs Myers (1980). All of these books are published by Consulting Psychologists Press, Inc., and certain material in the next chapter is reprinted with permission of Consulting Psychologists Press, Inc.

Note: For each profile, we provide an approximation of the percentage of this type found in the American population. These percentages were developed by Dr. Charles K. Martin of the Center for Applications of Psychological Type (CAPT), Gainesville, Florida.

3 | MIRROR, MIRROR
Verifying Your Personality Type

Included in this chapter are the sixteen Verifying Type Profiles. Your true type profile is among them.

Your type profile is not meant to be a totally comprehensive, all-encompassing description of your innermost thoughts and feelings. However, in a general way, it should ring true for you—perhaps not every word, but overall you ought to recognize a great deal of yourself in it.

The Verifying Type Profiles don't attempt to explain why different personality types behave the way they do. We'll get into these kinds of explanations in Part 2. For now, just concentrate on finding the type profile that best suits you.

In these profiles, we have deliberately avoided using descriptions from the workplace. This may strike you as a little odd, but remember, you are trying to pinpoint the "real you." How you are obliged to act at work may be very different from how you wish you were free to be. In Part 3 you'll find a list of the work-related strengths and weaknesses that are commonly associated with your personality.

You may read through several of the Verifying Type Profiles and think, "Wait a minute. I can see something of myself in *all* of these descriptions." Actually, this isn't unusual, but the point is to find your true type profile, not bits and pieces that sound like you. Most people find that their type profile is very accurate and extremely insightful.

We hope that by now we've convinced you of the validity of Type. However, if you are a skeptical sort who suspects that the personality types are all interchangeable, we suggest that you read both a type profile *and its opposite* (for example, INTP and ESFJ). You'll see that the two profiles describe two very different kinds of people.

In the Verifying Type Profiles we've included not only descriptions of personality strengths but also information on possible blind spots. You'll find that sometimes the flip side of your greatest strength is your worst shortcoming. For example, excellent reasoning power can be coupled with a tendency to overlook the feelings of others. By being aware of the weaknesses associated with your personality type, you can seek balance in your behavior—both on and off the job.

‖ ENFJ

Extraverted, Intuitive, Feeling, Judging
Approximately 3–5 percent of the American population

ENFJs are people-lovers. They place the highest importance on people and relationships and are naturally concerned about others. They take a warm approach to life and feel personally connected to all things.

Because they are idealistic and live by their values, ENFJs are very loyal to the people, causes, or institutions they respect and admire. They are energetic and enthusiastic, as well as responsible, conscientious, and persevering.

ENFJs have a natural tendency to be self-critical. However, because they feel responsible for the feelings of others, ENFJs are seldom critical in public. They are acutely aware of what is (and isn't) appropriate behavior, and are gracious, charming, personable, and socially adept. Even-tempered and tolerant, ENFJs are diplomatic and are good at promoting harmony around them. They are natural leaders, popular and charismatic. They tend to be good communicators, and usually use their expressive gift verbally.

ENFJs make decisions based upon how they feel about a situation, rather than how the situation actually stands. They are interested in possibilities beyond what is already obvious, and in the ways these possibilities might affect others.

Being naturally orderly, ENFJs prefer an organized world and expect others to be the same way. They like to have matters settled, even if someone else is making the decisions.

ENFJs radiate sympathy and understanding and are nurturing and supportive of others. They read people well and are responsible and caring. Since they are idealists, they generally look for the good in others.

Possible Blind Spots

ENFJs are so empathetic and caring that they can become overly involved with the problems or feelings of others. Sometimes they choose causes that aren't worthy of all the time and energy they pour into them. When things don't work out well, they can become overwhelmed, disappointed, or disillusioned. This can lead them to withdraw, feeling they weren't appreciated. ENFJs need to learn to accept their own limitations as well as those of the people they care about. They also need to learn how to "pick their battles" and how to maintain realistic expectations.

Because of their strong desire for harmony, ENFJs can overlook their own needs and ignore real problems. Because they avoid conflict, they sometimes maintain relationships that are less than honest and equal. ENFJs are so concerned about the feelings of others that they can be blind to important facts when the situation involves criticism or hurt feelings. It's important that ENFJs learn how to accept and deal with conflict as a necessary part of relationships.

Because they are enthusiastic and in a hurry to get on with their next challenge, ENFJs sometimes make incorrect assumptions or make decisions too quickly, without gathering all the important facts. They need to slow down and pay closer attention to the details of their projects. By waiting until enough information is known, they can avoid making mistakes.

ENFJs focus on emotions to the point that they can fail to see the logical consequences of their actions. Trying to focus on the facts, not just the people, involved in their decisions can be helpful.

ENFJs respond well to praise, but are easily hurt by criticism, which can make them appear touchy. They take even the most innocent or well-intentioned criticism personally, and they often respond by becoming flustered, hurt, or angry. Their responses can be illogical to the point that they appear downright irrational to others. ENFJs do well to stop, take a step back, and try to see a situation objectively before reacting. Trying to be less sensitive will enable an ENFJ to hear the important and helpful information that is contained in constructive criticism.

ENFJs are so idealistic that they tend to see things the way they wish they were. They are vulnerable to idealizing relationships, and they tend to overlook facts that contradict what they believe. ENFJs who don't learn to face facts they find disagreeable end up ignoring their problems instead of finding solutions for them. In general, ENFJs need to try to keep their eyes open as well as their hearts.

‖ INFJ
Introverted, Intuitive, Feeling, Judging
Approximately 2–3 percent of the American population

INFJs inhabit a world of ideas. They are independent, original thinkers with strong feelings, firm principles, and personal integrity.

INFJs trust their own ideas and decisions even in the face of skepticism. They are motivated by an inner vision that they value above all else, including prevailing opinion or established authority. INFJs often see deeper meanings and have intuitive insights into situations. Their inspirations are important and valid to them even if others don't share their enthusiasm.

INFJs are loyal, committed, and idealistic. They are quietly forceful in having their ideas accepted and applied. They value integrity and can be determined to the point of being stubborn. Because of the strength of their conviction and their clear vision of what is best for the common good, INFJs can be great leaders. They are often honored or respected for their contributions.

Because they value harmony and agreement, INFJs like to persuade others of the validity of their viewpoint. They win the cooperation of others by using approval and praise, rather than argument or intimidation. INFJs will go to great lengths to promote fellowship and avoid conflict.

Generally thoughtful decision makers, INFJs find problems stimulating and usually reflect carefully before they act. They prefer to focus in great depth on one thing at a time, which can result in periods of single-mindedness.

Empathetic and compassionate, INFJs have a strong desire to contribute to the welfare of others. They are aware of other people's emotions and interests, and often deal well with complicated people. INFJs themselves tend to have deep, complex personalities and can be both sensitive and intense. They can be reserved and hard to get to know, but are willing to share their inner selves with people they trust. They tend to have a small circle of deep, longstanding friendships, and can generate plenty of personal warmth and enthusiasm in the right circumstances.

Possible Blind Spots

Since they tend to be so absorbed with "the idea," INFJs can sometimes be impractical and are capable of neglecting routine details that need attention. Becoming more aware of what is around them and relying more on proven information helps INFJs anchor their creative ideas in the real world.

INFJs can be so committed to their own principles that they develop tunnel vision. They can be stubborn about change, and may resist changing a decision once it has been made. Sometimes they overlook important facts that don't support their position, or resist ideas that conflict with their values. They may not hear the objections of others because, to them, their position seems unquestionable. INFJs need to attempt to look at themselves and at their work more objectively, as others might.

Because they are so protective of their own vision, INFJs tend to overregulate. They are often perfectionists, and they can be hypersensitive to criticism. Although they are strong-willed, they also have difficulty dealing with conflicts in relationships and can become disappointed or disillusioned if conflicts develop. The more objective INFJs can be about themselves and their relationships, the less vulnerable they will be to these kinds of hurts.

‖ ENFP
Extraverted, Intuitive, Feeling, Perceiving
Approximately 6–7 percent of the American population

ENFPs are full of enthusiasm and new ideas. Optimistic, spontaneous, creative, and confident, they have original minds and a strong sense of the possible. For an ENFP, life is an exciting drama.

Because they are so interested in possibilities, ENFPs see significance in all things and prefer to keep lots of options open. They are perceptive and keen observers who notice anything out of the ordinary. ENFPs are curious; they prefer to understand rather than judge.

Imaginative, adaptable, and alert, ENFPs value inspiration above all else and are often ingenious inventors. They are sometimes nonconformists, and are good at seeing new ways of doing things. ENFPs open up new avenues for thought or action...and then keep them open!

In carrying out their innovative ideas, ENFPs rely on their impulsive energy. They have lots of initiative and find problems stimulating. They also get an infusion of energy from being around other people, and can successfully combine their talents with the strengths of others.

ENFPs are charming and full of vitality. They treat people with sympathy, gentleness, and warmth and are ready to help anyone with a problem. They can be remarkably insightful and perceptive, and they often care about the development of others. ENFPs avoid conflict and prefer harmony. They put more energy into maintaining personal relationships than into maintaining objects, and they like to keep a wide assortment of relationships alive.

Possible Blind Spots

Since they find it so easy to generate ideas, ENFPs have difficulty focusing on just one thing at a time and can have trouble making decisions. They see so many possibilities that they have difficulty selecting the best activity or interest to pursue. Sometimes they make poor choices or get involved with too many things at once. Carefully choosing where they will focus their energy helps ENFPs avoid wasting their time and squandering their considerable talents.

To an ENFP, the fun part of a project is the initial problem solving and creation of something new. They like to exercise their inspiration on the important and challenging parts of a problem. After this stage, they often lose interest and lack the self-discipline necessary to complete what they've started. They are likely to start many projects but finish few. ENFPs have more to show for their efforts when they follow through with the necessary but tedious parts of a project until it is completed. Often writing important facts or steps down on paper helps them keep from getting sidetracked.

Often ENFPs are not particularly well organized. They can benefit from learning and applying time management and personal organizational skills. They do well when they team up with other more realistic and practical people. This usually suits them fine anyway, since ENFPs don't like working alone, especially for extended periods of time. They find working with another person, even on a less interesting phase of a project, far preferable to working alone.

ENFPs are not much interested in details. Since they are more excited about using their imagination and creating something original, they may not bother to collect all the information they need in order to carry out a particular activity. Sometimes they just improvise on the spot, instead of planning and preparing ahead. Because they find information gathering tedious, ENFPs run the risk of never getting past the "bright idea" stage or, once started, never finishing. Always restless, they'd rather put off dealing with troublesome details and move on to something else new or unusual. ENFPs are more effective when they consciously attend to the actual world around them and gather more realistic impressions to make their innovations workable.

‖ INFP
Introverted, Intuitive, Feeling, Perceiving
Approximately 3–4 percent of the American population

INFPs value inner harmony above all else. Sensitive, idealistic, and loyal, they have a strong sense of honor concerning their personal values and are often motivated by deep personal belief or by devotion to a cause they feel is worthy.

INFPs are interested in possibilities beyond what is already known and focus most of their energy on their dreams and visions. Open-minded, curious, and insightful, they often have excellent long-range vision. In day-to-day matters they are usually flexible, tolerant, and adaptable, but they are very firm about their inner loyalties and set very high—in fact, nearly impossible—standards for themselves.

INFPs have many ideals and loyalties that keep them occupied. They are deeply committed to whatever they choose to undertake—and they tend to undertake too much but somehow get everything done.

Although they demonstrate cool reserve on the outside, INFPs care deeply inside. They are compassionate, sympathetic, understanding, and very sensitive to the feelings of others. They avoid conflict and are not interested in impressing or dominating others unless their values are at stake. Often INFPs prefer to communicate their feelings in writing, rather than orally. When they are persuading others of the importance of their ideals, INFPs can be most convincing.

INFPs seldom express the intensity of their feelings and often appear reticent and calm. However, once they know you, they are enthusiastic and warm. INFPs are friendly, but tend to avoid superficial socializing. They treasure people who take the time to understand their goals and values.

Possible Blind Spots

Since logic is not a priority for INFPs, they sometimes make errors of fact and can be unaware that they are being illogical. When their dreams become out of touch with reality, others may see them as flighty and mystical. INFPs do well to ask the advice of more practical people to find out if their ideas are workable and useful in the real world.

Because they are so committed to their own ideals, INFPs have a tendency to overlook other points of view and can sometimes be rigid. They are not particularly interested in physical surroundings, and often are so busy that they fail to notice what is happening around them.

INFPs may reflect on an idea much longer than is really necessary to begin a project. Their perfectionistic tendencies can lead them to refine and polish their ideas for so long that they never share them. This is dangerous, since it is important for INFPs to find ways of expressing their ideas. To keep from getting discouraged, they need to work toward becoming more action-oriented.

INFPs are so emotionally entangled in their undertakings that they are very sensitive to criticism. To complicate things further, they tend to demand too much of themselves as they aspire to their own impossibly high standards. This can lead to feelings of inadequacy, even though they in fact are capable of accomplishing a great deal. When INFPs are disappointed, they tend to become negative about everything around them. Trying to develop more objectivity about their projects will help keep INFPs less vulnerable to both criticism and disappointment.

Because INFPs tend to try to please many people at the same time, it can be hard for them to stand up for an unpopular position. They hesitate to criticize others, and they have a hard time saying no. When INFPs don't express their negative opinions about ideas or plans, others can be misled into thinking they agree with them. INFPs need to develop more assertiveness, and can benefit from learning how to offer honest criticism of others when needed.

‖ ENTJ
Extraverted, Intuitive, Thinking, Judging
Approximately 2–5 percent of the American population

ENTJs are great leaders and decision makers. They easily see possibilities in all things and are happy to direct others toward making their vision become a reality. They are ingenious thinkers and great long-range planners.

Because ENTJs are so logical and analytical, they are usually good at anything that requires reasoning and intelligence. Driven to achieve competence in all they do, they can naturally spot the flaws that may exist in a situation and see immediately how to improve them. They strive to perfect systems rather than simply accept them as they are. ENTJs enjoy working with complex problem solving and are undaunted in their pursuit of mastery of anything they find intriguing. ENTJs value truth above all else and are convinced only by logical reasoning.

Eager to continually add to their base of knowledge, ENTJs are systematic about planning and researching new things. They enjoy working with complex theoretical problems and work toward the pursuit of mastery of anything they find intriguing. They are much more interested in the future consequences of actions than the present condition of things.

Natural leaders with a hearty and frank style, ENTJs tend to take charge of any situation they find themselves in. They are good organizers of people because they have the ability to see ahead and then communicate their vision to others. They tend to live by a rather strict set of rules and expect others to do so as well. Therefore, they tend to be challenging and push others as hard as they push themselves.

Possible Blind Spots

Owing to their desire to move on to the next challenge or toward their larger goal, ENTJs sometimes make decisions too hastily. Slowing down occasionally will give them the chance to gather all relevant data, and consider both the practical and personal ramifications of their actions. Their action orientation propels them to act on their decisions as soon as they are made rather than stopping to double check their facts and the realities of the situation.

Because ENTJs take a logical approach to life, they can be tough, blunt, impatient, and insensitive to the needs and feelings of others when they don't see the logic of those feelings. ENTJs can be argumentative and difficult to approach and don't often welcome the commonsense advice of others. Rather than automatically being critical, they need to listen to the input of those around them and express their appreciation for their contributions. ENTJs need to make a conscious effort—in fact to make it a rule—to stop and listen to others before charging ahead with their own ideas, and avoid acting domineering and dictatorial.

ENTJs' impersonal approach to life leaves little time, tolerance, or compassion for emotions, even their own. When they allow their feelings to go ignored or unexpressed, they can find themselves overreacting emotionally. They are particularly prone to this if they perceive someone to be questioning their competence, especially someone they respect. They can have explosive reactions to seemingly insignificant situations, and these outbursts can be hurtful to those close to them. ENTJs are more effective and happy when they give themselves time to consider and understand how they really feel. Giving their emotions a constructive outlet, rather than allowing them to take over their personalities, will actually allow them to stay more fully in control, a position they enjoy and strive for. Surprisingly, ENTJs may actually be less experienced and competent than their confident style indicates. They will increase their personal power and rate of success by allowing themselves to take some reasonable and valuable assistance from others.

‖ INTJ
Introverted, Intuitive, Thinking, Judging
Approximately 2–4 percent of the American population

INTJs are perfectionists. Their strong need for autonomy and personal competence, as well as their unshakable faith in their own original ideas, drives them to achieve their objectives.

Logical, critical, and ingenious, INTJs can see the consequences of the application of new ideas and live to see systems translated into real substance. They are demanding with themselves and others, and tend to drive others almost as hard as themselves. They are not particularly bothered by indifference or criticism. As the most independent of all types, INTJs prefer to do things their own way. They are usually skeptical, decisive, and determined in the face of opposition. They are not impressed with authority per se, but can conform to rules only if they see them as useful to their greater purpose.

With original minds, great insight, and vision, INTJs are natural brainstormers. They are naturally theoretical and work well with complex and global concepts. They are good strategic thinkers and can usually see with clarity the benefits and flaws of any situation. In subjects that interest them, they are fine organizers with insight and vision. If the idea or project is of their own making, they can invest incredible concentration, focus, energy, and drive. Their many accomplishments are achieved through determination and perseverance toward reaching or exceeding their high standards.

Possible Blind Spots

Being visionaries with sometimes unrealistically high standards, INTJs may expect too much from themselves and others. In fact, they tend not to care how they measure up to others' standards; it is their own that are important. They may lack an understanding of how their behavior affects others and can be critical and blunt in giving recommendations for improvement. They don't often encourage others to challenge their views or express any personal feelings. Because INTJs have a rather impersonal style, they may erroneously assume others wish to be treated in the same manner. They need to learn to understand the seemingly "illogical" feelings of others, and accept that they are rational and valid. This will help keep them from alienating and offending those around them.

Because INTJs place so much value on their own visions and ideas for the future, they are vulnerable to missing some important realities and facts of the present moment. They may also fail to recognize practical weaknesses in their ideas that may make their execution more difficult. Gathering all the relevant and factual data will help ensure that their ideas are workable. INTJs need to simplify their often theoretical and complicated ideas so they can communicate them to others.

Because INTJs often choose to be alone and are single-minded in their efforts, they can neglect to invite others to participate or assist in their activities. Soliciting the input and suggestions of others can help them recognize an impractical idea earlier in the process, or help them make the necessary changes and improvements before investing huge amounts of time.

Increased effectiveness for INTJs lies in making an effort to yield on less important points to win the more important ones. This will also decrease the likelihood of the INTJ becoming too stubborn and controlling. When they make an effort to adopt a more accepting approach to life and their dealings with others, INTJs will achieve more balance and competence, and will succeed at having more of their innovations accepted by the world.

ENTP
Extraverted, Intuitive, Thinking, Perceiving
Approximately 2–5 percent of the American population

ENTPs love excitement and challenge. Enthusiastic and ingenious, they are talkative, clever, and good at many things and constantly strive to increase their competence and personal power.

ENTPs are born enterprising. They are fascinated with new ideas and are alert to all possibilities. They have strong initiative and operate on creative impulse. ENTPs value their inspiration above all else and strive to turn their original ideas into reality. They are inquisitive, versatile, adaptable, and resourceful in solving challenging and theoretical problems.

Alert and outspoken, ENTPs can easily see the flaw in any position and often enjoy arguing for fun on either side of an issue. They have excellent analytical abilities and are great strategic thinkers. They can almost always find a logical reason for the things that they want.

Most ENTPs like to test the limits around them and consider that most rules and regulations are meant to be bent, if not broken. They are sometimes unconventional in their approach and enjoy helping others to push past what is accepted and expected. They like to live freely and look for fun and variety in everyday situations.

ENTPs deal imaginatively with social relationships and often have a great number and variety of friends and acquaintances. They can display great humor and optimism. ENTPs can be charming and stimulating company and often inspire others to become involved in their projects through their infectious enthusiasm. They prefer to try to understand and respond to people rather than judge them.

Possible Blind Spots

Because ENTPs value creativity and innovation above all else, they sometimes ignore the standard way of doing something simply because it is not original. Their intense dislike for the routine and predictable can make it difficult for them to notice the necessary details. They sometimes neglect the needed preparation when, in their zeal to take on something fresh, they dive in too quickly. And once major problems are solved, they are often off to the next exciting adventure rather than sticking around to see the original project through. They need to work toward making commitments to fewer projects so they will complete more of the ones they start.

Often, ENTPs talk so quickly, and so much, they don't allow others to contribute. They are honest and fair but can be blunt and tactless in their ready criticism of others. ENTPs need to consider the feelings of others as valid and important, even if they don't share them. While they can be charming, funny, and entertaining, they can also be insincere. ENTPs need to resist the urge to simply adapt and perform, and instead share their genuine emotions.

ENTPs' reluctance to commit to one thing stems from the fear that they may miss other, more appealing opportunities. Their desire to remain open and responsive to new challenges can make them undependable and inconsiderate of the plans and schedules of others. Thinking through how their actions affect others will help them be more dependable.

ENTPs' natural quickness and ability to anticipate what is coming means they occasionally assume erroneously that they knew what the person was going to say, and may jump in to finish their sentences. Taking the time to pay closer attention to what is actually going on in the real world around them and listening carefully to the input and reactions of others will help them avoid appearing arrogant and rude.

‖ INTP
Introverted, Intuitive, Thinking, Perceiving
Approximately 3–5 percent of the American population

INTPs are conceptual problem solvers. They are intensely intellectual and logical, with flashes of creative brilliance.

Outwardly quiet, reserved, and detached, INTPs are inwardly absorbed in analyzing problems. They are critical, precise, and skeptical. They try to find and use principles to understand their many ideas. They like conversation to be logical and purposeful and may argue to the point of hairsplitting just for fun. INTPs are convinced only by logical reasoning.

INTPs are usually ingenious and original thinkers. They prize intelligence in themselves, have a strong drive for personal competence, and are interested in challenging other people to become more competent as well. INTPs are primarily interested in seeing possibilities beyond what is currently known, accepted, or obvious. They like to develop models for improving the way things are or solving difficult problems. They think in extremely complex ways and are better able to organize concepts and ideas than they are able to organize people. Occasionally, their ideas are so complex they have difficulty communicating and making others understand them.

Highly independent, INTPs enjoy speculative and imaginative activities. They are flexible and open-minded and are more interested in finding creative yet sound solutions to problems than they are in seeing those solutions made into reality.

Possible Blind Spots

Because INTPs rely so heavily on their logical analysis, they can overlook what matters to others. If something is not logical, INTPs run the risk of dismissing it, even if it is important to them. Admitting to themselves what they really care about will help them stay in touch with their true feelings.

INTPs are excellent at detecting the flaws in an idea but are more reticent about expressing their appreciation. They can get bogged down on a minor flaw in one part of a plan and keep the entire project from moving toward completion because they refuse to let one illogical point remain within the whole. When they turn their highly honed critical thinking skills on the people around them, their naked honesty may translate into unintended hurtfulness. They need to be told, and need to learn to ask, what matters emotionally to others.

Because INTPs are fascinated with solving problems, they tend to be impatient with routine details and may lose interest in a project and never complete it if it requires too much follow-through or detail. Turning their energy outward will enable them to gain sufficient practical knowledge to make their ideas workable and acceptable to other people.

INTPs sometimes feel inadequate when they try to live up to their own high standards of perfection. Learning to share those feelings with someone else can help them get a more realistic and objective view of themselves.

∥ ESTJ
Extraverted, Sensing, Thinking, Judging
Approximately 8–12 percent of the American population

ESTJs are great at getting things done. They like to run the show and make things happen. They are responsible, conscientious, and faithful to their commitments. They like structure and can remember and organize many details. They systematically set about achieving their goals on schedule and as efficiently as possible.

ESTJs are driven to make decisions. Often they base their decisions on their own past experience. They are logical, objective, and analytical and have great reasoning power. In fact, they are unlikely to be persuaded by anything but logic.

ESTJs are realistic, practical, and matter-of-fact. They are more interested in "real things" than in intangibles, such as abstract ideas and theories. They tend to not be interested in subjects for which they see no practical application. They know what's happening around them and are concerned primarily with the here and now.

Because they live by a certain set of rules, ESTJs are consistent and dependable. They tend to be traditional and interested in maintaining established institutions. They are consistent in their relationships, although their emotional and social life is not as important to them as other aspects of life. They are comfortable judging others, and can be crisp disciplinarians.

ESTJs are outgoing, sociable, direct, and friendly. They are usually easy to get to know, since "what you see is what you get."

Possible Blind Spots

Because ESTJs adopt a strict code of ethics for both themselves and others, they can be seen as dictatorial when they attempt to impose their standards of behavior on others. Attempting to be more flexible and open-minded will prevent an ESTJ from becoming rigid.

Being logical and impersonal analysts, ESTJs don't naturally consider the impact their decisions have on others. They can be seen as cold and uncaring, and often need to become more aware of their own feelings as well as more respectful of the thoughts and feelings of others.

Since they are naturally critical, ESTJs usually don't demonstrate their appreciation of the positive attributes or contributions of those around them. They need to try to become more aware of the talents and efforts of others, and then offer compliments and praise.

Sometimes ESTJs are so intent on their own plans that they don't stop to listen to what others have to say. They don't naturally ask "what if," so they often miss possible meanings, implications, connections, and patterns. An easy way to protect against being close-minded is to wait a few seconds before speaking, giving others a chance to offer input.

ESTJs often jump to conclusions without gathering all the necessary information or taking the time to fully understand a situation. They need to learn to consciously delay making decisions until they have considered more information, especially alternatives they may have overlooked.

ESTJs who have been able to relinquish some of the control they seek and who have learned to see that there are gray areas in life (rather than seeing things only in black and white) become more adaptable and successful.

‖ ISTJ
‖ Introverted, Sensing, Thinking, Judging
‖ *Approximately 11–14 percent of the American population*

ISTJs are the serious, responsible, and sensible stalwarts of society. They are trustworthy and honor their commitments. Their word is their solemn vow.

Practical and realistic, ISTJs are matter-of-fact and thorough. They are painstakingly accurate and methodical, with great powers of concentration. Whatever they are doing they accomplish with orderliness and reliability. They have unshakable, well-thought-out ideas and are difficult to distract or discourage once they have embarked on what they believe to be the best course of action.

Characteristically quiet and hardworking, ISTJs have great practical judgment and memory for details. They can cite accurate evidence to support their views and apply their past experiences to their present decisions. They value and use logic and impersonal analysis, are organized and systematic in their approach to following things through and getting them done on time. They follow necessary systems and procedures and are impatient with those who do not.

ISTJs are cautious and traditional. They listen well and like things to be factual and clearly stated. They are said to "Say what you mean and mean what you say." Private by nature, ISTJs appear calm even during times of crisis. They are duty bound and steadfast but beneath their calm facade, they may have strong yet rarely expressed reactions.

Possible Blind Spots

A common problem for ISTJs is their tendency to lose themselves in the details and daily operations of a project. Once immersed, they can be rigid and unwilling to adapt or accept another point of view. They tend to be skeptical of new ideas if they don't see their immediate and practical application. They need to take time to look at their overall objectives and consider alternatives they may not have considered. Gathering a wider range of information and consciously trying to anticipate the future implications of their behavior will increase the ISTJ's effectiveness in all areas.

ISTJs sometimes have trouble understanding the needs of others, especially those that are different from their own. Because they keep their reactions private, they can be perceived as cold and unfeeling. They need to express their appreciation for others directly, rather than keeping it to themselves.

Because they are logical, ISTJs tend to expect others to be so as well. They run the risk of imposing their judgments on others and overriding the opinions of less assertive people. They can demand conformity to their way of doing things and discourage more creative or innovative approaches. By staying open to untested or unconventional methods, they will develop more tolerance for differences in people, and also end up with more effective alternatives and options.

‖ ESFJ
Extraverted, Sensing, Feeling, Judging
Approximately 9–13 percent of the American population

ESFJs are motivated to help other people in real and practical ways through direct action and cooperation. They are responsible, friendly, and sympathetic.

Because ESFJs place such importance on their relationships with other people, they tend to be popular, gracious, eager to please, and talkative. They need harmonious relationships with others and work hard to achieve and maintain them. In fact, they often idealize whatever or whomever they admire. ESFJs need to be appreciated for themselves and their service, so they are highly sensitive to indifference or criticism. They usually express strong opinions and are decisive, and they like to have things settled.

Practical and realistic, ESFJs tend to be matter-of-fact and organized. They attend to and remember important facts and details and like others to be sure of their facts as well. They base their planning and opinions on their own personal experience or that of someone else they trust. They are aware of and involved with their physical environment and like to be active and productive.

Because ESFJs are conscientious and traditional, they are bound by their sense of duty and commitments. They nurture established institutions and tend to be active and cooperative members of committees and organizations. Their social ties are important and well maintained. They often go out of their way to do something helpful and nice for someone else and especially enjoy being responsive in times of trouble or great celebration.

Possible Blind Spots

Because ESFJs value harmony so highly, they tend to avoid conflicts rather than deal with problems head-on. They sometimes place too much importance and value on the opinions and feelings of those they care for. During tense or hurtful times, they can become blind to the facts of the situation. They need to learn to deal directly and honestly with conflict, trusting that their natural sensitivity to others' feelings will provide them with the necessary tact in even the most difficult situations.

ESFJs often overlook their own needs because of their desire to please or help other people. They have a difficult time saying no or asking for help because they don't want to risk offending or disappointing anyone. They usually have trouble giving or accepting constructive criticism because they take things so personally. They can become pessimistic and gloomy when they don't see ways to make changes in their lives. Taking a step back from their problems to get some objectivity usually helps them gain a fresh outlook.

In their efforts to help other people, ESFJs sometimes express their strong opinions in ways that are bossy and domineering. They do better to wait to find out if their help or suggestions are really wanted before offering them.

ESFJs often make decisions too quickly, before they've had adequate time to gather all the less obvious facts and consider the implications of their actions. They don't tend to look for new or different ways of doing things and can appear inflexible. Postponing judgments in favor of staying open to novel approaches to problems will give them a better base of information and help them make better decisions.

‖ ISFJ
‖ Introverted, Sensing, Feeling, Judging
‖ *Approximately 9–14 percent of the American population*

ISFJs are loyal, devoted, compassionate, and perceptive about how other people feel. They are conscientious and responsible and enjoy being needed.

ISFJs are down-to-earth and realistic people and prefer others who are quiet and unassuming. They absorb and enjoy using a large number of facts. With great memories for details, they are patient with the follow-through phase of tasks. ISFJs like things to be clearly and explicitly stated.

Because they have a strong work ethic, they accept responsibility for things that need to be done, if they can see that their actions will actually help. They are painstakingly accurate and systematic in handling tasks. ISFJs tend to be conservative, with traditional values. They use practical judgment in making decisions and lend stability through their excellent commonsense perspective.

Quiet and modest, ISFJs are serious and hardworking. They are gentle, sympathetic, tactful, and supportive of friends and colleagues. They like to care for others and prefer to help in practical and tangible ways. They use personal warmth to communicate, and they relate well to people in need. ISFJs tend not to show their private feelings but have an intensely personal reaction to most situations and events. They are protective and devoted to their friends, service-minded, and committed to meeting their obligations.

Possible Blind Spots

Because ISFJs live so completely in the present, they have trouble seeing events in global terms or anticipating the possible outcomes of a situation, especially when it is unfamiliar. They need help looking beyond the moment and imagining what might or could be if things were done differently.

ISFJs can become mired in the daily grind and the unending work around them, both their own and others' for whom they feel responsible. They can easily become overworked, doing everything themselves to be sure that tasks are completed meticulously. Because they are not naturally assertive or tough-minded, they risk being taken advantage of. They need to express their frequently bottled-up feelings of resentment so they don't find themselves in the rescuing role. They also need to let other people know their needs and their accomplishments.

ISFJs often need extra time to master technical subjects. They tend to plan excessively and need to develop strategies that will help them refocus the energy they often expend worrying. ISFJs need to find ways of getting the much-needed enjoyment and relaxation they deserve.

|| ESTP
Extraverted, Sensing, Thinking, Perceiving
Approximately 4–5 percent of the American population

ESTPs don't worry—they're happy! Active, easygoing, and spontaneous, ESTPs enjoy the present moment rather than planning for the future.

Extremely realistic, ESTPs rely on and trust what their senses tell them about their world. They are curious and keen observers. Because they accept things as they are, they tend to be open-minded and tolerant of others and themselves. ESTPs like real things that can be handled, taken apart, and put back together.

ESTPs prefer action to conversation and enjoy dealing with situations as they arise. They are good problem solvers because they can absorb necessary factual information and then find logical and sensible solutions quickly, without a lot of wasted effort or energy. They can be diplomatic negotiators, happy to try unconventional approaches and usually able to persuade other people to give their compromises a chance. They are able to grasp underlying principles and make decisions based upon what is logical, rather than on how they feel about things. Therefore they are pragmatic and can be tough when the situation warrants.

Friendly and charming, ESTPs are popular and at ease in most social situations. They are outgoing, versatile, and funny, and may have an endless supply of jokes and stories for whatever situation they find themselves in. They can be good at easing tense situations by lightening up the atmosphere and getting conflicting parties together.

Possible Blind Spots

ESTPs' preference for living in the moment and adopting an "emergency" style of responding to unexpected crises can result in a chaotic environment for those around them. They may miss opportunities through lack of planning. They sometimes take on too much at one time and find themselves overloaded and unable to keep their commitments. ESTPs need to look beyond the current moment and their interest in the material world to try to anticipate ways of finishing tasks on time.

ESTPs also tend to overlook other people's feelings and may be blunt and insensitive in their desire to be honest, especially when they are rushing from one experience to another. Their flamboyance can sometimes be perceived as crudeness and may alienate the people they are trying to entertain. ESTPs become more effective with other people when they direct their keen powers of observation to be sensitive to the people around them. They are more effective when they rein in their boldness, energy, and love of a good time to a level where other people are more comfortable.

More interested in solving problems quickly and effortlessly, ESTPs tend to jump directly into the next crisis and not follow through on the less-exciting portions of current projects. They do well to learn and apply time management and long-range planning techniques to help them prepare for and complete responsibilities. Slowing down to develop standards for their own behavior and considering the ramifications of their actions will make them more effective.

‖ ISTP
Introverted, Sensing, Thinking, Perceiving
Approximately 4–6 percent of the American population

ISTPs are straightforward, honest, and pragmatic people who prefer action to conversation. They are unpretentious and often have a good understanding of the way things work.

Because they are analytical, ISTPs are most interested in the impersonal and underlying principles of things. ISTPs have an innate understanding of how mechanical things work and are usually skilled at using tools and working with their hands. They tend to make logical and private decisions, stating things clearly and directly, just as they see them.

Curious and observant, ISTPs tend to be convinced only by hard, reliable facts. They have a great respect for facts and can be veritable storehouses of information on the things they know well and understand. Because they are realists, they are able to capitalize well on available resources, which makes them practical, with a good sense of timing.

Quiet and reserved, ISTPs tend to appear cool and aloof and are inclined toward shyness, except when with good friends. They are self-leading, egalitarian, and fair. They tend to operate on impulse, so they are quite adaptable and responsive to immediate challenges and problems. Because they thrive on excitement and action, they usually like the outdoors and sports.

Possible Blind Spots

Because ISTPs make judgments privately, they often keep even the most important issues to themselves, which leaves the people in their lives in the dark about what is going on. They have difficulty sharing their reactions, feelings, and concerns with others because it seems unnecessary to them. They need to accept that other people want and need to know what is going on in their lives and realize they are the only ones who can provide an accurate explanation.

ISTPs are so realistic that they can usually see ways of minimizing effort on almost all projects. Because of their desire to have free time, they often don't prepare more than is absolutely necessary or may not stick with a project to its conclusion. This can lead them to cut corners. Mapping out a plan, complete with all the steps and details, will help them curb their potential lack of initiative and reduce their apparent indifference.

Because ISTPs are constantly on the alert for new sensory information and prefer to keep all their options open, they may be indecisive. Their need for excitement can make them reckless and also easily bored. Setting goals and making serious commitments to people and things will help them avoid the common disappointments and dangers of such a potentially haphazard lifestyle.

‖ ESFP
Extraverted, Sensing, Feeling, Perceiving
Approximately 4–9 percent of the American population

ESFPs enjoy people and have a real zest for living. They are playful and vivacious, and make things more fun for others by their pure and unabashed enjoyment.

Adaptable and easygoing, ESFPs are warm, friendly, and generous. They are extremely sociable and are often "on stage" with others. They enthusiastically and cooperatively join in activities and games and are usually juggling several activities at once.

ESFPs are realistic observers and see and accept things as they are. They tend to trust what they can hear, smell, taste, touch, and see instead of theoretical explanations. Because they like concrete facts and have good memories for details, they learn best from hands-on experience. Their common sense gives them practical abilities with people and things. They prefer to gather information and see what solutions naturally arise.

Tolerant and accepting of themselves and others, ESFPs don't tend to try to impose their will on other people. Tactful and sympathetic, ESFPs are generally and genuinely liked by many people. They are usually able to get people to adopt their suggestions, so they are good at helping conflicting factions get back together. They seek out the company of others and are good conversationalists. They enjoy helping other people but prefer to assist in real and tangible ways.

Spontaneous and charming, ESFPs are persuasive. They love surprises and finding ways of bringing delight and unexpected pleasure to others.

Possible Blind Spots

Because ESFPs place such a strong priority on experiencing and enjoying life, they sometimes allow their other responsibilities to suffer. Their constant socializing can interfere and get them into trouble and because they are so easily tempted, they have difficulty disciplining themselves. ESFPs' tendency to become distracted from finishing the tasks they start can make them lazy. By working to prioritize their activities, and finding a balance between work and play, they will gain a broader perspective and longer-range vision for their lives. Using successful and accepted methods of organization and time management helps them overcome this natural predisposition.

Their active life keeps them so busy, they fail to plan ahead. This can leave them unprepared for life's changes that would be easier to cope with if clues of their approach had been noticed. ESFPs need to try to anticipate what might be coming down the road and develop an alternative plan in case things become unpleasant.

ESFPs also tend to make decisions without considering the logical consequences of their actions. Their own personal feelings are trusted and used to the exclusion of more objective data. Friends are so highly valued by ESFPs that they tend to look only at their positive sides. ESFPs need to take a step back to consider the cause and effect of actions and work toward becoming more tough-minded. Saying no will not be nearly as difficult if they do.

|| ISFP
|| Introverted, Sensing, Feeling, Perceiving
|| *Approximately 5–9 percent of the American population*

ISFPs are gentle, caring, and sensitive people, who keep much of their intensely personal ideals and values to themselves. They more often express their deeply felt passions through actions than through words.

Modest and reserved, ISFPs are really tremendously warm and enthusiastic people but tend not to show that side of themselves except with people they know well and trust fully. ISFPs tend to be misunderstood because of their tendency not to express themselves directly.

ISFPs are patient, flexible, and easy to get along with and have little need to dominate or control others. They are nonjudgmental and accepting of others' behavior in a rather matter-of-fact way. They are observant of people and things around them and do not seek to find motives or meanings.

Because ISFPs live completely in the present moment, they do not tend to prepare or plan more than is necessary. Good short-range planners, they are relaxed about getting things done because they are fully engaged in the here and now and like to enjoy the current experience without rushing on to the next.

Interested in what they learn and sense directly from their experiences and senses, they are often artistic and aesthetic, and seek to create beautiful and personal environments for themselves.

Without the need to lead, ISFPs are often loyal followers and good team members. Because they use their personal values to judge everything in life, they like other people who take the time to get to know them and understand their inner loyalties. Basically trusting and understanding, they need harmonious relationships in their lives and are sensitive to conflicts and disagreements.

Possible Blind Spots

The highly sensitive nature of ISFPs allows them to clearly see the needs of other people, and they sometimes work so excessively to fulfill those needs that they neglect themselves in the process. This can result in their becoming physically ill from exhaustion and overwork. They need to take time out from caring for others to take care of themselves.

Because they focus so completely on their experience in the moment, they tend not to look beyond the present, and miss the broader view. They sometimes have difficulty understanding things in a more complex context. Because they don't usually look for or see possibilities that don't exist at the present time, they don't tend to prepare in advance. They often have trouble organizing their time and resources. They may have to work hard to curb their impulse to go off and enjoy a quiet moment, or participate in a favorite activity.

ISFPs are vulnerable to the criticism of others because they tend to take feedback personally and become offended and discouraged. They may be seen as gullible and too trusting because they accept people and things as they are and don't expect a malicious motive or read anything else into them. They need to become more assertive about their own needs and consider the implications of another's behavior. By applying some objectivity and skepticism to their analysis, they can become better judges of character.

Part Two | THE "FOURMULA" FOR CAREER SATISFACTION

Now that you've discovered your true personality type, you may be wondering why we can't just point you to a career and send you on your way. Well, it isn't that simple. It is not true that certain personality types can find career satisfaction only in certain fields. People of your type, for example, don't "have" to be dentists, dog-catchers, or designers. People of all types can find success in all fields. What matters most is finding the best job for you within each profession. As we've already seen, this depends upon a solid understanding of yourself.

We've always known that Type is the key to career satisfaction, but it wasn't until recently that we realized— eureka!— exactly how to translate the intricacies of Personality Type into happiness and success in the workplace. We're now able to pinpoint the four aspects of Personality Type that are most important to people who are looking for career options that will be truly satisfying. Taken together, we call these four components the "Fourmula" for Career Satisfaction. The following four chapters examine each component in turn, as you will now see.

4 WHAT A CHARACTER!

The Four Different Temperaments

You don't need us to tell you that people have different natures. But did you know that everybody can be divided into just four basic human temperaments?

Suppose your cousin is intense and excitable, but your neighbor is a Steady Eddy. This is in large part due to differences in their innate temperaments. If your cousin the thrill seeker takes a number-crunching job at an insurance company, chances are he'll be bored out of his head. Big mistake. If, however, he works for the same company doing field investigations of buildings that have burned to the ground, he has a better chance of being interested in his work—and therefore satisfied with it. And what about your dependable neighbor? He might be perfect for the number-crunching job!

Throughout history, philosophers, writers, psychologists, and other observers of humanity have noticed that there are four distinct "natures" into which all people fit. As far back as 450 B.C., Hippocrates described four different dispositions, or temperaments. In the Middle Ages, Paracelsus described four natures whose behavior was influenced by four kinds of spirits. The American Indian Medicine Wheel suggests four spirit keepers, similar to the temperaments, and Hindu wisdom postulates four central desires.

Psychologist David Keirsey was impressed that these four different temperaments, observed independently by people from diverse cultures and from different periods of history, all described remarkably similar characteristics. When he learned about Type through the work of Isabel Briggs Myers, he became intrigued with the relationship between Type and temperament. Many different labels have been used to identify the four temperaments. The names we use in this book, some borrowed and some original, were chosen because we feel they best describe each temperament's most central characteristic.

Keirsey determined that four combinations of type preferences correspond to the four temperaments people have posited throughout history. The four combinations are:

"Traditionalists" (SJs) are people who prefer both **Sensing** and **Judging**.

"Experiencers" (SPs) are people who prefer both **Sensing** and **Perceiving**.

"Idealists" (NFs) are people who prefer both **Intuition** and **Feeling**.

"Conceptualizers" (NTs) are people who prefer both **Intuition** and **Thinking**.

Each of the sixteen personality types falls into one of these categories. In this book when we refer to temperament, sometimes we use the names, and other times the letter combinations (e.g., "Traditionalist" and "SJ"). We do this because some people find one easier to remember than the other. But *both* labels apply equally well. One way you can determine your temperament is to check the letters of your type. With SJs and SPs, they are the second and fourth letters. With NFs and NTs, they are the middle letters.

Traditionalists (SJs):	ESTJ	ISTJ	ESFJ	ISFJ
Experiencers (SPs):	ESTP	ISTP	ESFP	ISFP
Idealists (NFs):	ENFJ	INFJ	ENFP	INFP
Conceptualizers (NTs):	ENTJ	INTJ	ENTP	INTP

People with the same temperament have a great deal in common and tend to share certain core values. However, they are *not* all the same! People of each temperament come in four varieties. Their other preferences—Extraversion or Introversion, Thinking or Feeling, and Judging or Perceiving—give them very different personalities. Think of a particular temperament as a family of instruments. All stringed instruments, for example, have many important features in common, and yet there are obvious differences between a violin, a viola, a cello, and a double bass (not to mention a guitar and a piano). And they are *very* different from wind instruments.

Since it's important to find a job that suits your nature, we are now going to discuss the four human temperaments and how they best fit into the workplace. Within each discussion you'll find specific information regarding temperament-based strengths and weaknesses. This will help you see how different personality types flourish in different settings, and it will help you begin to focus on the kind of work you would find personally satisfying. You may want to mark (or highlight or copy) your particular section once you've found it, for easy reference.

Even if you are already certain of your personality type, we suggest that you read about all four temperaments before deciding which one best describes you. For the time being, *do not* concern yourself with whether or not the letters of the temperament you choose match those of your personality type. There's a good chance they will—but there's also a possibility they won't.

▌ Traditionalists (**S**ensing **J**udgers)
ESTJ ISTJ ESFJ ISFJ
Approximately 46 percent of the American population

You will recall that Sensors trust facts, proven data, previous experience, and the information their five senses bring them. Judgers prefer a structured, orderly world and are driven to make decisions. Taken together, these two preferences create a "Sensing Judger," a type of person who is down-to-earth and decisive, and whom we call a "Traditionalist."

The motto for Traditionalists might well be "Early to bed, early to rise." Traditionalists are the most traditional of the four temperaments. They value law and order, security, propriety, rules, and conformity. They are driven by a strong motivation to serve society's needs. Traditionalists respect authority, hierarchy, and the chain of command, and generally have conservative values. They are bound by their sense of duty and always try to do the right thing, which makes them reliable, dependable, and, above all else, responsible.

Now because Traditionalists come in both Thinking (STJ) and Feeling (SFJ) varieties, there are clearly differences between them. Frequently, ESFJs and ISFJs won't identify as strongly with the Traditionalist description as their ESTJ and ISTJ friends do. For ESFJs and ISFJs the connection with others and the people-oriented criteria for decision making are critically important. So while most Traditionalists (regardless of their judgment preference) are happiest in occupations where the structure is clear and the expectations explicit, those with a Feeling preference will strive for harmonious affiliations with others and seek opportunities to do work that lets them help others in tangible ways.

Traditionalists at Work

Traditionalists need to belong, to serve, and to do the right thing. They value stability, orderliness, cooperation, consistency, and reliability, and they tend to be serious and hardworking. Traditionalists demand a great deal of themselves on the job and expect the same of others.

Strengths. Traditionalists are practical, organized, thorough, and systematic. They pay attention to regulations, policies, contracts, rituals, and timelines. They are excellent at guarding, monitoring, and regulating. Traditionalists prefer to deal with proven facts and use them to further the goals of the organization to which they belong. They take great pride in doing something right the first time and every time. They are good at seeing what needs attention and at getting the job done with the available resources as efficiently as possible. Once they've committed themselves, Traditionalists always follow through. At their best, Traditionalists are solid, trustworthy, and dependable.

Potential Weaknesses. Traditionalists are not particularly interested in theories or abstractions, and the future doesn't attract their attention as much as the present. Long-range planning usually is not one of their strengths. Traditionalists sometimes make decisions too quickly. They tend to see things in black and white, rather than in shades of gray. They run the risk of being unable to change or to adapt quickly, and they tend to resist trying approaches that are new, different, or untested. They are likely to want to see proof that a solution will work before seriously considering it. At their worst, Traditionalists can be inflexible, dogmatic, and unimaginative.

A good job for a Traditionalist might be one that involves a relatively high level of responsibility within a stable company that has a clear-cut chain of command. Since they like structure, they are generally comfortable in organizations that have a fair number of rules and standard ways of doing things. Traditionalists prefer working in an environment where both regulations and rewards are certain. (They *don't* like positions or organizations where everything is in a state of flux or confusion!) They prefer colleagues who share their dedication and respect for authority and who pull their own weight.

Traditionalists usually make good managers. They appreciate the need for structure and are often the mainstays of organizations, either in leadership or support positions. The role they most often play is that of the stabilizer—the maintainer of traditions and the status quo.

Remember how we said that people of all types can find satisfaction in all fields? For the purposes of this chapter, let's use the field of law enforcement as an example. Some temperaments are more likely to gravitate to law enforcement than others, but all can find satisfaction in this area if they find a way of meeting their individual needs.

It's not unusual for Traditionalists to become police officers. In fact, in some studies, over 50 percent of police officers in a given area fit this temperament! This line of work appeals to them because a high priority of theirs is protecting and serving society. They find enforcing social rules, maintaining order, and aiding those in distress intrinsically satisfying.

Many police officers are also Experiencers—the next temperament we'll discuss—but they are attracted to law enforcement for different reasons, as you'll see.

‖ Experiencers (**S**ensing **P**erceivers)
ESTP ISTP ESFP ISFP
Approximately 27 percent of the American population

Sensors, you'll remember, concentrate on what can be seen, heard, felt, smelled, or tasted, and trust whatever can be measured or documented. Perceivers like to stay open to all kinds of possibilities and prefer to live in a flexible way. Taken together, these two preferences create a "Sensing Perceiver," a type of person who is responsive and spontaneous, and whom we call an "Experiencer."

The motto for Experiencers might well be, "Eat, drink, and be merry!" And they are the most adventurous of the four temperaments. They live for action, impulse, and the present moment. They focus on the immediate situation and have the ability to assess what needs to be done *now*. Since Experiencers value freedom and spontaneity, they seldom choose activities or situations that impose too much structure or too many rules. They are risk-taking, adaptable, easygoing, and pragmatic. They admire skillful execution in any field or discipline. Many, but not all, are thrill seekers who like living on the edge.

Experiencers at Work

Experiencers need to be active and free to act on their impulses. In their work, they focus on what can be accomplished in the here and now. They value heroic deeds and masterful acts and like moving from one challenge to the next.

Like Traditionalists, Experiencers also come in two varieties, STPs and SFPs. Like their SFJ friends, some SFPs don't fully agree with the description of Experiencer temperament because it doesn't include their natural desire to help others or make decisions that are congruent with their values. So while all Experiencers are typically most satisfied in careers that are relatively free of excessive rules, planning, and structure, SFPs usually want to respond primarily to the needs of others and feel their work is making a difference to people in ways that are immediate.

Strengths. Experiencers can see clearly what is happening and are agile at seizing opportunities. They are excellent at recognizing practical problems and approach them with flexibility, courage, and resourcefulness. They are not afraid to take risks or improvise as needed. Because they are not invested in tradition the way Traditionalists are, Experiencers enjoy making changes in response to some immediate need or crisis. However, like Traditionalists, they prefer to deal with facts and real problems rather than theories or ideas. Experiencers are keen observers of human behavior and can be good negotiators. They are efficient, and use an economy of effort in achieving their goals. Many Experiencers (but not all) are especially skillful with tools and instruments, things they can physically manipulate and which require precision. At their best, they can be resourceful, exciting, and fun.

Potential Weaknesses. Experiencers often are not predictable to others, and they sometimes fail to think things through carefully before acting. They are not much interested in the theoretical, abstract, or conceptual, and they may fail to see important connections or patterns linking events. Experiencers tend to lose enthusiasm once the crisis phase of any given situation is over. Since they prefer to keep their options open, they don't always follow established rules and they sometimes avoid commitments and plans. At their worst, they are irresponsible, unreliable, childish, and impulsive.

A good job for an Experiencer might be one that provides autonomy, variety, and action. They prefer work that brings immediate results, and they enjoy being able to execute tasks skillfully and successfully. Since they like to have fun, whatever they do must give them a high degree of pleasure if it is to be satisfying.

Although they are not naturally drawn to structured organizations, Experiencers can find a niche in the role of corporate "firefighter"—the person who notices and responds to crises. And they are often involved in occupations that allow them to use acquired skills, often involving tools, independently and spontaneously.

Now that you're familiar with this temperament, can you guess why many Experiencers are drawn to law enforcement? According to some studies, as many as 25 percent of many U.S. police forces are Experiencers. Many become police officers because of the excitement, the unpredictability, and even the danger that can await them with every new door they knock on or car they pull over. For many Experiencers, the job of police officer satisfies their need for action, spontaneity, and fully experiencing the moment.

‖ Idealists (i**N**tuitive **F**eelers)
ENFJ INFJ ENFP INFP
Approximately 16 percent of the American population

Intuitives, you'll recollect, are interested in meanings, relationships, and possibilities. Feelers make decisions based on personal values. Taken together, these two preferences create an "Intuitive Feeler," a type of person who is concerned about personal growth and understanding for themselves and others, and whom we call an "Idealist."

The motto of Idealists might well be, "To thine own self be true." They are the most spiritually philosophical of the four temperaments. It's as if they are on a perpetual search for the meaning of life. They place a very high value on authenticity and integrity in people and relationships and tend to idealize others. Idealists focus on human potential and are often gifted at helping others grow and develop, a task that gives them great satisfaction. They are often excellent communicators and can be thought of as catalysts for positive change.

Idealists at Work

Idealists enjoy using their natural ability to understand and connect with other people. They are naturally empathetic and focus on the needs of the people involved in their work—for example, employees, colleagues, patients, or clients.

Strengths. Idealists know how to bring out the best in others and understand how to motivate others to do their best work. They are excellent at resolving conflicts and at helping people work together more effectively, and have the ability to help people feel good about themselves and their jobs. When they praise a job well done, they usually praise the individual, rather than just the accomplishment. Idealists are good at identifying creative solutions to problems. They communicate well in speech and writing and can generate enthusiasm for their ideas and actions. At their best, they are charismatic, receptive, and accepting.

Potential Weaknesses. Idealists have a tendency to make decisions based exclusively upon their own personal likes and dislikes. They have trouble staying detached. They tend to take other people's problems to heart and can become too involved and overwhelmed as a result. Sometimes they are too idealistic and not practical enough. Idealists are not particularly good at disciplining or criticizing others, although they have a great capacity for self-reproach. Sometimes they will sacrifice their own opinion for the sake of harmony. At their worst, they can be moody, unpredictable, and overemotional.

A good job for an Idealist is one that is personally meaningful, rather than simply routine or expedient. They value harmony and do not flourish in a competitive or divisive arena. And they prefer organizations that are democratic and that encourage a high degree of participation from people at all levels.

Idealists gravitate toward organizations that promote humanistic values or toward jobs that allow them to help others find fulfillment. They are often found in human resources or personnel positions, as well as in teaching, consulting, counseling, and the arts.

Where do you suppose Idealists fit into the field of law enforcement? Studies show that they make up well under 10 percent of most police forces, and they usually don't end up "on the beat." Instead, they almost unfailingly find their way to the human resources department, community outreach programs, or training or development programs where they can use their natural gifts in reaching out to others.

▌ Conceptualizers (i**N**tuitive **T**hinkers)
ENTJ INTJ ENTP INTP
Approximately 10 percent of the American population

By now you know that Intuitives look for meanings in all things and focus on implications, and you'll remember that Thinkers make decisions impersonally and logically. Taken together, these two preferences create an "Intuitive Thinker," a type of person who is intellectual and competent, and whom we call a "Conceptualizer."

The motto for Conceptualizers might well be "Be excellent in all things." They are the most independent of the four temperaments, driven to acquire knowledge and setting very high standards for themselves and others. Naturally curious, Conceptualizers usually can see many sides to the same argument or issue. Conceptualizers are excellent at seeing possibilities, understanding complexities, and designing solutions to real or hypothetical problems. Their role is often that of the architect of change.

Conceptualizers at Work

Conceptualizers enjoy using their abilities to see possibilities and analyze them logically to solve problems. They are interested in constantly acquiring knowledge, either for its own sake or for a strategic purpose.

Strengths. Conceptualizers have vision and can be great innovators. They can see possibilities as well as the big picture, and they can conceptualize and design necessary changes within an organization. They excel at (and enjoy) strategizing, planning, and building systems to accomplish their goals. Conceptualizers understand complex, theoretical ideas and are good at deducing principles or trends. They enjoy being challenged, are demanding of themselves and others, and can usually accept constructive criticism without taking it personally. At their best, they are confident, witty, and imaginative.

Potential Weaknesses. Sometimes Conceptualizers can be too complex for others to understand. They have a tendency to overlook necessary details. They can be deeply skeptical and often challenge rules, assumptions, or customs. They also sometimes have trouble with authority and can be seen as elitist. Conceptualizers often fail to see how they affect others, and they may not be interested in either harmony or the importance of feelings. They can be fiercely competitive and will sometimes not bother with a project or activity if they don't think they will excel at it. At their worst, Conceptualizers can be arrogant, remote, and in a world of their own.

A good job for a Conceptualizer might be one that provides autonomy, variety, plenty of intellectual stimulation, and the opportunity to generate ideas, and they must find their work challenging to be satisfying. Since they can be impatient with others whom they consider less competent than they, Conceptualizers need to be surrounded by very capable supervisors, colleagues, and employees. Many Conceptualizers value power and gravitate toward powerful positions or people.

Because their need for competence is so strong, Conceptualizers are often found in leadership positions. They show up in college-level teaching positions, in upper management, in the sciences or computer fields, and in medicine or law in great numbers.

You can probably guess where Conceptualizers end up on the police force. Although not found in law enforcement in large numbers, they can represent as much as 20 percent of upper management. High-level positions give them a chance to tackle complex problems, the opportunity to apply their vision and logic to long-range strategic plans, and the power they enjoy.

Temperaments in a Teapot

A peek into a staff meeting at a hospital will illustrate the strengths of each of the four temperaments. You can see that the department heads have very different concerns, but that each makes a vital contribution to the meeting.

Susan, the director of planning and marketing, is a Conceptualizer (Intuitive Thinker). She presents a proposal for a new Women's Health Services unit at the hospital. A potentially lucrative source of revenue, the unit would offer a wide range of medical services exclusively for women. It would provide both diagnostic and surgical services and would offer procedures and equipment on the cutting edge of technology. Susan's plan includes marketing the unit's expert, well-respected staff of physicians and technicians; she thinks it's very possible that the unit would create a competitive environment among hospitals, putting them in a position to choose the best personnel and to be seen as a leader in health care.

Ross, the director of finance, is a Traditionalist (Sensing Judger). He recommends a full investigation of comparable centers around the nation to determine their operating costs and to establish realistic start-up costs for the new unit. He cautions the group about starting too quickly before feasibility studies and certificate-of-need applications have been fully researched and documented. *If* the data supports the creation of the new unit, Ross recommends that they commit only to a three-year trial operation to reduce the overall risk to the hospital's fiscal stability. He cites the need for cost comparison studies to determine the best pricing strategies, and cost containment plans to keep overhead low while maintaining a realistic operating budget.

Rachel, the director of operations, is an Experiencer (Sensing Perceiver). She suggests that a task force be mobilized immediately to begin gathering information about the staff, materials, and equipment already on hand that could be appropriated for the new unit before any new purchases are made. She recommends that bids be solicited from construction and contracting firms, and she suggests that all negotiations be handled through her office. Rachel is concerned that if the hospital does not open the new unit relatively quickly, it will lose its opportunity to be an innovator as other hospitals try similar approaches. She encourages the group to work expediently and efficiently without an excessive number of meetings and without a lot of memos—in other words, to strike while the iron is hot.

Mark, the director of human resources, is an Idealist (Intuitive Feeler). He is enthusiastic about the new unit and recommends that it be designed to serve women of all social and economic backgrounds. Mark reminds the group that some employees and members of the community may see the new unit as a threat to their jobs. He points out the need for employee and community support for the project, and recommends that the hospital make continuous efforts to maintain enthusiasm for the unit through a variety of communication activities, including employee meetings, individual questionnaires, and a public information campaign aimed at residents and neighboring hospitals. He also recommends groundbreaking ceremonies, grand opening tours, and similar community-oriented events.

Which Temperament Are You?

By now you have probably identified which of the four temperaments you relate to most closely. Which one suits you best?

Traditionalist (SJ)   Experiencer (SP)

Idealist (NF)   Conceptualizer (NT)

What personality type did you think fit you in Part 1? _____

If your type is consistent with your choice of temperament, this is further verification that you have found your true type.

If your personality type is *not* consistent with your choice of temperament, there's a chance that you did not correctly identify your true personality type in Part 1. For example, let's say you thought you were an ENFP, but you relate strongly to the Conceptualizer temperament. It's possible that you really *are* an ENTP and not an ENFP. We suggest that you go back to Chapter 3 and read the Verifying Type Profiles for both ENFP and ENTP to see which one sounds most like you.

Suppose you reread the Profiles in Chapter 3 and still think you're an ENFP. Don't despair! There's another possible explanation for your conflicting results. As we grow older, we all naturally "round out" our personalities by developing our weaker preferences. This process is called **type development**, and we explain it in detail in Chapter 7. Briefly, in this situation it means that you really could be an ENFP, but that you are busy developing your Thinking, which leads you to relate more strongly to the Conceptualizer temperament. By the time you've finished Chapter 7, you should have a good idea of how type development works, which will help you make your final decision about your true personality type.

Much of our own general knowledge about temperament has come from the excellent resource *Introduction to Temperament,* by Louise Giovannoni, Ph.D., Linda Berens, Ph.D., and Sue Cooper, Ph.D.

5 | WHO'S ON FIRST?

Identifying Your Innate Strengths

The second ingredient in the "Fourmula" for Career Satisfaction is understanding which aspects of your personality are strongest and which are weakest. Although all of your preferences play important roles, certain preferences within each personality type are more powerful than others. Since you want to operate from a position of strength while you're at work, it makes sense for you to identify carefully which preferences you use most easily and most successfully.

The Type Functions

You will recall that Extraversion and Introversion are the two different ways we interact with the world, and that Judging and Perceiving are the two different ways we prefer to construct our lives. These four preferences are reflected in the first and last letters of your personality type. We refer to them as the **attitudes**. The attitudes are discussed more fully in Chapter 6.

You'll also remember that Sensing and Intuition are the two different ways we take in information, and that Thinking and Feeling are the two different ways we make decisions. These four preferences are reflected in the two middle letters of your personality type. We refer to them as the **functions**. The functions are the core of Type, and in this chapter we'll show you why.

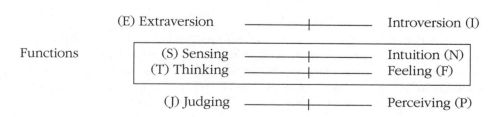

The Hierarchy of Functions

Each personality type has what is called a "hierarchy of functions." This hierarchy ranks your functions from strongest to weakest. Although you grow and change and develop your abilities over time, your hierarchy of functions stays the same throughout your life.

The hierarchy of functions does *not* rank all of your preferences (the letters of your personality type). It concerns only the functions (the middle two letters of your personality type). Since everyone uses all four functions to some extent, the hierarchy of functions includes both the functions you use most often (the preferences that are reflected in the letters of your personality type) *and* the functions you use less often (the letters that do not show up in your personality type).

For each personality type, there is one function that is the most important characteristic of that type—the captain of the ship, so to speak. We call this the **dominant function**. Any one of the four functions (Sensing, Intuition, Thinking, or Feeling) can be dominant, but for each personality type there is only one dominant function, and it always stays the same.

The next function in the hierarchy—the second-in-command—is called the **auxiliary function**. Again, there is only one auxiliary function for each personality type, and it never changes.

The dominant and auxiliary functions always refer to how you take in information (either Sensing or Intuition) and how you make decisions (either Thinking or Feeling). Since everyone needs to use both of these processes, the dominant and auxiliary functions never refer to the same process. If your dominant is an information-gathering function, then your auxiliary is a decision-making function, and vice versa.

The **third function** in the hierarchy of functions is always the opposite of your auxiliary function. The **fourth function** in your hierarchy of functions is always the opposite of your dominant function. In a way, it is a casualty of your dominant function. Since your dominant function is the most powerful preference in your personality, it figures that the opposite of this preference should be your weakest point. The fourth function is sometimes referred to as the inferior function—with good reason!

#1 Dominant Function
#2 Auxiliary Function
#3 Third Function (opposite of #2)
#4 Fourth Function (opposite of #1)

One way to understand the hierarchy of functions is to think of a family of four taking a car trip. There are two adults in the front seat: the dominant function is driving, and the auxiliary function is navigating. In the backseat are the two kids: the third function, who is about ten years old, and the fourth function, who is just a baby. Clearly, you want the dominant to be in charge (somebody has to drive!)

and the auxiliary to help navigate. But you still have to pay attention to the other two (breaking up fights, stopping to go to the bathroom…).

As long as your dominant and auxiliary are in command, you are functioning well. When your third and especially fourth functions take over, it's as if the kids climbed over the seat and started driving the car (with predictably disastrous results).

How do you know which functions are your dominant, auxiliary, third, and fourth? We'll tell you! Following is a table that shows the hierarchy of functions for each personality type. Take a moment to find yours.

The Hierarchy of Functions*†

ISTJ	ISFJ	INFJ	INTJ
1 Sensing	1 Sensing	1 Intuition	1 Intuition
2 Thinking	2 Feeling	2 Feeling	2 Thinking
3 Feeling	3 Thinking	3 Thinking	3 Feeling
4 Intuition	4 Intuition	4 Sensing	4 Sensing
ISTP	**ISFP**	**INFP**	**INTP**
1 Thinking	1 Feeling	1 Feeling	1 Thinking
2 Sensing	2 Sensing	2 Intuition	2 Intuition
3 Intuition	3 Intuition	3 Sensing	3 Sensing
4 Feeling	4 Thinking	4 Thinking	4 Feeling
ESTP	**ESFP**	**ENFP**	**ENTP**
1 Sensing	1 Sensing	1 Intuition	1 Intuition
2 Thinking	2 Feeling	2 Feeling	2 Thinking
3 Feeling	3 Thinking	3 Thinking	3 Feeling
4 Intuition	4 Intuition	4 Sensing	4 Sensing
ESTJ	**ESFJ**	**ENFJ**	**ENTJ**
1 Thinking	1 Feeling	1 Feeling	1 Thinking
2 Sensing	2 Sensing	2 Intuition	2 Intuition
3 Intuition	3 Intuition	3 Sensing	3 Sensing
4 Feeling	4 Thinking	4 Thinking	4 Feeling

*This chart is reproduced from *Introduction to Type in Organizations,* by Sandra Krebs Hirsh and Jean M. Kummerow, page 9 (2nd edition, 1990), reprinted with permission of Consulting Psychologists Press, Inc.

†The formula for determining each type's hierarchy is complex and requires an in-depth explanation that we feel would be an unwelcome and unnecessary distraction to most readers. Therefore, we present the hierarchy and refer readers who wish to learn about the underlying theory to *Manual: A Guide to the Development and Use of the MBTI,* by Isabel Briggs Myers and Mary McCaulley, published by Consulting Psychologists Press (Chapter 3, page 16).

Your Dominant Function

Your dominant function is the one in charge—the head honcho, the big enchilada, the top banana! It leads and directs your personality so that all of your functions are not constantly competing. Although everyone uses all four functions to some extent, the dominant function is the one you use most often and most naturally. People who have the same dominant function have a great deal in common, but they can also be very different, since their auxiliary functions and other preferences (don't forget the attitudes!) may vary.

If Sensing is the dominant function for your personality type, we call you a **Dominant Sensor**. You're not just a Sensor, you're a Super Sensor! Dominant Sensors usually pay extremely close attention to the facts and details of their experience. They trust and value above all else the data their five senses bring them, and their fundamental view of the world depends upon exactly what they see, hear, touch, taste, and smell.

If Intuition is the dominant function for your personality type, we call you a **Dominant Intuitive**. You're not just an Intuitive, you're a Super Intuitive! Dominant Intuitives are much more interested in the meanings, possibilities, patterns, and relationships in what they perceive than they are in specifics or facts. Intuition dominates most—even all!—of their perceptions. They look at a given situation and see implications and alternatives above all else.

If Thinking is the dominant function for your personality type, we call you a **Dominant Thinker**. You're not just a Thinker, you're a Super Thinker! Dominant Thinkers are driven to make decisions based upon logic and impersonal analysis. Their immediate and strongest inclination is to come to a conclusion by looking at a given situation objectively, and it's hard for them to do otherwise.

If Feeling is the dominant function for your personality type, we call you a **Dominant Feeler**. You're not just a Feeler, you're a Super Feeler! Dominant Feelers are most comfortable making decisions based upon their own personal values. They have a strong need to empathize, and they go through life constantly evaluating what is most important to themselves and to others.

Your Auxiliary Function

The auxiliary function balances the dominant function. It's the second-in-command, the counterweight, the Best Supporting Actor. It doesn't have a starring role, but it does play an essential one! As we've already mentioned, the auxiliary function is always a different process from the dominant function.

If your dominant function is either Sensing or Intuition (the information-gathering functions), your auxiliary function must be either Thinking or Feeling (the decision-making functions). Dominant Sensors and Dominant Intuitives naturally prefer to spend their time taking in information, rather than making decisions. If you're a Dominant Sensor, there's a risk that you'll spend all your time collecting facts but never coming to any conclusions. If you're a Dominant

Intuitive, you may be so preoccupied with considering the possibilities that you may never take any action. This is where the auxiliary function kicks in. As second-in-command, it pushes you to make decisions based upon the information you've gathered.

Most people have a reasonably strong auxiliary function, but occasionally you will meet a Dominant Sensor or a Dominant Intuitive who is unable to move from information gathering to decision making. Typically these people are either chronic procrastinators or are cripplingly indecisive. You can see why a strong auxiliary function is so important!

If your dominant function is either Thinking or Feeling (the decision-making functions), your auxiliary function must be either Sensing or Intuition (the information-gathering functions). Dominant Thinkers and Dominant Feelers naturally prefer to spend their time making decisions. If you're a Dominant Thinker, you are busy analyzing and critiquing everything. If you're a Dominant Feeler, you are eager to form opinions and determine how you feel about issues. Again, the auxiliary function helps balance your dominant function, in this case by pushing you to gather information before making judgments.

Occasionally you will meet a Dominant Thinker or a Dominant Feeler whose auxiliary function is extremely weak. These people are so driven to make decisions that they don't postpone making up their minds long enough to make sure they've collected all the information they need. They tend to be rigid, close-minded, and inflexible, whether their judgments are based upon principles or personal values.

Of the sixteen personality types, four are Dominant Sensors, four are Dominant Intuitives, four are Dominant Thinkers, and four are Dominant Feelers. Let's take a look at each group.

‖ Dominant Sensors
ISTJ ISFJ ESTP ESFP

Dominant Sensors—the Super Sensors!—trust facts and specifics above all else. However, Dominant Sensors come in four varieties, and they each do something a little different with data once they have gathered it.

ISTJs and ISFJs are both Dominant Sensors (they prefer facts), and they are both Introverted (they prefer to reflect on inner realities). Both types are traditional, practical, and organized. However, the auxiliary function for ISTJs is Thinking, which means that ISTJs focus on and gather impersonal facts, which they analyze. ISTJs tend to be matter-of-fact, sensible, and businesslike. The auxiliary function for ISFJs is Feeling, which means that ISFJs gather facts that relate to people and then base their decisions on their values, with a sensitivity to others. ISFJs tend to be loyal, patient, and service-minded.

ESTPs and ESFPs are both Dominant Sensors (they prefer facts), and they are both Extraverted (they focus on the specifics of the situation at hand). Both types are outgoing, adaptable, and energetic. Since the auxiliary function for

ESTPs is Thinking, they gather data and make decisions logically. ESTPs tend to be pragmatic, persuasive, and versatile. The auxiliary function for ESFPs is Feeling, which means that they make their decisions with more concern for others. ESFPs tend to be sociable, easygoing, and cooperative.

‖ Dominant Intuitives
‖ INTJ INFJ ENTP ENFP

Dominant Intuitives—the Super Intuitives!—see implications everywhere. Like Dominant Sensors, Dominant Intuitives come in four varieties, and they use the inferences they have gathered in different ways.

INTJs and INFJs are both Dominant Intuitives (they see implications), and they are both Introverted (they focus on inner meanings). Both types are original, visionary, and creative. However, the auxiliary function for INTJs is Thinking, which means that INTJs notice patterns and meanings and analyze them impersonally. INTJs tend to be logical, theoretical, and systems-oriented. On the other hand, the auxiliary function for INFJs is Feeling, which means that INFJs see connections and associations and analyze them in humanistic terms. INFJs tend to be sensitive, compassionate, and holistic.

ENTPs and ENFPs are both Dominant Intuitives (they see implications), and they are both Extraverted (they naturally see all the possibilities around them). Both types are creative, perceptive, and imaginative. But the auxiliary function for ENTPs is Thinking, which means they are logical. ENTPs tend to be strategic, challenging, and theoretical. The auxiliary function for ENFPs is Feeling, which means they are people-oriented. ENFPs tend to be curious, enthusiastic, and friendly.

‖ Dominant Thinkers
‖ INTP ISTP ENTJ ESTJ

Dominant Thinkers—the Super Thinkers!—have a strong drive to make logical decisions. However, the four varieties of Dominant Thinkers make their analyses in different ways.

INTPs and ISTPs are both Dominant Thinkers (they are very logical), and they are both Introverted (they use their own objective criteria to understand the world). Both types are independent and analytical. However, the auxiliary function for INTPs is Intuition, which means they are comfortable with the conceptual and abstract. INTPs tend to be original, speculative, and theoretical. The auxiliary function for ISTPs is Sensing, which means they are more application-oriented. ISTPs tend to be practical, adventurous, and spontaneous.

ENTJs and ESTJs are both Dominant Thinkers (very logical), and they are both Extraverted (they seek to organize people and events). Both types are decisive and organized. But since the auxiliary function for ENTJs is Intuition, they are able to see the big picture and possibilities for the future. ENTJs tend to be theoretical, critical, and plan-oriented. The auxiliary function for ESTJs is Sensing, which means they focus more on the specifics and concerns of the present moment. ESTJs tend to be efficient, practical, and conscientious.

‖ Dominant Feelers
ISFP INFP ESFJ ENFJ

Dominant Feelers—the Super Feelers!—have a strong drive to make decisions based on their personal values. Once again, this means something slightly different for each of the four types of Dominant Feelers.

ISFPs and INFPs are both Dominant Feelers (they care about what their decisions mean in human terms), and they are both Introverted (they focus on their inner personal values). Both types are gentle, adaptable, and loyal. However, the auxiliary function for ISFPs is Sensing, which means they focus on the specific and concrete. ISFPs tend to be modest, observant, and trusting. The auxiliary function for INFPs is Intuition, which means they focus on possibilities, both for themselves and others. INFPs tend to be compassionate, empathetic, and committed.

ESFJs and ENFJs are both Dominant Feelers (they make decisions based on their own values), and they are both Extraverted (they focus on others). Both types are loyal, personable, and social. However, the auxiliary function for ESFJs is Sensing, which means they focus on the specifics about people. ESFJs tend to be thorough, systematic, and traditional. The auxiliary function for ENFJs is Intuition, which means they focus on the potential in other people. ENFJs tend to be idealistic, enthusiastic, and persuasive.

Using Your Strengths (and Avoiding Your Weaknesses) at Work

Your greatest strengths are reflected in your dominant and auxiliary functions. Conversely, you are at your weakest when you use your fourth function and, to some extent, your third function as well. This is a vital little piece of self-awareness. It is exhilarating to be able to use your natural strengths, and it is very stressful to be made vulnerable by your innate weaknesses.

There are obvious advantages to knowing your natural strengths. Once you're aware of your talents, you can seek out situations that allow you to use them to best advantage. You'll be confident of your own potential for success, and it will be easier for you to choose work that will be stimulating and satisfying.

Dominant Feelers are excellent at evaluating situations in human terms. For example, take Kelly, a customer service representative. Kelly's top priority is to establish a warm and friendly rapport with her customers and to be sure they have a positive and long-lasting experience with the company. She listens to their complaints, supports their feelings, and then assures them that she will help straighten out any problems they have. She, in effect, becomes their friend and advocate at the company.

Dominant Thinkers are without equal when it comes to making impersonal analyses. The legal maneuvering and tough decisions Robert makes as an attorney call his excellent Thinking skills into action repeatedly during a typical day in court. He looks at situations coolly, with clear and detached objectivity. He evaluates the logical effects of different strategic moves and then chooses his approach decisively and calmly.

Dominant Intuitives see connections and implications that no one else does. Abby works in an advertising agency as a copywriter. She writes headlines and radio and television ads for commonplace products and services. Using her natural creativity and ability to see connections between seemingly unrelated things, Abby comes up with clever phrases that evoke the kind of image her clients want to project and the kind of image consumers want to buy.

Dominant Sensors are unparalleled at remembering facts and putting them to good use. Herb is a biology researcher. His job requires that he use his superior attention to detail to observe and document minute changes in experiments. To test the validity of hypotheses, Herb runs experiments repeatedly with the same careful skill and accuracy.

There are also obvious and practical advantages to recognizing your weaknesses—and we all have them. Acknowledging your innate weak points can help you avoid the types of circumstances or the kind of work that places you at the mercy of your lesser functions. Once you know where your own land mines are hidden, you know where to tread carefully! In unavoidably difficult situations, you can at least prepare an appropriate course of action while you are still relatively calm.

We are all stressed by having to use our fourth function too often or for too long. Dominant Feelers are at their weakest when they have to be impersonal and logical (use Thinking). Dominant Thinkers are at their weakest when they are called upon to deal with other people's feelings (use Feeling). Dominant Intuitives are driven crazy by having to attend to facts and details (use Sensing), and Dominant Sensors are at sea when they are obliged to find hidden meanings (use Intuition).

Let's use Jay, an ESFJ, as an example. Jay's dominant function is Feeling, which means he relies heavily on his values when he makes decisions. One of Jay's greatest natural gifts is his sensitivity to others. He is liked and appreciated for his caring, compassionate nature and his willingness to help others. As long as he makes decisions based on what he feels is the right thing to do, Jay feels good about himself and—not incidentally—receives reinforcement and support from others.

Jay's fourth function is Thinking. He finds it difficult to make decisions impersonally. When Jay is put in the position of having to think logically and disregard his feelings, he is operating out of his weakest function. This makes him nervous (it isn't the way his mind naturally works) and can also lead to poor decisions or behavior that seems irrational, overreactive, even childish.

Suppose Jay's boss criticizes one of his written proposals. In truth, this is not a reflection of how the boss feels about Jay. However, like many Dominant Feelers, Jay has great difficulty evaluating criticism objectively and impersonally, as it was intended. He just isn't wired for logical analysis. In this case, Jay misses all the constructive suggestions that his boss makes and responds with hurt feelings, as if his boss had made a personal attack.

Now, suppose Jay were aware of his dominant and auxiliary functions. He would recognize that he has a tendency to take things too much to heart, and he would know that being logical requires extra effort on his part. Instead of panicking and responding emotionally when confronted with criticism, he would remind himself to keep his feelings under control and his mind open, thereby getting the benefit of his boss's comments. Better yet, he would learn to write his next report as logically as possible so he wouldn't be placed in such a vulnerable position again.

We've Only Just Begun...

We'd like to say that you now know everything there is to know about your dominant and auxiliary functions, but in fact there's more essential information ahead. Next we'd like to show you how to use your dominant and auxiliary functions most effectively—and we'll also show you how important it is to find work that not only suits these functions but also suits the way you naturally prefer to use them.

6 | THE WAY YOU DO THE THINGS YOU DO

*Which Strengths
You Share and
Which You Use Privately*

The third ingredient of the "Fourmula" for Career Satisfaction has to do with the way you naturally prefer to use your dominant and auxiliary functions. By now, you know what these are for your personality type; you know why they're both important, and you know that throughout your life your dominant function will always be your most important process. This chapter will explain the special way you need to use your dominant and auxiliary on the job to make them most effective for you.

Extraverted and Introverted...Again!

Essentially you can use your functions in either of two ways: in the outer world or in the inner world. Extraverts use their dominant function in the outer world, with other people. They use their auxiliary function in their inner world, when they are alone, or when the situation relates more personally to them.

For Introverts, the opposite is true. Introverts use their dominant function in their inner world (which is why you have to get to know Introverts before you can appreciate their greatest strengths). They use their auxiliary function in the outer world (which places them at somewhat of a disadvantage, since what others see most is not their strongest function).

When you are using a function in the outer world, we call this "extraverting" a function. Usually this means that you are applying it to something or someone outside of yourself, or that you are using this function with others.

When you are using a function in your inner world, we call this "introverting"

74

a function. Usually this means that you are using it in a way that is related primarily to you, or that you are using it by yourself.*

To help readers understand this dynamic more clearly, Isabel Briggs Myers suggested that we think of the dominant function as a general, and of the auxiliary as his aide-de-camp. When you are dealing with an Extravert, it's as if you walk up to the general's tent and he or she is standing outside, ready to greet you. You get to deal with the top person immediately, while the aide-de-camp (the auxiliary) is inside the tent, ready to assist if needed.

When you are dealing with an Introvert, you are met by the aide-de-camp (the auxiliary) outside the general's tent. The general is busy inside, and you don't get to deal with him or her unless the matter is urgent.

How you use your dominant and auxiliary functions—that is, whether you extravert or introvert them—makes a tremendous difference in how these functions work best for you and how much you will enjoy using them. To achieve maximum satisfaction and effectiveness, you need to use your dominant function in your favorite world. Using it in the "wrong" world is more difficult for you; the result will not be as satisfactory, and you probably will experience a lot of stress as well.

Knowing that your dominant is Intuition, for example, is important, because it identifies the most central aspect of your personality. But your preference for *Extraversion* or *Introversion* is what determines *how* you like to use your dominant (in the outer or inner world). This is important because Introverted Intuitives and Extraverted Intuitives each need to use their Intuition in their most comfortable world to find satisfaction.

To clarify what we mean, let's look at Jonathan and Shelly, a husband-and-wife team who work together. Jonathan and Shelly use their dominants and auxiliaries in opposite ways. Shelly is an ENFJ. Her dominant is Feeling, which she extraverts, and her auxiliary is Intuition, which she introverts. Jonathan is an ENFP. His dominant is Intuition, which he extraverts, and his auxiliary is Feeling, which he introverts. Because they're both Extraverts, Intuitives, and Feelers, you might wonder how different can they be.

First, let's take Shelly. Her dominant is Feeling, which means she makes her decisions (and views the world) primarily on the basis of her personal values. She also *extraverts* Feeling, which means she naturally relates to the feelings of others and seeks to connect with other people. She is driven so strongly by her values, she tends to believe that what she values, others (in the outer world) should as well.

Because Shelly's auxiliary is Intuition, which she *introverts*, she sees patterns, relationships, and meanings, as they relate to her, and is most comfortable using her intuition when she can do it privately, thoughtfully, and by herself (in her inner world).

---

*A more thorough explanation of extraverting and introverting can be found in *Wholeness Lies Within: Sixteen Natural Paths Towards Spirituality*, by Terrence Duniho.

Now consider Jonathan. His dominant is Intuition, which means he sees possibilities, relationships, and meanings of things where he himself is not the focus. He *extraverts* Intuition, which means he naturally seeks to see what is "really" going on—reading between the lines and behind the scenes. Jonathan's primary motivation is to understand situations and people (in the outer world).

Because Jonathan's auxiliary is Feeling, which he *introverts,* he is more tuned in to his own feelings (the inner world) than those of others. And though his values dictate much of his own behavior, it is less important to him if others share the same values.

So how, on a practical, day-to-day basis, do these differences show up? Hearing Jonathan and Shelly talk about Intuition provides some insights:

Jonathan: New possibilities, ideas, and projects are the most exciting thing in the world to me. *Extraverting* my Intuition means I not only *see* things in the world, but like to *talk* about my ideas and inspirations out loud, to process them. Naturally, the first person I turn to is Shelly. Not only because she is extremely bright and perceptive, but I want and need to discuss it out loud to formulate the best solution. However, that can present a problem when I want to brainstorm my great ideas at 11:30 P.M.

Shelly: I'm an Intuitive like Jonathan, but I naturally prefer to *introvert* my Intuition. When Jonathan comes to me with an idea, I know he needs to talk about it to think it through, but I'm at my best when I can *think* about it first privately, going inside my own head to mull it over, then "come out" to discuss it. This is rarely possible to do when I live and work with such a strong extraverted Intuitive who is usually looking for immediate feedback and creative solutions at 11:30 P.M.

Remember that Shelly, a dominant and extraverted Feeler, uses her Feeling very differently than Jonathan, whose Feeling is his auxiliary and introverted. Here's what Shelly and Jonathan have to say about how the different ways they each use Feeling are demonstrated in their daily lives:

Shelly: I'm perfectly comfortable talking about feelings. It helps me to understand what someone's true motivations are. It usually can make resolving a problem with an associate easier and faster when we can let everyone express what's bothering them, and then I can help mediate a positive outcome. Like most extraverted Feelers, I need harmony, and strive to make other people feel good.

Jonathan: As a feeling type, I also make most of my decisions based upon how I feel about something. But I *introvert* my feelings. It's not that I don't feel things very deeply, it's just that I don't like to *talk* about my feelings. It's embarrassing and uncomfortable to make them public [the outer world]. In other words, it is difficult and somewhat stressful to extravert them, because that is not what I do naturally.

As you can see, Shelly and Jonathan, two people who share three of four preferences (E, N, and F), are really very different because they *naturally* use their different functions in opposite ways.

How Do You Face the World?

To help you visualize how you use each function, we've developed a chart we call a "Typogram." In each Typogram there are two figures. The figure in the foreground represents your "public" function—the one you share with the world (the one you extravert). The figure in the background represents your "private" function—the one you prefer to use primarily by yourself (the one you introvert).

Since your dominant is the most central part of your personality, the figure representing it is outlined with a solid dark line. The figure representing your auxiliary function is drawn with a dotted line. The auxiliary function is very important, but it is nonetheless secondary to your dominant function.

You'll notice that all eight of the Extraverted personality types extravert their dominant function. You can see this at a glance because the figures drawn with a solid dark line are all out in front. Similarly, all eight of the Introverted personality types introvert their dominant function. In their Typograms, the figure drawn with a solid dark line is in back.

Before you find the Typogram for your own type, let's look at Jonathan and Shelly's. Jonathan is an ENFP. (The official name for this type is "Extraverted Intuitive with Feeling.") His dominant—Intuition—is up front. His auxiliary—Feeling—is in the background. Remember, Intuition, like Sensing, is a perceiving function. We know Jonathan is a Perceiving type because his dominant is Intuition.

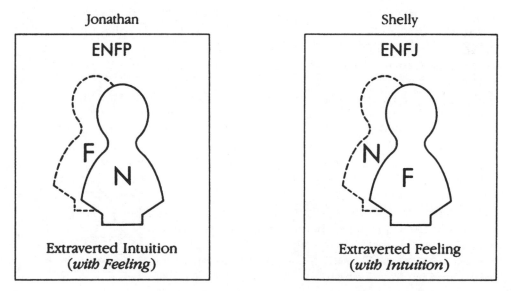

Jonathan

ENFP

F
N

Extraverted Intuition
(*with Feeling*)

Shelly

ENFJ

N
F

Extraverted Feeling
(*with Intuition*)

Shelly is an ENFJ. (Her type is called "Extraverted Feeling with Intuition.") In this drawing, the figure in front, outlined with a solid bold line, is her dominant—Feeling. In the background, represented by a finer, dotted line, is her auxiliary—Intuition. In Shelly's case, we know she is a Judging type because her dominant—Feeling—is a Judging function.

Because both Shelly and Jonathan are Extraverts, their dominants (although different from each other) are both "right up front" where they prefer to use them in the world. And their auxiliaries are in the background where they use them more privately.

What Does This All Mean in Real Life?

Next we'd like to show you just how the way you use your functions influences your daily life and work needs. In the following pages, we discuss the personality types two at a time. As you already learned in Chapter 5, each of the four functions (Sensing, Intuition, Thinking, and Feeling) is dominant for four personality types. However, of the four personality types, two extravert this dominant function, and two introvert it. This means that certain personality types can share the same dominant function but use it very differently.

Now it's time to locate your personality type and read about the unique way you extravert and introvert your dominant and auxiliary functions. On the following pages you will find the typogram for your type and for another that uses its dominant in the same way. When you read the section "Implications for Career Satisfaction," please keep in mind that you are *not* limited to the particular career we use as an example. In Part 3, you'll learn about many career options that all make good use of your personality strengths.

Although we expect you'll start by reading about your own personality type, reading about other types will help you understand why other people just naturally see things very differently than you do.

‖ ISTJ & ISFJ
Introverted Sensing types

Sensing is dominant and introverted for these types. But ISTJs extravert their auxiliary function, which is Thinking, and ISFJs extravert their auxiliary function, which is Feeling.

Implications for Career Satisfaction

Because ISTJs and ISFJs spend so much of their time reflecting on the realistic facts and details they personally experience, they derive the most satisfaction from performing work which allows them to use that data in a practical and useful way. Physicians, for example, need

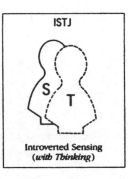

ISTJ

Introverted Sensing
(*with Thinking*)

to be able to internalize large amounts of very specific information. However, an ISTJ physician might be more inclined to go into medical research (to use his or her auxiliary function, Thinking, and work with the logical cause and effect of their work), whereas an ISFJ physician might be more likely to start a family practice (to use his or her auxiliary function, Feeling, to deal directly with the concerns and needs of people and to make personal connections with patients).

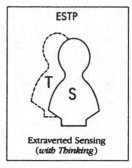

‖ ESTP & ESFP
Extraverted Sensing types

For both ESTPs and ESFPs, Sensing is dominant and extraverted. ESTPs introvert their auxiliary function, which is Thinking, and ESFPs introvert their auxiliary function, which is Feeling.

Implications for Career Satisfaction

In order for ESTPs and ESFPs to be happy, they must constantly be using their senses to experience the world. They like to be active, and they also like to be able to talk about and act on their observations. In general, the *process* is more important to them than the end result. ESTPs and ESFPs gain satisfaction just from the act of doing whatever it is they enjoy. An extraverted Sensing type would make a good basketball coach—jumping around, watching the game, keeping track of the opposing team, etc.—although an ESTP coach might focus more on strategy and winning (to use his or her auxiliary function, Thinking, and enjoy the competition of the game), and an ESFP coach might focus more on teamwork and the human experience (to use his or her auxiliary function, Feeling, and help develop the spirit of cooperation among the team members).

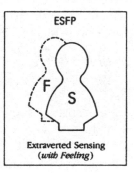

‖ INTJ & INFJ
Introverted Intuitive types

For both INTJs and INFJs, Intuition is dominant and introverted. INTJs extravert their auxiliary function, which is Thinking, and INFJs extravert their auxiliary function, which is Feeling.

Key: The figure drawn with the solid dark line represents your dominant function. The figure drawn with the dotted line represents your auxiliary function. The figure in the foreground represents the function you extravert. The figure in the background represents the function you introvert.

Implications for Career Satisfaction

Both INTJs and INFJs must have work that makes use of their gift for seeing inner meanings, implications, and possibilities. They also like to get things done. It's important to them to find a way of expressing their perceptions. Somehow their unique, inner vision of how things could be must be translated into reality. It's not unusual for college professors to be introverted Intuitive types, since this job allows them not only to ponder but also to express all kinds of intellectual possibilities. However, the INTJ professor would probably teach in the sciences (to use his or her auxiliary function, Thinking, to see the underlying principles at work), while the INFJ professor would probably teach in the humanities (to use his or her auxiliary function, Feeling, to help students develop and grow through an understanding of the material).

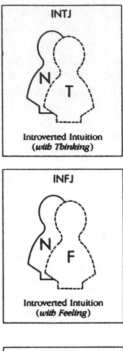

INTJ

Introverted Intuition
(*with Thinking*)

INFJ

Introverted Intuition
(*with Feeling*)

‖ ENTP & ENFP
Extraverted Intuitive types

For both ENTPs and ENFPs, Intuition is dominant and extraverted. ENTPs introvert their auxiliary function, which is Thinking, and ENFPs introvert their auxiliary function, which is Feeling.

Implications for Career Satisfaction

Because ENTPs and ENFPs love possibilities, they need to be free to pursue as many options as they can. To be satisfied, they also need to express their ideas or somehow make them real (for example, through a song, speech, or presentation). Psychology is a popular field for extraverted Intuitive types, since each patient or client presents a fascinating array of new possibilities and mysteries to be considered and discussed. However, the ENTP psychologist would be more likely to focus on logical problem solving (which makes good use of his or her auxiliary, Thinking), and the ENFP psychologist would be more likely to focus on each patient's feelings and values (using his or her auxiliary function, Feeling).

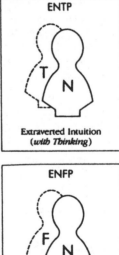

ENTP

Extraverted Intuition
(*with Thinking*)

ENFP

Extraverted Intuition
(*with Feeling*)

Key: The figure drawn with the solid dark line represents your dominant function. The figure drawn with the dotted line represents your auxiliary function. The figure in the foreground represents the function you extravert. The figure in the background represents the function you introvert.

‖ ISFP & INFP
Introverted Feeling types

For both ISFPs and INFPs, Feeling is dominant and introverted. ISFPs extravert their auxiliary function, which is Sensing, and INFPs extravert their auxiliary function, which is Intuition.

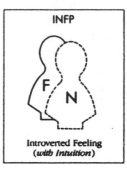

Implications for Career Satisfaction

Both ISFPs and INFPs need to feel good about what they do. They please themselves first, and others second. Although their work often has to do with helping others, it must first and foremost be something they believe in wholeheartedly. A possible career choice for introverted Feeling types would be physical therapy. However, the ISFP physical therapist would probably focus more on the mechanics of helping correct physical problems (to make use of his or her auxiliary function, Sensing), whereas an INFP physical therapist would probably focus more on each patient's total well-being, looking to help the client understand and work through the psychological or spiritual factors involved with his or her pain (to use the physical therapist's auxiliary function, Intuition).

‖ ESFJ & ENFJ
Extraverted Feeling types

For both ESFJs and ENFJs, Feeling is dominant and extraverted. ESFJs introvert their auxiliary function, which is Sensing, and ENFJs introvert their auxiliary function, which is Intuition.

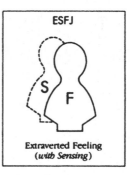

Implications for Career Satisfaction

Both ESFJs and ENFJs derive their greatest satisfaction from pleasing others and receiving their approval. It is especially important for extraverted Feeling types to work in a harmonious environment that is free from interpersonal tension. People who extravert Feeling can be very successful as college recruiters, since this kind of work allows them to connect with others. However, the ESFJ college recruiter would be more likely to

---

Key: The figure drawn with the solid dark line represents your dominant function. The figure drawn with the dotted line represents your auxiliary function. The figure in the foreground represents the function you extravert. The figure in the background represents the function you introvert.

focus on a prospective student's academic record and specific test scores and to share information about activities, programs, and schedules at the school (in order to make use of his or her auxiliary function, Sensing). The ENFJ recruiter might be more interested in focusing on the all-around potential of the prospective student, sharing information about the school's philosophy, social and intellectual climate, and opportunities for personal exploration, discovery, and growth.

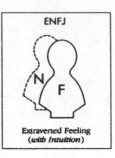

ENFJ

Extraverted Feeling
(*with Intuition*)

‖ ISTP & INTP
Introverted Thinking types

For both ISTPs and INTPs, Thinking is dominant and introverted. ISTPs extravert their auxiliary function, which is Sensing, and INTPs extravert their auxiliary function, which is Intuition.

ISTP

Introverted Thinking
(*with Sensing*)

Implications for Career Satisfaction

Because they want to understand and make sense of the world, ISTPs and INTPs need work which allows them to make analyses—whether they are considering an abstract idea or a concrete project—in the most logical way possible.

Introverted Thinking types are often drawn to computer-related work, although an ISTP is more likely to be interested in setting up, maintaining, and fixing computer systems (to be able to use his or her auxiliary function, Sensing, to attend to the accurate operations of the system), and the INTP is more likely to be drawn to programming (to be able to use his or her auxiliary function, Intuition, to learn about new programs and creative ways to use the system).

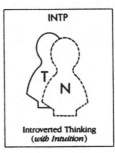

INTP

Introverted Thinking
(*with Intuition*)

‖ ESTJ & ENTJ
Extraverted Thinking types

For both ESTJs and ENTJs, Thinking is dominant and extraverted. ESTJs introvert their auxiliary function, which is Sensing, and ENTJs introvert their auxiliary function, which is Intuition.

Key: The figure drawn with the solid dark line represents your dominant function. The figure drawn with the dotted line represents your auxiliary function. The figure in the foreground represents the function you extravert. The figure in the background represents the function you introvert.

Implications for Career Satisfaction

Extraverted Thinking types need to be in charge. Both ESTJs and ENTJs need to be able to make logical decisions about the people and situations they encounter. Not content to merely observe the logic of things, they are happiest when they can use their skills to organize others to behave in the most logical and efficient way. Both ESTJs and ENTJs make natural corporate managers and executives, although the ESTJ manager will probably focus more on maintaining the standard for maximum efficiency (using his or her auxiliary function, Sensing), and the ENTJ manager will probably focus more on the future and determining ways of improving or changing the system (in order to use his or her auxiliary function, Intuition).

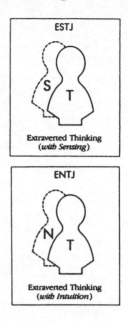

ESTJ

Extraverted Thinking
(*with Sensing*)

ENTJ

Extraverted Thinking
(*with Intuition*)

Here's Looking at You

Now that this chapter has given you an appreciation for the importance of how you naturally use your dominant and auxiliary functions, we hope you'll try to take note of how you use these functions both at work and in everyday life. The more you observe your own behavior, the more clearly you will see the dynamic between your dominant and auxiliary. Also, you will now be able to judge work situations with more discrimination and increased awareness of what will probably be most satisfying.

Key: The figure drawn with the solid dark line represents your dominant function. The figure drawn with the dotted line represents your auxiliary function. The figure in the foreground represents the function you extravert. The figure in the background represents the function you introvert.

7 | AGED TO PERFECTION

*Developing Your
Abilities Over Time*

The fourth ingredient in the "Fourmula" for Career Satisfaction is type development, the lifelong process during which we may gain access to *all* the Type preferences—even our weakest or least comfortable. This process occurs naturally in everyone, but it can also be undertaken deliberately.

What we think of as "good type development" allows you to make the most of your natural abilities, enables you to make better decisions, and helps prevent you from being sabotaged by your innate weaknesses.

We know someone who is fond of saying, "The trouble with getting old is that you get more like yourself!" Although we grow and change with age, we don't change our personality types, and our dominant and auxiliary functions remain the same. However, within each type it is possible—not just possible, but preferable!—to develop a well-rounded personality.

To some extent, people develop their personalities in predictable stages. Whether or not you've ever heard of Type, you are likely to have different interests at different times in your life. However, once you understand type development, you'll see that these changes don't just occur randomly. By recognizing where you are in your own type development, you'll be able to identify which functions you'll naturally find satisfaction using—and these might be very different for you at age forty-two than at age twenty-two. You'll also understand why certain activities that once satisfied you no longer do. Furthermore, you'll gain some insight into how you can expect to change as you grow older, and how your career choices may broaden.

The theory of type development was originated by an early user of Type, W. Harold Grant. Our experience confirms much of what Grant believed, although we've noticed a different timeline. We've found that the principles of type development can be very useful in helping people determine their immediate and future career-related needs.

From Birth to Age Six

As we've already said, each individual is born with a personality "blueprint" that stays the same throughout life. However, it takes some time for definite preferences to become apparent. In children's early years, it is more difficult to conclusively identify their type preferences because they don't yet have the language skills to accurately describe their mental processes. While one's preference for extraversion or introversion may be the easiest to spot early on, the other preferences may be more elusive, especially with introverted children because, as with introverts of all ages, they are more difficult to get to know! And because the four functions do not develop simultaneously, before the age of six, or so, it is usually difficult to determine most young children's full types with real accuracy. When we learn more about the cues and play behaviors of children of different types, the adults who care for them will be able to teach and parent according to the child's style, rather than requiring that she or he adapt to ours. An excellent resource for understanding children's developmental patterns and how to individualize parenting and teaching strategies is our second book, *Nurture by Nature: Understand Your Child's Personality Type and Become a Better Parent.*

From Age Six to Age Twelve

Starting at *about* age six, a child's dominant function starts to pull ahead of the pack, and patterns of behavior become clearer. A Dominant Sensor may show an inclination for mastering skillful gymnastics routines; a Dominant Intuitive may create surprising musical instruments out of household odds and ends; a Dominant Thinker may construct impressive arguments against being punished; a Dominant Feeler may demonstrate concern and empathy for others, especially those in trouble or those suffering a tragedy. Without constraints, children will always naturally start to strengthen their dominant function during this period of their lives.

It is crucial to a child's healthy development that the use of his or her dominant function be encouraged by parents and teachers. The dominant function is the driving force behind our personalities and the source of our natural strengths. When encouraged, it will flourish and help produce a competent, confident adult. If a child is discouraged from using his or her dominant function, he or she may grow up not trusting the most central part of his or her personality. This obviously interferes with having a fulfilling life.

From Age Twelve to Age Twenty-Five

From *about* the age of twelve, we start to strengthen our auxiliary function. As you learned in the previous chapter, the auxiliary function balances the dominant function and ensures that we are proficient at both information gathering and decision making.

Once the dominant and auxiliary functions are firmly established, the third and fourth functions fall into line (although they are still quite undeveloped). By the age of about twenty-five, our personality types are distinct. Happily, this is *not* the end of personal growth!

From Age Twenty-Five to Age Fifty

At some point after the age of twenty-five, we start to develop our third function. We've found that most people don't start to do this in earnest or with great success until closer to the age of forty or even after. You'll notice that this timing coincides with another phenomenon that can occur at this age: the mid-life crisis.

We believe that the connection between type development and mid-life crisis—let's call it mid-life reevaluation!—is more than coincidental. For the first half of our lives, we use primarily our dominant and auxiliary functions. We rely on them, we trust them, and they work well for us. After many years, we are generally proficient at using both. At this point, having reached the top of the proverbial hill, we may also reach some disturbing conclusions: first, that there may not be that much time left ahead, and second, that there isn't much challenge in spending the remaining years exactly as we spent our earlier years. It is not uncommon for people to reassess their values at mid-life and to change their priorities.

Based on our experience with our clients, we believe that mid-life marks the beginning of a new phase of type development. Unconsciously, we seek to round out our personalities and to become more effective and capable. We start to develop our third and, later, fourth functions.

For example, take Marty, an ISFP. Marty is a Dominant Feeler. His auxiliary function is Sensing, his third function is Intuition, and his fourth function is Thinking. Up until now, Marty has been pretty much a "meat-and-potatoes" kind of guy, taking things as they are, not wondering about how they got to be that way and not looking for any deeper meanings. Now that he's thirty-eight, however, Marty has become more curious. He has become interested in *why* he acts the way he does and what influence his parents had on his upbringing. He has been talking more with his sister about their childhood, and he is even considering some personal counseling in order to learn more about himself and his patterns of behavior. Marty has become more interested in connections and in the reasons why people behave the way they do—including himself. He is deepening his awareness of life's complexities, and he has a new appreciation for possibilities. These are all clear signs of developing Intuition.

Sometimes, developing your third function can be deeply unsettling. Naomi is a thirty-seven-year-old stockbroker. As an ENTP, she is a Dominant Intuitive. Her auxiliary function is Thinking, her third function is Feeling, and her fourth function is Sensing. Naomi is a brilliant wheeler-dealer. Her ability to analyze markets, anticipate trends, and persuade others that she is right have already made her very wealthy. Naomi finds the fast-paced, high-stakes, risk-taking financial arena exhilarating, and she has become very good at what she does. Lately, however, Naomi has been finding her work less satisfying. She has become somewhat less willing to work eighteen-hour days, especially now that she has a serious romantic partner who would actually like to see her once in a while. Worse, Naomi has become acutely aware of the ticking of her biological clock. She still enjoys the challenges of her career, and being successful still means a lot to her, but she is realizing that being alone with her money and her collection of expensive possessions is not entirely satisfactory. Naomi's third function—Feeling—is making itself heard, and she is probably going to have to make some changes in her lifestyle to accommodate it.

Mid-life doesn't always bring profound changes, as it did for Marty and Naomi. Many people quietly develop new interests or activities or simply start to live their lives a little differently. At mid-life, we often become more open to other interests, other points of view, and other ways of doing things. We may become more flexible in our attitudes and may start to pay attention to things we once overlooked or considered unimportant.

Some people will simply develop hobbies associated with their third function (for example, a sign of developing Sensing may be a new interest in exercise). Other people will be drawn to the mental perspective associated with their third function (for example, a sign of developing Thinking can be a new emphasis on objectivity and fairness). Many people develop *both* the recreational activities *and* the mental awareness associated with their third function. This can occur simultaneously, or by starting with one and progressing to the other.

Once you understand type development, you can consciously work on strengthening your third function at mid-life in order to add more depth, enjoyment, and capability to your life. How to go about doing this is unique to each individual.

Phil, an ENFP, is forty-one. He is a Dominant Intuitive. Phil's auxiliary function is Feeling, his third function is Thinking, and his fourth function is Sensing. Phil has always preferred harmony to conflict, and he has spent much of his life trying to make other people happy. Now, however, Phil is deliberately working on developing his Thinking.

Recently Phil purchased an expensive pair of sneakers that began to fall apart after only two weeks of use. When he brought them back to the store and explained the situation, the manager responded, "No problem! We'll just send these back to the factory, and if they can't be repaired, you'll be sent a new pair. It should only take a month or so."

Ten years ago Phil would have accepted this solution because he would have been so interested in having a positive, friendly interaction with the store manager that he wouldn't have been willing to risk a confrontation. At this stage of his life, however, Phil is more comfortable using his Thinking, and he is more willing to sacrifice harmony in order to be treated fairly. Instead, Phil answered, "That doesn't seem right to me. I don't want to stop my exercise program for a month because you sold me a pair of faulty sneakers. I didn't buy the sneakers from the factory, I bought them from you, and the extra markup I paid is for your service. I'd like you to replace the sneakers *now,* and you deal with the factory!"

The manager reluctantly complied. Without consciously planning to do so, Phil was drawn to use his emerging reasoning skills (his Thinking) and in the process, got better at doing so.

After Age Fifty

Later in life, we start to use our fourth function with more success. Some typologists believe that the fourth function is so underdeveloped that we are never really able to use it efficiently. However, we have found that many people are drawn to their fourth function at this stage in life, and that with conscious effort they can indeed make good use of it. Engaging your fourth function with some degree of success requires concentration—it is, after all, your weakest function—but it is worth the effort.

Steve, fifty-seven, does consulting for the manufacturing industry, as he has for most of his working life. He has also always been extremely active in volunteer work. An ESFJ, Steve is a Dominant Feeler. His auxiliary function is Sensing, his third function is Intuition, and his fourth function is Thinking. Steve works hard as a community leader, helping to create affordable housing for homeless people in his city. Over the years, Steve has become increasingly innovative at finding new funding sources and at thinking up alternative uses of space to create housing for the homeless (using his Intuition). While Steve has always been passionate about the homeless, his developing Thinking abilities are now enabling him to be more objective and thick-skinned about the political process. He has started to work on implementing programs and systems that operate within the larger city structure (using his Thinking). This is a challenge for Steve, but by using his head, he is more effective in solving the problems about which he cares deeply in his heart.

If you have experienced good type development throughout your life, you should be able to use all of your functions—Sensing, Intuition, Thinking, and Feeling—after the age of fifty or so, calling up the right one for the right situation. Your dominant and auxiliary functions are still the source of your greatest strengths, and your third and fourth functions require more supervision, but you'll have a wider range of skills at your command.

Remember the analogy comparing your functions to the family in the car? Well, with good type development, it's as if the third and fourth functions (the kids in the backseat) have grown up a little. The dominant and auxiliary are still in charge, but the third function is now a young adult, and the fourth function is an adolescent.

Interestingly enough, in the process of using all the functions, you'll find that you also gain access to all the type preferences, including the attitudes. (Remember them? The attitudes are Extraversion, Introversion, Judging, and Perceiving.) If you're an Introvert, you may find that you are more comfortable with Extraverted activities such as meeting new people or widening your area of interest. And if you're a Judger, you may find you are better able to use Perceiving—for example, to relax, play, and spend more time experiencing life instead of needing to control it.

Here's an example to show what we mean. Marian, an ENFJ, is a sixty-year-old woman serving on a jury for a medical malpractice case. As a Dominant Feeler, Marian might be expected to base all of her decisions on her personal beliefs and values, with special sympathy for the victim. Since Marian's auxiliary function is Intuition, she might also be expected to focus primarily on the implications of the evidence and the general patterns of the information she hears.

In fact, Marian is quite a different juror. Because she has gained better access to her Sensing, she pays close attention to the evidence, and during the jury's deliberations she remembers and recites specific relevant details. Perhaps surprisingly, she is able to stay impartial during the trial, using her fourth function, Thinking. She even cautions her fellow jurors not to base their decisions purely on empathy. Furthermore, although Marian is an Extravert, she has learned to listen closely before speaking (using Introversion) and to wait, reflecting carefully on all she has heard before rendering a final verdict (using Perceiving).

Has Marian changed from an ENFJ to an ISTP? No! But because she has good type development, she can call on all the preferences when she needs them. In this situation, it was clearly appropriate for Marian to work hard at gathering the facts and arrive at an impartial decision, something she would have had a very hard time doing twenty-five years earlier.

What Helps (and Hurts) Good Type Development

As we mentioned earlier in this chapter, it is essential that children be reinforced for using their dominant and auxiliary functions. We all know that how we were brought up has a profound effect on how well-adjusted we are today, but have you ever stopped to think of your life in terms of your own type development? Children who are encouraged to follow their natural abilities strengthen all of their functions over time and generally become fully functional adults. Children who are discouraged from using their innate strengths *can* grow up to be confused and ambivalent about their perceptions and inclinations—and this confusion can affect every aspect of adult life, including career issues.

Parents and teachers naturally value in children the qualities that they have themselves. Conversely, they can be mystified by—even disapproving of—behavior they don't naturally understand. This isn't malicious or even intentional; it's just natural for people to enjoy and feel more comfortable with others who are like them because they understand them more easily.

We know a woman who spent much of her young life playing with imaginary friends. She lived on a farm in a remote area, and as far as we know, the day-to-day challenges of farming meant little to her. She spent her time inventing playmates who talked, interacted, and even misbehaved. Some parents (particularly Dominant Sensors) might, in this situation, fear that their child was hallucinating, but fortunately Rebecca's parents were just happy that their daughter was keeping herself harmlessly occupied. Today Rebecca is a very successful romance novelist, and she attributes much of her success to her early practice with characterization!

Of course, not all stories are success stories. We also know a young woman named Erica who is definitely a Dominant Thinker—cool, independent, and undemonstrative. As it turns out, both of Erica's parents are Dominant Feelers. They have never been comfortable with Erica's impersonal manner, and they've always wondered if maybe they did something wrong to produce such a remote child. Despite their best efforts to deny their own need for affection, Erica's parents unintentionally communicated to her from infancy that they wished she were different. Although Erica's parents never actively interfered with her inclinations, Erica was always plagued by self-doubt. Fortunately, identifying her true personality type has been a liberating experience for her.

If you're a parent, we know what you're thinking: Oh, great! Just what I need...another expert telling me how I'm screwing up my kid! We can appreciate your feelings. (Honestly—we're both Feeling types, and parents, too!) But our point is not that you're doing anything wrong; it's simply that it is easy to forget that our children may be very different from us, just as we may be very much unlike our parents.

At this point, it might be helpful for you to reflect on how you were brought up. We're not suggesting that you necessarily try to "type" your parents and teachers, but do take a moment to think about your childhood. What natural talents did you exhibit when you were young? How were your efforts received by others? Do you think you were encouraged to develop your dominant function, or were you expected to behave in what was for you an unnatural way? Most people will be remarkably similar as adults to the way they were as children, but some people have a difficult time asserting their true personalities in the face of resistance or lack of understanding from others. Children are particularly vulnerable to others' expectations and often suppress their own natural preferences in order to fit in and be accepted.

Throughout life, circumstances can either work for or against your good type development. In addition to parents and teachers, we are also influenced by siblings, peers, and the culture in which we grow up. Consider this: Over 50 percent of the American population is made up of Extraverted Sensors. Only about 4 percent of the American population comprises Introverted Intuitives. Strong messages permeate our culture that it's better to be the former (action-oriented, social, pragmatic, and practical) than the latter (thoughtful, introspective, complex, and creative).

Pressure to be what you aren't can cause lifelong confusion. If you are obliged to fit into a certain group mentality that really doesn't suit you (this could be a family dynamic, a school or community setting, or a professional environment), you may end up denying your true nature and not enjoying your required role. If you spend twenty years at a job you don't enjoy, you may end up not only out of touch with your natural interests but—even worse—with a distorted view of your own competence.

If you were never encouraged to "be yourself," or if you are confused about your true nature, take heart. We have found that Type can help lead people to a productive, fulfilling life based on a sound understanding of their true natures.

Where Are You in Your Type Development?

There are two ways to find out how you are coming along in your own type development. Before you do either of the following exercises, you will need to refer to your hierarchy of functions on the table on page 67. We suggest that you write it down and keep it close by for easy reference. This will be helpful in translating our general information about type development into information that applies to your specific personality type.

To get a rough idea of where you stand in your own type development, locate your age on the timetable below. If you're following the general trend, you are probably developing the function that appears above your age. Remember, this is only a rough estimate. Everyone progresses at his or her own rate.

TYPE DEVELOPMENT TIMETABLE

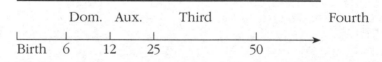

| Dom. | Aux. | Third | Fourth |

Birth   6   12   25   50

The Type Development Timetable is helpful really only in a general way. Nobody wakes up at age twenty-five and says, "Aha! Time to develop my third function!" People will focus on different dimensions of their personalities at different times in their lives. Even people who have the same personality type and who are the same age will not progress in exactly the same way. The age ranges given here are just approximate guidelines.

For another check on where you stand in your own type development, you'll need to examine your current interests and attitudes. It's usually best to focus on your behavior away from work, since during your "free time" you are more likely to pursue what you wish and be whoever you want to be.

Read through the following four descriptions of how people develop their Sensing, Intuition, Thinking, or Feeling and see which one sounds like you. Can you tell which function you are strengthening at this stage in your life? In making your decision, it might be helpful for you to write down a list of your latest interests, or to ask someone who knows you well if he or she has seen any evidence of a new perspective on your part.

After you've pinpointed the function you're currently developing, refer to your hierarchy of functions. Is it your auxiliary, third, or fourth function? If you want, you can check your results against the Type Development Timetable.

Evidence of Type Development

Developing Sensing

In general, people who are developing their Sensing start to focus more on the present moment, taking things day by day.

New attitudes may include:

- Becoming more aware of how things look, sound, smell, taste, and feel
- A new appreciation of nature
- Becoming more interested in facts and details; becoming more precise and accurate
- Becoming more realistic; becoming more concerned with how long projects take and with the realities of getting them done

New interests may include:

- Cooking
- Building
- Arts and crafts
- Listening to music
- Exercise
- Hiking, camping
- Gardening
- Reading nonfiction
- Careful attention to details
- Greater interest in numbers

Developing Intuition

In general, people who are developing their Intuition become more open to change and to seeing things in new ways.

New attitudes may include:

- Becoming more interested in underlying meanings and in what symbols represent
- Developing or deepening an interest in spiritual matters and the meaning of life
- Becoming more open to using imagination
- Thinking about how people or things are related to each other; focusing on the big picture

New interests may include:

- Art, design
- Religion
- Research, study, returning to school, advanced degree
- Problem solving, brainstorming
- Inventing
- Creative writing
- Reading fiction
- Travel to learn about different cultures
- Long-range planning/thinking

Developing Thinking

In general, people who are developing their Thinking become better able to stay objective when considering data.

New attitudes may include:

- A greater emphasis on fairness and equality, even at the expense of harmony
- A new awareness of cause and effect and the logical consequences of actions
- Becoming more critical in evaluating people and things
- Greater interest in efficiency and competency

New interests may include:

- The rights of others
- Negotiating, arbitration
- Strategy games (Scrabble, chess, etc.)
- Debating
- Consumer awareness
- Political interests
- Elevating one's standards
- Being aware of others' standards
- Striving to be consistent

Developing Feeling

In general, people who are developing their Feeling gain a new awareness of how their actions affect others. They often reassess their priorities in more human terms.

New attitudes may include:

- Providing more emotional support for others; showing concern for other people's needs
- Cultivating friendships; sharing personal experiences and feelings
- Greater interest in communication and listening skills
- Greater appreciation for the contributions of others

New interests may include:

- Volunteer work
- Mentoring
- Rekindling past relationships
- Initiating or attending reunions
- Personal therapy
- Open, thoughtful conversation
- Writing
- Keeping a journal
- Expressing gratitude
- Praising others

As an example, let's assume you are an INFJ and that you are fifty-two years old. Your hierarchy of functions is as follows:

#1 (Dominant)	Intuition
#2 (Auxiliary)	Feeling
#3 (Tertiary)	Thinking
#4 (Inferior)	Sensing

You've always been adept at seeing implications and meanings (Intuition), and you have learned how to use this information in making sound decisions based upon your personal values and your understanding of others (Feeling). Over the years you've gotten better at anticipating the logical consequences of your decisions (Thinking). Recently, you've found yourself leafing through catalogues for gourmet cooks and you've signed up for a cooking course. You're also more determined to find that ten-cent discrepancy in your bank statement. These may both be signs of developing Sensing.

Sensing is your fourth function. According to the Type Development Timetable, you are likely to start developing your fourth function after age fifty.

Still Confused?

If you started this chapter with a very clear idea of your true personality type, and if you have been thoughtful about these exercises, chances are you found that you are pretty much "on schedule" in your own type development. You should have a sense of some of the ways you've changed over the years, as well as an understanding of why these changes occurred. However, if you're having trouble trying to figure out which function you are currently strengthening, don't despair.

If you're not certain about your personality type, try plotting the function hierarchies of the other personality type(s) you might be. (To do this, go back to the hierarchy of functions table on page 67.) This exercise can help you clarify your type as well as where you are developmentally.

Another possibility is that you've correctly identified your personality type, but that you are developing in a unique way that has nothing to do with our Type Development Timetable. You're allowed! But don't throw this chapter out the window just because you're on your own private schedule. The concept of type development will still be useful to you; you'll just have to do a little more independent research to find out where you've been and where you're going.

Type Development and Problem Solving

You'll find that the more you develop your functions—Sensing, Intuition, Thinking, and Feeling—the better you'll be at making good decisions. This is a significant skill, especially when it comes time to make important, far-reaching decisions such as selecting a career. Luckily it is a skill you can consciously develop.

When you are faced with a decision, first use *both* information-gathering functions (Sensing and Intuition), and then use *both* decision-making functions (Thinking and Feeling). Don't automatically start with your dominant function (whichever it is). It will be easier for you to use your dominant and auxiliary functions, but make a special effort to use your third and fourth functions as well. Each function makes a valid and important contribution to the problem-solving process, and overlooking any one of the four can result in a seriously flawed decision.

The ideal approach to problem solving looks like this:

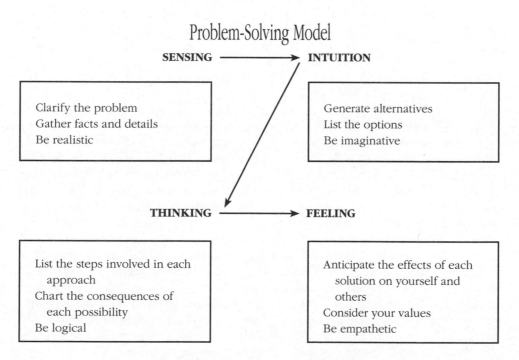

Problem-Solving Model

SENSING ⟶ **INTUITION**

Clarify the problem
Gather facts and details
Be realistic

Generate alternatives
List the options
Be imaginative

THINKING ⟶ **FEELING**

List the steps involved in each approach
Chart the consequences of each possibility
Be logical

Anticipate the effects of each solution on yourself and others
Consider your values
Be empathetic

Decide on a course of action!

Note: Even if you make a conscious effort to use all of these functions, you probably won't use them in this order in "real life." The important thing is to *consult* them, even if you don't follow this pattern exactly.*

We all make a thousand decisions a day, so you should have plenty of opportunities to practice good problem-solving skills. If you are faced with a particularly important decision, it may be a good idea to consult someone you respect *who has different strengths than you do.* For example, if you're a Thinking type, ask a Feeler for his or her views. You might be amazed at how differently he or she sees the situation. Seeking this kind of input from time to time will help you develop your weaker functions, resulting in more effective decision making. Strengthening your mental functions is just like building up muscles: The more you exercise them, the stronger they become.

Type Development and Career Satisfaction

Wherever you are in your career, whether you're starting out or starting over, keep in mind that type development is a natural process you can take advantage of. If you choose career options that fit into your own natural type development, you'll find your work more satisfying on many levels because it will provide you with opportunities for professional growth and enjoyment. Professionally, this translates into greater competency and, ultimately, greater success.

From the beginning, it's important to choose work that suits your dominant and auxiliary functions. This doesn't change with age. However, at some point you can also expect your third function to become more important. Sooner or later—preferably sooner!—you will want to exercise and express it in your work. Your fourth function, on the other hand, may never play a significant role in your professional life, except to the extent that you should avoid situations that require using it for too long.

Throughout your working life, you'll need to make constant career updates. These don't have to be dramatic changes (although for some personality types they probably will be). Expect to lose interest in certain professional activities you have mastered even as you become more interested in new challenges, approaches, or skills. This is all part of good type development. The stronger your third function becomes, the more viable career options you'll have at your disposal. Later in life, you may even gravitate toward work that would have been unsuitable for you ten or twenty years earlier.

Maureen, an ISTJ, is a Dominant Sensor. Her auxiliary function is Thinking, her third function is Feeling, and her fourth function is Intuition. Shortly after Maureen graduated from college, she accepted a job in medical research. Once she mastered the different procedures involved in the lab work, she grew to love her job and she excelled at it. Maureen was always precise and observant, her reports were detailed and accurate, and she enjoyed verifying data firsthand and

*Adapted by Elenor Corlett from *People Types and Tiger Stripes*, by Gordon Lawrence.

recording it in neat notebooks for later review. Maureen was glad that her work might someday result in a medical breakthrough, but mostly she was interested in the step-by-step progress on the different experiments going on in the lab. She was a steady, quiet, dependable worker, and for many years was quite content.

When Maureen's boss quit unexpectedly, Maureen was offered a supervisory position. She would be responsible for overseeing the work of all the lab technicians, making sure they did their jobs, helping them with difficult procedures, and training new technicians as needed. Maureen wasn't sure whether or not she should accept the job, and because she knew somebody who knew us, she came to us for advice.

We were certain that Maureen would do well with the new job. By means of exercises and discussion we helped her see that she was developing her third function—Feeling—and that this professional opportunity would mesh nicely with her personal timetable. We urged her to try it.

To her own surprise, Maureen turned out to be an excellent supervisor. She developed a supportive managerial style and successfully kept her staff working together. She also continued with her own lab work, focusing in particular on cancer research.

Over the next several years, Maureen became more interested in the human consequences of her research. She formed many connections with doctors, hospitals, and organizations associated with finding and funding a cure for cancer. Eventually these relationships brought Maureen directly into contact with cancer patients, and she started volunteering some time on weekends to visit them. This would not have appealed to Maureen at all ten years earlier, but at this stage in her life she found that it added new meaning and urgency to her research.

Today, Maureen is exceedingly busy. She does far less hands-on lab work, and instead is concentrating on evaluating new developments in cancer research and treatment. In this latest phase of her career, Maureen is actively engaging her Intuition. She travels a great deal, learning new procedures and familiarizing herself with breakthroughs and advances occurring all over the world. Now an acknowledged expert in her field, she also lectures frequently—something she would never have felt comfortable doing when she was younger—and still finds time to visit the patients to whom her work means so much.

At this point, it would be difficult to separate Maureen's personal and professional lives, just as it would be impossible to separate her personal and professional growth. By choosing a career path that engaged her natural interests at different points in her life, Maureen has become not only an extremely capable professional but also an exceptional human being.

Recapping the "Fourmula"

Now you have it: the complete "Fourmula" for Career Satisfaction! Here, for your review, are the four things you must understand in order to find a career you can love:

1. Your innate temperament (Chapter 4)
2. Your hierarchy of functions (Chapter 5)
3. How you extravert or introvert your functions (Chapter 6)
4. Where you are in your type development (Chapter 7)

In Part 3, you'll meet people of your same personality type who are a lot like you. After you've read their stories, we'll show you how they've found work that is consistent with their temperament, that makes good use of their dominant and auxiliary functions, allows them to use their strengths in the most effective way, and is in sync with their type development.

After you've finished reading this book, you'll be able to do the same!

Part Three | GETTING TO WORK

Profiles of Career-Satisfied People

It is said that the best way to learn is by one's own mistakes. If that's so, perhaps the next best way to learn is through the mistakes and successes of others, especially those who are a lot like us. The case studies that follow are the real-life career experiences of people from many different and varied professions, income levels, ages, and backgrounds. What they all have in common is that each one has found career satisfaction. For some it took many years and several different jobs; for others the path was carefully planned and more direct.

For each of the sixteen type chapters that follow, there are profiles of people who really enjoy their jobs— and have found the right match between their personality type and their career. Following the profiles, we provide an analysis to help you understand how their jobs let them use their natural strengths and therefore are satisfying. As you read these profiles, think about how you are similar to the people described. This will help you to identify what you require to find career satisfaction.

Following the case studies you will find a section called Common Threads, which lists specific and important criteria for career satisfaction for people like you. Popular Occupations contains a list of specific careers and the reasons why they offer the best potential for career satisfaction for people of your type.

After identifying a potentially satisfying career, you will need to conduct a successful job search campaign. Recognizing that people of different types will naturally approach this process differently, we provide specific and practical pointers to help you capitalize on *your strengths and minimize your possible weaknesses to conduct the most effective job search possible.*

By the time you have finished reading your type chapter, you will be ready to *identify and evaluate one (or maybe more than one) career option that can give you real satisfaction— work that will finally let you Do What You Are!*

8 | ENFJ
Extraverted, Intuitive, Feeling, Judging
"The Public Relations Specialists"

Profile 1: Anna

"Putting love and ability together."

Anna loves seeing an institution that she deeply believes in flourish as the result of her efforts. She is the director of development at an independent school and spends her days supervising a team of people, both volunteers and trained professionals, who raise money for the school. Anna's day typically consists of creating strategies for how best to ask people to make significant contributions as well as figuring out how much to ask for. This involves research into potential donors' capabilities but also less factual investigations into their interests and tendencies. "It's the propensity, not just the capacity, for giving that I look into." In this way, Anna forms connections with donors and helps them find the perfect outlet for their largesse.

Before taking this job, Anna worked as an independent consultant and a freelance special events coordinator. She often found herself involved in public relations work for causes that appealed to her values, such as planning functions for children's charities. An event that she is especially proud of is a black-tie dinner she arranged for the local chapter of Ronald McDonald House Charities, a fund-raiser that included an auction of original artwork by children's picture book illustrators. Anna approached approximately forty big-name illustrators and asked them to donate their work, and the auction turned out to be an enormous success. She also worked in an advertising agency, as a management consultant, and as a workshop facilitator.

Anna explains that she never intended to become a director of development; rather, she says, "I fell into it—fell in love with the institution. My children were attending the school, and, like a lot of volunteers, I felt that I wanted to be a part of it. One nice thing about most nonprofits is that they allow people to get involved." So Anna began as a volunteer—as a member of the school's board of trustees—and in that role she helped shape the bigger picture for the school. This led to her involvement in various special projects for students, parents, and faculty, until Anna proved her mettle: "I was supportive of the administration, a hard worker, and it was clear that our values were in sync." People close to Anna encouraged her, noticing that the work was making her happy. When a part-time development job opened up at the school, Anna decided to give it a try. Four months in, it became clear that the job was a good match for Anna's skills, and she says, "I threw my hat into the ring for the director job."

What Anna loves about development is the challenge of connecting the right person to the institution and seeing the joy that both parties derive from the interaction. Anna is energized by the positive change that occurs by putting love and ability together, a combination that typifies much of her work. She also admits to enjoying the "thrill of the hunt," the prospecting side that includes calling people and asking for gifts for the school, the sales mode. Anna's wholehearted enthusiasm for the institution makes her a persuasive salesperson, capable of sharing her passion with others and infecting them with the same insight for possibility that she has. Her attitude about what most people see as a terrifying aspect of the job—that is, asking for money—is "If I feel good about the institution, what's the worst that can happen? They can always say no, but I want to give them the opportunity to say yes and make a real impact with their generosity." Other features of the job that Anna likes are the collegial atmosphere, being part of a team, and the leadership role that her position affords. She loves helping people feel inspired and empowered about the future.

What Anna is less inclined toward is the management that comes with leadership. She dislikes having to remind co-workers of their responsibilities and finds it frustrating when people don't maintain high work standards. Anna also dislikes the politics that can arise in any institution and is frustrated with pettiness. "With nonprofits, there are always volunteers who occasionally believe they know better, even when they have little experience. It can be hard for those on the inside to be overridden by well-meaning but sometimes uninformed people. But for the most part, a little education and patience can go a long way."

Nevertheless, Anna is not discouraged about these occasional bothers because she maintains her optimism and sense of what's possible. "If you believe in the mission and respect the people, then it's all good. I have to care deeply about what I'm doing and about the long-term possible results, because no matter how much they pay you, in the long run it won't work unless you really believe in the place."

Why This Career Works for Anna

Anna's mission of matching people with an institution that they feel good about supporting is right in line with her values. Her drive to help people find meaning and joy in giving, and her belief in nonprofits, reflect her Idealist temperament, which is naturally inclined to make humanistic connections. Her skills as a communicator and her deep belief in her mission allow her to reach donors and appeal to their sense of purpose, resulting in satisfaction for all parties.

As a dominant extraverted Feeler, Anna is driven by making connections with people, and her career choices reflect her value system. Her people skills are highly developed, and she naturally enjoys meeting people and discovering what matters to them. Like many extraverted Feelers, she is articulate both in person and in writing, and she knows how to get the best out of people by making them feel good about themselves and their association with the cause.

Anna's auxiliary function, introverted Intuition, is evidenced by her grasp of the big picture and her focus on what is possible in the future. Development requires a long-range mind-set, and Anna spends a great deal of time envisioning and assessing the implications and potential results of her work five, ten, and fifteen years from the present. This allows her to create strategies and plans that incorporate both long- and short-term goals.

Extraverted Sensing, Anna's third function, is beginning to emerge for her. In her thirties, Anna finally began to notice seasonal changes. "I remember opening my eyes one day and thinking, *Oh my God, it's spring!*" She finds herself exclaiming over budding trees, blooming flowers, and the reappearance of birds. Anna has also developed a new appreciation for specificity. "Increasingly now, I remember personal details about people, like how they take their coffee, and people are flattered by that level of attention."

More and more, Anna is seeing evidence of her Introversion and Perceiving, especially in her ability to let processes run their course. "I start my day with my plan. I start everything with a plan, but when someone walks in with a problem, I am able to appreciate that that is what I need to be doing in the moment. The person trumps the plan." Anna notices in herself a newfound patience for letting a situation arrive at its natural course rather than hurrying it to a conclusion. As for Introversion, Anna has grown more comfortable with being inside her own head. In fact, she finds herself craving solitude where once she would have sought company. "I value and look forward to my commute time alone, and instead of opting for an exercise class that involves a lot of frenetic activity, I'll choose a yoga class that allows me to concentrate on my own process and my individual goals."

Meet the Millennial

Name: Madeline
Age: 26
Special education teacher

"Making a difference every day."

Backstory

Madeline always knew she wanted to be a teacher, like her mom. Throughout her childhood, even when she considered other possibilities such as marine biologist or actress, teacher never left the list. But in high school, as she watched her mother become burned out at the end of a thirty-five-year-long career in the classroom, Madeline shifted her career goals. She ended up going to school for film, then quickly changed her major to communications. After a series of internships that Madeline found "shallow

(continued)

and terrible," she realized she had drifted far from the mission that was important to her—being able to really help people.

Upon graduating, Madeline began work at an urban nonprofit centered on nutrition education, and in her free time, she volunteered with her friend June at a program for homeless children. Once a week, as they drove the thirty minutes to the playgroup, June would tell Madeline about the courses she was taking in general and special education. Suddenly, a light bulb went on for Madeline: "I was on the path for this all along, and somewhere I fell off. Of course I'm supposed to be working with kids!"

Madeline immediately applied for a national teaching corps and that fall was placed at an inner-city charter school while working toward her dual master's degree in general and special education. But the environment at Madeline's school was toxic: there was little trust between leadership and teachers, and a pervasive negativity that she found constantly draining. After struggling for two years in a school environment that felt all wrong, Madeline moved to her current position as a first-grade teacher in an independent school focused entirely on special education.

A Good Fit

Madeline's new school is a huge shift in environment. Instead of being micro-managed, Madeline is trusted, and was given responsibilities right off the bat. Her dominant Feeling function is satisfied by the positive and harmonious working environment, as well as the belief that she is making a real difference—something that matters to most Idealists.

Madeline works with students who have speech, language, and attention disabilities. She loves trying, and succeeding, to get through to kids for whom conventional methods have just not worked. With special education, innovation is the name of the game, and Madeline's auxiliary Intuition function leads her to find new and creative ways to reach her students. As both an Extravert and a Judger, Madeline is in control in the classroom, able to work the room and feed off of the energy of her students. She is both nurturing and tough, and her high expectations show her students that she has confidence in their capabilities.

Looking Ahead

While Madeline is much happier in her new school, she doesn't feel that her values are being completely fulfilled by her work just yet: "I would really like to find a school that serves a minority population, but with a progressive model of education. What I liked about the charter school was that I was serving a population that most people don't want to work with, and that felt really good. But I didn't think that they were doing it well. And at this school it's the opposite. The teaching is phenomenal, but everyone is rich and white. And I feel like it's so unfair that this great teaching is being given to kids who already enjoy so many advantages, and not to the other kids who need it, too." In the next five to ten years, Madeline would love to find a school that meets both of these criteria, and continue to reach all kinds of children with special needs, regardless of class or race.

Profile 2: Mitch

"Helping people achieve their fullest potential."

During lunch at a local restaurant one afternoon, Mitch was approached by a woman he recognized as a former career counseling client. She told him, "You're the person who turned my life around!" He remembers the experience and the feeling it gave him and today counts it among his most prized accomplishments. Helping other people has been a motivation and a theme for all of Mitch's career. At thirty-five, he is the manager of executive staffing and development in the human resources department of a large insurance company. What he enjoys best is the opportunity he has every day to assist other people in the development of their own careers and their competency and leadership skills.

Mitch's job entails three major areas: recruitment of executives, the "outplacement" or assistance offered when an individual's job is eliminated, and development of special programs to increase executives' effectiveness, usually through workshops and seminars. With the fluctuation of the economy, the amount of recruiting and outplacement he performs varies. But he enjoys all of the work, especially the "competencies program" he initiated, developed, and now is the spokesperson for. He works independently, without a staff, but as a member of a task team. He leads the group in developing ways to increase their personal competency on the job. He is featured on a videotape about the program, which is shown to employees company-wide.

When he is wearing his recruiting hat, Mitch spends time developing strategies to get the right person for the right job. He works with several "headhunter" firms or conducts the search himself. He meets with and evaluates candidates and then makes his recommendation to the department that will supervise the new executive.

On the other end of the employment cycle, Mitch works with employees who are losing their jobs. He sometimes helps them process and express their feelings about the loss, and helps them move ahead by preparing them for the job market or a new opportunity. "I spend time with them, I get to know them, and make recommendations that are right for them as individuals." He likes to stay close and monitor their cases until they are recruited and hired for another company. "The best part of my job, the part that I find energizing, is the counseling I do to help other people become more successful in their jobs. I enjoy the coaching I do with executives to help them develop their skills with their staffs. And I get a big charge out of the training sessions I conduct. I love to get up in front of people in a variety of audiences and give them some helpful information. I get big strokes and reinforcement for that."

The least interesting part of Mitch's job is the more routine matters, like completing monthly reports and the paperwork required when he fills a job. He once taught himself a computer spreadsheet program that automated much of the statistical elements of the job. He enjoyed learning the program but, once mastered, he no longer liked using it.

Mitch is drained by the redundant sales pitches he hears from recruiting firms. "When I consider them to be less than reputable, I find that wears me out. But the hardest thing for me to deal with personally is direct conflict with a co-worker. It's especially true when we're disagreeing about a policy decision that's really about values. I want to make changes that will make life easier or better for other people and some of the more organizational people make decisions just based upon the bottom line. I see them as rigid and unable to see what I see—what makes sense to people." Conflict that others are experiencing is something Mitch likes helping with; conflict he is personally embroiled in is much more difficult for him.

Mitch came to his job in the corporate world as part of his overall career plan. His first job, however, was as a manager of a ceramic studio. He had worked there during his college years and upon graduation filled in as manager while the owner recuperated from a serious car accident. After a year, he returned to college to work toward a master's degree in guidance counseling and personnel. During the program, he participated in an internship in the career counseling department at a university, which "helped me get my feet wet in the world of counseling." Upon graduation, he accepted a position at another university as a career counselor. Within two years, Mitch was promoted to director of career development. "Here I was telling people how to prepare résumés for work in the big world, and I hadn't ever experienced the corporate world. So I took a job at a big insurance company in the human resources department. I fully intended to get a couple years' experience and return to university life as the big expert! But I felt at home and stayed for seven years!" Since joining the insurance company, Mitch has been promoted to the position of manager of staffing and then to the more autonomous position he holds now. His career goals are mapped out: assistant vice president within two years, vice president in five.

From the very start, Mitch knew he wanted a job where he was able to help people. He considered becoming a psychiatrist or a lawyer "because I perceived them as helping professions. But I learned

more about them and realized there was a whole lot more to them. And I considered being an entertainer because I value my sense of humor and love to make people laugh. I still do, and I believe that I bring my sense of humor to bear on so much of my life and job. It helps me to not take things so seriously."

But Mitch considers his communication skills to be among his best talents. "I approach every project with an attitude that asks, how can I do what I need to do and help someone along the way? I have an empathy for others and an ability and desire to really listen to what the other person is needing." Mitch also is pleased with his writing skills and is told by others that his style of written and oral communication makes even the dry or technical material interesting and understandable to others. "I'm proud of some of the less formal work-related things I've done like a mentoring program I started some years ago. On our own time, I met with a small group of people I was helping with their leadership skills to try to work on areas that could contribute to our own success."

Equally important in Mitch's life is his relationship with his wife. "It's rewarding to watch our relationship change from simply a romantic love to a deeper friendship, too. And I feel good about helping to reconcile my family, who have been estranged for several years. That's a great satisfaction for me. I like when other people count on me." In his free time Mitch likes to exercise. He lifts weights, jogs, and takes karate, all new interests for him.

Mitch sees the changes in himself primarily in his professional life. "I'm much more realistic about the world of work and about my own strengths and weaknesses. I'm more ambitious, and I realize now that money *does* matter. I also have a broader vision; I can see there are a lot of ways and a lot of places to help people. And I'm much thicker-skinned than I was ten years ago because I can take criticism and be less defensive about it. I've even learned how to be tough when I need to be. Firing someone used to just be unbearable for me. Now, I still feel for the person and I present bad news in a gentle way, but I can also do the hard stuff."

Mitch's ability to work hard and to be productive and "results-oriented" is a quality he values. "I work hard because it's the right thing to do, not only because there's a paycheck. My employers always know they get their money's worth out of me!" But building and sustaining relationships is the real secret to Mitch's success. "I hope people remember me as someone who went the extra mile for someone else and helped others reach their potential."

Why This Career Works for Mitch

Mitch is in the business of helping people develop their fullest potential. Whether working as a career counselor on a college campus or as a manager in human resources for a large corporation, he is naturally drawn to helping people see possibilities about themselves, figure out what is right for them, and develop the necessary skills to be their best. Like most Idealists, his genuine affection for and enjoyment of people helps him to be an excellent communicator.

A natural counselor, Mitch extraverts his Feeling (dominant) by establishing relationships with clients and colleagues. He demonstrates his empathy by reaching out to people who have lost their jobs and helping them understand and express their feelings. Whether he is coaching executives to be more effective or conducting general training workshops, he enjoys giving helpful information and receiving the positive

reinforcement that often accompanies his presentations. Mitch is also a harmonizer. He puts people together who can benefit each other and in the process is himself rewarded for his efforts.

Since a large part of his work involves interviewing people and matching them to the right job, Mitch calls on his introverted Intuition (auxiliary) to make connections and see possibilities. It also helps him to understand people's motivations. He expresses his creativity in many ways—one example is the mentoring program he developed for employees. Another way Mitch uses his Intuition is to take complex and sometimes dry technical information and figure out a way to make it understandable and even interesting to others.

Recently, Mitch has begun using his Sensing (third function) more. For him it has taken the form of physical activity—practicing karate, running, and lifting weights. He has also become more realistic about the world of work, his own strengths and weaknesses, and is more interested in seeing tangible results. As he has tuned in to his senses, he has become more interested in the physical possessions that making more money allows him to have. There is some evidence that Mitch has also developed some access to his Thinking (fourth function); he is much "thicker-skinned," can take criticism more easily, and although he still dislikes doing so, he can be tough with employees when necessary.

Common Threads

Although Anna, Mitch, and Madeline have different backgrounds, experiences, and careers, there are certain common threads woven through their stories. Specific interests, abilities, and values may differ, but owing to their similar temperament values, the *same hierarchy* of their psychological functions, and the "world" they naturally use them in (inner or outer), there are certain observations we can make about the needs of many ENFJs.

What follows is a list of the most important elements—the formula, if you will—for ENFJ satisfaction. Given the uniqueness of all individuals—even those who share the same type—this list will not describe each ENFJ equally well. The important thing is that these ten elements, with varying degrees of intensity and in different orders of importance, identify what ENFJs need to be satisfied.

After you have reviewed this list, we recommend that you go back and prioritize the elements in order of *their importance to you*. When doing this, think of past work experiences as well as your present job, and what you found particularly satisfying or unsatisfying. Try to look for *themes* that run through several experiences, not just the events which might be true for one work situation but not for another.

As an ENFJ, career satisfaction means doing work that:

1. Lets me establish and maintain warm and supportive interpersonal relationships with co-workers, clients, customers, etc.
2. Lets me develop creative solutions to problems on projects that I believe in and where I can see the positive results of my efforts for other people
3. Is done in an environment where expectations are clear, contributions are appreciated, and personal and professional growth and development are encouraged
4. Lets me be a part of a team of other creative people I trust as well as being busy and productive
5. Allows me time to develop creative solutions to problems and then share them with other supportive and caring people
6. Is done in an active and challenging environment where I am able to juggle several projects at once
7. Lets me use my organizational and decision-making skills and have control and responsibility for my own projects
8. Gives me a variety of activities but allows me to work in a relatively orderly and well-planned manner
9. Is done in an environment that is free from interpersonal conflicts and ongoing tension
10. Exposes me to new ideas and lets me explore new approaches, especially those that will improve the lives of other people

Popular Occupations for ENFJs

Because of their combination of preferences, ENFJs are naturally drawn to a wide variety of occupations.

In listing occupations that are popular among ENFJs, it is important to note that there are successful people of all types in all occupations. However, the following are careers ENFJs may find particularly satisfying and some of the reasons why. This is by no means a comprehensive listing but is included to suggest possibilities you may not have previously considered. Although all of these occupations offer the potential for career satisfaction, the future demand for some careers is anticipated to be greater than for others. Based upon our research, the occupations that are italicized below are forecast to enjoy the fastest rate of growth over the next several years.

COMMUNICATIONS
- *Advertising account executive*
- *Public relations specialist*

- *Social media manager*
- Communication director
- Writer/journalist
- Entertainer/artist
- Fund-raiser
- Recruiter
- Recreational director
- TV producer
- Newscaster
- Politician
- Marketing executive: radio/TV/cable broadcast industry
- Informational-graphics designer
- Magazine editor
- Graphic artist
- Website content editor
- Multimedia producer
- Copywriter
- Reporter and correspondent
- *Interpreter/translator*
- Managing editor

ENFJs are masterful communicators. They are motivated to understand and please others, so they often possess great tact and diplomacy. They sometimes prefer the spoken word to the written word but many ENFJs are good writers as well. They enjoy the process of gathering information by meeting and interviewing people and coming to understand the underlying and personal side of a story or issue. The world of advertising, public relations, and fund-raising is often a satisfying one, especially when the ENFJ believes in the product, service, or cause involved and if the atmosphere does not become too competitive or conflict-ridden. ENFJs establish relationships quickly with clients, customers, and co-workers and can be persuasive and effective agents, producers, recruiters, and politicians. They are natural and charismatic leaders and enjoy facilitating large and small groups.

COUNSELING
- Psychologist
- Facilitator
- Career counselor
- *Life coach*
- *Marriage and family therapist*
- *Mental health counselor*
- Clergy/ministry
- *Corporate outplacement counselor*
- *Substance abuse counselor*
- Employee assistance counselor
- Vocational rehabilitation counselor
- Educational psychologist
- Guidance counselor

Great numbers of ENFJs find career satisfaction helping others find happiness and contentment in their lives through self-understanding. They enjoy helping their clients become aware of personal issues and then overcome obstacles. ENFJs are usually warm, compassionate, and influential therapists. They often enjoy careers in the ministry, as they are able to share their own values with others and to help themselves and others reach their full potential. They easily see possible options or solutions and can help their clients see them as well.

EDUCATION/HUMAN SERVICE
- *Teacher: health/art/drama/English*
- *College professor: humanities*
- Dean of students
- Librarian
- *Social worker*
- Nonprofit organization director
- Special education teacher
- *Early education teacher*
- *Bilingual education teacher*
- *Online educator*
- Child welfare worker
- *Elder care specialist*
- *Director of assisted care living facility*
- *Director of child care center*
- Planned-giving officer

- Philanthropic consultant
- Educational program director
- *Social services coordinator*
- Parent instructor, child development
- Music director
- *Public health educator*
- College and university administrator
- Director of religious activities
- Urban and regional planner
- Sociologist
- Adult day care coordinator

ENFJs are often drawn to education because it gives them an opportunity to work directly with other people, helping them to grow and develop. They prefer teaching subjects where they can focus on the meaning of material and teach through interpretation and expression. They need a harmonious and cooperative work environment that is tolerant of all views and fosters the open sharing of opinions and feelings.

Human service organizations are often appealing to ENFJs because they provide an opportunity to work toward improving the quality of life for themselves and others. They like to be leaders, in control of their projects as much as possible, and to see positive results from their efforts.

HEALTH CARE
- *Holistic health practitioner (alternative medicine)*
- *Dietitian/nutritionist*
- *Speech-language pathologist/audiologist*
- *Occupational therapist*
- Chiropractor
- Corrective therapist

Within the rapidly expanding field of health care, these occupations make the best use of an ENFJ's ability to view, diagnose, and treat the whole person. ENFJs are usually interested in the psychological, emotional, and spiritual causes of disease and are often intrigued with new and alternative methods of treatment. They frequently enjoy the creative problem-solving elements of occupational therapy and speech and language pathology.

BUSINESS/CONSULTING
- *Human resource development trainer*
- *Customer service representative*
- *Employment specialist*
- *Sales trainer*
- Personnel recruiter
- Travel consultant
- Executive: small business
- Program designer
- *Sales manager*
- Management consultant: diversity/team building
- *Corporate/team trainer*
- *Outplacement consultant*
- Eco-tourism specialist
- Labor relations manager
- *Meeting, convention, and event planner*
- Industrial-organizational psychologist
- *Advertising account executive*
- *Marketing manager*
- Set designer
- Hotel and restaurant manager
- Talent director
- Print designer
- Interaction designer

The many varied jobs within the consulting profession can provide satisfaction to ENFJs because they offer independence while maintaining a close affiliation with others. ENFJs are excellent presenters and trainers, especially when working with individuals or groups to help them improve their own effectiveness. They can be creative and energetic designers of new programs and services, but only if those programs benefit others. They tend to prefer executive positions in smaller companies or organizations where they can have a positive impact, enjoy variety and opportunities to explore new ways of doing things, and still maintain a certain amount of control.

Remember, these are only some areas that provide satisfying expression for the unique natural talents of the ENFJ.

TECHNOLOGY
- *Customer relations manager*
- Staff advocate (technology consultant)
- Project manager
- Engagement manager
- Human resources recruiter

With the proliferation of technology, there is a rapidly growing need for people who understand technology but also have good people and communication skills. Being the liaison between the technology people and the end users appeals to many ENFJs, who find these jobs satisfy their need to help and be connected with their co-workers.

Customizing Your Job Search

Knowing the particular strengths and blind spots of your type can afford you a tremendous advantage in your job search campaign. In all aspects of the process, from conducting research into available positions, identifying and contacting prospective employers, developing personal marketing tools such as résumés, arranging and conducting job interviews, negotiating salaries to finally accepting a position, people will act true to their type. Being able to capitalize on your assets and compensate for your liabilities can make the difference between a successful or unsuccessful job search.

The differences between types are sometimes subtle and other times dramatic. It is the subtle variations in advice we offer that make the real difference between success and failure in a job search. The concept of networking, or meeting with and talking to people to gather information about potential jobs, serves as a good example. Extraverts will naturally enjoy networking and are advised to do so on a large scale, while Introverts find more limited and targeted networking, especially with people they already know, easier. Sensors tend to network with people in a defined scope, while Intuitives will go far and wide to find people often seemingly unrelated to their field of interest. Further, Feelers take networking, like everything else, very personally and enjoy establishing warm rapport, while Thinkers will be more objective and detached in their style. Finally, Judgers tend to ask fewer and more structured questions during their networking, while Perceivers could ask questions of all sorts all day long! One valuable search technique, many ways to implement it.

Pathways to Success: Using Your Strengths

Because of the combined strengths and talents of an ENFJ, most find it fairly easy and often fun to conduct a job search. In fact, ENFJs are great job searchers! And because many career counselors are also ENFJs, it comes as no surprise that some of the classic recommendations offered to job searchers seem tailor-made for ENFJs.

As an ENFJ, your most effective strategies will build on your abilities to:

Plan and execute a creative and well-organized job search plan.

- Establish your criteria for a satisfying job ahead of time and adhere to the most important items on that list to be sure you stay true to what you originally determined was critical. Research potential options by talking with people and using other resources to learn as much as you can before an interview.

- Use your creativity to anticipate and then demonstrate the best way to sell yourself.

As a result of helping a good friend search for a new job, Michael decided to change from a career in secondary school administration to one in career counseling. Because he had no paid experience, he decided to use the help he had given his friend as a case study to demonstrate his ability and skills in the process of looking for a new job. Before meeting with the director of a small counseling service, Michael sent an articulate cover letter and enclosed his résumé and the case study he had written about his friend. The study detailed the steps Michael had advised and assisted his friend with and the final result of his friend's finding a great new job. He finished the letter by stating he was eager to offer the same energy and insightful direction and assistance to others.

Impress interviewers with your enthusiasm and self-confidence.

- Establish warm and friendly rapport quickly to demonstrate your ability to make others feel at ease with you.
- Express yourself articulately when discussing your skills, past work experiences, and reasons for interest in the position.

Benjamin was great at helping bolster other people's confidence. But when it came to preparing himself for an important job interview, he learned to seek out support and encouragement from his wife. Before the interview he would talk through his feeling of nervousness and then review his strengths and accomplishments. Then he would arrive

for his interview early, park a distance from the building, and spend a couple of minutes reciting several self-confidence affirmations. He used this little routine to give his self-esteem a needed shot in the arm.

Develop and use a large and active network.

- Conduct the majority of your research in the form of informational interviews— meeting other people who have careers in fields of interest or who have jobs of specific interest to you.
- Call on friends, family, and past associates to let them know that you are looking for a job and ask them to refer you to anyone they know who might be able to help you.

When Evelyn wanted to change careers to training in human resource development, she called on everyone she knew. But most of her friends were connected to other industries and careers and weren't able to offer contacts in her newly chosen field. So Evelyn joined a professional organization for trainers and consultants. She knew no one at the first dinner meeting but set a goal for herself that she would leave the meeting with at least three contacts whom she would call to conduct an informational interview. She left with four.

See job possibilities that don't already exist.

- Brainstorm jobs that you might enjoy, and delay making quality judgments on any until you have a lengthy list. Ask friends who know you well to help you list jobs they think you would succeed at.
- During interviews, demonstrate your ability to see ways of matching your skills and experience to meet the needs of a potential employer.

Lindsey had been a volunteer for most of her life, even as a child. After her children started school, she decided it was time to get a job for which she would be paid for her hard work. But she wasn't sure what marketable skills she had, having never received a paycheck for her work before. When she came to us, we suggested she do some brainstorming with a friend. She and her sister decided to brainstorm over drinks one night. Lindsey returned to our office with a list of jobs that sounded appealing. During our session, we developed another list of jobs that used the skills she had perfected during her volunteer assignments for various civic, church, and health care organizations. The most obvious was her love of the theater and organizing and promoting productions. After making contact with many of her old friends in the arts around town, she was hired to coordinate fund-raising for the city's arts council on a part-time basis. It was a dream job and one she turned into a full-time success in a matter of months.

Follow through on all phases of the job search, especially the courtesies.

- Honor all commitments, be on time or a bit early for appointments, and send thank-you notes or other notes to follow up all appointments.
- Use your great memory for personal details to remember people's names and recall any personal information from your research or a common experience.

Debbie developed a foolproof system for tracking her prospects during her search for a job as a recruiter for a college or university. She used a series of index cards for each prospective employer and each person with whom she interviewed. Because in some cases she interviewed before a search

committee, she kept a card for all members and then color-coded the whole batch to correspond with the college or university. She added notes when she learned something new or after a contact, so she was always up to date on where she stood with each prospect. Her system helped her avoid letting anyone or any detail of her search slip through the cracks. And when she ultimately found the position she wanted and was hired, she was able to write announcement notes to everyone she had met.

Possible Pitfalls

Although all people are unique, there are certain *potential* blind spots that many ENFJs share. We underscore "potential" because some of the following may clearly be true of you, while others may not apply. While considering them, you may notice that these tendencies do not relate just to the job search, but rather describe pitfalls that you may have experienced in other aspects of your life as well. It is therefore helpful to consider each one in terms of your past experiences by asking yourself, "Is this true for me?" And if so, "How did this tendency prevent me from getting something that I wanted?" You will probably notice that the key to overcoming your blind spots is the conscious and thoughtful development of your third and fourth functions (Sensing and Thinking). Many of the suggestions will be challenging to implement, but the more you use these functions, the fewer problems they will cause you in the future.

Try not to make decisions based only on your personal feelings.

- Use objective analysis to help you see the logical results of potential actions. Remember that cause and effect are not what you naturally see, so seek some assistance from a friend who does.

- Don't dismiss an option because of your personal dislike for one person in the organization. Also resist the temptation to judge a whole job or organization on the basis of one positive interaction.

Don't take criticism and rejection personally.

- Take constructive criticism and feedback as they are intended. Relying on the support and encouragement of friends and family can help you avoid the tendency to become discouraged during the sometimes stressful career search time.
- When rejected for a job or interview you want, try to suspend the tendency to become self-critical. Make it a personal challenge to rise to the occasion and see it as an obstacle to be overcome.

Concentrate on collecting all the necessary facts.

- Pay attention to the details and realities as well as the people you meet. Don't ignore the less interesting tasks of your job search in favor of only making new contacts.
- Rather than simply accepting what you are told at face value, be prepared to ask plenty of questions to learn what the job or company is really like.

Try to be more realistic about potential careers and about other people.

- Look at people as they really are, and recognize their limitations. Consciously guard against idealizing people or expressing unquestioning loyalty to others.
- Confront conflict or misunderstandings quickly and directly rather than avoid-

ing them and allowing them to become larger or more complicated.

Don't make decisions too quickly.

- Conducting plenty of research will help keep you from leaping before you have looked things over carefully. Ask for time to think things through before responding to any offer to be sure it is really right for you.
- If you don't resist your tendency to rush to closure, you may miss other potentially good options still on the horizon, or accept a job that in reality isn't what you want.

The Final Piece: Changing or Keeping Your Job . . . the Key to Success for ENFJs

Now that you have a solid understanding of your type, you can see how your natural preferences make you better suited for certain kinds of jobs. You can also see how knowing your type-related strengths and weaknesses can help you conduct a more successful job search. But as an ENFJ, you've already realized that you are not equally drawn to *every* career or field listed in the Popular Occupations section. The next and final step is to narrow down the field and find the work you were meant to do.

In addition to Type, several other factors—such as your values, interests, and skills—also contribute to your level of satisfaction on the job. The more compatible you are with your job, the happier you'll be. So prepare to use everything you've learned (in this book and in life) to create *your strategic career plan*. The exercises in Chapter 24, Putting It All Together, are designed to help you do just that.

However, you may have decided it makes more sense (if perhaps only temporarily) to stay in your present job or with your current employer. There may be many valid reasons—financial pressures, family considerations, a tough job market for your specialty, or just bad timing. But take heart! What you've learned in this book can also help you be more content and successful *in your current job.* And should the time come when you're ready to make a major career move, you'll have a much better idea of where you want to go, and how to get there.

"So, if you can't have the job you love (yet!)...love the one you've got."

The simple truth is, with the exception of work on a factory assembly line, the vast majority of jobs allow a good deal of flexibility in the way tasks are performed. Here are some ways you may be able to "massage" your current job into one that better fits your needs:

- Take and conduct communication workshops.
- Try not to get enmeshed in personality conflicts between co-workers.
- Volunteer to help draft your organization's/department's mission statement.
- Create a support group to help people with personal and/or work-related issues.
- Volunteer to do public relations for your department/organization.
- Limit your "informal counseling" of co-workers, especially when you begin to feel overwhelmed or before you feel caught in a no-win situation.
- Try (harder!) to leave your work at the office.
- Consider becoming a trainer or coach in your field of expertise.
- E-mail a friend with an inspirational message of support daily, weekly, or when the spirit moves you.

- Let your boss know that feeling appreciated is what really motivates you.
- Stay in the same occupation but switch employers.

One ENFJ turns lemons into lemonade:

Sarah worked as an administrative assistant for a nonprofit health agency. Although she loved the company and believed in its mission, she did not enjoy many of the detail-heavy aspects of the job. Since she was always touting the agency's work and objectives everywhere she went, she thought it would be great to be paid for it. At the time, there were no openings in the public relations department, so in her spare time, Sarah visited schools as a volunteer to talk about the agency. She did a great job. Six months later a full-time position opened up, she applied, and she was hired.

Use what you've got to get what you need.

Simply put, the best advice on how to succeed is to *capitalize on your strengths and compensate for your weaknesses.* Learning how to do this can make the difference between succeeding or failing and loving or hating your work. To help you, we include the following inventory of your potential strengths and weaknesses. And while every individual is unique, as an ENFJ, many of the following should apply to you.

Your work-related strengths may include:

- Excellent communication and presentation skills
- Charismatic leadership and ability to build consensus
- Enthusiasm and ability to enlist cooperation from others
- Decisiveness and organizational skills
- Eagerness to "think outside the box" and consider new possibilities

- Empathy and ability to anticipate others' needs; a genuine concern for people
- Varied interests and being a quick study
- Ability to see the big picture and the implications of actions and ideas
- Drive to be productive and reach your goals
- Deep commitment to work you really believe in

Your work-related weaknesses may include:

- Reluctance to work on projects that conflict with your values
- Tendency to idealize people and relationships

- Difficulty working in competitive or tension-filled environments
- Impatience with structures or people who are inefficient or uncooperative
- Avoidance of conflict and tendency to ignore unpleasantness
- Tendency to make decisions too quickly, before gathering adequate information
- Reluctance to discipline subordinates
- Tendency to make errors due to haste
- Tendency to micro-manage and resist relinquishing control

Using your strengths is easy.
The secret to success for an
ENFJ
is learning to:

Slow down, relinquish some control, and take things less personally.

9 INFJ
Introverted, Intuitive, Feeling, Judging
"Catalysts for Positive Change"

Profile 1: Helen

"Doing something that is really worth doing—and doing it right."

Helen works all day with two things that she loves: words and ideas. She especially enjoys taking concepts and theories that matter to her and making them accessible to a wide range of people. From her small, home-based publishing company, Helen does just that: she creates illustrated materials that present innovative ways to involve families in Christian education. Helen's press produces modestly priced booklets, calendars, and other items for use in Episcopal churches nationwide. Her clientele figure in at about one thousand, with three hundred ordering on an annual basis. Helen now makes all transactions through her website, where customers can order from an array of about thirty products. Because churches (her principal customers) print the materials themselves after ordering them,

Helen's business has very low overhead costs, with no need for staff or shipping and no warehousing fees. This independence is appealing to Helen, who delights in making biblical stories relevant and channeling them into activities that engage families, especially those with young children. Her work is deeply rooted in her personal values, and she is gratified by remaining connected to those values, as well as by the positive feedback she receives from clients who purchase her products. Helen appreciates the human interaction when clients order by telephone, and she describes herself as "addicted" to the warm gratitude expressed by her customers. Highly adept at and oriented to customer service, Helen is eager to advise her clients about tailoring products to their needs, and she enjoys the problem-solving aspects of consultation.

Helen's is a nontraditional career history. She worked as a secretary prior to marriage and then as a homemaker for fifteen years.

During her time as a homemaker, Helen served in a variety of volunteer positions, including precinct chairwoman, coordinator of volunteers for a hospital clinic, Sunday school teacher, and then superintendent of Sunday school responsible for curriculum development. Her next paid position was as administrative assistant to a diocesan bishop and editor of a diocesan newspaper. She then became administrative assistant in an education think tank run by the federal government. She served as the coordinator of a publishing project that a year later became a for-profit publishing corporation. After leaving that organization, Helen created the Christian educational press that is her current pursuit.

One of the things that Helen finds most rewarding about her job is sitting down with an idea that has energized her and crafting words to express a fresh message. "It's so fun for me to get an idea based on a theological principal or concept and make it accessible and usable and fun for families." Many of the booklets that Helen produces integrate spiritual questions with activities that families can undertake together. For instance, inspired by the occasion of Lent and its focus on sacrifice, Helen designed a soup can bearing the question "What Can We Do?" Families are encouraged to keep the can in a conspicuous place in their homes, to devise a variety of ways to collect or save spare change, and then at the end of each year to turn the money over to a charitable organization they select. Helen is driven to produce work that she is proud of and to create products that can really have an impact on people.

Another satisfying aspect of Helen's work is collaborating with illustrators. After Helen generates the concepts and does the writing, the next stage is taking her work to one of several illustrators with whom she has a long history and close connection. Because of their mutual understanding and similar aesthetic sense, Helen and the illustrators share a sort of shorthand that enables them to move swiftly and pleasurably through the collaborative process because they really "get each other." An editor provides an outside eye and gives Helen the polish and perspective that makes her work ready for sale.

Although Helen cherishes the independence that her situation affords, she can sometimes feel the strain of working alone. When an idea pops into her head, there is no critical sounding board immediately available to help her test her idea and determine whether it really is up to snuff. Helen satisfies her need for collegial companionship by traveling often to attend Christian education conferences around the country. She represents her region of the United States at the Christian Educators Association, where she makes new contacts and extends her customer base.

Why This Career Works for Helen

Helen's work is a perfect vehicle for the expression of her Idealist values. Her mission, or calling, is to spread God's word and to help facilitate people's spiritual growth. Adhering to her fundamental value system in her work satisfies Helen's need for integrity and meaning in her career. Helen's dominant introverted Intuition provides her with a vision of the way things can be. It leads her also to draw connections between concepts and to see alternative applications for ideas. The work that Helen does requires access to her intuitive imagination and creativity—producing artistic work that engages a broad spectrum of age groups. The constant presence of creativity and innovation keeps Helen interested in her work.

It is Helen's auxiliary, extraverted Feeling that drives her to share her beliefs and values with others. Not content just to keep her ideas and findings to herself, she strives to help others find the kind of opportunities for spiritual growth that she herself finds so compelling. Helen also exercises her extraverted Feeling in her skillful dealing with customer service situations. Her diplomacy and ability to negotiate with a range of different types of people is a testament to her auxiliary function.

The introverted Thinking that is Helen's third function has developed over time, owing to situations in which she has been forced to confront logical and logistical quandaries. Running her own business has required Helen to use a particular set of tools, and she finds that she must sometimes exercise certain Thinking traits as she deals with the more practical aspects of her business. Helen has noticed a growing interest in Thinking areas. "The subjects that I had no interest in in college, like physics and mathematics, I now find fascinating. I have no interest in becoming a physicist, but I am eager to get a solid layperson's understanding of it."

Helen's extraversion has also developed through her experiences traveling and her newfound willingness to make presentations at conferences. She often stays in the homes of people within the church community who are at first strangers but soon become dear friends.

Finally, Helen is beginning to see evidence of the development of her Sensing (fourth function), a sign of type maturation. Once hesitant to deal with technology and afraid of computers, she now faces the technological frontier with a much more adventurous attitude, opting to troubleshoot on her own and to "crawl under the desk" to see what she can do. Rather than throw up her hands at the Sensing details of mechanical problems, Helen feels competent and proficient enough to try fixing things herself, which fuels pride in her natural independence.

Meet the Millennial

Name: Maggie
Age: 23
Fulbright grant recipient

"Radio for social change."

Backstory

"How can I get paid to travel?" This was the phrase that Maggie Googled in the spring of her senior year of college. Maggie had enjoyed the true liberal arts experience at Sarah Lawrence College, pursuing a wide, interdisciplinary course load of politics, literature, gender studies, and Spanish. Then she studied abroad in Barcelona during her junior year and fell

(continued)

in love with travel, which is what brought her to Google. Google brought her to the prestigious Fulbright grant, which Maggie applied for and received. The following fall she headed to Argentina for ten months to teach English in a university while designing and executing an independent research project.

Although Maggie originally planned on teaching creative writing workshops, her project evolved when she met another girl who shared her interest in radio. Maggie had explored radio production in college, and the two girls set up a radio series through a website — a sort of call-and-response between two cities several hundred miles away. When they began the series, their stories centered on finding a sense of place as outsiders: two girls from Brooklyn in the heart of Argentina. But when Maggie met people engaged in grassroots social activism, the series evolved even more — as did Maggie's project. She made radio pieces championing the causes of the people she'd met while teaching mini-workshops on how her new friends could create radio of their own. Since radio is fairly easy and cheap to produce, it makes an ideal vehicle for sharing stories and communicating ideas. For Maggie, the experience was a two-way street. "It really became a partnership of teaching them about radio and making my own to spread their messages."

A Good Fit

Because Maggie is an INFJ, her dominant function is Intuition. In radio, she uses her Intuition constantly, sifting through interviews to find the story she wants to tell, always keeping her eye on the larger picture. She continually makes connections between seemingly disparate stories to elucidate a larger theme. Maggie is driven, like most Idealists, to tell stories that are in sync with her values and have a social impact. Her auxiliary function of Feeling is evidenced by the kind of stories that interest her — stories about people and the things that matter to them. Maggie is warm, personable, and charming, able to connect with the people she interviews and exceptionally adept at drawing them out. Her natural empathy and sensitivity allow her to connect with others — especially in a one-on-one setting, which she prefers.

Looking Ahead

At the end of the ten-month Fulbright grant, Maggie came back to New York City to look for full-time work while she became a part of the radio community in the city. For the time being, she works as the front desk manager — her official title is Queen of the House — at a company that does innovation consulting, which she describes as all of the work an in-house creative team would do in a big company, only outsourced to them. "It's nice to be in an environment where creativity is king," she explains. Maggie is now beginning a radio series through her blog called *Are You There, God? It's Me, Margaret,* which will focus on questions of faith and spirituality. Ideally, she would love to continue to travel, working freelance in radio journalism, meeting new people, and telling their stories in the increasingly popular form of radio podcasts.

Profile 2: Delia

"I naturally empathize with people in pain and am highly motivated to help solve problems in a compassionate way."

Delia moves at a pace that is thoughtfully slow and deliberate. In some professions, this tendency toward reflection might be deemed secondary to action. But in Delia's career, her natural qualities are just what the doctor ordered. Delia is a clinical social worker in a private geriatric psychiatric practice. About 80 percent of the patients whom Delia sees suffer some type of dementia. Her job is centered on working with patients and their families to educate them about the process, what to expect, and the available resources for treatment and coping. Delia also helps families deal with behavior problems that arise from dementia, and she supports families through the depression and other issues that sometimes accompany such conditions.

Delia visits with six to eight patients daily, usually seeing a patient together with a family member, and spends time in conversation assessing the current situation and then consulting with two staff psychiatrists to create strategies for managing the various implications of these tricky diagnoses. She talks the patients through the doctors' recommendations, medicine and treatment changes, and suggestions for how to manage behavior, and she helps break through the natural and inevitable denial that accompanies these diseases. Delia's ability to listen to patients and to let the natural process unfold make her extremely effective at what she does.

Delia began her work in this field with a master of science degree in social work in adult psychology. She worked in hospitals and in community mental health offices, and

as a therapist in private practice. After these various experiences, Delia spent eleven years as a therapist in a social service agency, where she commuted to her patients' homes, as most of the patients were aging adults with limited mobility. The strain of constant commuting and the atmosphere at the agency were not what Delia was looking for, however, and she left the practice.

But Delia loves both the environment and the mission of her current place of work. Geriatrics is rapidly expanding, and it is an exciting field to be in. As dementia becomes much more widespread due to the general aging of the population, people in the field are constantly discovering new permutations of the disease, which keeps Delia interested. "Most people who work in this field had an older person in their life who was really important to them—for me, that was my uncle Frank." Delia has a genuine interest in the people she treats. "This particular generation is so interesting: they were born at the beginning of the twentieth century, and they lived through the Great Depression and World War II. It is such a grateful generation, so appreciative of attention and support." Aside from the patients, Delia feels supported and appreciated by her colleagues. She has two great bosses who recognize her strengths and play to them and who also encourage her professional growth. Delia is gratified by the sense that she is part of a great, collegial team. In addition to working with patients, Delia conducts research into the ever-expanding types of dementia and the particular manifestations in her patients. She loves the opportunity to delve deeply into fascinating research that could make a difference in people's lives.

Less interesting to Delia are the pressures to document everything and the low-grade fear of being faced with a lawsuit. Dealing with insurance companies that question diagnoses or treatment is draining to Delia, and she hates the interference in her work. In her previous employment, Delia felt rushed and harried by the pace, a feeling exacerbated by the endless paperwork and documentation. Now, however, there is a clerical team to manage those important details, and the pace is much more professional and respectful of Delia's need for time to think.

Why This Career Works for Delia

Delia's Idealist temperament is well suited to the field of social work and therapy. Her instinctual drive to help and understand people coincides with her empathy and her grasp of larger connections. This makes her a born nurturer of people in pain as well as an effective problem solver.

Delia is a dominant Intuitive, and she sees this as a huge element in her work. Much of her job is based on interpreting symptoms and behavior, a skill that relies on the connections she makes between pieces of information. Delia must be adept at paying attention to cues and tones of voice while building a story or pattern in her mind and then figuring how best to respond. Her intuitive grasp of the larger picture is instrumental in making sense of seemingly disparate or unrelated bits of information.

Delia's auxiliary function, extraverted Feeling, makes her extremely empathetic. "People feel comfortable with me—I've always been told that." Her nonjudgmental attitude and utter concentration while listening causes people to believe that she really hears them and cares about what they are saying. Delia's unconscious style of mirroring people allows all kinds of people to feel comfortable with her. Also important to her line of work is the fact that Delia doesn't treat elderly people as though they're invisible—something that tends to happen

in our society. Instead, she is respectful and never talks down to them. Her mother had dementia, and Delia admits to having struggled with depression, so she understands her patients and can relate to their circumstances.

Introverted Thinking, Delia's third function, has emerged for her as a necessity in her job. She has developed the ability to disengage emotionally from her patients and not respond on a personal level, a skill that is critical to Delia's maintenance of her own emotional strength and well-being. She is better able to analyze clinical information and feels competent in all areas of her work.

Recreation is where Delia sees most of her fourth function, extraverted Sensing. She loves the outdoors and is deeply appreciative of beauty in the natural world. Much more than she used to, Delia enjoys outdoor recreational activities and seeks to be exposed to nature as often as she can. In development of her Perceiving, Delia enjoys the level of passivity that necessarily characterizes her work life and is increasingly comfortable with the inevitably slow disease process that her patients and their families confront.

Common Threads

Although Helen, Delia, and Maggie have different backgrounds, experiences, and careers, there are certain common threads woven through their stories. Specific interests and abilities may differ, but owing to their similar temperament values, the *same hierarchy* of their psychological functions, and the "world" they use them in (inner or outer), there are certain observations we can make about the needs of many INFJs.

What follows is a list of the most important elements—the formula, if you will, for INFJ satisfaction. Given the uniqueness of all individuals—even those who share the same type—this list will not describe each INFJ equally well. The important thing is that these ten elements, with varying degrees of intensity and in different orders of importance, identify what INFJs need to be satisfied.

After you have reviewed this list, you might find it useful to go back and try to prioritize the elements in order of *their importance to you*. When doing this, think of past work experiences as well as your present job, and what you found particularly satisfying or unsatisfying. Try to look for *themes* that run through several experiences, not just *events* which might be true of one work situation but not of another.

As an INFJ, career satisfaction means doing work that:

1. Lets me consider and create new ideas and/or approaches to a variety of problems, mostly those that help others to grow and develop
2. Lets me produce a product or service that I believe in and am proud of
3. Recognizes my authorship and ownership and my unique contributions
4. Lets me express myself and see the results of my vision
5. Lets me implement my ideas for the good of people or in the service of others; lets me work with others on a one-to-one basis
6. Is done in a friendly and tension-free environment where my ideas are seriously considered and where I am psychologically supported for my efforts
7. Can be done independently but with the opportunity to share frequently with others in an environment that is friendly and free of interpersonal conflict

8. Lets me organize my own time and work environment and exert significant control over both the process and product
9. Gives me adequate time to formulate and process my ideas so they are thoroughly prepared
10. Is in harmony with my personal values and beliefs and lets me maintain a high degree of personal and professional integrity

Popular Occupations for INFJs

In listing occupations that are popular among INFJs, it is important to note that there are successful people of all types in all occupations. However, the following are careers INFJs may find particularly satisfying and some of the reasons why. This is by no means a comprehensive listing but is included to suggest possibilities you may not have previously considered. Although all of these occupations offer the potential for career satisfaction, the future demand for some careers is anticipated to be greater than for others. Based upon our research, the occupations that are italicized in the lists below are forecast to enjoy the fastest rate of growth over the next several years.

COUNSELING/EDUCATION
- Career counselor
- Clinical psychologist
- High school teacher: English/art/music/ social sciences/drama
- *College professor: English/art/music/ social sciences/drama*
- Educational consultant
- Curriculum designer
- Librarian
- Special education teacher
- *Bilingual education teacher*
- *Early education teacher*
- *Online educator*

- Employee assistance counselor
- *Elder care specialist*
- *Marriage and family therapist*
- Child welfare counselor
- *Substance abuse counselor*
- *Social worker (elderly and child day care issues)*
- Sociologist
- Museum research worker
- *Public health educator*
- *Occupational therapist*
- Educational program director
- Parenting instructor, child development course
- Museum educator
- Developmental psychologist

These occupations allow INFJs to use their ideas and knowledge to help others. The counseling and teaching fields require very personal interaction, often on a one-to-one basis, allowing INFJs to make in-depth connections with others. INFJs also enjoy studying, learning, and the growth opportunities found in an educational context, so they are usually quite comfortable in an academic setting.

RELIGION
- Priest/clergy/monk/nun
- Religious worker
- Director of religious education

Religious work requires a deep and personal commitment and a work philosophy that can be characterized as a mission. INFJs frequently see their work that way and find deep satisfaction in sharing their philosophy and beliefs with others.

CREATIVE
- Artist
- Playwright
- Novelist

- Poet
- Interior designer
- Informational-graphics designer
- Universal design architect
- Freelance media planner
- Editor/art director (magazine)
- Genealogist (family tree researcher)
- Print designer
- Interaction designer
- Multimedia producer
- Editor/art director (website)
- Film editor
- Documentary filmmaker
- Set designer
- Educational software developer
- Exhibit designer
- Costume designer
- Merchandise designer and displayer

The appeal of the arts to the INFJ is the ability to create unique works, using their own ideas and vision. The arts enable INFJs to express themselves in a personal way, and the result is often to have an impact on others. With these occupations, the work is generally done independently, allowing the INFJ to organize and control the environment, the process, and the product.

HEALTH CARE/SOCIAL SERVICES
- Director, social service agency
- Mediator/conflict resolver
- Social scientist
- *Social worker*
- *Mental health counselor*
- *Dietitian/nutritionist*
- *Speech-language pathologist/audiologist*
- *Holistic health practitioner (alternative medicine)*
- Massage therapist
- *Occupational therapist*
- Chiropractor
- Grant coordinator
- Health care administrator

- Fund-raising director
- Legal mediator
- Adult day care coordinator
- Corrective therapist
- Crisis hotline operator
- Legislative assistant

The social service occupations require a commitment to helping others, often within an organizational structure. Most INFJs enjoy working in such a setting, especially when it involves a small and close-knit staff. Social service enables the INFJ to consider and develop new approaches to the problems of individuals or society. Many times social workers work independently on a caseload, allowing them to have frequent and one-on-one interaction with clients and colleagues.

BUSINESS
- *Human resources manager*
- Marketer (of ideas and/or services)
- *Organizational development consultant*
- Employee assistance program coordinator/counselor
- Job analyst
- *Diversity manager: human resources*
- *Corporate/team trainer*
- *Preferred customer sales representative*
- Merchandise planner
- Environmental lawyer
- *Interpreter/translator*
- Planned-giving officer
- Philanthropic consultant
- Curator
- Literary agent or editor
- Online publisher (e-books)
- *Outplacement consultant*

Although INFJs do not tend to gravitate toward business careers in large numbers, there are areas of business in which INFJs may find satisfaction.

Human resources, or personnel, and organizational development consulting are the "people" parts of business, requiring an interest in and facility with many different types of people. These occupations enable the INFJ to help others find jobs, structure effective work environments, and engage in creative problem solving in which people are the focus.

The marketing occupations enable INFJs to use their creative problem-solving abilities, often working on a team. If INFJs have significant input into the process and are able to maintain a comfortable level of personal and professional integrity, they can find this type of work satisfying.

Remember, these are only some of the areas that provide satisfying expression for the unique natural talents of the INFJ.

TECHNOLOGY
- *Customer relations manager*
- Staff advocate (technology consultant)
- Project manager
- Engagement manager
- Human resources recruiter

With the proliferation of technology, there is a rapidly growing need for people who understand technology but also have good people and communication skills. Being the liaison between the technology people and the end users appeals to many INFJs, who find these jobs satisfy their need to help and be connected with their co-workers.

Customizing Your Job Search

Knowing the particular strengths and blind spots of your type can afford you a tremendous advantage in your job search campaign. In all aspects of the process, from conducting research into available positions, identifying and contacting prospective employers, developing personal marketing tools such as résumés, arranging and conducting job interviews, negotiating salaries, to finally accepting a position, people will act true to their type. Being able to capitalize on your assets and compensate for your liabilities can make the difference between a successful and an unsuccessful job search.

The differences between types are sometimes subtle and other times dramatic. It is the subtle variations in advice we offer that make the real difference between success and failure in a job search. The concept of "networking," or meeting with and talking to people to gather information about potential jobs, serves as a good example. Extraverts will naturally enjoy networking and are advised to do so on a large scale, while Introverts find more limited and targeted networking, especially with people they already know, easier. Sensors tend to network with people in a defined scope, while Intuitives will go far and wide to find people often seemingly unrelated to their field of interest. Further, Feelers take networking, like everything else, very personally and enjoy establishing warm rapport, while Thinkers will be more objective and detached in their style. Finally, Judgers tend to ask fewer and more structured questions during their networking, while Perceivers could ask questions of all sorts all day long! One valuable search technique, many ways to implement it.

Pathways to Success: Using Your Strengths

As we will detail in the following pages, your strength and talent for the job search lie in thoughtful planning, creative problem solving, and your ability to communicate your commitment to what you believe in. But beware your tendency to become single-minded in your research and unrealistic in your objectives.

As an INFJ, your most effective strategies will build on your abilities to:

Think through and formulate an innovative, organized job search plan.

- Use your creativity to plot out a campaign in a new and different way — setting you apart from other candidates to potential employers.
- Use your organizational skills to stay on top of the project, make a plan, be on time, remember to send a note after the interview, follow up with prospective employers, etc.

While working with us to make a career switch from corporate law to the more specialized area of environmental law, Sue easily saw possibilities that could incorporate her legal skills and her interests. She brainstormed the names of organizations she might like to work for, then researched them thoroughly. Having attempted to determine their needs, she "packaged" herself in a way that made her attractive to prospective employers. An organized person by nature, Sue designed and conducted her search true to her type, by following up interviews with letters, calling people back at the times they asked her to, and keeping good records of her progress.

Network on a limited basis.

- Enlist the help of people with whom you have developed relationships over the years and who know you well to identify people to contact about career opportunities.
- During each interview, ask for additional recommendations of other people for you to see to more fully research the field or a particular job.

When Helen was looking for more fulfilling work — work that would serve her sense of mission—she began by speaking with friends and priests within the church. These informational interviews led her to discuss her job plans and interests with the then acting coordinator of the educational publishing project. In talking to him, she learned he was only serving temporarily, and, therefore, the job was about to become available. For Helen, talking to friends and associates on a one-on-one basis helped her to find a satisfying position which (like many of the best jobs) was never advertised in the public job market.

Establish rapport with interviewers and potential employers.

- Use your extraordinary ability to "read" people's needs and motivations.
- Let employers sense your natural warmth and enthusiasm, and demonstrate your ability to listen and communicate articulately.

A client of ours, John, was in the running for a personnel manager position at a small company. He learned that he was one of four applicants asked to return for a second interview and felt he needed to set himself apart from the other candidates. In preparation for this important interview, John spent some time rereading background information on the company with an eye for more personal details about the staff.

Being a father of two young children, John was interested to discover that two of the principals were parents of school-aged children in his hometown. During the first moments of the interview, while everyone was getting seated, John asked how the children were enjoying the new playscape recently constructed on their playground. Thus, he was able to establish something they had in common while creating a friendly and relaxed atmosphere. The

conversation also allowed John to demonstrate his knowledge of and interest in community activities and his ability to get along well with people.

Consider options thoughtfully, without rushing to judgment.

- Capitalize on your propensity for thinking things through in a careful way.
- Decide to give yourself a few minutes to keep open options you might have eliminated at first thought.

Upon relocating to New York City, Cynthia began interviewing for positions in art departments of advertising agencies. She found herself with a "good" problem: after completing interviews at four agencies, she was offered positions at two. Both would provide steady work at competitive salaries. Instead of making a hasty decision that would result in job security and an end to the search process, Cynthia asked both agencies for one week's time to consider her options. During that week she spent time carefully weighing the pros and cons of each opportunity until she came to a surprising decision: she declined both offers and instead began working on a freelance basis at all four agencies! Her decision gave her the flexibility, free time, and independence she would have given up had she accepted either of the staff positions.

Create a position that will meet your specific needs.

- Use your vision to anticipate trends, where people with your talents will be needed in the future, etc.
- Demonstrate that talent to prospective employers by letting them know how you will help them achieve goals or solve problems.

While working as a kitchen designer, Bob used his natural Intuition to see the need for a system that would allow his customers to actually see on paper what their redesigned kitchens would look like before spending the enormous amount of money it would take to have the work done. Imagining that the technology might be available to create such a system, or might already be in existence, he began his research. First he talked to a computer-whiz friend, which ultimately led him to the company he now represents. His ability to see the possibilities and then demonstrate that vision to the potential employer won him the job he now loves.

Find creative solutions to obstacles that arise.

- Approach temporary setbacks as problems to be solved rather than rebuffs or insurmountable obstacles.
- Use your natural ability to look ahead, focus on the next opportunity, or recover from a disappointment.

Another client, Sandy, tried unsuccessfully for six weeks to get an appointment with the director of human resources of a company he wanted to work for. In discussions with a neighbor who worked for the company, Sandy discovered that the director was an avid sailor. On a long shot, Sandy sent a copy of an article listing new and innovative gadgets and supplies for outfitting sailboats. He attached a personal note saying he was trying to get an appointment to see the director and would like to talk with him further about the other creative ways Sandy might be able to make his life easier. When Sandy called to follow up three days later, the director not only remembered his name but interviewed him the following week.

Possible Pitfalls

Although all people are unique, there are certain *potential* blind spots which many INFJs share. We specify "potential" because some of the following *may* be true of you, while others may clearly not apply. While considering them, you may notice that these tendencies do not relate just to the job search, but rather describe pitfalls that you may have experienced in other aspects of your life as well. It is therefore helpful to consider each one in terms of your past experiences by asking yourself, "Is this true for me?" And if so, "How did this tendency prevent me from getting something that I wanted?" You will probably notice that the key to overcoming your blind spots is the conscious and thoughtful development of your third and fourth functions (Thinking and Sensing). Many of the suggestions will be difficult to implement, but the more you use these functions, the fewer problems they will cause you in the future.

Concentrate on the facts and details of the situation, not just the more interesting big picture.

- This requires a conscious effort to tune in to what is actually before you—to read what is on the lines, not just what is *between* them.
- Make notes ahead of time to be sure you ask the practical questions about what a job is really like, including hours, duties, salary, benefits, reporting structure, etc.

Try to establish realistic expectations about the job search process and the potential outcome.

- Engage in "reality testing" to make sure you are being realistic about the market, your skills, and the amount of time a search will take. Ask a friend to help you by playing devil's advocate with your plan.

- Try to set more realistic goals to avoid the tendency to become overly perfectionistic and then experience the disappointment that comes from not accomplishing all you hoped.

Try to avoid making decisions based solely on your personal feelings rather than on more objective data.

- Remember that you naturally see things from a personal perspective and need to consciously engage your logical thinking skills.
- Don't confuse rapport established during an interview with personal friendship. Keep yourself a bit detached from the situation, deciding not to make a permanent connection until you know a lot more.

When discussing your skills and abilities, focus on how you can meet the prospective employer's needs rather than your own.

- Show the prospective employer you have done your research by incorporating information about the company's current challenges and then demonstrate how you might help meet them by recalling your past experiences and accomplishments.
- Express the willingness to take some necessary risks to handle a new challenge and prove yourself. Take an extra few seconds to consider another way, especially after you think you have made up your mind.

Avoid spending too much time considering possibilities and not enough time acting on them.

- Develop a reasonable list of options to pursue and a timetable in which to research them. Hold yourself accountable for meeting an established quota of letters written, phone calls made, or interviews completed within a particular time frame.
- Try to be flexible in setting job criteria and throughout the negotiation process, remembering that sometimes unexpected benefits appear when you stay open to another point of view.

The Final Piece: Changing or Keeping Your Job . . . the Key to Success for INFJs

Now that you have a solid understanding of your type, you can see how your natural preferences make you better suited for certain kinds of jobs. You can also see how knowledge of your type-related strengths and weaknesses can help you conduct a more successful job search. But as an INFJ, you've already realized that you are not equally drawn to *every* career or field listed in the Popular Occupations section. The next and final step is to narrow down the field and find the work you were meant to do.

In addition to Type, several other factors—such as your values, interests, and skills—also contribute to your level of satisfaction on the job. The more compatible you are with your job, the happier you'll be. So prepare to use everything you've learned (in this book and in life) to create *your strategic career plan*. The exercises in Chapter 24, Putting It All Together, are designed to help you do just that.

However, you may have decided it makes more sense (if perhaps only for the moment) to stay in your present job or with your current employer. There may be many valid reasons—financial pressures, family considerations, a tough job market for your specialty, or just bad timing. But take heart! What you've learned in this book can also help you be more content and successful *in your current job.* And should the time come when you're ready to make a major career move, you'll have a much better idea of where you want to go, and how to get there.

"So, if you can't have the job you love (yet!)...love the one you've got."

The simple truth is, with the exception of work on a factory assembly line, the vast majority of jobs allow a good deal of flexibility in the way tasks are performed. Here are some ways you may be able to "massage" your current job into one that better fits your needs:

- Make sure you have plenty of uninterrupted time to think; close your office door and occasionally take a break from answering your phone.
- Volunteer for planning committees where you can give your creative input.
- Try not to get enmeshed in personality conflicts between co-workers.
- Try to work on one major project at a time.
- Volunteer to help draft your organization's/department's mission statement.
- Seek out other creative people to hear your ideas.
- Try to put your ideas and thoughts on paper and get them published somewhere.
- Make sure to strike a balance between your work and personal life.
- Consider becoming a trainer or coach in your field of expertise.
- E-mail a friend with an inspirational message of support daily, weekly, or when the spirit moves you.

One INFJ turns lemons into lemonade:

Although Mark was a successful internist, he was extremely frustrated that the bureaucracy of managed care had severely limited the amount of time he could spend with each patient. While he had always valued having time to discuss with his patients their concerns, he realized what he missed most was the teaching aspect of these sessions. Mark ultimately decided to teach a course in family medicine at a nearby college, which he found extremely rewarding.

Use what you've got to get what you need.

Simply put, the best advice on how to succeed is to *capitalize on your strengths and compensate for your weaknesses.* Learning how to do this can make the difference between succeeding or failing and loving or hating your work. To help you, we include the following inventory of your potential strengths and weaknesses. And while every individual is unique, as an INFJ, many of the following should apply to you.

Your work-related strengths may include:

- Integrity that inspires people to value your ideas
- Focus and single-mindedness about projects that are important to you
- Decisiveness and strong organizational skills
- Creativity and ability to come up with original solutions
- Empathy and ability to anticipate others' needs
- Perspective to see the big picture and the future implications of actions and ideas
- Ability to understand complex concepts

- Genuine interest in others and talent for helping others grow and develop
- Independent streak and strong personal convictions
- Drive to be productive and reach your goals
- Deep commitment to work you believe in

Your work-related weaknesses may include:

- Single-mindedness that can result in inflexibility
- Unrealistic sense of how long things take
- Difficulty working on projects that conflict with your values

- Tendency to be impractical about viability and/or feasibility of some ideas
- Difficulty working in competitive or tension-filled environments
- Reluctance to revisit or reverse decisions once they've been made
- Difficulty dealing with conflict and tendency to ignore unpleasantness
- Trouble disciplining subordinates with objectivity and directness
- Difficulty changing plans or directions quickly
- Difficulty communicating complex ideas simply
- Tendency to be judgmental

Using your strengths is easy.
The secret to success for an
INFJ
is learning to:

Pay attention to details, be flexible, and be willing to act spontaneously.

10 | ENFP
Extraverted, Intuitive, Feeling, Perceiving
"Anything's Possible"

Profile 1: Joyce

"I have the life that everyone else wants!"

Joyce laughs a lot. And so do the hundreds of people who come in contact with her through her two occupations. She is a college professor of special education at a community college and a national lecturer on the subject of humor. Each year she gives approximately three hundred talks and workshops to corporations, schools, hospitals, and associations on the value of humor and laughter. Lots of people are laughing with Joyce.

"There's no question that what I love most about my work is the people I spend time with and the fact that it's so much fun!" She loves group interaction—all her classes are taught in the round, with people using only first names. Joyce is like an energy magnet: people are drawn to her and she is energized by them. So much so that after her class ends, at 10:00 P.M., she'll frequently go back to her office and work until 1:00 A.M. because

she's so charged up, there's no way she can sleep.

Specifically, what energizes this forty-seven-year-old mother of two is "being with students, kibitzing, talking to people about their problems and experiences." Teaching still excites her and because every class is so different, it's as if she were teaching it for the first time. "I love being in front of and part of a group, doing very experiential things, not knowing exactly what will happen until it does—all that is exciting!"

What Joyce enjoys least about her work is doing research, writing recommendations for students, and advising students on their course schedules. Also draining is reviewing the increasingly complicated contracts she is asked to sign as a speaker, filling out forms, and writing the detailed "behavioral objectives" required for her special education graduate courses.

Joyce's work history is unusually linear for an ENFP. She received a bachelor's degree in education, then completed two master's degrees, the first in special education, the second in counseling. (Later on, she also picked up a sixth-year certificate.) Unable to find a job teaching the physically disabled when she began her career, she taught general special education for three years. She left the field for seven years to raise her two children and returned to teach special education part-time at the community college. Joyce has become a kind of local legend—she is so popular that her classes are always filled early, and students are delighted with what she delivers. She has been teaching at the college for fifteen years.

Joyce has a great many strengths and abilities. "I'm a terrific teacher; I have a high energy level and I put in a tremendous number of hours; I'm creative and perceptive, with good insight into people; I'm very friendly and I have a good sense of humor." Every class is an accomplishment because she is making a difference in what people understand about themselves and their students. Not surprisingly, the greatest satisfaction in her life comes from her work and her relationships with her students. "I tend to get depressed in January and June because, although I'm still very busy lecturing, that's when school lets out for vacation, and I can't wait for it to start again!"

Joyce doesn't experience much work stress, primarily because she is in a department with people who like each other and share the same disdain for structure and bureaucracy. When she does have tasks that she dislikes—like paperwork and research—she is often able to hire a graduate student to do them. What little stress she does allow in is relieved by losing herself in back-to-back movies with her husband, shopping for spontaneous gifts and cards for her many friends, and doing unconventional things like eating bridge mix in bed for breakfast.

Not surprisingly, Joyce has a large and varied collection of friends whom she likes to visit. She is particularly close to her family, who get together frequently. "Teaching is really my favorite thing in the world. As a result, my only career goal is to do what I'm doing, only better." She admits that she would like to be famous on a national level, and one day hopes to write a book that she thinks might make her so. In the meantime, she has enrolled in a doctoral program in adult higher education. She anticipates how rigorous working on this degree will be for the next several years but feels the need to be challenged by learning something new, stretching her intellectual faculties.

Joyce has no career regrets. She believes in the truth of the advice her brother gave her years ago: "Life is a series of breaks, and either you're ready for them or you're not." Although she never thought she would be an international lecturer (or perform as a stand-up comic at a local comedy club, for that matter), she sees how all her experiences have led her to where she is now.

She defines career satisfaction as "having fun, involving people, and making a difference." Consistent with her philosophy is the fact that her favorite course to teach is "How to Make Small Talk," which she particularly loves because her students (frequently many on the shy side) end up learning how to open themselves to new experiences. Joyce, like many ENFPs, enjoys being a catalyst—helping others grow and develop. In fact, she considers the secret of her success to be her ability to be open to different people and different opportunities that were not in her plans.

Joyce would like to be remembered as a good friend, a lighthearted person, and someone who helped others to take things less seriously. "It's really a pretty funny world we live in, and laughing can be very therapeutic when things aren't so funny."

Why This Career Works for Joyce

Joyce has a wonderful sense of humor. She is also very perceptive about people. She has found a unique way to combine these two qualities to carry out the mission of so many Idealists (NFs)—to help people gain self-awareness and live happier lives. Joyce uses humor to entertain and educate— whether she is lecturing to her graduate school students or speaking before any one of the hundreds of audiences she is hired to address each year. Challenging people to open themselves up to new experiences, she makes people laugh and learn at the same time.

Everything is possible to Joyce. Her extraverted Intuition (dominant) is always tuned in to the new and different, which almost guarantees that something special will happen every day. She is clever, witty, and has boundless energy; her enthusiasm quickly infects whomever she is interacting with. Because she is so tuned in to people, she "knows" what will and won't work and is able to pick up subtle cues and adapt her style to connect with very different types of people.

The single most satisfying part of her job is the deep personal relationships that Joyce develops with her students. As an introverted Feeler (auxiliary), Joyce thrives on these close friendships. Once she has taken someone "inside," he or she becomes a friend for life. Likewise, she values the relationships she has with her colleagues. Joyce's family is a central part of her life, and her college teaching schedule allows her lots of time to spend with them. Run by her values, Joyce believes that laughter is therapeutic and can make a serious impact on a person's physical and mental health. She helps people to "lighten their load" and enjoy their lives more fully.

There is ample evidence that Joyce is developing greater access to her Thinking (third function). Professionally, she has enrolled in a very challenging doctoral program, her objective being to exercise her brain—to develop competency in something she is not already good at. In her personal life she has also made dramatic changes. For eighteen years she did volunteer work as often as four days a week! Although she still supports these organizations, she has learned to say no to their constant requests for volunteer help and instead has reexamined her priorities to spend more time with her husband. As a mother, she has stopped blaming herself for the inadvertent mistakes that all parents make. She is also tuning in to her Sensing (fourth function) more by becoming more consciously grateful for the really important things in her life.

Meet the Millennial

Name: Eddie
Age: 29
Activist video producer

"Making politics fun."

Backstory

All throughout college, Eddie loved to make people laugh. He studied improvisation and stand-up comedy, and after school moved to Los Angeles to try his hand in the big leagues. But the rat race started to get to Eddie, and something seemed to be missing. He'd always had his eye on a different goal— to do something important, effect political change, even become a senator.

Eddie had switched tracks and decided to go to law school, with the end goal of working for the American Civil Liberties Union, when the 2010 midterm elections brought a slew of Republicans into Congress. He read an article about the new political climate posing a risk to Internet neutrality, and made a post to Reddit suggesting a Reddit political action committee. The next morning he woke up to a huge response, and his life in activism began in earnest.

Eddie quickly realized he could use his background in comedy to garner a wider audience for the issues he cared about. Using parody and satire to make videos, Eddie caught the attention of a progressive Democratic lobby. He moved to New York City to work as a writer and producer of videos that brought awareness to meaningful political topics.

Having worked in New York for a couple of years, Eddie is now in the midst of an exciting change. His dream is to form a satiric organization in the vein of Stephen Colbert that is centered on campaign finance reform. He has been in talks with another activist organization that is interested in helping to make his dream a reality. Eddie's goal is to reverse activism's stigma as serious and boring. He'd particularly love to create "a comedy show you actually want to come to, not because you feel like you should support this issue, but because it would just be fun."

A Good Fit

As a writer and producer, Eddie gets to use his natural creativity and originality on a daily basis. A dominant Intuitive type, Eddie is constantly absorbed with the big picture—the social and political issues that matter to him. He loves being the person in the room to pitch ten new ideas that no one else has thought of. Eddie's values as an Idealist are front and center in his job, and he gets to tackle big problems through a medium that is actually fun. He enjoys seeing the various parts of producing and writing come together in service of his message.

(continued)

Looking Ahead

Whatever Eddie accomplishes in the next five years, he hopes to do it through this comedy organization. "I'd love to be a politician if the system wasn't so god-awful." Eddie wants to effect real political change, but he is put off by how much of a politician's time must be spent raising money and kowtowing to special interests. The medium of comedy seems to be a way to wield cultural power and raise awareness about issues that matter, without experiencing firsthand the Washington meat grinder. While he enjoys producing, Eddie doesn't want to stay behind the scenes forever: "I do have a desire to be a leader. I have a desire to express my voice."

Profile 2: Daniel

"Instantaneous innovation and sharing my gifts to help others empower themselves."

At thirty-five, Daniel finds his work as an independent management consultant exhilarating and fulfilling. "Fun, and empowerment, and seeking the personal challenges in life are what it's all about for me." In fact, work and leisure are one and the same to Daniel. He honestly doesn't see where one ends and the other begins.

As an independent management consultant, Daniel conducts training workshops and seminars designed as continuing education for executives. Most of his programs include Personality Type as a foundation for understanding and improving employees' effectiveness. He works with leaders of business in health care, banking, law, and high-tech industries. He conducts full-day workshops on team building, problem solving, developing creativity, and understanding value differences. He also offers courses for enhancing interviewing and listening skills. After the initial consultation to determine what the real problem is from the client's point of view, Daniel designs the workshop to meet the specific needs of the client. "I'm extremely detailed in my design, down to the right colors of all materials, the graphics I choose, the food to be served, the music I play—everything to set and keep the atmosphere most conducive to learning. Once I design the program and print out the script, I never look at it again. I don't refer to it in the workshop because it is limiting. It's much more exciting to extemporize, inspired by the personalities of the individuals in the workshop."

During the training, Daniel enjoys the element of surprise. He often opts to play music when the participants arrive—something they would never expect, like a provocative rock ballad. The sessions are highly confrontational. "I get into people's faces, but in a very loving way. And the imperative is always to have fun. If it isn't fun, I simply don't have any energy for it."

The best part of Daniel's job is "seeing eyes light up, no matter what the reason, and it's different for everyone." He is energized by leading the group, facilitating the discussion, and helping others to see new and more positive ways of living and working. He is constantly revamping his materials to make each session new, but "the people really make it different each time. I try to stay in the moment. I say to myself: I'm here *today*. I'm going to give it everything I have, *today*. If I can be sensitive and present for each workshop, it will never be the same because I'll be responding to the new people who will make it fresh."

Daniel enjoys almost everything he does in his work. The few exceptions are writing proposals, which he finds dull, and some of the necessary follow-through. He tends to put those tasks off, sometimes having several invoices sitting on the edge of his desk for weeks after a workshop. "I'm obviously not motivated by the money, or I'd manage to get the energy to do the accounting tasks to get paid!" Daniel also doesn't enjoy the act of selling himself or "pounding the pavement," which, fortunately, he doesn't have to do much anymore. Most of his business is repeat business or referrals from satisfied clients.

There are, because of the nature of his business, some sources of stress for Daniel. "Because I use examples from my personal life during my workshops, if there's discord in my personal life, it's hard for me to forget it and do my job effectively." Also, the lack of long-term job security can be stressful because "I'm essentially unemployed when I finish each session. So sometimes I feel some anxiety about what's coming next. But it's not where my next paycheck is coming from, but rather, where's my next opportunity to give my gift, to empower others, and to have fun. The money is really secondary." Finally, working alone can be difficult for Daniel so he tries to use the telephone as much of the day as he can, to establish contact and connection with other people and keep himself invigorated. Daniel also participates in regular, vigorous exercise, roller skating and attending aerobics classes. But it's his spiritual life that best helps him cope. "I have

faith in God and in myself that I am good at what I do and that the pie is huge. I just really believe God will lead me to my next opportunity. It's pretty simple."

Daniel has experienced many transitions in his career to date. He went to a small engineering college to obtain a degree in mineral sciences. He knew he was misplaced, "like a fish in peanut butter." During the summer between graduation and his first job, he attended clown school. But he took his first job as a metallurgical engineer at a large aluminum manufacturer in the quality assurance division. "I was never a good engineer because I really didn't know what I was doing, but I did excel at some of the other responsibilities I took on, including college recruiting each spring and organizing the company picnics and softball team." Deciding he needed to make some changes after two years, Daniel set out to make one transition at a time. He started by moving to a new regional office, and then to a new company. Next he went to work as the national coordinator for a temporary employment and placement firm, specializing in engineering managers. The work was easier for him because it wasn't as technical, but he still found he was longing for more interaction with different kinds of people. So he returned to school and obtained his MBA, knowing only that he wanted to use the entrepreneurial spirit he felt. The week before graduation, he happened to hear a speaker from a major training company speak at a college function, and he knew immediately that he wanted to pursue training as a career. He applied and was hired immediately.

The job required him to travel around the country conducting two-day seminars on management development and leadership training. While the job showcased his training talent, it was exhausting work. He quit and, always eager for a new challenge, gutted and remodeled an entire house, which was later featured in a national magazine. That gave him the confidence to strike out again. He met his first client on an airplane flight and began his own management and training consulting business five years ago.

Daniel believes his greatest strength is his ability to change and help others to change by providing an arena in which to change safely. "My unbridled enthusiasm, energy, and humor make the trainings really fun. The compassionate side of me has made the programs richer and mellower because I can tap into my own deep feelings. And I'm really creative—capable of instantaneous innovation. I see that as God's presence in me."

One of Daniel's greatest work-related accomplishments is a series of team-building workshops he recently conducted for a law firm to help them work effectively together. "We got the whole room of lawyers to create a hug line. And not those 'slap-on-the-back' hugs either. I'm talking about the kind where you stand with bodies touching and take a few breaths together. It was really wild." Daniel is also pleased about the opportunity he recently had to conduct a team-building program for a renowned human resources development office of a local corporation. "It was a real compliment to be asked by my peers to teach them something new."

Being appreciated for his gifts and talents is the source of greatest satisfaction for Daniel. "Witnessing or hearing about a life change someone has made as a result of my influence really touches me. For me, this life is about individuation, and self-actualization. The most important thing in my life is the pursuit of self-understanding. It's a quest, and unless I'm actively working on it, I can't help anyone else on their way, either."

Daniel finds himself more secure and centered these days. He even changed his name to reflect that change. "I used to go by Dan, which means judge. I changed to Daniel because adding the letters 'iel' adds the meaning 'of God.' I don't spend the time or energy worrying about what other people think of me. I'll walk away from a client, even a big job, if they won't let me do my work my way. I see myself and others around me more objectively. But that doesn't mean I'm less compassionate. I believe if anything, I am more so. I'm able to work alone easier than I used to, and I have a clearer focus about what's important to me in my life. And I have a better understanding of the meaning of pain. Life is a combination of both joy and pain. If you don't ever experience pain, you can't really be *in* your life. So it doesn't make me as uncomfortable anymore.

"The best advice I could give someone who is also an ENFP is to trust your dreams to guide you, your own vision of what's right for you. I know it's been said before, but ENFPs more than maybe other types need to follow their passion. I know I followed mine, after some detours along the way! And I believe if I *really* keep listening to it, I'll always find work that is fun and fulfilling."

Why This Career Works for Daniel

Many Idealists share Daniel's quest in life—the pursuit of self-understanding. He seeks meaning in everything he does and quite naturally uses his talents and gifts to help others do the same. As a trainer, the topics he chooses to teach reveal much about what he values: creative problem solving, understanding value differences, listening skills, and personal growth. Daniel has an infectious enthusiasm and an irreverence which people find refreshing. He uses his creativity and sense of humor to make his points and help people see new and more positive ways of working and living.

Daniel's extraverted Intuition (dominant) expresses itself in his creativity in designing training experiences that are enlightening, fun, and challenging. He is particularly good at creative problem solving and enjoys responding to others in a crisis. His Intuition helps him get new business as well. His attitude: "Anyone I haven't met is a potential client" keeps him ever alert to new possibilities.

Making connections with people is very important to Daniel. He shares personal examples from his own life and loves knowing he's really touched and helped somebody. Daniel's spiritual life is central to him. He has a deep faith in God and is always looking for an opportunity to share his gifts with others. He is most gratified to see the positive life changes that a person has made as a result of his influence.

As he has gained better access to his Thinking (third function), Daniel has become less concerned about what others think of him. He has even turned down business when it would have meant compromising his principles. He now sees himself and others more objectively—not idealizing people the way he used to. Daniel has a clearer focus on what's important to *him*—he is better able to make decisions out of choice, rather than obligation, another sign that he has developed better use of his Thinking.

Common Threads

Although Joyce, Daniel, and Eddie have different backgrounds, experiences, and careers, there are certain common threads that weave through their stories. Their specific interests and abilities may differ, but owing to their similar temperament values, the *same hierarchy* of their psychological

functions, and the "world" they naturally use them in (inner or outer), there are certain observations we can make about the needs of many ENFPs.

What follows is a list of the most important elements—the formula, if you will, for ENFP satisfaction. Given the uniqueness of all individuals—even those who share the same type—this list will not describe each ENFP equally well. The important thing is that these ten elements, with varying degrees of intensity and in different orders of importance, identify what ENFPs need to be satisfied.

After you have reviewed this list, we recommend that you go back and prioritize the elements in order of *their importance to you*. When doing this, think of past work experiences as well as your present job, and what you found particularly satisfying or unsatisfying. Try to look for *themes* that run through several experiences, not just the events which might be true for one work situation but not for another.

As an ENFP, career satisfaction means doing work that:

1. Lets me work with a diverse group of people on a variety of projects, motivated by creative inspiration
2. Lets me create new ideas, products, services, or solutions to problems that will help other people, and then see my projects become reality
3. Is fun, challenging, and always varied
4. Rarely requires me to handle the follow-through, routine details, or maintenance of a system or project
5. Lets me work at my own pace and schedule, with a minimum of rules or structure and the freedom to act spontaneously

6. Lets me meet new people, learn new skills, and continually satisfy my curiosity

7. Is consistent with my personal beliefs and values and lets me create opportunities that benefit others

8. Is done in a friendly and relaxed environment with humor, goodwill, and a minimum of interpersonal conflict

9. Allows me the freedom to follow my inspirations and participate in exciting and intriguing adventures

10. Is done in an environment that appreciates and rewards enthusiasm, ingenuity, and imagination

Popular Occupations for ENFPs

Because of their combination of preferences, ENFPs are naturally drawn to a wide variety of occupations.

In listing occupations that are popular among ENFPs, it is important to note that there are successful people of all types in all occupations. However, the following are careers ENFPs may find particularly satisfying and some of the reasons why. This is by no means a comprehensive listing but is included to suggest possibilities you may not have previously considered.

Although all of these occupations offer the potential for career satisfaction, the future demand for some careers is anticipated to be greater than for others. Based upon our research, the occupations that are italicized in the lists below are forecast to enjoy the fastest rate of growth over the next several years.

CREATIVE
- Journalist
- Screenwriter/playwright
- Columnist
- Blogger
- Character actor
- Musician/composer
- Newscaster
- Interior decorator
- Artist
- Reporter/editor (magazine)
- Informational-graphics designer
- Print designer
- Interaction designer
- Editor/art director (website)
- Creative director on a multimedia team
- Developer of educational software
- Multimedia producer
- Director of regional/community theater
- Documentary filmmaker
- Costume designer
- Television producer
- Radio/podcast producer
- Broadcast news analyst
- Cartoonist/animator
- Exhibit designer

The obvious appeal of these creative careers is the opportunity to continually develop new and original approaches. ENFPs enjoy the creative process, especially if it offers opportunity for collaboration and to be inspired by working with others. The more unconstrained and flexible the working environment, the better ENFPs like it. They work well independently but need frequent, spontaneous interaction with others to keep their creative juices flowing and to keep their work fun.

MARKETING/PLANNING
- *Market research analyst*
- *Public relations specialist*
- Marketing consultant
- *Advertising account executive*
- Copywriter/publicity writer
- *Advertising creative director*
- Strategic planner
- *Social media manager*
- Publicist

- Research assistant
- Editor/art director (magazine)

ENFPs usually are excellent long-range thinkers and can easily see the possible effects of an idea, program, or service on others. They take the needs and concerns of other people into consideration in their planning and often devise innovative and humane solutions to problems. They enjoy creative problem solving, especially as part of a lively and energetic team. Often clever and funny, many ENFPs find satisfaction in writing advertising copy for print or broadcast media. The fast pace and constantly changing face of advertising is also appealing. And they can be great spokespeople for organizations in the role of a public relations manager.

EDUCATION/COUNSELING
- Special education teacher
- *Bilingual education teacher*
- *Early childhood education teacher*
- *Teacher: art/drama/music/English*
- Child welfare counselor
- *Substance abuse counselor*
- *Social worker (elderly and child day care issues)*
- *Marriage and family therapist*
- *Mental health counselor*
- *Development director*
- Career counselor
- Residential housing director
- Ombudsperson
- Pastoral counselor
- *Rehabilitation counselor*
- Social scientist
- Educational psychologist
- Planned-giving officer
- Philanthropic consultant
- Social psychologist
- Counseling psychologist
- Anthropologist

- Parent instructor, child development course
- High school guidance counselor

Many ENFPs find work that has a positive impact on others to be intrinsically satisfying. They can be compassionate and supportive psychologists and creative and enthusiastic career counselors, helping their clients find new and original solutions to problems. Their focus is on possibilities, especially for others, and they have an infectious and energizing style that motivates their clients to try to make positive changes in their lives. They enjoy helping others develop their own spirituality and often are attracted to careers in some form of ministry. As ombudspersons, they are effective and innovative catalysts for change within organizations, helping individuals by serving as a guide to available resources.

HEALTH CARE/SOCIAL SERVICE
- *Dietitian/nutritionist*
- *Speech-language pathologist/audiologist*
- *Holistic health practitioner (alternative medicine)*
- Massage therapist
- Employee assistance program counselor
- *Physical therapist*
- Legal mediator
- Chiropractor
- Urban regional planner
- *Public health educator*
- *Occupational therapist*

These fields in health care and social service are generally appealing to ENFPs, in part because of their helping nature and opportunity to use creative approaches but also because these tend to be careers one can self-manage while remaining independent and flexible. ENFPs in these careers are most satisfied when they are able to work outside of a rigid traditional structure, perhaps as consultants serving a variety of clients.

ENTREPRENEURIAL/BUSINESS
- Consultant
- Inventor
- Sales: intangibles/ideas
- *Human resources manager*
- *Human resources development trainer*
- *Meeting, conference, and event planner*
- Employment development specialist
- Restaurateur
- Management consultant: change management/team building/diversity
- Merchandise planner
- *Diversity manager: human resources*
- *Corporate/team trainer*
- *Advertising account manager or account executive*
- Public relations specialist
- Marketing executive: radio/TV/cable broadcast industry
- *Outplacement consultant*
- Environmental lawyer
- Personnel recruiter
- Labor relations specialist

ENFPs are born entrepreneurs! They enjoy working for themselves because it gives them the freedom and flexibility, and the opportunity, to choose the projects they wish to work on and the people they want to work with. They usually have an abundance of ideas they want to see turned into reality, particularly those that will affect other people. Many ENFPs enjoy consulting in the areas of team building, conflict resolution, or increasing effectiveness in the workplace. They also enjoy being independent salespeople, especially selling intangibles— ideas, rather than products.

The conventional business world is usually not appealing to ENFPs because they dislike excessive rules, regulations, or standard operating procedures. However,

within traditional organizations, ENFPs flock to the human resources departments in the role of trainers and counselors. They find that a career as an employment development adviser uses their abilities to plan ahead and devise creative ways for people to do their work while keeping the organization's goals in mind.

Remember, these are only some areas that provide satisfying expression for the unique natural talents of the ENFP.

TECHNOLOGY
- *Customer relations manager*
- Staff advocate (technology consultant)
- Project manager
- Engagement manager
- Human resources recruiter

With the proliferation of technology, there is a rapidly growing need for people who understand technology but also have good people and communication skills. Being the liaison between the technology people and the end users appeals to many ENFPs, who find these jobs satisfy their need to help and be connected with their co-workers.

Customizing Your Job Search

Knowing the particular strengths and blind spots of your type can afford you a tremendous advantage in your job search campaign. In all aspects of the process, from conducting research into available positions, identifying and contacting prospective employers, developing personal marketing tools such as résumés, arranging and conducting job interviews, negotiating salaries to finally accepting a position, people will act true to their type. Being able to capitalize on your assets and compensate for your liabilities can make the difference between a successful and an unsuccessful job search.

The differences between types are sometimes subtle and other times dramatic.

It is the subtle variations in advice we offer that make the real difference between success or failure in a job search. The concept of networking, or meeting with and talking to people to gather information about potential jobs, serves as a good example. Extraverts will naturally enjoy networking and are advised to do so on a large scale, while Introverts find more limited and targeted networking, especially with people they already know, easier. Sensors tend to network with people in a defined scope, while Intuitives will go far and wide to find people, often seemingly unrelated to their field of interest. Further, Feelers take networking, like everything else, very personally and enjoy establishing warm rapport, while Thinkers will be more objective and detached in their style. Finally, Judgers tend to ask fewer and more structured questions during their networking, while Perceivers could ask questions of all sorts all day long! One valuable search technique, many ways to implement it.

Pathways to Success: Using Your Strengths

As an ENFP, your strength and talent for the job search lies in your unlimited ability to see alternatives and creative approaches, and your endless energy for gathering information by talking with people. But while you will love the data collection phase, beware of your tendency to become overwhelmed by details and paralyzed by your lack of organization.

As an ENFP, your most effective strategies will lie in your abilities to:

Create your own job opportunities.

- Use your ability to see opportunities that don't presently exist, and tailor your current job to meet your changing needs, or the changing needs of your employer.
- Invent an entirely new job for yourself that will fill a need you see or predict in the market.

Elizabeth began to feel restricted by the amount of red tape and rules being implemented in the rapidly growing advertising agency where she worked as a copywriter. She decided she needed a more relaxed environment in which to be creative. So she got together with a group of copywriter friends of hers and developed an idea for a small agency of copywriters. They realized that while the idea sounded great, they would need to hire at least a part-time person to help them schedule jobs, bill clients, and pay their own bills so each of the writers would be free to meet new clients and write.

They found someone who had some of the business strengths they lacked and started their own firm.

Develop and use your active network of contacts.

- Conduct lots of helpful informational interviews. Constantly enlarge your circle of contacts each time you meet with someone by asking him or her to refer you on to someone else.
- Tell everyone you meet and all of your friends that you are looking for a new career or job. You'll spread the word quickly and learn helpful information along the way.

Gil was shopping in the supermarket with his family when he literally bumped into an old friend from graduate school. Joe told Gil that he was considering leaving the hospital where he worked for a position out of state. Gil replied that he was interested in Joe's marketing-and-planning-director job himself. Gil arranged to call Joe at the end of the week and was able to interview for the position the day after Joe offered his resignation.

Impress your interviewer with your natural enthusiasm and confidence.

- Establish instant rapport and demonstrate your ability to meet people and make them feel comfortable with you.
- Use your sense of humor to change the interview from a formal and basically stilted experience to one where you and the interviewer enjoy yourselves. It will be a welcome breath of fresh air for the interviewer.

Maggie credited her offbeat sense of humor for getting the job she loves as a trainer in the human resources department of a major insurance company. She went through the typical interview process and arrived at the final interview. It was a very stormy day and Maggie went directly into the ladies' room to try to dry off and do something with her hair. A woman entered, also soaked to the skin, hair dripping, makeup running down her cheeks. Maggie immediately struck up a humorous conversation with the woman about their comical situation. They got to laughing and talking as they pulled themselves together. A few minutes later, they started laughing all over again when Maggie discovered that the woman was the vice president of human resources and Maggie was her nine o'clock interview!

Consider and keep several options open.

- Adapt to changing situations and improvise when you find yourself against an unexpected obstacle.

- Use your natural curiosity to gather a great deal of information about potential careers, jobs, and organizations.

Pat was about at the end of his career search. But he went ahead and conducted yet one more informational interview at a university even though he thought he might accept a job offered to him at an in-house conference planning department for a major company. He learned during the interview that the university was creating a position for a new faculty ombudsman—a job he had always wanted but had not figured possible because the position is so rare. He realized if he had not kept his options open, he would already have accepted one of the other positions before this dream job came along.

Be resourceful in getting job interviews.

- Use creative approaches to get yourself noticed and remembered, especially if you are one of many candidates for a job you are sure you want.
- Use the same energy and ability to see options to help you get around barriers or resistance you encounter during your search.

Jenna had decided that she wanted the highly sought-after job of director of creative arts for a program for gifted and talented children. After several calls to inquire into getting an interview with the supervisor of special education, she was told the position was only being posted within the school system, and outside applicants would not be considered unless the position could not be filled internally. She did not let that obstacle deter her; in fact, she felt energized by the challenge. She created a series of mailings to be received by the supervisor of special education each day for a week. Each used a different medium (photography, painting, music—she enclosed a cassette tape—

writing, and sculpture), and each detailed her experience, past work experience, and her interest in the position. She didn't have to call to follow up because she received a call for an interview after the final piece was received.

Possible Pitfalls

Although all people are unique, there are certain *potential* blind spots that many ENFPs share. We specify "potential" because some of the following may clearly be true of you, while others may not apply. While considering them, you may notice that these tendencies do not just relate to the job search, but rather describe pitfalls which you may have experienced in other aspects of your life as well. It is therefore helpful to consider each one in terms of your past experiences by asking yourself, "Is this true for me?" And if so, "How did this tendency prevent me from getting something that I wanted?" You will probably notice that the key to overcoming your blind spots is the conscious and thoughtful development of your third and fourth functions (Thinking and Sensing). We recognize that many of the suggestions will be difficult to implement, but the more you use these functions, the fewer problems they will cause you in the future.

Pay attention to the realistic facts of a career or job.

- Focus your energy and attention on seeing what is really in front of you rather than just what might be. Use resources like the library, trade publications, and other people to learn what a job is really like.
- Be realistic in planning your job search in terms of how long it will take, what will be required, how much it will cost, and how you will afford to live (and eat) while you are involved in it. Make con-

tingency plans so you are ready if it takes longer than you hope.

Curb your tendency to leap before you look!

- Develop a job search plan in advance so you don't squander your inspiration and energy in areas that aren't right for you.
- Generate a list of criteria for the right job, including what you can't live without as well as what would be nice but not imperative. Continue to use that list as a guide, comparing potential opportunities to it before pursuing them fully.

Work on developing self-discipline.

- Use proven time management skills and systems to help you get and stay organized. Ask an organized friend to help you (and to make it more fun).
- Prioritize the most important tasks, issues, and activities so you can't become distracted as easily. Try not to let impromptu socializing take you away from the less exciting but nevertheless important parts of the search.

Don't put off making a decision.

- Procrastinating may mean that you lose out on potentially satisfying opportunities because you took too long to decide.
- Decide when you have enough information rather than go on indefinitely gathering more.

Follow through on all phases of the job search.

- Remember that some people use and respect established organizational procedures and expect others to as well.

Consider it an opportunity to demonstrate your ability to adapt rather than viewing it as a repressive limitation.

- Develop and then *use* a system of your choosing to help you check your progress so that nothing slips through the cracks. Stick with whatever you decide, rather than dropping it to try a more intriguing system before giving the first one a chance to help you.

The Final Piece: Changing or Keeping Your Job...the Key to Success for ENFPs

Now that you have a solid understanding of your type, you can see how your natural preferences make you better suited for certain kinds of jobs. You can also see how knowledge of your type-related strengths and weaknesses can help you conduct a more successful job search. But as an ENFP, you've already realized that you are not equally drawn to *every* career or field listed in the Popular Occupations section. The next and final step is to narrow down the field and find the work you were meant to do.

In addition to Type, several other factors—such as your values, interests, and skills—also contribute to your level of satisfaction on the job. The more compatible you are with your job, the happier you'll be. So prepare to use everything you've learned (in this book and in life) to create *your strategic career plan.* The exercises in Chapter 24, Putting It All Together, are designed to help you do just that.

However, you may have decided it makes more sense (if perhaps only for the moment) to stay in your present job or with your current employer. There may be many valid reasons—financial pressures, family considerations, a tough job market for your specialty, or just bad timing. But take heart!

What you've learned in this book can also help you be more content and successful *in your current job.* And should the time come when you're ready to make a major career move, you'll have a much better idea of where you want to go, and how to get there.

"So, if you can't have the job you love (yet!)...love the one you've got."

The simple truth is, with the exception of work on a factory assembly line, the vast majority of jobs allow a good deal of flexibility in the way tasks are performed. Here are some ways you may be able to "massage" your current job into one that better fits your needs:

- If possible, delegate routine tasks to others.
- Team up with co-workers and/or work on teams.
- Find other creative people to brainstorm ideas with.
- Work different shifts, arrange more flexible hours, or job-share.
- Change your focus if you're not stimulated or challenged; work on something else.
- Make sure you have a variety of projects to work on.
- Talk through detailed projects with someone.
- Join or start organizations for people with similar expertise or interests.
- Attend conferences and get involved in professional organizations.

One ENFP turns lemons into lemonade:

A corporate trainer for a large service company, Alan longed for the autonomy and freedom of being a private consultant, but he knew he didn't want to work alone all day. Realizing it would take a long time to establish his own lucrative business and that his boss was under pressure to reduce costs, Alan convinced him he could save a substantial amount of money (a full-time salary plus benefits) if he hired Alan as an independent contractor. With this creative proposal, Alan managed to stay connected to his friends and colleagues and secured a well-paying, steady client. And most important, he bought the time he needed to develop his own business.

Use what you've got to get what you need.

Simply put, the best advice on how to succeed is to *capitalize on your strengths and compensate for your weaknesses.* Learning how to do this can make the difference between succeeding or failing and loving or hating your work. To help you, we include the following inventory of your potential strengths and weaknesses. And while every individual is unique, as an ENFP, many of the following should apply to you.

Your work-related strengths may include:

- Eagerness to "think outside the box" and consider new possibilities
- Courage to take some risks, try new things, and overcome obstacles
- A broad range of interests and ability to quickly learn things that interest you

- Natural curiosity and skill for getting the information you need
- Ability to see the big picture and the implications of actions and ideas
- Excellent communication skills and ability to rouse others' enthusiasm
- Adaptability; you can shift gears and change directions quickly
- Perceptiveness about people; you understand their needs and motivations

Your work-related weaknesses may include:

- Difficulty setting priorities and making decisions
- Impatience with uncreative people
- Reluctance to do things in traditional or routine ways
- Lack of discipline when attending to and following through on important details
- Tendency to become bored or sidetracked, especially after the creative process is done
- Dislike for doing repetitive tasks
- Impatience working with systems or people who are too rigid
- Propensity to always focus on what's possible rather than what's doable or probable
- Tendency to be disorganized

Using your strengths is easy.
The secret to success for an
ENFP
is learning to:

Prioritize, focus, and follow through.

11 | INFP
Introverted, Intuitive, Feeling, Perceiving
"Still Waters Run Deep"

Profile 1: Emily

"My best work is what I am personally pleased with; the pieces that really say what I wanted them to say."

Emily has been an artist since the sixth grade and has earned her living through her art her whole adult life. Today she is a freelance illustrator specializing in editorial illustrations that accompany articles in magazines and newspapers. She works for a large number of different clients and exclusively from the studio in her home. She wouldn't have it any other way.

Nearly all of Emily's assignments come directly to her from the art directors of publications. When she first started illustrating, she used to travel to the publications but now uses the mail and her fax machine to send sketches back and forth. In fact, she never has to leave her studio if she doesn't want to. Usually, Emily is sent the text of an upcoming article to read and told about any size or color elements she

must accommodate. Next she decides upon the approach and style she wishes to use to communicate her message. Then she develops a sketch of her illustration and sends the sketch to the art director, using her trusty fax machine. Any changes or alterations are made at the sketch stage. After the editor of the article reviews her sketch, Emily makes any necessary changes and produces the finished artwork. Again, she ships her work to the publication and doesn't see it again until it appears in the magazine or newspaper.

Emily engages in only limited marketing because after twelve years her clients come to her, primarily through word of mouth from other art directors and as a result of people seeing her work in other publications. Occasionally she places a small ad in a directory of specialty artists. And she handles her own bookkeeping, which is a very informal, handwritten list of projects, bills, and expenses.

"My favorite part of the job is the stimulation and challenge of solving a problem in a creative way. Working within the confines of the text I'm given, I can express my ideas and really say something that adds to the article." She is also gratified when the work she does pleases her clients. "They almost always like what I do and they tell me so. Then I see it in print and get a check. That's reinforcement!" Finally, Emily likes the fact that her client contact is almost always with people who are trained in art. "Anyone else involved, like a copy editor, I don't deal with directly, so I seldom have to hear any negative criticism."

Emily finds the most energizing projects to be the ones that involve text that is of excellent quality. "When I personally respond to the text, I especially love the job. But the very best is when an art director tells me to just have fun with the piece. That means I can use humor and there are virtually no limits to my creative expression."

Predictably, the opposite type of project is Emily's least favorite. "When people fuss with my ideas, suggesting that it would be cute to add something or other here or there, it really diminishes my work. Or if an agency has the idea worked out completely, with too many specifications so I end up doing no creating, just executing their idea, then it's no fun." Sometimes those situations go to an extreme and Emily finds her work so diluted by changes or outside controls that she begins to disassociate herself from it. "Too many changes, especially changes in style rather than concept, are really bad for me. It's not my work anymore. In those cases, I begin to hate the piece; I've compromised myself and I'm not proud of the work anymore. If I'm not proud of it, I don't want to do it."

For the most part, Emily has little job stress in her career, but that which she does experience comes from the unpredictability of her work. "I'm a very flexible person and can adapt well to changes but when I get too busy, I feel stress. This is especially true when a good client needs me to squeeze in a job when I already have a full schedule. Or if a problem arises with a project and that throws everything else off schedule. That's difficult but I've learned to be more realistic about the time and potential difficulty with new jobs, so I don't get caught too often."

Emily came to a career in illustration after a series of less fulfilling jobs. She began work after college as a layout and paste-up artist putting together advertisements for several large department stores. These jobs allowed her to do a lot of doodling, and since she didn't have to finish the ads, she was able to concentrate on design rather than production. Next she went to work for a publisher as an assistant to the art director. It was another learning experience where she designed a book and did other freelance designs in her spare time. When she and her husband decided to move, she found a job in another department store, this time working on women's fashion ads. "That was great training. I learned how to make fast production decisions. But I was still free to experiment and doodle and didn't have to execute the finished drawings." Eventually, Emily decided to try to make her living as a working artist. She began creating art and entering it in shows. She won several prizes and enjoyed the process of learning how to exhibit her work. She set up a studio in her home and for seven years made art, showed it in galleries, and sold it. "But the complete lack of outside stimulation began to bog me down. I wasn't productive because I wasn't trying anything really new. So I took a graduate painting course and started producing a different type of art. I wanted to try new techniques and styles, but, unfortunately, they turned out not to be very marketable." Finally, she realized she needed to change directions. She was encouraged by an illustrator friend to put together a portfolio. She took her portfolio in to several magazines and was hired immediately by a prestigious national magazine that continues today to be one of her favorite clients. "I realized that dealing with the agencies was much better for me. I could talk about my work because they were judging my work, not my soul. There aren't the same politics in agencies as there are in galleries. It felt pure—I was filling a need the art director had. I could be a little less personally involved."

Emily's work and her relationship with her husband are the most important things in her life. "I've always been an artist and being an artist shapes everything about you. It's who you are, not just what you do." But the importance of her work has shifted in intensity over the last couple of years as she has become successful. "I feel like it's OK to let up on it a bit. I want to pursue some new interests, like piano, my weight lifting, and taking Italian lessons. I can now justify time away from the studio, and I want to learn new things. I'm less focused on getting recognition for my work." In fact, Emily believes she is much more objective and realistic about her work today. She is more self-confident and tolerant of other people in their interaction with her.

But she remains as uncompromising about her work as ever. "I have shaped my life to be the way I wanted it to be. Sometimes that has meant taking a risk or making what looked to others like a crazy mistake. But I always trusted myself and my convictions first. Even the boring jobs gave me a chance to build my skills, even if they didn't challenge me creatively. I'm better because of it. I tell young art students not to be

discouraged if it takes a long time. Someday, maybe they'll find the satisfaction I've found—being able to do work that lets them express themselves and get recognition from their peers."

Why This Career Works for Emily

Like most Idealist artists, Emily defines herself not by what she does, but what she is. In effect, her work and her life are so intertwined as to be almost indistinguishable. Her life's work is about creative expression, creative problem solving, and communicating through her art. It is important to her that both her clients and the readers of the books and articles she illustrates feel something special as a result of her work.

Because she is an introverted Feeler (dominant), Emily must, above all else, be true to herself. In her case, this means being able to exercise almost total creative control. By being in business for herself, she has few rules to follow other than those she lays out for herself. She is therefore free to do things her own way. This is an important theme for introverted Feelers because they are most concerned about pleasing *themselves*—in Emily's case, doing what is right for her and her husband. She also enjoys the close relationships she has with some longstanding clients and the mutual respect and trust they have developed over the years.

Emily draws her creative ideas from the outside world. Through her extraverted Intuition (auxiliary), she constantly perceives things—especially the new and unusual. She then figures out ways to represent these ideas in interesting and different ways. Her Intuition also helps her interpret what she experiences and to characterize it so that it will have meaning for the reader. Most of her work is subtle and witty—she suggests meanings to the reader, rather than hitting them over the head with the obvious.

Not surprising, most of the interests Emily has developed in recent years require the use of her Sensing (third function). She has begun taking piano lessons, lifting weights, doing aerobics, and learning to speak Italian. Most of these are physical activities that call on her to use her body. She has also become more realistic, though she regrets that she may have lost some of her innocence and idealism in the process. As she has become more successful, she has grown more self-assured and realizes that she has made a certain place for herself and that she is in demand.

Meet the Millennial

Name: Darren
Age: 25
Video game designer

"The creator of fun."

Backstory

Darren had been making video games in his spare time since elementary school, but it wasn't until a senior project in high school that he first showcased his work to a large audience. The experience was life changing, and Darren began to realize that he could pursue a career in video game design, starting with a college degree. Savannah College of Art and Design fit the bill, and Darren began the BFA program in interactive design and game development.

During his junior year, Darren completed an internship working on a fantasy online role-playing game (RPG). Afterward, Darren was offered a permanent position, but he declined in order to finish his degree. It was a tough decision, but one that he doesn't regret, even though by the time he graduated, the position had already been filled.

Darren spent a couple of months working on his portfolio and applying for jobs, but the economic climate in 2009 was bad news for recent grads. In the fall he finally got his opportunity when he was offered his previous mentor's position.

The design team for an RPG often consists of content designers, who focus on story and narrative, and systems designers, who are in charge of the logistics, numbers, and strategy. Darren worked as an associate game systems designer for almost two years before being promoted to the midlevel position of game systems designer. By that time he was beginning to feel the need for change and new challenges. He transitioned to a new company, and his current position is that of game designer on a kid-oriented toys-plus-video-game experience.

Now Darren gets to work on a broader

(continued)

view for the game, which he enjoys. He designs environments for the game and works with both engineers and artists to fulfill his vision and shape the player experience.

A Good Fit

Like many Idealists, Darren has the soul of an artist. "What I've wanted to do since I was little is to craft these interactive experiences and to make things that people can get immersed in, like the way I did with games when I was young." Darren's job gives him the power to create and bring to life entire worlds that previously existed only inside his mind. His dominant function of Feeling is constantly rewarded by the fact that he gets to make art that has a direct impact on others and lets them enjoy his world. Working on a team with colleagues who respect his vision, Darren is upbeat and enthusiastic, inspiring them with his dedication. Darren's auxiliary Intuition is constantly in play as he dreams up new worlds and explores the realm of

possibility. As a designer, Darren has an eye on the greater whole and works to make the component pieces come together.

Looking Ahead

When asked what his dream job is, Darren laughs, since in some ways he is already doing it. "But I think if you're ever in the position where you can't see yourself going further, then you should rethink things." Like many designers, Darren can imagine opening his own studio five or ten years down the road and creating an environment in which he would have greater control over all the projects. And this may be more possible now than ever: "The game industry is currently undergoing a revolution, with crowd-sourcing allowing new start-up studios to get funded." Darren is excited by changes coming to the industry, pleased by the fact that about half of all gamers in the world are now female and that games are marketed toward increasingly broader audiences.

Profile 2: Dan

"Love and meaningful work—I can't have either in my life if I don't have both."

Dan always dreamed of being successfully self-employed. He liked the idea of being a college professor because he imagined the job would allow him a high degree of personal autonomy and independence. But once he had the job, he knew he needed even more. Today, Dan is a very successful independent consultant, specializing in

conflict resolution through the process of mediation. He trains others how to use the methods and materials he has created, and he serves as a mediator with his corporate and business clients to help employees resolve interpersonal conflicts in the workplace. Dan is forty-five years old and enjoying the chance to have a positive impact on others and to strike a balance between the professional status and freedom he has attained and a rich and meaningful personal life.

Dan's business comprises three different components. The first involves conducting training seminars, both public registration seminars and those sponsored by organizations. They are full-day programs where he teaches people how to understand and implement the conflict resolution techniques and methods he has developed. Dan especially likes to use role-playing, small-group discussions, and discovery exercises "where participants become aware of something new about themselves." To conduct the training seminars, Dan travels an average of two days a week, working with groups of fifteen to thirty people.

In addition to offering skills training to others, Dan also provides his services as a mediator to corporations and business. In these situations, he travels to the organization, meets with the individuals experiencing the interpersonal strife, and works with them to reach a satisfying agreement to both parties. "These are people who don't get along. Often they just don't like each other. But the purpose is to reach an agreement, and we stay at it until we have one. I facilitate the dialogue, help them to reframe the issues in question, and run up trial balloons that might serve as the point of agreement. It usually takes two or three hours working together." Then Dan writes up whatever agreement the two people have created that spells out how they agree to work or interact in the future. "It's not a legal document, but is a public commitment to interact in a more positive way. That's pretty rewarding, to help people work out difficult personal challenges."

The final area of Dan's business is the process of marketing his services and products, developing new products and services, giving speeches that promote the two books he has written on the subject of conflict resolution, and all the more routine matters of operating a small business.

Dan enjoys the mix of things he does, as long as none of them becomes too time-consuming. "I enjoy the variety and the absence of routine. I can keep myself propelled all by myself. But it's really thrilling to receive a phone call inviting me to come speak to a group because it's so affirming of my work and of me and because it also means a large chunk of money!" Having an opportunity to talk to interested and admiring audiences about his original ideas and creations *and* to be paid handsomely for it is an energizing element of Dan's work.

"There's not a lot in my work that I don't like, which is lucky, I know. But I don't like the anxiety I feel when cash flow is tight and I have to either put off buying something like a new printer because I can't justify it, or being late to pay a vendor of mine. That's terribly uncomfortable for me. But the uncertainty of life as a self-employed consultant doesn't bother me. I was raised on a farm, where life itself is uncertain. I grew up learning to trust that things will work out and to survive amid great uncertainty." The routine, menial, or boring activities like running errands or going to the post office are draining for Dan. He now has an assistant to help organize and follow through on tasks like mailings and paying bills. "But some things I just can't get organized enough to delegate. They require judgments along the way, so I have to do them." Dan experiences stress when he doesn't have enough time before a deadline to prepare himself adequately. To cope, he insists on getting enough sleep and proper nutrition, no matter how rushed he may be.

Dan's career was long in the making. After two years in college, he left to serve in the army in Vietnam and Panama. After the service, he returned to college to find he could concentrate better and make high grades. He switched majors three times, from math to philosophy to psychology, where he received his degree. He continued on to obtain a master's and then a Ph.D. in counseling psychology. While writing his dissertation, he became inspired by a self-help career guidance book and moved, without a job, from a rural state to Washington, D.C. He conducted countless informational interviews until he got a job setting up an employee assistance program for the Office of Education. "I was terribly naive, but it was a great big adventure."

After one year, a friend told him about a teaching opportunity at a small private university. He was hired as assistant professor of management, and taught organizational behavior courses there for the next seven years. While he enjoyed fulfilling his early ambition of being a college professor, he found the job too easy and decided after four years that he would not attempt to become tenured. "I've never been a good subordinate. I got into several scrapes in the army because of that. I just can't make myself do unpleasant things just for someone else's purposes. And I like the idea of being self-determining, so I used the final three years at the university to begin to develop my own consulting practice." He left the university on a positive note and still teaches a conflict resolution course there twice each summer.

His consulting practice has grown considerably over the past five years, primarily because of the book he wrote in 1985, a source of great pride and satisfaction for Dan. That book and his second one have created opportunities and added to his credibility as a speaker and as a mediator and trainer. His first book is now translated into five languages, and Dan recently returned from a speaking trip to Russia and is planning a book tour in India. "I've evolved a lot in my level of understanding, not just added to my stature on paper. Each accomplishment has led to greater opportunities—sort of a snowball effect."

One of Dan's great strengths is his ability to concentrate intensely and be creative. So he structures his day to make the most of this energy, using the mornings exclusively for the tasks that require concentration. "I have a lot of faith in myself. I have confidence that I can make things work out by persevering even in the face of apparent failures, like the ups and downs I've experienced in my own business."

But the most important things to Dan, in addition to doing meaningful work, are the personal relationships in his life—his wife of twelve years and his seventeen-year-old daughter from a previous marriage, who came to live with him a few years ago. "While my career has become progressively more important to me over the past ten years, my primary relationship has mellowed to the point of being more consistently meaningful and enjoyable now. People have always seen me as a calm and easygoing person but I often didn't feel that way on the inside. Perhaps I appeared that way but now I'm really feeling more so. I'm more and more aware of my feelings and can be clear and direct about them."

A major change in Dan is his ability to spend a good deal of his professional life standing up before large groups of people. "I used to have anxiety attacks if I had to speak to groups. So I actually volunteered for a teaching assignment when I was in my last year of college. I remember feeling panic before that class, afraid no one would listen to me or I'd forget my material. But I gradually desensitized myself to the anxiety. I came to enjoy it, and now, unless the group is huge, I don't feel any nervousness before a talk. But as much as I enjoy it, my strength is really in small group interaction."

Dan has also developed a better sense of what is realistic and has, out of necessity, become more organized in running his business "I never have been able to manage money and I would probably be much more financially successful by now if I had. But I get great pleasure from being productive and goal-oriented because it keeps me moving on to new opportunities."

Moving and changing are the keys to happiness for Dan. "Doing meaningful work that benefits others, being regarded with respect by my clients and audiences, and being financially rewarded so I can enjoy life and feel successful, all come together to mean career satisfaction for me. The major decisions in my life have almost been unconscious. I didn't set out with a goal of getting one particular job to make me happy. I think you need to find work that is personally enjoyable and meaningful to you and then make a career out of it. It worked for me!"

Why This Career Works for Dan

Although promoting harmonious relationships between people comes naturally to most Idealists, Dan has made it his life's work. His specialty—helping people resolve interpersonal conflicts—is an outgrowth of his more general Idealist interest in helping people understand themselves and each other. Being self-employed, Dan has the flexibility and variety he needs. His time is divided between working with individuals, training groups, writing, and spending time enjoying his rewarding and meaningful personal relationships with his wife and daughter—which provides a satisfying balance in his life.

To an introverted Feeler (dominant) such as Dan, work must be personally meaningful. He has become successful because he believes so deeply in the value of mediation and the effectiveness of his techniques. Since he places such a high value on interpersonal harmony, he experiences great satisfaction when he sees the positive results of his work, just as he does when he feels the respect and affection from the people he works with. Dan's relationships with his family are central to his life. And because he travels extensively, he keeps expanding his own level of understanding, which he uses to improve his relationships.

Dan owes his success in developing his creative programs and materials to his extraverted Intuition (auxiliary). His Intuition also helps him integrate different techniques such as role playing, small-group discussion, and discovery exercises into his programs to help participants increase their self-awareness and interpersonal effectiveness. He has developed innovative marketing techniques to sell services and products that he continuously works to improve. Developing his Sensing (third function) has helped Dan become more realistic in running his business. He is better at some of the specifics of managing money and financial planning. Dan finds he is much more organized than he was in earlier years. He also enjoys the tangible proof of his success—the possessions and vacations he can now afford.

Common Threads

Although Emily, Dan, and Darren have different backgrounds, experiences, and careers, there are certain common threads that weave through their stories. Specific interests and abilities may differ, but owing to their similar temperament values, the *same hierarchy* of their psychological functions, and the "world" they naturally use them in (inner or outer), there are certain observations we can make about the needs of many INFPs.

What follows is a list of the most important elements—the formula, if you will—for INFP satisfaction. Given the uniqueness of all individuals—even those who share the same type—this list will not describe each INFP equally well. The important thing is that these ten elements, with varying degrees of intensity and in different orders of importance, identify what INFPs need to be satisfied.

After you have reviewed this list, we recommend that you go back and prioritize the elements in order of *their importance to you*. When doing this, think of past work experiences as well as your present job, and what you found particularly satisfying or unsatisfying. Try to look for *themes* that run through several experiences, not just the events which might be true for one work situation but not for another.

As an INFP, career satisfaction means doing work that:

1. Is in harmony with my own personal values and beliefs and allows me to express my vision through my work
2. Gives me time to develop substantial depth to my ideas and maintain control over the process and product
3. Is done autonomously, with a private work space and plenty of uninterrupted time, but with periodic opportunities to bounce my ideas off people I feel respect me
4. Is done within a flexible structure, with a minimum of rules or regulations, letting me work on projects when I feel inspired
5. Is done with other creative and caring individuals in a cooperative environment free from tension and interpersonal strife
6. Lets me express my originality and in which personal growth is encouraged and rewarded
7. Does not require me to present my work frequently in front of groups of people or be called upon to share before it is completed to my satisfaction
8. Allows me to help others grow and develop and realize their full potential
9. Involves understanding people and discovering what makes them tick; allows me to develop deep one-to-one relationships with others
10. Allows me to work toward fulfilling my ideals and not be limited by political, financial, or other obstacles

Popular Occupations for INFPs

In listing occupations that are popular among INFPs, it is important to note that there are successful people of all types in all occupations. However, the following are careers INFPs may find particularly satisfying and some of the reasons why. This is by no means a comprehensive listing but is included to suggest possibilities you may not have previously considered. Although all of these occupations offer the potential for career satisfaction, the future demand for some careers is anticipated to be greater than for others. Based upon our research, the occupations that are italicized in the lists below are forecast to enjoy the fastest rate of growth over the next several years.

CREATIVE/ARTS
- Artist
- Writer: poet/novelist
- Journalist
- Graphic designer

- Architect
- Actor
- Editor
- Musician
- Informational-graphics designer
- Editor/art director (magazine)
- Multimedia producer
- Video game designer
- Editor/art director (website)
- Composer
- Film editor
- Set designer
- Interior designer
- Print designer
- Interaction designer

- *Online educator*
- Employee assistance counselor
- Child welfare counselor
- *Substance abuse counselor*
- *Social worker (elderly and child day care issues)*
- *Interpreter/translator*
- Legal mediator
- Planned-giving officer
- Philanthropic consultant
- Career counselor/coach
- Grant coordinator
- Genealogist
- Curator
- *Public health educator*

The appeal of the arts to INFPs is the ability to express themselves and their ideas in creative and personal ways. The personal freedom and flexibility of a working artist is a lifestyle often embraced by INFPs. Whether they work with the written word, a paintbrush or other medium, use their building designs or their own bodies as actors or musicians, INFPs strive to create original products that are authentic expressions of their inner voice. Many INFPs describe themselves as artists "deep down," even if that is not how they earn their living. Some INFPs would even say that being an artist is not something they would choose to be, rather that it's a cross they have to bear.

EDUCATION/COUNSELING
- *College professor: humanities/arts*
- Researcher
- Clinical psychologist
- *Mental health counselor*
- *Marriage and family therapist*
- *Social worker*
- Librarian
- Educational consultant
- Special education teacher
- *Bilingual education teacher*
- *Early childhood education teacher*

Both teaching and counseling are career areas that enable the INFP to work with others to help them grow and develop their human potential. INFPs can be truly noble in their desire and efforts to improve the quality of life for others. They often prefer the college atmosphere to elementary or even secondary education because the motivation of the students is higher. They enjoy the process of learning and enjoy exploring deeper and more meaningful levels of understanding as researchers or librarians. INFPs make compassionate and insightful counselors, psychologists, and social workers and strive toward helping their clients gain self-understanding and harmony within their relationships and their lives. As counselors, they enjoy the process of understanding others as they come to understand themselves.

RELIGION
- Minister/priest
- Religious educator
- Missionary
- Church worker
- Pastoral counselor

For many INFPs the commitment of a religious career is rewarding. INFPs enjoy helping other people develop their spiritual side and receive pleasure from striving for and attaining their vision for themselves and others. They often prefer a one-on-one setting but with experience can come to enjoy preaching or lecturing. The bottom line for an INFP is to do work that is in harmony with their inner values and beliefs, and often careers within religion provide that.

HEALTH CARE
- *Dietitian/nutritionist*
- *Physical therapist*
- *Home health social worker*
- *Occupational therapist*
- *Speech-language pathologist/audiologist*
- Massage therapist
- *Holistic health practitioner (alternative medicine)*
- Arts therapist
- Geneticist
- Ethicist

The appealing aspects of these health care fields for many INFPs is the ability to work closely and intimately with clients or patients. INFPs generally prefer the autonomy that most of these careers provide them, working in their own practice or as a consultant to a larger health care institution. The creative and often spiritual elements of diagnosis and treatment of physical therapy, holistic therapies, and massage are satisfying uses of an INFP's intuition and feeling preferences.

ORGANIZATIONAL DEVELOPMENT
- *Employment development specialist*
- *Human resources development trainer*
- Social scientist
- *Diversity manager: human resources*
- Consultant: team building/conflict resolution
- Industrial-organizational psychologist

- *Outplacement consultant*
- *Labor relations specialist*
- *Corporate/team trainer*

Although INFPs are not usually satisfied in business careers, there are some selected fields that offer potential for success and satisfaction. Some INFPs enjoy a corporate setting when their work involves helping other people find jobs that are right for them. They often enjoy jobs in personnel, or human resources development, or designing and instituting jobs within a company. They need to work with other supportive people and feel that their contributions are valued and unique in order to find satisfaction in the tough and competitive world of business.

TECHNOLOGY
- *Customer relations manager*
- Staff advocate (technology consultant)
- Project manager
- Engagement manager
- Human resources recruiter
- Educational software developer

With the proliferation of technology, there is a rapidly growing need for people who understand technology but also have good people and communication skills. Being the liaison between the technology people and the end users appeals to many INFPs, who find these jobs satisfy their need to help and be connected with their co-workers.

Customizing Your Job Search

Knowing the particular strengths and blind spots of your type can afford you a tremendous advantage in your job search campaign. In all aspects of the process, from conducting research into available positions, identifying and contacting prospective employers, developing personal marketing tools such as résumés, arranging and conducting job interviews, negotiating salaries to finally accepting a position, people will act true to their type. Being able to capitalize on your assets and compensate for your liabilities can make the difference between a successful and an unsuccessful job search.

Differences between types are sometimes subtle and other times dramatic. It is the subtle variations in advice we offer that make the real difference between success or failure in a job search. The concept of "networking," or meeting with and talking to people to gather information about potential jobs, serves as a good example. Extraverts will naturally enjoy networking and are advised to do so on a large scale, while Introverts find more limited and targeted networking, especially with people they already know, easier. Sensors tend to network with people in a defined scope, while Intuitives will go far and wide to find people often seemingly unrelated to their field of interest. Further, Feelers take networking, like everything else, very personally and enjoy establishing warm rapport, while Thinkers will be more objective and detached in their style. Finally, Judgers tend to ask fewer and more structured questions during their networking, while Perceivers could ask questions of all sorts all day long! One valuable search technique, many ways to implement it.

Pathways to Success: Using Your Strengths

As we will detail in the following pages, your strength and talent for the job search lie in your ability to know what is important to you and to work tirelessly to find a career that will be an expression of your values. Beware of your tendency to be swept away by your idealism and, in the process, ignore practical realities.

As an INFP, your most effective strategies will build on your abilities to:

Readily see possibilities that don't presently exist.

- Use your creative energy to look beyond what is known, and imagine jobs that you might be satisfied with that meet the needs of the market or employer.
- Generate as long a list as possible of all the ways you can use your skills in fields that interest you. After you have created a lengthy list, research each option so you will be able to put together a more realistic plan of attack.

The staff at the magazine where Sarah worked as a research assistant was being cut back. Instead of waiting to hear whether the ax would fall on her, Sarah came up with an innovative staffing solution that would save her job and the job of another research assistant. Sarah and her co-worker offered to job-share the research position, thus saving the magazine the cost of two full-time researchers. In exchange, Sarah would write freelance articles for the magazine on an as-needed basis and be free to write for other publications as well. Her solution enabled her co-worker finally to have time to finish her master's degree. The magazine accepted the proposal and Sarah saved her job.

Give thoughtful consideration to all potential career opportunities.

- Your patience with complex tasks will serve you well if you give time and thought to each possible career avenue, and you will be better prepared to talk about why you are the right person for the job.

- Time spent in reflection will give you the chance to clarify your true feelings and motivation before accepting or rejecting an option.

Greg was in the enviable position of having received job offers from three architecture firms. However, he felt overwhelmed by the decision he had to make. So he asked each for two weeks in which to consider the offers. One firm said they needed his answer immediately, so he declined, confident in the knowledge that a firm in that much of a hurry was not a place he wanted to work. He spent the next two weeks carefully thinking through the advantages and disadvantages of the remaining options and what was most important to him in a work environment. Because he took the time, he was able to recall some factors about each office that he had forgotten in the excitement of the interviews. When the two weeks were over, he was able to make a thoughtful and confident decision.

Express yourself well, especially after thinking things through ahead of time.

- Whenever possible, find ways to express yourself in writing through letters of inquiry, cover letters sent with a résumé, or follow-up letters.
- Use words to help you verbalize your vision for your career or for the ways in which you see yourself adding to the growth and development of an organization.

Timothy, a career counselor, found *himself* looking for work after cutbacks at the community college where he had worked left him unemployed. Though Timothy certainly knew the tricks of the trade, the tight job market made his job search difficult.

We suggested that he target a private career consulting firm and sell himself by what he could offer the company. Because he had many of the same skills as other candidates, he decided to set himself apart by expressing his personal motivation to help others find truly fulfilling work which would result in more referral business. The partners of the firm were impressed by his genuine concern and decided he would take the time to be sure their clients were well served, and increase the bottom line as well.

Demonstrate your motivation and commitment to causes you believe in.

- Allow prospective employers to see and hear your enthusiasm for a position you want. Most employers are impressed with a candidate who is direct and clear about his or her interest in a job.
- When discussing how a potential job fits with your ideals, use your natural persuasiveness to convince potential employers of the intensity of your desire for the position.

Each applicant was told to prepare a selection of music suitable for three church choirs for an audition for the position of choir director. Melissa chose to let her words and musical selections not only fill an assignment but also express her desire for the job. She spent hours going over her selections so they would reflect her love of music, her eagerness to work with singers of all ages, and her own personal faith. She wrote a statement that she read to the selection committee which explained her choices of music and how each was thematically connected to the other pieces so the choir was, essentially, singing chapters of a book. She went a step farther and left copies of her statement, hand calligraphed, with her résumé and references. The committee was impressed with her diligence, care, and devotion, all the characteristics Melissa hoped they would associate with her.

Use limited, targeted networking.

- Start with close friends from your professional or personal life. Carefully select other people to help you, relying on people who know you well or are directly involved in the field you seek.
- Plot out your strategy, including a timetable for accomplishing objectives to keep you from becoming overwhelmed or discouraged.

Before she even got started on her job search, Lilly felt that she was in over her head. She knew she wasn't very organized and wasn't even sure how to begin finding out about available jobs. Her sister suggested she attend a time management seminar being offered through the continuing education department in their town. Lilly at first resisted the idea of a prepackaged program but finally succumbed to her sister's urging and went. She found that while parts of the seminar were too regimented, it gave her an excellent framework. She modified and adapted the basic program to work for her. She also gained some added confidence because she now had a way of ensuring that she wouldn't let things slip through the cracks. She was able to get started, and feel as if she was much more in control of the process.

Possible Pitfalls

Although all people are unique, there are certain *potential* blind spots that many INFPs share. We specify "potential" because some

of the following *may* be true of you, while others may clearly not apply. While considering them, you may notice that these tendencies do not relate just to the job search, but rather describe pitfalls that you may have experienced in other aspects of your life as well. It is therefore helpful to consider each one in terms of your past experiences by asking yourself, "Is this true for me?" And if so, "How did this tendency prevent me from getting something that I wanted?" You will probably notice that the key to overcoming your blind spots is the conscious and thoughtful development of your third and fourth functions (Sensing and Thinking). We recognize that many of the suggestions will be difficult to implement, but the more you use these functions, the fewer problems they will cause you in the future.

Develop realistic expectations for yourself and your job search.

- Realize that finding the right job takes more time than you expect or wish. Paying attention to the facts of the situation and including them in your vision of the right career choice will make you more efficient during your search.
- You may have to decide to compromise some of your less central personal values from time to time. There may not be the "perfect" job for you at the salary level or in the geographic area you live in—at least not at this time. Learning when to compromise on the less critical points is a valuable lesson.

Try not to take criticism or rejection personally.

- Bear in mind that many people offer criticism in a very objective fashion and expect that you will take it as it was intended. Try to look at it as *constructive* criticism and use the knowledge to improve your approach.

- Draw some boundaries and don't try to please too many people at the same time. A career search is a time-consuming task. Being willing to say no to others when necessary will help you conserve needed energy and maintain your focus.

Look at the logical consequence of your actions.

- Try not to make important decisions relying exclusively on your personal feelings. Get input from trusted, more objective friends.
- Take a break from the situation to think more clearly about it. Imagine what might be the logical cause and effect of your choices so you will have a more balanced picture.

Resist the tendency to avoid eliminating options and to put off making decisions.

- Take charge of your job search by eliminating less desirable options rather than waiting so long that more attractive options are eliminated for you. You may find the whole process less overwhelming if you remove from consideration those possibilities that don't fit with your most important criteria for career satisfaction.
- Don't spend so much time in reflection that you leave no time for action! Develop a timetable and stick with it. Remember that getting started is often the hardest part, but once you do, you will gain momentum from your actions.

Concentrate on getting better organized.

- Use time management techniques to be sure you get things done on time. Employers will judge you on how well you follow through with commitments.
- Beware that you are naturally prone to perfectionism, which may delay you from completing tasks, hoping to find some way to improve them.

The Final Piece: Changing or Keeping Your Job . . . the Key to Success for INFPs

Now that you have a solid understanding of your type, you can see how your natural preferences make you better suited for certain kinds of jobs. You can also see how knowledge of your type-related strengths and weaknesses can help you conduct a more successful job search. But as an INFP, you've already realized that you are not equally drawn to *every* career or field listed in the Popular Occupations section. The next and final step is to narrow down the field and find the work you were meant to do.

In addition to Type, several other factors—such as your values, interests, and skills—also contribute to your level of satisfaction on the job. The more compatible you are with your job, the happier you'll be. So prepare to use everything you've learned (in this book and in life) to create *your strategic career plan.* The exercises in Chapter 24, Putting It All Together, are designed to help you do just that.

However, you may have decided it makes more sense (if perhaps only for the moment) to stay in your present job or with your current employer. There may be many valid reasons—financial pressures, family considerations, a tough job market for your specialty, or just bad timing. But take heart! What you've learned in this book can also help you be more content and successful *in your current job.* And should the time come when you're ready to make a major career move, you'll have a much better idea of where you want to go, and how to get there.

"So, if you can't have the job you love (yet!)...love the one you've got."

The simple truth is, with the exception of work on a factory assembly line, the vast majority of jobs allow a good deal of flexibility in the way tasks are performed. Here are some ways you may be able to "massage" your current job into one that better fits your needs:

- Volunteer to help draft your organization's/department's mission statement.
- Delegate certain details or routine tasks to others.
- Take a course in conflict resolution and become a mediator.
- Consider becoming a trainer or coach in your field of expertise.
- Work a different shift or arrange more flexible hours, or job-share.
- Do more of your work from your home.
- E-mail a friend with an inspirational message of support daily, weekly, or when the spirit moves you.
- Stay in the same occupation but switch employers.
- Go back to school for more or specialized training.

One INFP turns lemons into lemonade:

As a result of an unfortunate experience his sister had with her supervisor, Jason became aware of the pervasiveness of sexual harassment in the workplace. He felt so strongly that people should absolutely feel safe in their jobs that he began researching the workplace harassment problem and what was being done about it around the country. Jason was fast becoming something of an expert in the subject, so he offered to conduct a short workshop for his department. It was so well received that the director of the Employee Assistance Program offered Jason the chance to repeat the workshop, this time for the entire company.

Use what you've got to get what you need.

Simply put, the best advice on how to succeed is to *capitalize on your strengths and compensate for your weaknesses.* Learning how to do this can make the difference between succeeding or failing and loving or hating your work. To help you, we include the following inventory of your potential strengths and weaknesses. And while every individual is unique, as an INFP, many of the following should apply to you.

Your work-related strengths may include:

- Thoughtfulness and the ability to focus on one issue or idea in depth
- Eagerness to "think outside the box" and consider new possibilities
- Deep commitment to work you believe in
- Ability to work well alone if necessary
- Natural curiosity and skill for getting the information you need
- Ability to see the big picture and to see implications of actions and ideas
- Perceptiveness about peoples' needs and motivations
- Adaptability; you can shift gears and change directions quickly
- Ability to work extremely well with people one-on-one

Your work-related weaknesses may include:

- Need to control projects or you may lose interest
- Tendency toward disorganization and difficulty setting priorities
- Difficulty working on projects that conflict with your values
- Reluctance to follow traditional ways of doing things
- Natural idealism, which may prevent you from having realistic expectations
- Dislike of doing things in traditional or routine ways
- Difficulty working in competitive or tension-filled environments
- Lack of discipline about attending to and following through on important details
- Impatience working with structures or people who are too rigid
- Tendency to be unrealistic about how long things take
- Reluctance to discipline direct-reports and criticize others

---

Using your strengths is easy.
The secret to success for an
INFP
is learning to:

Develop realistic expectations, value compromise, and not take things quite so personally.

12 | ENTJ
Extraverted, Intuitive, Thinking, Judging

"Everything's Fine—I'm in Charge"

Profile 1: Ted

"Developing the potential of existing organizations."

Ted is a hard worker and values that about himself. He puts in long hours at his job as the president of a community leadership development program as well as working hard as a volunteer on various community improvement projects. Ted loves accomplishing things, having events and projects work well, achieving his goals, and successfully advocating a cause he believes in. But he also strives to achieve a balance between his busy work life, his active volunteer life, and his home life, which he shares with his wife and two young daughters.

In his job as president of the community leadership program, Ted strives toward "getting people from different parts of the community to work together to improve the community while developing their own skills." He administers and coordinates a year-long training program that is aimed at

issue awareness, as well as skill and network building for the participants. His day is filled with phone calls, written communication, and meetings of all sorts. "Basically I put people together who might not ordinarily get together, matching the available skills with the existing needs and interests. That's what building a community and making it work better are all about." Ted also oversees the production of periodic newsletters, annual reports, and evaluations, and the planning and organization of a variety of events and meetings.

Ted enjoys his role as a "broker" and his "broker instinct" the job fulfills. He is energized by being the one whom others think of as having the information, and he is confident that the information he has can help others. He enjoys solving difficult and abstract problems, thinking logically, and determining what steps are necessary to meet the defined goals.

It's the routine jobs that Ted likes least. He used to enjoy proposal writing, but now that he has done it and has mastered that skill, he finds himself either putting it off or delegating it to a member of his staff. He knows the latter works better for him. "It's a double-edged sword—all of the tasks, even fund-raising, are easy for me now, but once something is too simple, I have no patience with it." And, as a result, he is less thorough.

Ted's career path reads, in some ways, like a career-planning textbook case study. With a degree in sociology, Ted worked his first few years out of college with severely and profoundly retarded adult men. There he learned how important it was for him to work as part of a team, trying to make a difference. But after a while, the work became too routine and stressful, so he returned to school to obtain his master's degree in social work with a specialty in community organization and a minor in administration. He obtained an internship in a business-backed think tank/resource center working with a coalition of housing groups. He was offered a staff position at that organization and found his mentor there. "He was a really smart man, politically smart, and was great at putting people together and moving a common agenda forward." Next Ted moved on to an executive directorship of a community-based social service agency, a job he was initially unqualified for but for which he rose to the challenge and found tremendous satisfaction and success. "I was really over my head, but I'm a survivor. It was a great learning experience." It was there that he learned how to write grants, supervise others, and use his creative thinking for fund-raising. After five years, he was ready for a change and a new challenge because "everything was settled." He found out about the job he now holds through his network. "At first I wasn't crazy about the environment because it was sponsored by the business community, but being part of a talented staff, being in a new

and challenging position, and being able to take risks made it worth it." Ted's been enjoying the job for the past five years.

Ted is good at making connections: "people with people, the past with the future, what is with what could be." He is a good abstract thinker, listens well, and recognizes good ideas when he sees them. And he can evaluate ideas, the good and the not-so-good. Ted gets the greatest satisfaction from getting things done, from seeing projects succeed and hearing from other people that what he's accomplished was done well and meant something to others. He works hard to earn the respect of others.

The rare on-the-job stress Ted experiences comes from the personnel management tasks he occasionally must handle. "Dealing with difficult interpersonal situations and relationships is very taxing. Luckily I have a very effective staff and they don't need a lot of discipline." To cope with the occasional stress that Ted does experience, he seeks the support of a very few close friends, "someone I can talk openly with and get support and honest feedback." Ted also enjoys the adventures he takes with his children and the fun he has playing on a softball team. He coaches T-ball, helping kids to develop a team spirit and learn how to win and lose.

Ted's family life has remained a constant over the years. His values haven't changed much, either. But his view of work has become more practical, he's more pragmatic, and he has a better sense of how the world works. He realizes that he has fulfilled much of his ambition to "work hard in a meaningful job, to play an important role, and make substantive changes in the community."

The secret of Ted's success in reaching his goals is that he strives first to do a good job and then to receive the recognition he deserves for his achievements. He networks extensively and constantly, letting people know what he's doing. He finds that those who work in the same groups become not only his friends but his advocates. Those connections have proved invaluable to him as he has progressed from challenge to challenge. "That, and a bit of luck!"

Why This Career Works for Ted

Ted's job is developing potential, in organizations and in people. True to his Conceptualizer temperament, he likes taking on huge challenges and enjoys finding new solutions to complex and difficult problems. Ted works hard at increasing his own and others' competency, as is demonstrated by the community leadership program. It is important to him that others respect him for the quality of his work.

Extraverting his Thinking (dominant) is how Ted evaluates and analyzes which approach will be most effective in meeting his goals. He enjoys planning and making decisions based upon sound, objective criteria. He is logical and very good at thinking through the consequences of proposed plans. His Thinking also comes in

handy in helping him to organize his time so that he can prioritize the very diverse types of activities that require his attention on any given day.

Through his introverted Intuition (auxiliary), he sees the implications of actions, the big picture, and how all of the individual pieces of the puzzle fit together. Attracted to new ideas, he naturally sees connections: between people, between the past and the future, and between how things are and how they can be improved.

As someone who is developing his (third function) Sensing, Ted has become more practical and pragmatic about getting things done in the work world by increasing his awareness and memory of realistic details. Ted is more likely to know exactly which steps need to be taken in what order to put a new program in place. As a source of recreation and relaxation, Ted enjoys physical experiences such as engaging in sports and playing with his children—also possible evidence he is using his Sensing more often and with greater enjoyment.

Meet the Millennial

Name: Skip
Age: 26
Creative producer of communication design at a social networking site

"Connecting the world."

Backstory

Skip has been obsessed with telling stories for as long as he can remember. "I started writing little movies with my friends, and every class assignment that could remotely be related to film I made into a movie project." Despite some ambivalence from parents who weren't

(continued)

exactly sure how practical a film degree was, Skip went to college for film in 2005. Simultaneously, Skip was becoming fascinated by a fledgling website for college students that in a matter of years would become the predominant social networking site in the world.

At the time, the site had been around for only a year and had less than one million users. "I just loved it—I thought it was the future." In the fall of his freshman year, Skip saw in an ad on the site that they were looking for a filmmaker in New York. At that point, the company had less than fifty employees and was trying to gauge public opinion of the website on college campuses. Skip was hired to produce a short holiday film capturing how students felt about the site, which was the beginning of his long relationship with the company. He continued making videos for the sales and marketing teams, and in the summer after his freshman year Skip moved out to their Palo Alto headquarters, where he worked to design and craft creative campaigns for companies looking for advertising opportunities.

That summer Skip watched the team in Palo Alto grow to over 150 people, and when the summer ended, he struggled mightily with whether he should drop out of school and join the team full-time. "It was the hardest decision I've ever made." Ultimately, Skip decided to go back to school, a decision he doesn't regret. He continued to contract for the company almost full-time while attending school, and after graduation he pursued work with other clients—a start-up, script development—before returning to the website to work on directing product

launch films for the company and then broadening his scope to branding.

Now in the Communication Design Department—an in-house creative team that conceives, produces, and designs all creative communication—Skip is responsible for producing projects that tie the website "to a cultural sphere, so that when people experience that cultural sphere, there's a personal resonance with the brand." One project that exemplifies this is the real-time election map they produced for the 2012 presidential election that showed millions of users voting at the same time. "For the first time ever, we were able to visualize democracy in action. Through the simple act of clicking 'I Voted,' we helped present this website as a real-time network where people could express what they believe in."

A Good Fit

Skip's specialty is envisioning new ideas and then seeing them through to fruition. "It's about making sure that the team is working toward the overall vision and goals we had from the beginning and that we actually get the thing built." His dominant Thinking function gives him an architectural mind-set and helps him make his ideas a reality. Like most Conceptualizers, Skip has a natural gift for problem solving. "I can't think of many other companies that are trying to solve a problem bigger than the one we are working to solve in the world: trying to connect humanity." Skip's auxiliary function of Intuition is very much in evidence in branding, as he works to make connections between his product and the cultural resonance he wishes to create. Skip's Extraversion explains both his initial draw to a social networking website as well as his belief in its mission to connect the world. Goal-oriented, ambitious, and driven, Skip uses his Judging function to help him close the deal and focus on the end product.

Looking Ahead

While Skip loves the website and his role in the company, his end goal is to move into producing feature films, and more specifically, to run a production company that is vertically integrated. "I want to be on the ground floor of development and sourcing for material, conceiving and developing that material, producing it, and then distributing it in totally new ways that we haven't seen before."

Profile 2: Jane

"Having the authority, autonomy, and resources to accomplish important things."

Jane has a double Rolodex on her desk that is bulging and ready to be expanded. So when she started her own consulting business a few years ago and "called a few friends," she soon had more business than she could handle. Knowing lots of people has been a career enhancer for Jane. She's not only been in the right place at the right time to be hired for most of the jobs she's held, but she has the "ability to recognize the right thing." So it was with the job she enjoys now.

Jane serves as president of a nonprofit council of foundations. The organization analyzes the funding requests of nonprofit groups seeking support and provides information about the grant seekers to the corporations and foundations that make grants available. She started the job a year ago after the organization had been run exclusively by one person for the twenty years since its founding. Jane was "hired to find out what the organization was doing and to change it by determining what kind of information was needed and how it should be disseminated." That means collecting a great deal of data. She reviews grant applications, researches the grant seekers, and becomes familiar with the grant giver's goals and objectives and with their available resources. She does most of this through site visits, which are her preferred way of gathering information. But she also spends a great deal of time on the telephone simply because there aren't enough hours in the day to visit all the people she'd like to. In fact, she is currently trying to cut her sixty- to seventy-hour-per-week schedule down to forty to fifty hours to give her the personal life she now realizes she wants. Jane is thirty-six and recently married.

"The best part about the job is that I get to give my advice and opinions all day and people listen to me!" She enjoys the planning, especially long-range planning, involved in dealing with large and complex issues like "affordable housing" or "AIDS in the community." She readily sees the connections between vastly different members of the community. "I can hear what the problems are from the consulting role I play with both the grant makers and grant seekers. And I can help them see the solutions."

What Jane enjoys least are the details and endless small tasks required of someone working alone because, at present, there is no one to delegate to. These activities include short correspondence, acknowledgments, thank-you letters, and referrals she receives during a busy day. She often leaves them in an ever growing stack until a weekend day, when she spends five or six hours tackling the entire pile and completes it all in one sitting.

"I'm also drained by the politicking I am required to do with the board of directors. Because everything I've done since I started has involved change, it's required a whole lot of time preparing the board members individually—a lot of hand-holding, which is a new experience for me and one I'm finding to be difficult."

Jane is a good delegator and misses the camaraderie of working with others. Now that she has analyzed the needs and potential of the organization, she is in the process of hiring a staff.

Jane went to college to become an elementary school teacher but decided midway through that she liked the concept better in the abstract. So instead she got a degree in English and went to work immediately after graduation as an admissions counselor for her alma mater. "I traveled, interviewed applicants, gave advice, talked to hundreds of people—it was a wonderful job." She decided after two years that she was ready for a new challenge, and since she had enjoyed the responsibility of designing the school's admissions publications, she went to work as an account executive at a New York City public relations firm. "I handled mostly nonprofit accounts, which was OK, but I was in over my head. I had much more responsibility than my experience warranted." After one year she left and returned to her home city.

Her next position was as associate director of an arts council, doing fund-raising. After a year, when the directorship became available, she applied for the position. The board considered her to be too young for the position but offered her a huge salary increase in exchange for her commitment to stay one year and help train the new director. She agreed, even though it meant she did two jobs.

She moved on to a director's position at another arts organization and then to director of development and public relations for a private school for deaf children. "I loved that job, mostly because of the great staff I assembled. We're still all very good friends. That's where I learned to build and appreciate a team. We all grew professionally and personally without outgrowing the jobs." But finally she left "on principle" because she saw that the school was unwilling to take the necessary direction to survive in a changing marketplace. "I took a year to try everything that interested me and kept everything open, which was extremely difficult." She began consulting on public relations and fund-raising projects and for two years had more business than she could handle. "I really just called a few friends, but I guess I know a lot of people!" It was during that time that she was approached to apply for the foundation presidency. "I was so relaxed in the interview because I didn't think I'd actually get it. I was never more surprised than when they offered me the job. Winning this job is probably my greatest accomplishment, so far."

Seeing relationships between ideas and being an analytical, strategic thinker are among Jane's greatest strengths. "But because I think in pretty complex ways, I'm not always able to communicate what I see in ways others can understand. Sometimes I can get impatient." Jane also experiences stress when she can't put all of her ideas into practice immediately. She is learning to manage stress better and finds she now confides in her husband and close friends to avoid getting sick, which she is prone to do when stress becomes too intense. "I'm trying to exercise more and to accept the reality that everything can't always be done perfectly."

Jane expects to stay at this job for approximately four years, or "until I've perfected the organization and then it'll be time for me to leave." She anticipates that she might go into business for herself again, working in a less structured fashion, allowing her to travel and spend time with her husband. Or she might work toward being appointed Secretary of Education for the U.S. government. "I've learned to accept without embarrassment the fact that I want to be in charge, I want to be the boss, I'm good at it, and that's OK! I value the fact that I'm honest and direct. I make reasonable and balanced decisions. And I am accurate and just."

Jane is a more secure person than she used to be, more tuned in to the values of others and sensitive to their needs, a quality she developed through working with the private school team. "I'm also less radical than I used to be, I've softened a bit. And I'm much more realistic. I've had a lot of lucky breaks, but I recognize good opportunities when I see them. My natural curiosity has led me to the best learning situations. But I was always willing to do whatever it took to get the job done right. And of course, I like to network, although I never called it that. I just meet people, and I never throw away a name and phone number!"

Why This Career Works for Jane

Jane was recruited for her current position in order to "fix the organization." Like most Conceptualizers, she thrives on solving problems—the more challenging, the better. She also enjoys being the boss and having a position that couples great responsibility with enough control to make things happen her way.

Jane uses her extraverted Thinking (dominant) to make the many decisions required of her. She also uses her Thinking to analyze an organization and provide honest and direct feedback as to its strengths, weaknesses, and what it must do to improve. She must objectively evaluate an organization's needs and engage in the long-range planning necessary to help the organization develop resources to meet those needs—activities which come naturally to her and which she enjoys.

To perform her job, Jane must collect a tremendous amount of data about the people she works with. She uses her introverted Intuition (auxiliary) to understand the motivations and operating styles of diverse types of people and to come up with creative approaches to solving the many problems associated with putting the fund givers and seekers together.

Evidence that Jane has become more comfortable with her Sensing (third function) can be found in her assessment that she feels her decisions are more workable—more realistic now than in the past. She has also become more aware of her body, the effect of stress on it, and how useful exercise is at reducing stress. And for the first time, she is making time for her personal life by arranging to spend more time with her husband—a possible sign of the influence of her emerging Feeling function.

Common Threads

Although Ted, Jane, and Skip have different backgrounds, experiences, and careers, there are certain common threads woven through their stories. Their specific interests, abilities, and values may differ, but owing to their similar temperament values, the *same hierarchy* of their psychological functions, and the "world" they use them in (inner or outer), there are certain observations we can make about the needs of many ENTJs.

What follows is a list of the most important elements—the formula, if you will—for ENTJ satisfaction. Given the uniqueness of all individuals—even those who share the same type—this list will not describe each ENTJ equally well. The important thing is that these ten elements, with varying degrees of intensity and in different orders of importance, identify what ENTJs need to be satisfied.

After you have reviewed this list, we recommend that you go back and prioritize the elements in order of *their importance to you*. When doing this, think of past work experiences as well as your present job, and what you found particularly satisfying or unsatisfying. Try to look for *themes* that run through several experiences, not just the events that might be true for one work situation but not for another.

As an ENTJ, career satisfaction means doing work that:

1. Lets me lead, be in control, organizing and perfecting the operating systems of an organization so that it runs efficiently and reaches its goals on schedule
2. Lets me engage in long-range strategic planning, creative problem solving, and the generation of innovative and logical approaches to a variety of problems
3. Is done in a well-organized environment where I, and others, work within a clear and definite set of guidelines
4. Challenges and stimulates my intellectual curiosity and lets me work with complex and often difficult problems

5. Gives me opportunities to meet and interact with a variety of other capable, interesting, and powerful people
6. Gives me the opportunity to advance within the organization and to increase and demonstrate my competence
7. Is exciting, challenging, and competitive; where I am in the public eye and where my accomplishments are seen, recognized, and fairly compensated
8. Lets me work with other intelligent, creative, ambitious, and goal-oriented individuals whose competencies I respect
9. Lets me set and meet goals and implement my organizational skills to keep myself and others focused on the larger goal while accomplishing all my objectives in a timely and efficient manner
10. Lets me manage and supervise others, using logical and objective standards and policies that utilize each person's strengths but without having to deal daily with interpersonal squabbles

Popular Occupations for ENTJs

In listing occupations that are popular among ENTJs, it is important to note that there are successful people of all types in all occupations. However, the following are careers ENTJs may find particularly satisfying and some of the reasons why. This is by no means a comprehensive listing but is included to suggest possibilities you may not have previously considered. Although all of these occupations offer the potential for career satisfaction, the future demand for some careers is anticipated to be greater than for others. Based upon our research, the occupations that are italicized in the lists below are forecast to enjoy the fastest rate of growth over the next several years.

BUSINESS
- Executive
- Senior manager
- Office manager
- Administrator
- Personnel manager
- *Management analyst*
- *Business development director*
- *Market research analyst*
- Network integration specialist (telecommunications)
- Technical trainer
- Information services–new business developer
- Logistics consultant (manufacturing)
- Management consultant: computer/ information services, marketing, reorganization
- *Advertising account manager*
- Marketing executive: online/radio/TV/ cable broadcast industry
- Media planner/buyer
- International sales and marketing
- *Franchise owner*
- *Sales manager*
- *Health care administrator*
- College and university administrator
- Managing editor
- Theater producer
- Police and detective supervisor
- *Human resources manager*
- Association manager and adviser
- Program director
- Project manager
- Retail manager
- Real estate manager
- Restaurant and food service manager

The world of business is often enjoyed by ENTJs. They prefer to be in positions of authority, control, and leadership. As business executives, they are able to use their long-range thinking to develop contingency plans and map out the best course to meet their goals. ENTJs use a style of direct management, able to make tough yet fair decisions and set policies for employees. They like to surround themselves with other independent, results-oriented people who can work without a lot of supervision or intervention. ENTJs usually rise to the top of organizations by using their ability to influence people and their ease at meeting and networking with people.

FINANCE
- *Personal financial adviser*
- Economic analyst
- Mortgage broker
- Credit investigator
- Stockbroker
- Investment banker
- Corporate finance attorney
- International banker
- Economist
- Treasurer, controller, chief financial officer
- Venture capitalist

ENTJs often excel in the field of finance. They enjoy making money and enjoy working with other people's money, too! They are energized by the competition of the field and take charge quickly and easily. These careers enable ENTJs to use their ability to forecast trends and design ingenious ways to take full advantage of opportunities for themselves and their clients. They do best when they have little work that involves details and follow-up, but instead can delegate to a competent support staff.

CONSULTING/TRAINING
- Business consultant
- Management consultant
- Educational consultant
- Program designer
- *Management trainer*

- *Employment development specialist*
- Labor relations manager
- Cyber security consultant
- Corporate/team trainer
- Technical trainer
- Legislative assistant
- Political consultant

The variety and independence offered in careers in consulting appeal to ENTJs. The field has grown tremendously in recent years, giving ENTJs the chance to satisfy their entrepreneurial spirit, work with a variety of people in a variety of business settings, and be compensated in proportion to the work they put in. ENTJs often excel in business or management consulting and can be excellent and stimulating trainers. They usually create a structured and challenging environment with creative designs and active sessions. They almost always prefer to take on new projects, and enjoy teaching other ambitious people ways to increase their competence.

PROFESSIONAL
- Attorney
- Judge
- Psychologist
- *College professor: science/social science*
- Chemical engineer
- Intellectual property attorney
- *Biomedical engineer*
- Psychiatrist
- *Surgeon*
- *Medical scientist*
- *Environmental engineer*
- Attorney (specialty: nonprofit charitable giving)
- Attorney (specialty: estate planning)
- Political scientist
- Pathologist
- Pilot

These professions offer the degree of status and level of influence ENTJs strive for in their careers. ENTJs often enjoy the field of law and have success as practicing and administrative attorneys and judges. The intellectual challenge of psychology and psychiatry appeals to many ENTJs, as do the complex field of chemical engineering and the growing fields of environmental and biomedical engineering. In education, ENTJs usually prefer teaching in the upper grades, especially secondary education, adult education, and at the college level. They enjoy applying their knowledge in the world around them and often have careers that let them expand their teaching responsibilities into other areas— like politics or political consulting.

TECHNOLOGY
- *Computer programmer: software and applications*
- *Mobile application developer*
- Network and computer systems administrator
- *Networking specialist*
- *Software and web development engineer*
- *Information and design architect*
- Computer and information systems manager
- *Robotics network manager*
- *Artificial intelligence technologist*
- *Construction and development engineer*
- Database administrator
- Project manager
- Engagement manager

Many ENTJs are ideally suited to careers in the ever-changing and expanding tech world. These jobs require several qualities that come naturally to most ENTJs: the ability to understand and process complex information, an extremely logical mind, the ability to grasp the big picture, and superior organizational skills.

Customizing Your Job Search

Knowing the particular strengths and blind spots of your type can afford you a tremendous advantage in your job search campaign. In all aspects of the process, from conducting research into available positions, identifying and contacting prospective employers, developing personal marketing tools such as résumés, arranging and conducting job interviews, negotiating salaries, to finally accepting a position, people will act true to their type. Being able to capitalize on your assets and compensate for your liabilities can make the difference between a successful and an unsuccessful job search.

Differences between types are sometimes subtle and other times dramatic. It is the subtle variations in advice we offer that make the real difference between success or failure in a job search. The concept of "networking," or meeting with and talking to people to gather information about potential jobs, serves as a good example. Extraverts will naturally enjoy networking and are advised to do so on a large scale, while Introverts find more limited and targeted networking, especially with people they already know, easier. Sensors tend to network with people in a defined scope, while Intuitives will go far and wide to find people often seemingly unrelated to their field of interest. Further, Feelers take networking, like everything else, very personally and enjoy establishing warm rapport, while Thinkers will be more objective and detached in their style. Finally, Judgers tend to ask fewer and more structured questions during their networking, while Perceivers could ask questions of all sorts all day long! One valuable search technique, many ways to implement it.

Pathways to Success: Using Your Strengths

As we will detail in the following pages, your strengths and talents in the job search lie in your ability to take command of the process, impressing others with your competence and inspiring them by your confidence. To avoid being perceived as overbearing, try to make a conscious effort to listen and ask questions as well as talk and give answers.

As an ENTJ, your most effective strategies will build on your abilities to:

Develop and follow an effective job search strategy.

- Establish your goals, including the criteria for the career or job you want, and map out your plan for obtaining it.
- Keep copies of your letters, log your appointments, and keep track of people you have followed up with or still need to contact to keep you organized and on time.

As Bruce began his job search, he used the same time management and organization techniques that had served him well in his previous job as an administrator. He put together a notebook with a coding system to denote which people he had seen, was scheduled to see, or had yet to arrange a meeting with. After each interview, he made notes about the meeting and what his next step was to be. Then he sent a note thanking the individual for his or her time, and moved that card from the "pending" section to "next step" section. Using this system, Bruce stayed on top of nearly twenty-five prospects and dozens of contacts without letting a single one slip.

Anticipate trends and forecast future needs.

- Use your ability to look at current situations and project how they will need to be different in order to meet the changing context.
- Demonstrate your ability to forecast future needs of potential employers by explaining how you see the market changing and how your input and involvement can help the employer meet those new demands.

During an interview at a small, newly formed market research company, Diane noticed that the president seemed distracted and was, in fact, interrupted several times by frantic-looking members of her staff. When the president realized she was being rude, she explained to Diane that her company was short-staffed and was in the middle of preparing a proposal for a major new client. Diane suggested several vendors with whom she might subcontract to get her through the crunch. The president was impressed with Diane's quick thinking, contacts, and understanding of the business. Then Diane explained that she had experience trouble-shooting similar projects and would be willing to freelance on the project as a way of demonstrating her abilities. The president was taken aback by the offer but after taking a minute to consider it, realized she was looking at the solution to her immediate problem and perhaps long-term improvement in the operation of her business. Diane was hired on the spot.

Solve problems creatively.

- Approach obstacles as challenges, rather than roadblocks. Rise to the challenge of overcoming them by using your creativity.
- Demonstrate your ability to develop innovative strategies by preparing an assessment of the prospective employer's biggest problems and how you would help to solve them.

Doris was beginning to think she had hit a brick wall. She had made repeated attempts to reach the new business manager by phone and had also written two letters following up on a recommendation by a mutual business associate. His secretary told Doris that he was interested in seeing her for the position that was soon to become available, but his schedule was just impossible. Doris decided to do something about that. Since she and the secretary had established a friendly telephone relationship, Doris found out that the personnel manager was scheduled to return to town later that afternoon. The secretary told Doris that her boss usually took a cab from the airport back to his office. So Doris drove to the airport, and met the manager at his gate. Having never met him, she wore a sign around her neck with his name, as if she were a chauffeur. On the ride back to town, she introduced herself and said that with her as a member of his company, he would be freed up to tend to more pressing matters and leave much of the traveling and client relations to her. He was so impressed with her clever approach that they went directly to his office upon returning, where Doris proceeded to have a great interview.

Network extensively.

- Develop a list of everyone you know who knows you and your abilities, and make appointments to meet with them to discuss your career goals.
- Ask the people who know you to refer you to other people who might either be interested in your area of expertise or might have some knowledge that you will find helpful.

Remember Jane's double Rolodex? It's her habit not ever to throw away a name, even if she doesn't have an immediate need or use for it. Jane used all those names to start her own business. She preferred to take people out for coffee, but because her time was at a premium, she also found that with a few minutes on the phone, she could usually reach several new contacts. Jane makes a point of returning the generosity shown her by agreeing to conduct informational interviews as often as possible, which results in an even greater network of contacts.

Become knowledgeable about the organization and the position of interest.

- Do some research at the library through industry trade publications or by talking to people already in the field or organization to find out as much as you can about what's happening at the company and in the field. Also find out what you can about your interviewer so you can find a common ground upon which to establish rapport.
- Synthesize the information you have collected and distill it into a mini-report to review before a subsequent interview or to refer to during the interview to demonstrate your interest in and knowledge of the business.

After working unhappily in a bank for twelve years, Ed decided that he wanted to make a career change to investment brokerage. He took a couple of training seminars offered through continuing education from a banking association of which he was a member. In one of the classes, he met an investment broker and queried him about the industry. Ed's new friend introduced him to several other investment brokers and suggested Ed read a trade publication that published helpful articles about the business and listed available jobs throughout the region. Later, in job interviews, Ed was able to refer to interesting information he had learned about the industry and also to call on his new contacts to help make inroads at investment firms.

Possible Pitfalls

Although all people are unique, there are certain *potential* blind spots that many ENTJs share. We underscore "potential" because some of the following *may* be true of you, while others may clearly not apply. While

considering them, you may notice that these tendencies do not just relate to the job search but rather describe pitfalls that you may have experienced in other aspects of your life as well. It is therefore helpful to consider each one in terms of your past experiences by asking yourself, "Is this true for me?" And if so, "How did this tendency prevent me from getting something that I wanted?" You will probably notice that the key to overcoming your blind spots is the conscious and thoughtful development of your third and fourth functions (Sensing and Feeling). We recognize that many of the suggestions will be difficult to implement, but the more you use these functions, the fewer problems they will cause you in the future.

Avoid making decisions too quickly.

- Take time to gather all the relevant, albeit mundane, facts about a job or career before deciding whether you are interested in it. Refer to your list of criteria and be sure to ask all the necessary questions so that you have an accurate and realistic picture of the job and its opportunities.
- Be sure to reflect before acting. Ask yourself what you really want and how a potential job fits with the things you believe are important to you. Be honest with yourself and add those values and desires to your list of criteria.

Try not to appear aggressive and pushy.

- Be aware that other people may be put off by your energy and drive and consider you too aggressive. Take time to establish rapport, finding some common personal ground early on in an interview. Take time to recognize the contributions of those around you.
- Try to be understanding of the unpredictable delays and postponements that are a

fact of life. These may slow down your journey toward your goal, but try not to let them frustrate or discourage you.

Don't discount opportunities you consider to be below your competency level.

- Realize that you may appear overconfident and arrogant and unintentionally insult a potential employer by refusing to consider a position you see as beneath you.
- Think of everyone you meet as someone with whom you may have to work one day and do all that you can to establish good relations with them.

Be patient with all phases of the process, even the details.

- Don't overlook the practical considerations of a job search in favor of the more interesting aspects. Check out the time investment and costs associated with a quality job search and be sure they are budgeted into your overall plan.
- Delay starting your job search until you have fully researched your resources and are sure you will be able to complete it to your high standards before plowing ahead.

Work on developing active listening skills.

- Realize that you sometimes may interrupt others before they finish speaking because you have anticipated (correctly or incorrectly) what they are about to say. Instead, wait a few seconds after they have finished speaking and check with them to make sure you understood what they meant.
- Remember that, rather than appearing confident and competent, you may come across as impatient and domineer-

ing. Make a conscious effort to curb that tendency by giving the other people plenty of time to gather their thoughts and finish their sentences.

The Final Piece: Changing or Keeping Your Job . . . the Key to Success for ENTJs

Now that you have a solid understanding of your type, you can see how your natural preferences make you better suited for certain kinds of jobs. You can also see how knowledge of your type-related strengths and weaknesses can help you conduct a more successful job search. But as an ENTJ, you've already realized that you are not equally drawn to *every* career or field listed in the Popular Occupations section. The next and final step is to narrow down the field and find the work you were meant to do.

In addition to Type, several other factors—such as your values, interests, and skills—also contribute to your level of satisfaction on the job. The more compatible you are with your job, the happier you'll be. So prepare to use everything you've learned (in this book and in life) to create *your strategic career plan*. The exercises in Chapter 24, Putting It All Together, are designed to help you do just that.

However, you may have decided it makes more sense (if perhaps only for the moment) to stay in your present job or with your current employer. There may be many valid reasons—financial pressures, family considerations, a tough job market for your specialty, or just bad timing. But take heart! What you've learned in this book can also help you be more content and successful *in your current job*. And should the time come when you're ready to make a major career move, you'll have a much better idea of where you want to go, and how to get there.

"So, if you can't have the job you love (yet!)...love the one you've got."

The simple truth is, with the exception of work on a factory assembly line, the vast majority of jobs allow a good deal of flexibility in the way tasks are performed. Here are some ways you may be able to "massage" your current job into one that better fits your needs:

- Try to get appointed to strategic planning committees.
- Find a mentor (if you are new to the field or organization).
- Create opportunities to be a leader (volunteer to chair a committee, etc.).
- Develop a "critical friends group" (people that help critique each other's ideas).
- Seek professional development opportunities on a regular basis.
- Sign up for advanced training or a degree in your area of specialty.
- Join and/or become a leader in a professional association.
- Invite more input from direct-reports.

One ENTJ turns lemons into lemonade:

Josh was the managing partner in a small law firm. Although he had reached the top of the ladder at his company and had even greater ambitions, he was not yet experienced enough to get the same position in a larger firm. He ran for office for his State Bar Association, worked hard, and within two years assumed its presidency. This added leadership experience and statewide exposure made him a great candidate for the kind of position he sought.

Use what you've got to get what you need.

Simply put, the best advice on how to succeed is to *capitalize on your strengths and compensate for your weaknesses.*

Learning how to do this can make the difference between succeeding or failing and loving or hating your work. To help you, we include the following inventory of your potential strengths and weaknesses. And while every individual is unique, as an ENTJ, many of the following should apply to you.

Your work-related strengths may include:

- Ability to see possibilities and implications
- Aptitude for creative problem solving; ability to examine issues objectively
- Understanding of complex issues
- Drive and ambition to succeed
- Confidence and natural leadership ability
- Strong motivation to be competent and to excel
- High standards and strong work ethic
- Ability to create systems and models to achieve your objectives
- Courage to take bold steps and the drive to reach goals
- Logical and analytical decision-making skills
- Decisiveness and strong organizational skills
- Comfort with technology; you're a quick learner

Your work-related weaknesses may include:

- Impatience with others who are not as quick as you are
- Brusqueness and lack of tact and diplomacy
- Tendency toward hasty decision making
- Lack of interest in mundane details
- Tendency to want to improve something that doesn't need improving

- Tendency to intimidate or overpower others
- Tendency to not take the time to adequately appreciate and praise employees, colleagues, and others

- Reluctance to reexamine issues already decided
- Propensity to overemphasize work life to the detriment of home life

Using your strengths is easy.
The secret to success for an
ENTJ
is learning to:

Slow down, focus on the details,
and tune into others' needs.

13 | INTJ Introverted, Intuitive, Thinking, Judging

"Competence + Independence = Perfection"

Profile 1: Kathleen

"Planning strategies excites the dickens out of me!"

Kathleen is a self-professed perfectionist. In her work, she "creates masterpieces" no matter what she's doing. She serves as coordinator and staff assistant to a city commission on women's issues and affairs. And she also runs her own business providing training, education, and consulting in management planning and development. It's a full plate and Kathleen works constantly. "I get turned on by my work. Career satisfaction for me means I can do my work any day of the week and never say, 'Hey! Isn't this my day off?!'"

Kathleen coordinates and manages the planning activities of a city human service and political commission. Her work involves research and analysis of proposals for potential programs, the writing of policy reports, and preparation and grooming of public officials to help identify and overcome potential obstacles to new policies. She facilitates internal task forces and handles negotiations among commissioners. "Lately I've been doing more and more politicking; I'm finding that I'm good at it and I like it." And Kathleen supervises one staff member, something she enjoys because that individual is "a lot like me and we each have a lot of freedom."

In her own business, which she runs after traditional work hours, Kathleen creates management planning and development programs for companies. Her consulting work is designed around helping teams work more effectively together. She works long hours keeping track of "the details nobody else thinks of. I'm the consummate planner, and I'm known for my prototypes, which pleases me."

"I enjoy almost everything I do: planning strategies excites the dickens out of me; creating proposals and getting other people to accept them, especially when there is initial resistance, is challenging; and anything having to do with theories and the future implications of *anything* is exciting." Kathleen is also energized by making presentations, and she often receives standing ovations for her "performances." But she's exhausted when they're over and finds the preparation process "painful, because I'm so demanding and perfectionistic about them."

It's the routine tasks of her job that she finds boring and ultimately draining. "Writing monthly reports, documenting time, rethinking what I've already thought about, that's the worst for me." And major decisions are difficult for Kathleen to make. She once took two years to decide what kind of new car to buy because she needed so much information in order to make a perfect decision.

One of the things Kathleen values most about herself is her competency. Throughout her work history it seems that she has always worked toward that end. Her first job after college was as administrative account specialist at an international business corporation. She was naive about the norms of working in a large organization but was learning so much she didn't mind all the detail work of administering the sales accounts. Soon she realized she wanted to be in a smaller work environment and accepted a job at a very small consulting firm where she developed the training programs they marketed. While she loved being "responsible for everything," the company couldn't offer her the salary she needed. She next went to work for the U.S. government courts system as arbitration and deputy clerk. It was a highly technical

position, and while it paid her a good salary, she was bored and hated every minute. She heard about a scholarship opportunity at a small university and entered the graduate program, where she obtained her MBA. "I loved being a student. The program let me explore and manipulate all kinds of information." It was in school that she decided to start her own business, which she has continued to run on a part-time and full-time basis for the past nine years. After completing the degree, she operated her business out of her home and also taught marketing management and human resources management at a community college. Typically taking on several challenges at once, she became director of communication for a local chapter of the United Way while still running her own business. After only a year at the United Way Kathleen was offered the job she has now.

Her career evolution has been a surprise to Kathleen. She had never expected to attend college and would not have, were it not for a bet made with her boyfriend that she could out-score him on the college aptitude tests. While she didn't win the bet, the challenge encouraged her to try college. She found out that she was bright and that when information was presented systematically, she understood it.

Even today, she dislikes working in large groups because they are rarely systematic and without that logical organization, she sometimes has difficulty understanding what is being presented. That area of insecurity is the only real source of stress Kathleen faces in her work. "I need to see things visually to learn them. Although I have always tested poorly, I now know it's a problem with how the information is organized." This insecurity comes as a surprise to those around

Kathleen, who describe her as cool and confident. She has a hard time asking for help or admitting to having a rough time. So she internalizes stress.

Kathleen admits to not having much of a personal life. She has a small group of close friends with whom she has very deep connections and to whom she is extremely loyal. "They understand me and know that when I'm blunt, I'm just being honest and don't mean to hurt." She is active in local town politics and collects all kinds of books: "I'm driven by information." And since the death of her mother two years ago, she is committed to taking care of her father. Her career goal is to start a liberal arts college for people of color. "I want to teach critical thinking skills." The school would have a strong economic and historical focus. And true to form, Kathleen has already begun the research to make her dream a reality.

"I've become more of a team player over the years. I'm more mature and have learned to take an emery board to tone down my sharp tongue." She hopes to continue developing her skills in facilitating group process, a skill she recognizes needs more work. She's able to express her feelings more freely now. "I still internalize most of it, but I'm learning to count on my friends to share that side of me with. I'm not there yet, but I hope someday people remember me as a person with spurts of genius in her; someone who was demanding of herself and others but was extremely loyal and compassionate to friends. Those are my goals."

Why This Career Works for Kathleen

Kathleen's career provides a rich example of the Conceptualizer temperament. She is driven to increase her competence, constantly acquiring new information and mastering new concepts. Hers is a quest for perfection, striving to be the best at everything she tries. She is motivated by any kind of challenge; working hard and single-mindedly to exceed even her own high standards.

Her introverted Intuition (dominant) allows—no, demands!—that she see possibilities. The possibilities that receive the most attention are those which spring from her own mind and vision. Her dream to start a college is one example, which she will pursue with dogged persistence. She loves planning strategies, considering theories, and anticipating the potential implications of her new ideas.

Kathleen uses her extraverted Thinking (auxiliary) to analyze, coordinate, and manage her ideas into concrete and workable programs. She identifies problems in the systems and uses her logical thinking to analyze and organize solutions. She coordinates strategic planning sessions and facilitates the implementation of her projects.

Although Feeling is not her strength, Kathleen is clearly developing more access to it. She is getting better at facilitating groups, handling negotiations, politicking, and supervising others (especially people similar to her). She is finding it easier to express her feelings with close friends. Kathleen is also becoming more comfortable in the extraverted world through making the painstaking presentations she finds so validating and rewarding.

Meet the Millennial

Name: Phil
Age: 27
Entrepreneur

"Creating something from nothing."

Backstory

Phil bought his first stocks when he was ten years old. He and a younger brother began investing money from odd jobs in the booming '90s stock market, even turning a profit. Ever since then, Phil knew he wanted to be in finance, and he went on to study business in college and spend several summers interning at different large investment banks. But it was Phil's experiences interning in the world of start-up companies that really inspired him: "It's the most direct way to change the world around me and see my work have an impact."

His first job out of college was in sell-side mergers and acquisitions. But when the recession hit hard and Phil was laid off a year later, it felt more liberating than disappointing. "Now I can go off and do something I'm more interested in," Phil remembers thinking. He launched a full-court press and landed his dream job working at one of the oldest and largest venture capital firms in the world. In the back of his mind, Phil always sensed that he wanted to be an entrepreneur, and what better way to confirm, he reasoned, than to talk to as many CEOs as possible and learn from them. Two years later, Phil had talked to over a thousand CEOs

and started to strategize the next move toward his own start-up. Now midway through his first year at Harvard Business School, Phil is lining up summer internships, largely in technology entrepreneurship. He sees himself either joining a start-up or starting his own new business after graduation.

As a side project—one of many for Phil—he is developing a website to help others use self-reflection in the internship process. A self-described journal writer since fifth grade, Phil saved himself from a potential career misstep in college by going back to his journals and remembering what he hated about the work environment at the big investment firm that offered him a job. The website acts as a virtual time capsule to help interns remember at the end of the process what their goals were, what they thought of the work-life balance, and other critical factors.

A Good Fit

Many Conceptualizers are drawn to the competitive, intellectual world of entrepreneurship. Phil's work is idea driven, and innovation is essential in a field where a new idea can have big payoffs. Because Phil is a dominant Intuitive, his brain is wired to see the big picture, make connections, and seek creative solutions. In investing, this meant having the vision to see opportunities and possibilities others might pass over. As for many INTJs, independence is the name of the game with Phil, who trusts his own judgment and ideas more than institutions or traditions. He is a born problem solver, and his auxiliary Thinking function makes him logical, analytical, and objective. Phil's Judging function makes him solution oriented, and driven to achieve his goals. An extremely hard worker, he's put in as many as 120 hours per week at some jobs—sometimes working 40 hours at a stretch. He excels in one-to-one interactions and exudes confidence and competence—one of the reasons he was able to make personal connections with so many CEOs.

Looking Ahead

Ideally, in five years Phil will be running a decent-size division at a company he's passionate about—that is, if he's not running his own company. In ten years, he would like to be firmly established as the CEO of his own company, then eventually transition into a role as a board member or another mentorship role where he can share his experience and help others to realize their ambitions. Phil's focus and drive thus far make it easy to imagine him meeting, and exceeding, these goals.

Profile 2: Jim

"I enjoy winning a really tough case on the strengths of my lawyering, not merely on the strengths of the case."

Odd as it may sound, Jim is at home in a courtroom. As a civil trial lawyer, he's in a courtroom a lot, and when he's "on trial," he feels a strong sense of belonging. "I know I'm right where I want to be. It's my sole responsibility, and I relish the opportunity to achieve success in such a public forum." Jim is considered tough, bright, insightful—a top-notch trial lawyer. It's his work, but it's also a great part of his life and his identity.

At forty-four, Jim is a partner in a plaintiff law firm, representing people who have been injured in a variety of ways. Medical malpractice and personal injury cases are his firm's specialty. "My clients come to me to help redress their injuries through the court system." His focus is entirely on the potential court case, yet he spends nearly 90 percent of his time preparing for the 10 percent of time he actually spends in court. This is due to the large number of cases that settle out of court and the relatively few that make it all the way to a jury trial. Jim's duties include taking depositions (interviewing potential witnesses to find out their side of the story), preparing witnesses, finding and obtaining testimony from expert witnesses, negotiating cases with opposing counsel, and the myriad phone calls and correspondence surrounding each of these functions. "I spend what often seems like a great deal of my time on the phone with a client, helping solve problems that may seem mundane to me but are nevertheless very important to my client."

The court time, however, is what makes Jim enjoy his work as much as he does. "My goal is to do my job so well that I never make mistakes. That's obviously impossible, but I try to put the other side in a position to make errors and then I capitalize on those mistakes." Jim is also a teacher in court. "My role is to echo the jury's possible questions before a witness, imagining what they will find unclear, and asking the witness to address issues that I know members of the jury have on their minds. My aim is to provide the jury with an educational experience. I want them to look back and say, 'That was fascinating. I really learned something.'"

Finally, court time gives Jim the control and autonomy he enjoys most. "When you're on trial, everybody in the office knows and accepts that as your sole responsibility. There are no interruptions, no phone calls in the middle of a meeting. I can concentrate fully, and I am able to make independent decisions in the best interest of the case. I am able to be my own boss."

The energizing part of Jim's work is the strategizing. He loves playing out the case in his head. He takes different parts of it and anticipates where problems will pop up. Wherever he see a problem, he labels it an opportunity. For Jim, it's a giant chess match.

But along with the job come enormous pressures. Jim is sometimes frustrated by the volume of work he has and the pressures it creates. The paperwork and the interruptions inherent in a busy law firm take away some of the control Jim wants over his own schedule. "The act of juggling priorities, deciding which are the tasks I should be addressing myself to at any one moment, means there are important things I will not get to. But I've found it's worth it because I really need the focus and it's the only way I can achieve that."

Interpersonal conflicts within the office are a drain for Jim. "Conflicts in the courtroom are handled in such an objective and fair way. In the end, it's the decision of the jury that counts. But personal confrontations usually mean someone is going to get hurt." Jim doesn't enjoy "playing the heavy" and is not very effective in a disciplinarian role. Fortunately, those occasions are rare.

Jim handles stress in an extremely intellectual manner. He uses a system of time management and self-improvement that he learned by using a series of audiotapes. He adopted the program a couple of years ago and still relies on it to help him manage the causes of stress. "When I'm really wound up I do a little self-talk and remind myself of my past experiences with the same problem. I tell myself this, too, shall pass."

Jim entered law school after first attempting divinity school. He thought he wanted to teach philosophy and theology but discovered he wasn't devoted to his subject area to the extent he ought to be in order to make it his life's work. He also realized that the market for theology or philosophy professors was a limited one, so he applied to law school and was accepted even though his LSAT scores were not current. During law school he clerked in several different law firms and found the subject matter (real estate, or zoning and sewer work) too boring. At another firm he wasn't comfortable with the strong emphasis on socializing. Then he clerked at the firm of his trial practice teacher and liked the subject area, the people, and the attitude of the firm. He was hired upon graduation, and except for a few times over the years when he has considered offers from other firms, he has been happily and steadily increasing his position and interest in his firm for fifteen years.

The moments Jim considers great accomplishments are when he has won a case nobody considered winnable. "The really tough cases that I have won on the strengths of my lawyering rather than on the strengths of the case are most rewarding to me." He is also proud of the articles he has published in professional journals, and the status he has attained within important professional organizations.

His work, rather than his personal life, is the focus of his life. While he values his family, his job has become more important to him as he continues to invest more and more of himself in it. His goals are to continue to win bigger and bigger cases, but he sees the risks involved. "When you roll the dice on the really big ones, with big numbers, you have to be prepared to get a goose egg sometimes. That takes courage." In fact, the only regrets Jim has are the cases he has settled that he might have won and would have resulted in large awards. And sometimes Jim wonders if it might have been both fun and more challenging to be a litigator with a wider range of subject areas, including business law.

But without any limitations, Jim would still choose to be a trial lawyer. "It's the right choice for me. And I see now that it gives me some of the elements I would have enjoyed in education. The opportunity to do research is here; the chance to stand up in front of people and teach them something is here; the intellectual stimulation and the theatrics are all here when I'm arguing a case."

Jim has returned to the classroom recently, teaching courses at the law school. "I think I've become more interested in incorporating positive reinforcement and mentoring some of the students. I feel as though I am making a contribution, and that's rewarding." He is finding more time to spend with his wife and children without the anxiety he used to experience when taking time off from work. He recently bought a boat and uses it

weekly; it is where he and his wife entertain friends. "I seem to be much more interested in socializing as well as enjoying the sheer physical elements of learning to navigate and handle the boat." Jim is finding himself tuning in to the present moment more than ever before. He makes a conscious effort to really focus on one thing at a time and be fully involved with that one task. He even sees how he has become more meticulous about the details of his work — insisting that he carefully review all the details of a client's file to be sure he hasn't missed anything.

"I think I have developed an ability to get along with all kinds of people. I have increased my level of self-awareness and can appreciate my strengths and also take responsibility for my failures. Whatever I do, I want to do it well. My work affords me the chance to do something I really enjoy, providing a service that is recognized as important and I am rewarded for being the best."

Why This Career Works for Jim

Jim's goal to be the best trial lawyer possible is consistent with his Conceptualizer temperament. His drive for competency pushes him hard to keep trying to improve his skills and to maintain extremely high standards. He is motivated to learn the tremendous amount of new material necessary to try cases often involving complex medical testimony. With practically every case, he is required to become an expert in some field. Like many Conceptualizers, he is drawn to being in positions of power that increase his stature, professional standing, and financial status.

As an introverted Intuitive, Jim is constantly strategizing in his head. Playing the ultimate chess match, he anticipates problems, forecasts his opponents' tactics, and tries to discover their weaknesses to figure out ways to overcome obstacles. His (dominant) Intuition is particularly useful in helping him to look at an issue (or a case) as his opponent might see it, turning it over in his mind, enabling him to prepare more effectively.

Jim uses his extraverted Thinking (auxiliary) to help him deal coolly, objectively, and dispassionately with the many conflicts that occur during trials. He views the inevitable and necessary conflicts between opposing counsel as "just business, nothing personal," and as a result, is able to maintain good working relationships with other lawyers. His Thinking also keeps him from getting so emotionally involved with the plight of his clients that he loses sight of the bigger picture—a verdict or settlement that is in their best interest.

Jim's development of his Feeling side (third function) shows up in his recreational life. He has become much more interested in socializing than he was in the past. He enjoys teaching and mentoring law students, gets along better with many different types of people, and has become more self-aware in recent years—all activities that engage his Feeling. He is also conscious of using his Sensing to live more in the present moment, to pay greater attention to, and be more meticulous about, details.

Common Threads

Although Kathleen, Jim, and Phil all have different backgrounds, experiences, and careers, there are certain common threads woven through their stories. Their specific interests, abilities, and values may differ, but owing to their similar temperament values, the *same hierarchy* of their psychological functions, and the "world" they use them in (inner or outer), there are certain observations we can make about the needs of many INTJs.

What follows is a list of the most important elements—the formula, if you will—for INTJ satisfaction. Given the uniqueness of all individuals—even those who share the same type—this list will not describe each INTJ equally well. The important thing is that these ten elements, with varying degrees of intensity and in different orders of importance, identify what INTJs need to be satisfied.

After you have reviewed this list, we recommend that you go back and try to prioritize the elements in order of *their importance to you.* When doing this, think of past work experiences as well as your present job, and what you found particularly satisfying or unsatisfying. Try to look for *themes* that run through several experiences, not just the events that might be true of one work situation but not of another.

As an INTJ, career satisfaction means doing work that:

1. Lets me create and develop original and innovative solutions to problems to improve existing systems
2. Lets me focus my energy on the implementation of my good ideas, working in a logical and orderly way and in a setting that rewards my perseverance
3. Lets me work with other conscientious people whose expertise, intelligence, and competence I respect
4. Gives me credit for my original ideas and lets me maintain authorship and control over their execution
5. Allows me to work independently but with periodic interaction with a small group of intellectual people within a smooth-running environment free from interpersonal squabbles

6. Exposes me to a steady stream of new information, providing me with new ways to increase my proficiency and competence

7. Lets me produce a product that meets with my own high standards of quality rather than with the personal likes or dislikes of others

8. Does not require the repetitive execution of factual and detail-oriented tasks

9. Provides me with a high degree of autonomy and control, with the freedom to effect change and develop people and systems

10. Is judged by uniform and fair standards for all, where performance evaluations are based on established criteria rather than on personality contests and that compensates me fairly for my contributions

Popular Occupations for INTJs

In listing occupations that are popular among INTJs, it is important to note that there are successful people of all types in all occupations. However, the following are careers INTJs may find particularly satisfying and some of the reasons why. This is by no means a comprehensive listing but is included to suggest possibilities you may not have previously considered. Although all of these occupations offer the potential for career satisfaction, the future demand for some careers is anticipated to be greater than for others. Based upon our research, the occupations that are italicized in the lists below are forecast to enjoy the fastest rate of growth over the next several years.

BUSINESS/FINANCE
- Cyber security specialist
- Management consultant: computer/ information services, marketing, reorganization
- Economist
- Pharmaceutical researcher (R&D)
- *Personal financial adviser*
- *Market research analyst*
- *Management analyst*
- Investment banker
- International banker
- Credit analyst
- Financial analyst
- Strategic planner
- Budget analyst
- Treasurer or controller
- Private sector executive
- *Real estate appraiser*

The business and financial careers listed all require highly developed analytical abilities that many INTJs possess. The intellectual challenge so necessary for satisfaction for INTJs is available in abundance in the high-tech and growing field of pharmaceutical research and telecommunications security. The constantly changing worlds of investment and international banking make good use of many INTJs' global perspective and ability to plan long range.

TECHNOLOGY
- Scientist/scientific researcher
- *Network systems and data communications analyst*
- *Software developer: applications, systems*
- *Computer programmer*
- *Networking specialist*
- *Information and design architect*
- *Robotics and manufacturing engineer*
- *Artificial intelligence technologist*
- Technician: electrical/electronic
- Astronomer
- Environmental planner
- *Biomedical researcher/engineer*
- Operations research analyst
- Information services developer
- Information services–new business developer

- Network integration specialist
- *Database administrator*
- Computer animator
- *Network and computer systems administrator*
- *Computer software engineer, systems software*
- *Computer software engineer, applications*
- Print designer
- Interaction designer
- Java programmer
- Computer security specialist
- Broadcast engineer

The technical fields appeal to the INTJ's interest in logical systems. These fields offer an opportunity to work with rapidly developing high-tech equipment and products. Often INTJs are able to use their creativity to develop ingenious and inventive systems.

EDUCATION
- *College professor: computer science/ math*
- Academic curriculum designer
- Administrator
- Mathematician
- Anthropologist
- Curator
- Archivist

Higher education appeals to the INTJ much more than elementary or secondary education because it usually involves teaching complex theories and systems with a more global perspective. Developing educational curricula or systems and making sure they are run efficiently allow the INTJ to make improvements. The world of higher education also exposes INTJs to an environment where they can gather and manipulate information and interact with other intellectual people with whom they can expand their own level of competence.

HEALTH CARE/MEDICINE
- Psychiatrist
- Psychologist
- *Medical scientist*
- Neurologist
- *Biomedical researcher/engineer*
- Cardiologist
- Pharmacologist
- Pharmaceutical researcher
- Coroner
- Pathologist
- Microbiologist
- Geneticist
- *Surgeon*
- Cardiovascular technician

The more technical areas of medicine are fields in which many INTJs often find success and satisfaction. These fields include highly complex systems, and allow the INTJ to work independently, with minimal outside intervention or input.

PROFESSIONAL
- *Attorney: administrative/litigator*
- Management consultant
- Strategic planner
- Investment/business analyst
- Manager
- Judge
- News analyst/writer
- Engineer
- Metallurgical engineer
- Intellectual properties attorney
- Civil engineer
- Attorney (specialty: nonprofit charitable giving)
- Attorney (specialty: estate planning)
- Aerospace engineer
- Nuclear engineer
- Architect
- Environmental scientist
- Intelligence specialist
- Criminalist and ballistics expert
- Pilot

The professional occupations offer a variety of appealing aspects for the INTJ. All but "manager" require independent research and planning. The development of strategies, systems, and long-range plans utilizes INTJs' future orientation (Intuition) and their ability to plan out how to reach their goals in a sequential and logical manner. The INTJ manager often finds the most satisfaction when working in a fairly small organization with employees who are a lot like him or her. If the staff does not require a great deal of personal support or hands-on supervision, the INTJ is more likely to find satisfaction in management.

CREATIVE
- Writer/editorial writer
- Artist
- Inventor
- Graphic designer
- Architect
- Universal design architect
- Informational-graphics designer
- Freelance media planner
- Editor/art director (magazine)
- Columnist, critic, commentator
- Blogger
- Exhibit designer and builder

The appeal of the creative occupations is the ability to do original work. Writers and artists use their Intuition to create new expressions and statements. Inventors are able to create new systems or devices that improve current ways of living or solve vexing problems. All three of these jobs require that INTJs work independently, meeting their own goals and standards, with themselves as the ultimate critic.

Customizing Your Job Search

Knowing the particular strengths and blind spots of your type can afford you a tremendous advantage in your job search campaign. In all aspects of the process, from conducting research into available positions, identifying and contacting prospective employers, developing personal marketing tools such as résumés, arranging and conducting job interviews, negotiating salaries, to finally accepting a position, people will act true to their type. Being able to capitalize on your assets and compensate for your liabilities can make the difference between a successful and an unsuccessful job search.

The differences between types are sometimes subtle and other times dramatic. It is the subtle variations in advice we offer that make the real difference between success or failure in a job search. The concept of "networking," or meeting with and talking to people to gather information about potential jobs, serves as a good example. Extraverts will naturally enjoy networking and are advised to do so on a large scale, while Introverts find more limited and targeted networking, especially with people they already know, easier. Sensors tend to network with people in a defined scope, while Intuitives will go far and wide to find people often seemingly unrelated to their field of interest. Further, Feelers take networking, like everything else, very personally and enjoy establishing warm rapport, while Thinkers will be more objective and detached in their style. Finally, Judgers tend to ask fewer and more structured questions during their networking, while Perceivers could ask questions of all sorts all day long! One valuable search technique, many ways to implement it.

Pathways to Success: Using Your Strengths

Because many of the tasks involved in the job search are not usually enjoyed by INTJs, you may not find this process to be particularly enjoyable. Remaining focused on your larger goal of finding challenging and interesting work will prevent you from becoming too impatient with the necessary details and seemingly frivolous social niceties required.

As an INTJ, your most effective strategies will build on your abilities to:

Anticipate trends, forecast future needs.

- Use your ability to look at current situations and project how they will need to be different in order to meet the changing context.
- Demonstrate ability to forecast future needs by explaining how your involvement can help employers meet their new demands.

When Jim was debating a career as a college professor, he did a little research and learned there were very few colleges with large philosophy or theology departments. He realized that the trend would continue and the opportunities for good jobs would decline further, making the competition fierce. Recognizing his waning interest in his field of study, he looked instead to where he might find the challenge, intellectual stimulation, and opportunity to use his excellent analysis and strategizing skills and decided upon a career in law.

Synthesize information.

- Engage your ability to understand and assimilate complex information to become fully versed in the technology of the discipline.
- Demonstrate that ability by summarizing what you see as the strengths and weaknesses of the market or industry, explaining how your unique skills will help the employer by meeting his/her goals.

Monica's skills at understanding the "big picture" helped her get the job at the children's hospital. In fact all of the jobs she has enjoyed are those where she had no predecessor and was hired because of her ability to sell her vision of a needed position. When she interviewed for the job as telethon coordinator, she explained that she saw her role as one who would see what needed to be done, find the existing flaws in the system, and pull the people together who would create a successful event. She described her role and how she would manage those around her. She was able to see and then communicate her vision to others.

Create your own career options, design your own job.

- Use your natural ability to see opportunities before others do and put yourself in an advantageous position early on in the interviewing process.
- Use your creativity to develop a unique career opportunity, selling a potential employer on how that job will help meet goals and solve problems.

Frustrated with the way his original ideas were so altered during the production process, Jack left the world of advertising copy writing to become a news writer. Even though he lacked news writing experience, Jack devised a plan to get himself where he wanted to go. He looked up an old friend in Arizona who was the editor of a small magazine. Jack wrote a couple of freelance articles that led to an offer as a staff writer. Instead of taking the job, he relocated to a larger city and took the experience and his portfolio with him. He was able to create a job as a reporter based on only a few articles and the letter of recommendation from his past employer.

Develop an innovative career plan.

- Use your creativity to plot out a campaign in a new and different way—

setting you apart from other candidates with potential employers.

- Use your organizational skills to stay on top of the project, make a plan, be on time, remember to send a note after the interview, follow up with prospective employers, etc.

Margaret's situation was not unique. As a single working mother with two young children, she could not afford to quit her administrative job at a large hospital to go on an all-out job search. She decided what she lacked in free time, she would make up for in innovation. She determined that she wanted to use her skills and experience in finance to become an investment analyst. So in an effort to gain some real experience, and also to market herself, she developed a newsletter on her personal computer at home. She worked on the newsletter in the evenings, designing it to be professional-looking, interesting, and valuable to potential employers. She focused each issue on a particular industry and then on several new rising companies. She did analysis of their markets, looked into the major shareholders, and made predictions about their movement in the stock market. She sent the newsletter to a very focused list of potential employers with cover letters that said she was interested in providing these kinds of insights for them should a position become available. She so enjoyed working on the newsletters that the next seven months flew by. When she was offered a job at one of the targeted companies, she persuaded them to let her continue to produce a newsletter, this time for their clients.

Make decisions.

- Organize your ideas into thoughtful and systematic work plans and stick with your agenda.

- Use your skills at critical analysis to eliminate unfavorable options along the way, reorganizing your plan when necessary.

When his wife accepted a job in a new city, it meant job search time for Stuart. He had been an assistant art director at a large advertising firm and decided he would look for an art director position. Stuart developed a list of criteria for the job, made an organized plan of attack, and began to call on agencies in the area.

After only a couple of days, he was offered an assistant art director job at another large agency. After thinking it over, he declined the offer because it would not give him the creative control or autonomy he had decided were critical to him. Finally, he received an offer from a small firm, whose growth necessitated the creation of a new department devoted to consumer advertising, his area of expertise. While the position was still assistant art director, Stuart accepted because he would have the autonomy and control he wanted as the head of the new division. He was willing to trade off the title because he was getting all that he had wanted in a director position.

Possible Pitfalls

Although all people are unique, there are certain *potential* blind spots that many INTJs share. We underscore "potential" because some of the following *may* be true of you, while others may clearly not apply. While considering them, you may notice that these tendencies do not relate just to the job search, but rather describe pitfalls that you may have experienced in other aspects of your life as well. It is therefore helpful to consider each one in terms of your past experience by asking yourself, "Is this true for me?" And if so, "How did this tendency prevent me from getting something that I wanted?" You will probably notice that the key to overcoming your blind spots is the conscious and thoughtful development of your third and fourth functions (Feeling and Sensing). We recognize that many of the suggestions will be difficult to implement, but the more you use these functions, the fewer problems they will cause you in the future.

Attend to all necessary and relevant facts, not just the new and novel ones.

- Spend time focusing on the realities and practical applications of your ideas rather than just on the innovative implications.
- Concentrate on not letting things fall through the cracks because you assume they are already taken care of.

Use tact and diplomacy in getting others to buy your ideas.

- Try to be persuasive in your approach rather than being unyielding in your style, allowing others to comment or challenge your viewpoint.
- Try to consider the ramifications and impact a decision or comment may have on another person, understanding that others often take criticism personally.

Avoid appearing arrogant and condescending to potential employers.

- Remember you are in a selling position, attempting to portray yourself as part of a team of workers, someone who can and will contribute to the goals of the whole organization.
- Take time to listen fully and completely to other people and repeat back to them what they said to be sure you haven't made incorrect assumptions.

Try to remain flexible and open-minded when making decisions.

- Try to be willing to give in on less important points while still holding firm to the elements that are truly vital to you.
- Decide to give everything a second look, even after you discount it. Some opportunities may appear more attractive when you give yourself the extra time to get all the information.

The Final Piece: Changing or Keeping Your Job . . . the Key to Success for INTJs

Now that you have a solid understanding of your type, you can see how your natural preferences make you better suited for certain kinds of jobs. You can also see how knowledge of your type-related strengths and weaknesses can help you conduct a more successful job search. But as an INTJ, you've already realized that you are not equally drawn to *every* career or field listed in the Popular Occupations section. The next and final step is to narrow down the field and find the work you were meant to do.

In addition to Type, several other factors—such as your values, interests, and skills—also contribute to your level of satisfaction on the job. The more compatible you are with your job, the happier you'll be. So prepare to use everything you've learned (in this book and in life) to create *your strategic career plan.* The exercises in Chapter 24, Putting It All Together, are designed to help you do just that.

However, you may have decided it makes more sense (if perhaps only for the moment) to stay in your present job or with your current employer. There may be many valid reasons—financial pressures, family considerations, a tough job market for your specialty, or just bad timing. But take heart! What you've learned in this book can also help you be more content and successful *in your current job.* And should the time come when you're ready to make a major career move, you'll have a much better idea of where you want to go, and how to get there.

"So, if you can't have the job you love (yet!) . . . love the one you've got."

The simple truth is, with the exception of work on a factory assembly line, the vast majority of jobs allow a good deal of flexibility in the way tasks are performed. Here are some ways you may be able to "massage" your current job into one that better fits your needs:

- Try to get appointed to strategic planning committees.
- Develop systems and work to get them implemented at your organization.
- Make sure you have enough uninterrupted time to think and work on projects that interest you.
- Develop a "critical friends" group to critique each other's ideas.
- Seek professional development opportunities.
- Sign up for advanced training (or a degree) in your area of specialty.
- Publish research and articles in your field.
- Invite more input from direct-reports.

One INTJ turns lemons into lemonade:

Several months ago, Roger—a design engineer—was promoted to manager of his department, and he soon designed several new systems to make the department more productive. The problem was, he was not especially skilled at managing *people,* and he was having a hard time getting certain staff on board. Recognizing this weakness, he

asked three more experienced managers he knew to meet with and critique his plans and approach. The initial meeting was so helpful to him, the group decided to meet monthly and take turns consulting with each other.

Use what you've got to get what you need.

Simply put, the best advice on how to succeed is to *capitalize on your strengths and compensate for your weaknesses.* Learning how to do this can make the difference between succeeding or failing and loving or hating your work. To help you, we include the following inventory of your potential strengths and weaknesses. And while every individual is unique, as an INTJ, many of the following should apply to you.

Your work-related strengths may include:

- Ability to focus and concentrate deeply on issues
- Ability to see possibilities and implications
- Enjoyment of complex theoretical and intellectual challenges
- Aptitude for creative problem solving; ability to examine issues objectively
- Single-minded determination to reach your goals even in face of opposition
- Confidence and commitment to your vision
- Strong motivation to be competent and excel
- Ability to work well alone; independent and self-directed
- High standards and strong work ethic
- Ability to create systems and models to achieve your objectives
- Comfort with technology
- Logical and analytical decision-making skills
- Decisiveness and strong organizational skills

Your work-related weaknesses may include:

- Loss of interest in projects after the creative process has been completed
- Tendency to drive others as hard as you drive yourself
- Impatience with others who are not as quick as you are
- Difficulty working with or for others you consider less competent
- Brusqueness and lack of tact and diplomacy, especially when you are rushed
- Lack of interest in mundane details
- Inflexibility about your ideas

- Tendency to want to improve things that don't need improving
- Tendency to be too theoretical and not consider practical realities
- Tendency to not adequately appreciate and praise employees, colleagues, and others
- Reluctance to reexamine issues already decided
- Propensity to overemphasize work life to the detriment of home life
- Impatience with "social niceties" required of some jobs

Using your strengths is easy.
The secret to success for an
INTJ
is learning to:

Consider practical realities, recognize the value of input from others, and balance your work and personal life.

14 | ENTP
Extraverted, Intuitive, Thinking, Perceiving
"Life's Entrepreneurs"

Profile 1: Brent

"What I love about this industry is that we can turn on a dime."

Brent was born to be a marketer. A natural and persuasive communicator and creative thinker, Brent runs a design and marketing business with a partner. Brent's forte is working the creative side of the team, developing logos and websites. He is chief creative officer, as well as co-president of the company, so his role leads him to meet with clients and help them realize their vision of what their company could become if promoted with smart marketing. Brent says his mission is to "discover what that tiny nugget is that makes a company unique and to figure out how to tell a whole story around that. From there, the goal is to discover the voice of the organization and the visual vernacular to best describe their business."

Brent has always had an artistic sensibility, coupled with an abstract, logical mind. He describes feeling torn between physics and illustration. He attended a highly creative arts school where he changed his major three times, vacillating between the two poles of his nature. From illustration, Brent moved to sculpture, but his pragmatic side forced him to acknowledge that he would struggle to find a use for that major. So he moved into graphic design. Once out of college, Brent began working as a graphic designer and quickly found himself "hitting the ceiling," learning all he could and then constantly seeking new challenges. He worked as a freelance designer on the Internet and for print publications until one evening he simply decided to start his own business. He began his graphic web design firm the next day and expected to work alone for a year or two, but with the dot.com boom, Brent found himself with six full-time employees within three months.

Working with a team to develop innovative and creative solutions to clients' problems gets Brent's juices flowing. He loves the creative process and finds that his energy rises in direct response to working with abstract concepts. Seeing the possibilities in everything, Brent becomes animated by opportunities that play to this strength. One of Brent's favorite activities is walking around the office to see what people are doing. "The next thing I know, we have five people in the conference room with some crazy idea, and we'll run with it to build it." This organic and spontaneous method is right up Brent's alley. And his natural charisma, charm, and enthusiasm make other people feel valued and excited about their work.

"What I love about the marketing industry is that it can turn on a dime. We may be a hundred hours into a concept, prepared to pitch to a client in three days, and in the middle of the afternoon we decide to scrap it to come up with a brilliant new direction. That's the kind of business we're in. I'm not afraid to launch into something that's not completely polished yet. It's always a work in progress; it's the constant change. I like to make beautiful things—that's what makes me run."

Most draining to Brent's high energy is dealing with the minutiae inherent in any business: "Taking notes when meeting with clients is a nightmare." Brent doesn't enjoy the bureaucratic details of running a business, nor does he relish the required bookkeeping side of things, like taxes and other paperwork. Personal relationships are both a joy and a burden for Brent. He loves mentoring a team but agonizes about having to make a tough decision to fire or discipline someone. Once it's done, however, Brent is energized, because he says, "you don't realize how stressful it is, dragging you down, until you've done something about it."

Another disappointing situation for Brent is working with clients who are unimaginative or overly cautious, who don't fully utilize his company for what it's good at and are unwilling to take any kind of leap. Negotiating with clients over pricing is also uncomfortable for Brent, as he wants and needs to be appreciated but ultimately hates the degradation he feels when he is required to ask for what he's worth.

Why This Career Works for Brent

Brent is a creative strategist. His Conceptualizer temperament endows him with a thirst for inventive problem solving that makes this career a perfect match for him. The daily challenge of responding to clients with varied needs keeps him interested, and he enjoys flexing his creative muscles as he constantly adapts to new and exciting situations.

A dominant extraverted Intuitive, Brent sees possibilities everywhere, so he is constantly imagining new and better ways to do business. When meeting with clients, Brent quickly assesses where a business is and then leaps to where they want to go. His capacity for problem solving takes him and his clients from A to Z. Best in a brainstorming session where he can bounce ideas off his team, Brent is poised to explore an idea at any moment to see its possibilities and its limitations, with a fully open and curious attitude about the outcome. He has no advanced "need" for it to land one way or another, as long as it is a smart, creative, and ultimately workable landing.

Introverted Thinking is Brent's auxiliary function, and it is abundantly evident in his work. His grasp of logic and systems is reflected in his ability to plot strategy, and his cool understanding of the way things work enables him to remain impartial and objective about his own ideas. Brent follows his logic and abandons projects that are not coming together, and he never lets his own emotional attachment to one idea cloud his view of its place and necessity in the overall scheme of things. Technology is key to

Brent's work, and he finds it both a challenge and a friend. He naturally understands the way most software and computer systems operate, and he enjoys untangling their mysteries.

Brent's third function is extraverted Feeling, which comes into play primarily in his relationships with his staff and his family. He strives to balance his career with his family and works hard to maintain a business that allows him to be home every night at six o'clock and leaves weekends open for family time. Brent's preference for Perceiving compels him to highly value playtime. The development of his extraverted Feeling sometimes comes with

growing pains for Brent, however. When financial relationships with clients become strained, Brent can be slow to take action to correct them. Or when he needs to reprimand or, worse, fire an employee, Brent may put off that difficult conversation, especially if he fears it will jeopardize a relationship. On the positive side, Brent sees his people skills improving with the development of his third function (Feeling), which makes clients comfortable with him. Brent sees development of his fourth function, Sensing, in recreational aspects of his life, in such hobbies as woodworking, furniture building, and landscaping, as well as in his interest in race cars.

Meet the Millennial

Name: George
Age: 26
Online sports video producer

"What problems have I solved today?"

Backstory

Most cinematographers are at least thirty-five before they find success. George wasn't willing to wait that long. Although he had loved film throughout high school and his first year at film school, by his sophomore year George had begun to reconsider, changing his major first to neuroscience and then to casting. The problem was that George knew he was good at a lot of different things, but he didn't know how those interests and skills translated into a career, or even what a "career" might mean.

In his senior year he got an internship at a casting agency, which turned into a position after graduation as a casting assistant. In 2008, two months after the fall of Lehman Brothers, George felt lucky to have a job at all. "But it became boring." George thought he might want to work as a copywriter or as part of a creative team, in advertising, and also considered business school. Then, through a friend, he met Graham, who had moved to the East Coast to build a video department for a sports and pop culture website. George helped to cast the

(continued)

four shows Graham was developing, and a few months later he saw on Graham's Tumblr blog that he was looking for an associate producer for the site's sports and pop culture show. George responded, interviewed, and had a job offer within the day. When the site was acquired by a larger sports conglomerate, George pitched an NBA show to his bosses. He now works as producer on the show, putting out ten to fourteen videos about basketball per week.

A Good Fit

As an ENTP, George is a dominant Intuitive type. As a producer, he is the big-picture person in the room. His overarching vision shapes the product, and he is always looking for the idea or thread that ties it all together. When producing a video, he combs through content with his eye on the end goal: "I want this hook out of it. I want people to get this feeling or think about this when they see it." Like most Conceptualizers, George is an ace strategist and problem solver. He describes looking back at the end of a day with great satisfaction at "all the different problems that had to be solved or handled." As an Extravert and a Perceiver, George is outgoing and flexible, and loves to think on his feet and roll with the punches. He gets along well with a variety of people and enjoys a good rapport with the many people who depend on him. George's job is fast paced and exciting, which is fulfilling to a person who considers boredom and downtime the ultimate drain on his energy.

Looking Ahead

George enjoys his current gig but describes his dream job as "something involving overarching strategy. I love the idea of reaching the level of senior vice president." He'd like to be with the thinkers and creators in a job that involves making large-scale problem-solving decisions, like how to brand a product or design a show. To be "the person who could integrate all those ideas" would be thrilling to George. Whether this job ends up being in the field of sports and entertainment, advertising, or entrepreneurship is just a matter of detail.

Profile 2: Alicia

"Making ideas come to fruition."

You might say that Alicia really has three jobs. As co-owner of a successful sports camp in New England with her husband, Jackson, Alicia finds that her life changes with the season. While camp is in session, she's primarily responsible for supervising the staff and making sure everyone has an excellent, happy experience. "People describe me as the glue that keeps the staff together. I listen to them, and if they have an idea, they know they can talk to me and I'll make it happen. It's not about keeping just the campers happy—it's the staff as well."

Because Alicia lives on the camp property, hers is really a twenty-four-hour job, and she has an open-door policy. Even though she has lots of paperwork to attend to during the day, she sees her main function as motivating her staff: "Keep it happy, keep it positive, keep it moving forward."

The absolute best part of the camp season is the daily interactions with people. "With a key staff of twenty, it's a fun place to be—full of positive energy." Alicia counts among her top skills her empathy and her ability to connect with people. "I love that others think of me as a really good leader who people like to follow, and a get-it-done person." The best compliment she ever received was, "Alicia is never satisfied with having an idea; she needs to see it come to fruition." And although she is fun and funny, she is also very organized and has extremely high standards.

Alicia's second job is co-running the camp during the off-season. It isn't quite as much fun, since Alicia is a people person and there just aren't that many people in the small, rural New England town where she and her family live. Still, there is much to do: helping Jackson hire staff, developing programs, creating marketing materials, writing staff manuals, and keeping the books. The off-season is also when she and Jackson have time to take a breath, think big thoughts, and come up with ways of improving how they do things at camp and how they market themselves.

Alicia's third job is as a very active volunteer and as a full-time mom to her two young daughters. Because of her resourcefulness, she has been able to find great outlets for her ample energy and impressive creativity. One example is when the director of the small school her daughters attend asked Alicia to chair the annual fund-raising auction. "Whenever I'm presented with a new task, the first question I ask is, how can I make it better than it's ever been before?" Given a goal of raising $10,000, she set the bar much higher. "I looked at what they had done in the past and immediately

saw how it could be improved." Some of the changes she implemented? "We added sponsorship and advertising in the program for the first time. I got the committee to meet once a week, rather than once a month; appointed classroom reps, with a goal of one hundred percent involvement; and a bunch of other things." As a result, the committee raised $17,000, and that number continued to grow for the three years Alicia was chair. She is most proud of the fact that, because of her leadership, teachers are now able to have health insurance—something they never had before.

Although she was not born into the camping world like her husband, whose family has been involved in this camp for one hundred years, Alicia's personality type, education, and experiences converged to provide her with work that is intrinsically satisfying and at which she excels.

Alicia graduated in 1988 with honors from Rollins College with a bachelor's degree that she designed herself, which combined art, philosophy, sociology, and literature. She spent a year volunteering as a child care worker in a Kentucky shelter. After that, she managed small retail shops for a few years before going back into social work full-time to serve people with special needs. One facility served clients with profound disabilities who needed physical care 24/7. "I was the activity director—the 'fun girl.' When they saw me, they lit up because they knew they were going to do something fun." She loved making people feel better about themselves. "One girl had never seen the ocean, so I took her down to the water's edge, sat down, and held her in my arms as she experienced the feel of the waves for the first time."

In 1997, she met Jackson, who had recently purchased the camp and was in the process of turning it into a premier sports camp. "I was drawn to his enthusiasm and work ethic—it was so stimulating! I decided that if I was going to date this man, his camp was going to be a part of my life." While they worked on the transition, Alicia took a job at the writing center of a local college. Soon they married, and now with two small children, Alicia and Jackson made the decision to move up north and live at the camp permanently, instead of just during the camp season, as they had been doing.

Although running the camp alongside Jackson has been tremendously rewarding, as with all jobs there are parts Alicia would give up if she could. What drains her most are combative relationships and times when people get angry because they don't like a particular decision. "And when business is tough and not doing as well as I want it to, each bill feels like an assault on my character—that I'm not successful enough." In the off-season, she finds that working in isolation, especially having to do so much detail-oriented work, can be very draining. Fortunately, the many pluses outweigh any minuses, and this has been a very rewarding career for Alicia.

Why This Career Works for Alicia

ENTPs are particularly adept at finding or creating situations that make good use of their natural abilities, and Alicia is no exception. As is true of most Conceptualizers, Alicia is a lifelong learner who strives to be successful. Her self-designed quadruple college concentration—art, philosophy, sociology, and literature—speaks to her natural curiosity and desire to understand how things are related to each other. ENTPs are the kind of people who continually seek new challenges. When Alicia realized that she was going to be involved in the camp business, she jumped in with both feet, learning everything she could about what it

takes to create the very best experience possible. Of course, it doesn't hurt that she extraverts her dominant function—Intuition—which enables her to immediately see possibilities everywhere!

Alicia prides herself on her creativity. Not only is she a talented visual artist, but she is able to use her creativity to solve problems. She is simply wired to see alternative—and often better—ways of executing an idea or project.

Alicia's auxiliary function is Thinking, which is introverted. This provides her with important balance and the ability to "go inside" and analyze her ideas logically and objectively, ensuring that they really are as good as when they first come to her with a rush of extraverted energy. Alicia's third function—Feeling—is extraverted. This means that, although she is a Thinker, she engages her Feeling when she is interacting with others. This contributes to her sensitivity and empathy, and helps to explain why she so values harmony and positive relationships with others.

Common Threads

Although Brent, Alicia, and George have different backgrounds, experiences, and careers, there are certain common threads woven through their stories. Their specific interests and abilities may differ, but owing to their similar temperament values, the *same hierarchy* of their psychological functions, and the "world" they naturally use them in (inner or outer), there are certain observations we can make about the needs of many ENTPs.

What follows is a list of the most important elements—the formula, if you will—for ENTP satisfaction. Given the uniqueness of all individuals—even those who share the same type—this list will not describe each ENTP equally well. The important thing is that these ten elements, with varying degrees of intensity and in different orders of importance, identify what ENTPs need to be satisfied.

After you have reviewed this list, we recommend that you go back and prioritize the elements in order of *their importance to you*. When doing this, think of past work experiences as well as your present job, and what you found particularly satisfying or unsatisfying. Try to look for *themes* that run through several experiences, not just the events that might be true for one work situation but not for another.

As an ENTP, career satisfaction means doing work that:

1. Gives me opportunities to engage in creative problem solving and/or generating new and innovative approaches to problems
2. Lets me implement my innovative solutions in the creation of more efficiently functioning systems
3. Acknowledges and encourages my creativity, competency, and ability to improvise
4. Lets me experience a variety of situations filled with fun, action, and excitement
5. Follows a logical order and is based upon objective and fair standards, rather than the likes or dislikes or one individual
6. Lets me increase my professional and personal power and interact frequently with other powerful people
7. Lets me meet and have constant interaction with many different people, especially those I respect
8. Can be done in a rapidly changing, high-energy environment with significant interaction with others
9. Is done in an environment that is casual and unstructured; where I can experience a high degree of personal freedom, time off, and the opportunity to operate in a spontaneous way
10. Allows me to design or start projects but does not require me to follow through with tedious details

Popular Occupations for ENTPs

In listing occupations that are popular among ENTPs, it is important to note that there are successful people of all types in all occupations. However, the following are careers ENTPs may find particularly satisfying and some of the reasons why. This is by no means a comprehensive listing but is included to suggest possibilities you may not have previously considered. Although all of these occupations offer the potential for career satisfaction, the future demand for some careers is anticipated to be greater than for others. Based upon our research, the occupations that are italicized in the lists below are forecast to enjoy the fastest rate of growth over the next several years.

ENTREPRENEURSHIP/BUSINESS
- Entrepreneur
- Inventor
- Management consultant
- Venture capitalist
- Literary agent
- Photographer
- Journalist
- Owner: restaurant/bar
- Actor
- *Outplacement consultant*
- Technical trainer
- *Diversity manager/trainer*
- *Management consultant: compensation/benefits/job analysis*
- University/college president
- Property manager: commercial/ residential
- Attorney: litigator
- Sales agent: securities and commodities

- Agent and business manager
- Urban and regional planner
- Human resources recruiter
- Ombudsman
- Security analyst
- Manufacturer's service representative
- Hotel general manager
- Employee relations specialist

ENTPs are born entrepreneurs! The appeal of these careers to the ENTP is the ability to create a work environment that is new, flexible, and changing. These careers often involve the interaction and participation of many people, creating new concepts and approaches, thinking in innovative ways, and engaging in a certain amount of risk-taking. The projects are often large-scale, requiring the development of big budgets and the participation of powerful and influential people.

Remember, these are only some areas that provide satisfying expression for the unique natural talents of the ENTP.

MARKETING/CREATIVE
- *Advertising creative director*
- *Market research analyst*
- *Public relations specialist*
- *Social media manager*
- *Marketing researcher/planner*
- *Marketing manager*
- Sports marketer
- Radio/TV talk show host
- Producer
- Art director (magazine)
- International marketer
- Informational-graphics designer
- New business development: information services
- Creative director on multimedia team
- Print designer
- Interaction designer
- Internet marketer
- Blogger

- Website content creator
- Creative writer
- Copywriter
- Director: stage, motion pictures
- Columnist, critic, commentator
- Reporter, correspondent
- Broadcast news analyst

The fields of marketing, advertising, and public relations allow the ENTP to be involved with other creative people, developing and implementing their ideas, often in creative and exciting ways. ENTPs enjoy the fast-paced, sometimes glamorous world of public relations and advertising and are able to use their charm and people skills selling their ideas and concepts. Market research requires ENTPs to use their abilities to spot trends. It also stimulates and satisfies their insatiable curiosity and active imagination.

PLANNING AND DEVELOPMENT
- Strategic planner
- *Business development director*
- Personnel systems developer
- Real estate agent/developer
- Special projects developer
- Investment broker
- Computer analyst
- Industrial design manager
- Logistics consultant (manufacturing)
- *Networking specialist*
- *Personal financial adviser*
- Investment banker
- Urban planner

Careers in planning and development require the ability to use one's vision and anticipate trends and formulate creative plans. Developers work on speculative projects, often needing to convince others of their merit and potential for success, an activity ENTPs enjoy and often excel at. Developers also need to remain flexible, adapting to new opportunities, ready to put together new "deals" without much preplanning or notice. ENTPs enjoy careers in strategic planning if they are allowed to focus on the development of innovative solutions to problems and then delegate the follow-through of the details to others.

POLITICS
- Politician
- Political manager
- Political analyst
- Social scientist

These occupations allow ENTPs to use their ideas, knowledge, and personal sophistication in a highly charged, fast-paced, and powerful arena. ENTPs are able to use their abilities to see trends, themes, and public opinion shifts and adapt to those changes. ENTPs are drawn to the powerful and enjoy working with a variety of different people. The world of politics requires they meet and establish rapport quickly with those whom they wish to influence. ENTPs often enjoy public speaking and can be excellent orators, using figurative, expansive language, and expressing great vision.

MISCELLANEOUS
- Chiropractor
- Environmental scientist
- Educational psychologist
- *Athletic coach and scout*
- Criminalist and ballistics expert
- Detective

Customizing Your Job Search

Knowing the particular strengths and blind spots of your type can afford you a tremendous advantage in your job search campaign. In all aspects of the process, from conducting research into available positions, identifying and contacting prospective employers, developing personal marketing tools such as résumés, arranging and conducting job interviews, negotiating salaries, to finally accepting a position, people will act true to their type. Being able to capitalize on your assets and compensate for your liabilities can make the difference between a successful and an unsuccessful job search.

Differences between types are sometimes subtle and other times dramatic. It is the subtle variations in advice we offer that make the real difference between success or failure in a job search. The concept of "networking," or meeting with and talking to people to gather information about potential jobs, serves as a good example. Extraverts will naturally enjoy networking and are advised to do so on a large scale, while Introverts find more limited and targeted networking, especially with people they already know, easier. Sensors tend to network with people in a defined scope, while Intuitives will go far and wide to find people often seemingly unrelated to their field of interest. Further, Feelers take networking, like everything else, very personally and enjoy establishing warm rapport, while Thinkers will be more objective and detached in their style. Finally, Judgers tend to ask fewer and more structured questions during their networking, while Perceivers could ask questions of all sorts all day long! One valuable search technique, many ways to implement it.

Pathways to Success: Using Your Strengths

As we will detail in the following pages, your strengths and talents will serve you well in the information-gathering stages of the job search. Your innovative approach and energetic and charming style will be great assets. Beware, however, of your tendency to underestimate the importance of following through on necessary details in your excitement to pursue yet another option.

As an ENTP, your most effective strategies will build on your abilities to:

Generate enthusiasm for yourself and your ideas.

- Use your natural enthusiasm for your ideas and inspirations when describing your abilities, success with past projects, and potential contributions.
- Express your confidence in yourself and your ability to master any project or challenge.

When ENTP Steven faces the challenge of winning over a skeptical potential client, he lets his imagination and enthusiasm for the project and its potential for positive change lead the discussion. He speaks about past successes and also talks about what he will be able to accomplish for the client. Sometimes, those are goals the client didn't even imagine were attainable before Steven pointed them out.

See new and exciting possibilities.

- Develop ideas for ways you might bene-fit an organization or company using your ingenuity and imaginative use of systems.
- Discuss how those changes will solve present and future problems.

Jeff used his imagination and vision to see ways he could help make a developer friend's health club project a reality. During the first casual conversation about the project, the light went on for Jeff and he began to brainstorm ways to improve and extend the original scope of the project. His enthusiasm was so infectious, he essentially sold himself to the developer as a vital element in the future success of the club. The fact that the job didn't formally exist yet did not deter Jeff from seeing its potential. Because he was able to communicate that energy to the developer he secured an excellent career opportunity.

Create your own job opportunities.

- Use your "vision" to anticipate trends, where people with your talents will be needed in the future, and so on.
- Use your energy and ability to meet people and introduce yourself to those who might best connect you with other influential people.

When Ann's job was about to be phased out, she used her vision and personal charm to find out which areas of the firm would be expanding over the coming months. She developed a friendship with an upper-level manager and soon learned about a new, experimental project being designed. She made a proposal over lunch to her friend and was able to get in on the ground floor of the new venture before her current job ended.

Collect a great amount of information from talking to people.

- Network extensively, especially with those who know many people with whom you might talk to identify possi-ble career opportunities.
- Ask others to brainstorm with you to develop a list of options you might research later.

When Marcia relocated to Chicago, she developed a list of contacts through her old college friends in the Chicago area and the advertising club of Greater Chicago. Marcia called on everyone. She enjoyed the process of meeting new people and found that in four weeks, she had a large roster of contacts. She ultimately met with a creative director of a large firm specializing in high-tech clients, which appealed to her because it was a new interest area to tackle. They hit it off, and she was offered a job. It was her twenty-second informational interview.

Understand what motivates others.

- Tune in to what others are saying and not saying about their needs as employers so you can discuss how your skills and abilities can assist them.
- Express your natural charm and sense of humor to create rapport and a positive working relationship.

Mike was applying for a high-paying job as special projects developer at a growing real estate development firm. He knew he was up against another candidate with more experience and a strong background in the financial market. He decided that he would use his natural charm to make friends with the interviewers. He immediately created a friendly, light atmosphere where all members of the group were laughing and sharing "war stories" from past projects. Mike was offered the job because, as he was later told, the group viewed him as a member of the team from the very start.

Improvise: show others how you can think on your feet.

- Demonstrate your ability to deal imaginatively with unexpected situations.
- Discuss your abilities and experience with crisis management and other emergencies, generating confidence in your capacity for responsibility.

While Gail was interviewing at a management consulting firm, the interviewer's assistant announced that proposals being prepared for a big presentation that afternoon were in a truck that had been disabled on the highway. Gail offered to call a friend who operated a personal delivery service. Gail arranged for a driver to meet the disabled truck, load the

proposals, and deliver them to the meeting. The interviewer and the firm's new client were impressed with Gail's quick thinking and ability to avert a potential disaster.

Analyze long-range implications.

- Demonstrate your ability to anticipate consequences, and to logically analyze products and processes.
- Demonstrate your ability to be objective by offering honest critiques of past work situations.

Possible Pitfalls

Although all people are unique, there are certain *potential* blind spots that many ENTPs share. We specify "potential" because some of the following may clearly be true of you, while others may not apply. While considering them, you may notice that these tendencies do not relate just to the job search but rather describe pitfalls which you may have experienced in other aspects of your life as well. It is therefore helpful to consider each one in terms of your past experiences by asking yourself, "Is this true for me?" And if so, "How did this tendency prevent me from getting something that I wanted?" You will probably notice that the key to overcoming your blind spots is the conscious and thoughtful development of your third and fourth functions (Feeling and Sensing). We recognize that many of the suggestions will be difficult to implement, but the more you use these functions, the fewer problems they will cause you in the future.

Avoid the tendency to generate so many options that it is impossible to make a decision and follow through on necessary details.

- Try to pay close attention to the facts, details, and timeliness of a project. Eliminate unrealistic options along the way and stick with your established list of priorities.

Try not to dismiss as illogical and unimportant the feelings of other people, therefore appearing arrogant and/or rude.

- Try to focus on how a project or statement will affect others. Try to offer positive feedback before negative criticism, knowing that some people may take criticism very personally.

Discipline yourself and try not to procrastinate; don't put off decisions so long that options are eliminated for you.

- Establish and adhere to deadlines. Try to be conscious of the schedules and timetables of others and to notify people when you expect to be late.

Don't interrupt others before they have finished speaking because an idea has come to you.

- Engage your listening skills; wait until you are sure the person has finished speaking before offering your ideas and input.
- Try the trick of repeating back what the person has said so you are sure you understood what they *actually* said.

The Final Piece: Changing or Keeping Your Job . . . the Key to Success for ENTPs

Now that you have a solid understanding of your type, you can see how your natural preferences make you better suited for certain kinds of jobs. You can also see how knowledge of your type-related strengths and weaknesses can help you conduct a more successful job search. But as an ENTP, you've already realized that you are not equally drawn to *every* career or field listed in the Popular Occupations section. The next and final step is to narrow down the field and find the work you were meant to do.

In addition to Type, several other factors—such as your values, interests, and skills—also contribute to your level of satisfaction on the job. The more compatible you are with your job, the happier you'll be. So prepare to use everything you've learned (in this book and in life) to create *your strategic career plan*. The exercises in Chapter 24, Putting It All Together, are designed to help you do just that.

However, you may have decided it makes more sense (if perhaps only for the moment) to stay in your present job or with your current employer. There may be many valid reasons—financial pressures, family considerations, a tough job market for your specialty, or just bad timing. But take heart! What you've learned in this book can also help you be more content and successful *in your current job*. And should the time come when you're ready to make a major career move, you'll have a much better idea of where you want to go, and how to get there.

"So, if you can't have the job you love (yet!) . . . love the one you've got."

The simple truth is, with the exception of work on a factory assembly line, the vast majority of jobs allow a good deal of flexibility in the way tasks are performed. Here are some ways you may be able to "massage" your current job into one that better fits your needs:

- If possible, delegate routine tasks to others.
- Take courses and seminars to continue to expand your expertise and credentials.
- Team up with co-workers and/or work on teams.

- Hire an assistant or secretary who is good with details and follow-through.
- Find other creative people with whom to brainstorm ideas.
- Join professional associations and attend conferences.
- Work a different shift, arrange more flexible hours, or job-share.
- Join or start organizations for people with similar expertise or interests.
- Change your focus if you're not stimulated or challenged; work on something else for a while.
- Make sure you have a variety of projects to work on.
- Develop a "critical friends" group to critique each other's ideas and plans.

One ENTP turns lemons into lemonade:

Debbie realized her shortcomings. Although she was a great idea person, she frequently lost her enthusiasm and energy for projects once the creative stage was finished. So when she was promoted to a new position, she made sure that the person she hired to be her assistant was very organized and detail-oriented, qualities she lacked but needed. With the right assistant, she was able to spend less time fixing her own mistakes and more time seeing her many creative ideas come to life.

Use what you've got to get what you need.

Simply put, the best advice on how to succeed is to *capitalize on your strengths and compensate for your weaknesses.* Learning how to do this can make the difference between succeeding or failing and loving or hating your work. To help you, we include the following inventory of your potential strengths and weaknesses. And while every individual is unique, as an ENTP, many of the following should apply to you.

Your work-related strengths may include:

- Excellent communication skills and the ability to get others excited about your ideas
- Eagerness to "think outside the box" and consider new possibilities
- Great creative problem-solving skills
- Courage to take some risks, try new things, and overcome obstacles
- Broad range of interests and ability to learn new things quickly
- Ability to withstand rejection and maintain optimism and enthusiasm
- Great confidence and drive to continually increase your knowledge
- Natural curiosity and skills for getting the information you need
- Ability to see the big picture and the implications of actions and ideas
- Ability to juggle several projects at once
- Perceptiveness about people—their needs and motivations
- Adaptability and ease in shifting gears and changing directions quickly
- Great social ease and ability to fit comfortably into most social situations

Your work-related weaknesses may include:

- Trouble keeping yourself organized
- Difficulty setting priorities and making decisions
- Overconfidence; you may misrepresent your abilities or experience
- Propensity to always focus on what's possible rather than what's doable or probable
- Tendency to promise more than you can deliver
- Impatience with unimaginative or inflexible people
- Tendency to lose interest in projects once problems are solved

- Dislike of doing things in a traditional, established, or routine manner
- Lack of discipline when it comes to attending to and following through on important details

- Tendency to become bored or easily sidetracked
- Dislike of repetitive tasks
- Impatience with people whose competence you question

Using your strengths is easy.
The secret to success for an
ENTP
is learning to:

Prioritize, focus, and follow through—
especially with commitments
made to others.

15 | INTP
Introverted, Intuitive, Thinking, Perceiving

"Ingenious Problem Solvers"

Profile 1: Jaye

"There's something very satisfying about running a business that is completely self-supporting."

Forty-one-year-old Jaye prefers the title career consultant to the more popular career counselor, primarily because she has created a job and a business that are more dynamic and varied than the average counselor's day of one-on-one client sessions. Jaye thinks of her role as more of an architect, helping to develop creative strategies using logical and efficient processes to meet her clients' goals. And after ten years her thriving practice is completely referral-based, a source of pride and great satisfaction.

Jaye spends about 75 percent of her time providing individual career counseling to adult job changers aged thirty to sixty. Most are dissatisfied with their work or are interested in exploring what else they might do, having been typically "sucked into a job

without any informed career planning." Jaye provides a structured system of information gathering and testing. She helps her clients identify their personality type, skills, values, and interests to end up with what she calls the "recipe" with potential for long-term success. Next she helps her clients "package" themselves, beginning with the development of a résumé. She teaches her clients how to have effective interviews, use a network, and become educated about all the possibilities in the market. Jaye sees interviewing as a life skill, one that empowers you to get access to whatever information you need and not have to wait for someone else to provide it. During this phase, Jaye becomes more than a teacher; "I act as coach, supporter, adviser, evaluator, cheerleader, and kicker-in-the-pants." She describes this part of the process as a "treasure hunt." Her clients join a "research club" of other "hunters" to share information, contacts, and ideas, and offer support and validation to one another. Jaye meets with her clients throughout this process and also helps when the time comes to consider a job offer, negotiate a salary and benefits package, and adjust to the new job.

It's a process-lover's dream. Jaye admits that besides being independent and calling her own shots, her favorite part of her work involves brainstorming. That's the time when she and her client look for patterns and find connections between what the client has enjoyed and succeeded at in the past and what might be satisfying for his or her future. It's that creative problem solving and the application of a logical and expedient strategy that Jaye finds most energizing, followed closely by the time she spends working alone, creating new materials and "letting the ideas flow." She structures her schedule to keep each Friday free of appointments so she can work independently and not be interrupted or pressured.

Jaye spends the remaining 25 percent of her time consulting for small businesses in the areas of analyzing management teams, enhancing communication and problem solving, and performing employment-needs analysis. She has successfully helped start nine new businesses, and all but one are still thriving.

Looking back on her work history, Jaye has always been a teacher, beginning with her high school days as a swimming instructor and camp counselor. In college she designed her own major, a combination of biology and psychology, and minored in English and sociology. She received a teaching certificate. After college she served in Vietnam with the Red Cross for a year as a field counselor and recreational leader. Upon her return, she fell into a job teaching science and English in a middle school. "I liked all the creative stuff about

teaching, and my classroom always had big models hanging from the ceiling. But I couldn't stand the structure and bureaucracy, and I was bored with the routine." She relocated and enrolled in graduate school, designing a major in career counseling for adults, with lots of field work and internships. After graduation, she was hired as a career counselor at a small private university with a growing program and staff and "a philosophy that embraced the importance of preparing students for working in the real world." Within two years, she had been promoted to director and created an "exciting and unique four-year career experience for students." She began to tire of the supervisory demands of the job and decided to start a private career consulting business with a colleague. The business flourished for seven years and grew to a total of five associates.

During this time, Jaye began to confront her alcoholism and eventually left the partnership. In recovery she decided to once again strike out on her own and has been working in her own business for four years, the first three alone and the past year with an associate who Jaye feels complements her skills and style. Generally, Jaye says, "I never have a bad day." But she is sometimes drained by what she calls "all the loose ends"—phone calls to return, appointments to reschedule, and details like proofreading materials from the printer. She lacks time management skills, and her "piling" system is not as efficient or logical as she'd really like it to be.

"The only real source of stress is that I can't do all of my ideas." Indeed, if she could create any job in the universe, it would be one where she would be required to come up with good ideas for other people to implement and follow through on.

Jaye deals with stress by leaving work at work and getting involved in a great many activities, including volunteer work with a national self-help group for recovering alcoholics, hiking, biking, and camping, playing with her dog, reading, and an array of arts and crafts from photography to wood carving.

"I derive great satisfaction from empowering others: helping them change their lives, take risks, and make choices that are right for them." Through her own recovery from alcoholism, Jaye has found a new spirituality in her life and has been able to develop a stronger and healthier view of herself. She used to think that being successful must involve "big bucks" but now wants a simpler life. "I've been blessed in my career because most of the jobs I've had were really all accidents that worked out well."

Jaye has changed a lot over the past ten years. In addition to a sober lifestyle that has allowed her to intensify her important relationships, she is becoming a really good counselor. She is becoming less directive in her approach and more sensitive to her clients. The notes and cards of thanks and appreciation she receives from clients are very meaningful to her. "There's a better balance in me, and as a result, I'm better at my work. I'm very lucky to be able to honestly say I'm a happy person and I really love my days."

Why This Career Works for Jaye

As with many Conceptualizers (NTs), Jaye works with possibilities—in her case helping her clients discover satisfying career options. Valuing competence, Jaye is constantly increasing her own knowledge and working to help her clients become more competent, effective, and successful. She enjoys the independence that comes with being an entrepreneur and the risk-taking associated with being in business for oneself.

Although she likes people, Jaye enjoys working alone where she can put her introverted Thinking (dominant) to good use by developing strategies for her own business and her clients' career advancements. She applies depth and logic to analyze her clients' needs and skills and to identify career opportunities that offer the potential for a good match between the two. In her business consulting, she uses her critical Thinking to evaluate clients' staffing needs and figure out ways to get those needs met.

Jaye uses her Intuition (auxiliary) to imagine and brainstorm possible satisfying job options for her clients. Generating ideas, making connections between past jobs and activities that her clients engaged in with future possibilities, and creative problem solving are also ways she uses her highly developed Intuition. She enjoys making connections between people—matching up the most helpful people for her clients to talk to—and helping her people to start new businesses.

In recent years, Jaye has plugged into her Sensing (third function) by developing greater consciousness of herself and her *immediate* world. She is striving for a simpler life, realizing that becoming rich and powerful is not as important as she once thought it was. She uses her senses more often in her hands-on recreational activities and by spending more time enjoying nature while hiking and camping. She has also become more aware of the importance of her Feeling side (fourth function). Expressions of appreciation from her clients mean a lot to her, and she is able to express her own feelings more easily. She believes her increased sensitivity to the feelings of others has made her a better counselor.

Meet the Millennial

Name: Anna
Age: 25
Sales and digital marketing manager

"Marketing books in the digital age."

Backstory

When she was a kid, Anna wanted to grow up to be an artist. In high school, she wanted to be a mathematician. And in college, she wanted to be a journalist. "After college, I realized that none of these are jobs that are typically available for a twenty-two-year-old." Instead, Anna started doing editorial work for a food website, an experience that taught her a lot about the editorial process, publicity, marketing, and copy writing. She made a lot of connections with bloggers, writers, business owners, and book publicists, opening up a network of people who would later hire her for freelance work and recommend her for future jobs.

A year after college, Anna took a job as the marketing director for a craft beer start-up. The prospect of pioneering a start-up company's online platform was exciting to her, but she quickly found herself missing both the creative and intellectual aspects of editorial work. She left this job to pursue freelance copy writing and editing. After a few months, she was hired at an independent publishing house to do a combination of marketing and editorial work.

Now Anna is the sales and digital marketing manager. Her job consists mainly of getting a strong sense of the books to be published and figuring out how best to market them. She then equips the sales team with the key points and facts they need to convince wholesale book buyers to purchase the books. Anna also manages the company's online presence, curating the website and running social media to promote their catalogue of books.

A Good Fit

As a Conceptualizer, Anna is an extremely strategic and architectural thinker. This is central to her role in marketing, as she calculates which moves will best ensure each project's success. "These days, any sort of editorial work has to be anchored with a sense of the business and marketing that sustains it. You have to understand how books are marketed and sold on a large scale." A dominant Thinking type, she is analytical and intellectual in her editorial duties, able to see both the flaws in a project as well as how best to problem-solve them. With Intuition as her auxiliary function, Anna is adept at seeing the big picture of a book, task, project, or company's mission, and then effectively communicating those ideas to others.

One of the results of her well-developed Intuition is her skill at composing superior promotional materials for books: "It is easy for me to assess the style, aims, appeal, and target audience of a book and to articulate them." She has a keen and creative sense of aesthetics, which also makes her good at managing the company's online appearance.

Looking Ahead

Anna really appreciates the creative and intellectual sensibilities that go into editorial work. In five to ten years she sees herself in some sort of editorial leadership role either for a publication, like a magazine or website, or for a publishing company. She would like to take a larger role in the big-picture decision making and use her talents to envision and shape a long-range view of a book, publication, or season's content. As an editor or even editor in chief, Anna would have greater control and discretion over a product's outcome, a prospect she finds satisfying. Most of all, Anna would like to continue to work on publications she is proud of, and to see how the work takes on a life of its own.

Profile 2: Bert

"I value the process; it's the process that creates success."

At first glance it would seem that forty-one-year-old Bert is a producer of entertainment shows, audiovisual presentations, and custom marketing programs. But he's really first and foremost an entrepreneur. "The day-to-day functions are totally incidental to what I do for a living. I'm always changing"—changing himself and helping create change for others around him, especially those people Bert respects and enjoys working with. "It doesn't feel like an occupation."

Each year Bert creates programs, entertainment shows, marketing presentations and corporate meetings, audiovisual presentations, and custom marketing programs for large corporate clients around the country. He runs a small office and supervises a full-time staff of four and countless independent contractors on an as-needed basis. Sometimes he contracts with a major Broadway, film, or musical star, arranges for all the technical and musical equipment and support, and makes complete travel and accommodation arrangements. Other times he may develop a multiscreen audiovisual program to showcase a corporation's new marketing strategy during a national sales conference. The details are endless, the pressure intense. And as Bert says, "I'm only as good as my last show."

But the man loves his work. He thrives on the freedom he has to work on the kinds of projects he enjoys and with the people he enjoys and respects. His work requires that he be as creative as possible and have continuous opportunities to build his network. It's the networking that energizes Bert most. "The more competent people I work with, the easier it is to be successful at what I do." Bert enjoys the fact that the process of working with "great people" helps him and them fulfill their goals. He believes he helps others share and take risks they wouldn't ordinarily take on their own, work to their potential, and create an excellent product. "I get people to stretch, to understand the importance of 'going for it,' and to understand how great it will be to be successful at what they are reaching for."

This is not the kind of talk one might expect from a trained accountant. Bert received his college degree in accounting with the full, conscious knowledge that he would never be an accountant. It was a strategic decision because he knew that he would someday run his own business and would need those skills. The practical skills he gained during his first job as business manager of his father's dental lab have been invaluable. But the lack of creativity of that position was too limiting, so he left to start a company that manufactured furniture kits. After one and a half years, Bert accepted a job as business manager of a screen printing company. He left that job because his boss was "running the company into the ground." He decided to start his own screen printing company, which he ran successfully for six years until the recession of the early 1980s hit and interest rates soared. Business dropped 85 percent in one month. His next venture was a special events company that created and marketed events and activities to colleges, universities, and corporations. He ran the business with two partners for five years and continues it on his own, in a different form, today. Now his market is exclusively corporations and businesses. Bert's greatest strengths are his childlike enthusiasm, the fact he doesn't get trapped by society's expectations of what he should do, or what's proper to do, his willingness to experiment and take risks, and his ability to organize his work efficiently even though he is not a very organized person. Bert is also

resourceful, meticulous about the details required to make his project succeed, and a great alternative thinker.

Bert takes pride in the fact that he has a reputation for being good at whatever he does, from creative concepts and presentations and shows that receive standing ovations from their audiences to brilliant business consulting. "The key word is competence. If the client is happy with the results of my work, that's great. But if there's an audience involved, then *their* satisfaction is more important than the client's. The best combination is when my client takes a risk, based on my recommendation, and it succeeds. That's the biggest high of all."

As with all work, there are the downsides too. Bert dislikes the routine, day-to-day details, the record keeping, and the accounting necessary to keep track of his business. He's drained by the preparation of tax returns and any time he needs to act as a "gofer" for anybody.

And because the projects are often very large, so are some of the stresses. Bert is stressed about the things over which he has no control, like entertainers arriving at the last minute, equipment that doesn't show up, or planes that don't take off. However, most of the time he is able to combat and relieve the stress by the confidence he has in his own resourcefulness. Stress reduction, like most processes, is an intellectual one for Bert. He also participates in physical outdoor activities like riding his motorcycle, biking, lifting weights, and in other activities like playing or listening to music, tinkering with things, and photography.

Bert hasn't really changed much over the past few years. His three children and strong friendships are as important now as they have always been. But he is learning to use and trust his "gut" instinct about people more and with better results. He used to spend too much time doing work himself because he couldn't trust other people to do it right. Now he is better able to select the right people to work with, making his work easier and more fun. "I'm not there yet and may never really be there. But my goal is to increase my insight about others so I work less by myself and more with people I trust and know are competent."

Bert continues to work toward the optimum process: creating unique concepts, working with excellent people, achieving competent executions of his concepts and the satisfaction of those he works with to create them, and wowing his audience. For him, that *is* career satisfaction.

Why This Career Works for Bert

Bert's Conceptualizer temperament drives him to constantly seek out new challenges. He has built his business around developing programs and services that continuously present him with new problems to solve. Being an entrepreneur satisfies his need for independence and his desire to surround himself with people whose competence and talents he respects. Bert thinks big, takes on huge and complex projects, and enjoys the status and power his success gives him. He also enjoys being highly respected for his creativity and integrity.

"Noodling things over" in his head is how Bert describes using his introverted Thinking (dominant). It allows him to see the logical consequences of actions, anticipate problems and identify solutions, and organize the competent execution of his concepts. As an introverted Thinker, he is also less concerned about what others think of his ideas. He is run by his own principles and sets very high standards for himself because it is what *he* thinks that is most important to him rather than what others think.

It is Bert's extraverted Intuition (auxiliary) that helps him to see possibilities out in the world. He lives to provide exciting and original ways to meet clients' goals, generate enthusiasm for his vision, and get his clients excited about how positively the end result will be received. He naturally sees connections between the right people for the right job, and enjoys putting them together. Being innovative and shaking up the establishment are important to Bert. He has a gift for helping people stretch and exceed their own expectations.

Bert uses his Sensing (third function) to keep track of the myriad details involved in his projects and to make sure things are done right. Recreationally, he has plugged into his Sensing by taking up many physical activities, such as bike riding, weight lifting, downhill skiing, and snorkeling. Evidence that he is developing better access to his Feeling side (fourth function) can be seen in the fact that all of his personal relationships have become more important to him. He expresses his feelings more openly and easily and trusts his gut more in evaluating other people.

Common Threads

Although Jaye, Bert, and Anna have different backgrounds, experiences, and careers, there are certain common threads woven through their stories. Their specific interests, abilities, and values may differ, but owing to their similar temperament values, the *same hierarchy* of their psychological functions, and the "world" they naturally use them in (inner or outer), there are certain observations we can make about the needs of many INTPs.

What follows is a list of the most important elements—the formula, if you will—for INTP satisfaction. Given the uniqueness of all individuals—even those who share the same type—this list will not describe each INTP equally well. The important thing is that these ten elements, with varying degrees of intensity and in different orders of importance, identify what INTPs need to be satisfied.

After you have reviewed this list, we recommend that you go back and prioritize the elements in order of *their importance to you.* When doing this, think of past work experiences as well as your present job, and what you found particularly satisfying or unsatisfying. Try to look for *themes* that run through several experiences, not just the events which might be true for one work situation but not for another.

As an INTP, career satisfaction means doing work that:

1. Lets me develop, analyze, and critique new ideas

2. Lets me focus my attention and energy on a creative, theoretical, and logical process, rather than on an end product

3. Is challenging and deals with complex problems, where I am able to try unconventional approaches, and take risks to find the best solution

4. Lets me work independently with plenty of quiet, private time to concentrate and complete my thinking process

5. Lets me set and maintain my own high standards for my work and determine how my performance will be evaluated and compensated

6. Is done in a flexible, nonstructured environment, without useless rules, excessive limitations, or unnecessary meetings

7. Lets me interact with a small group of highly regarded friends and associates, all of whom I respect

8. Gives me opportunities to constantly increase my own personal competence and power and lets me meet and interact with other powerful and successful people

9. Lets me develop ingenious ideas and plans and lets me delegate the implementation and follow-through to an efficient support staff

10. Does not require me to spend time directly organizing other people or supervising or mediating interpersonal differences

Popular Occupations for INTPs

In listing occupations that are popular among INTPs, it is important to note that there are successful people of all types in all occupations. However, the following are careers INTPs may find particularly satisfying and some of the reasons why.

This is by no means a comprehensive listing but is included to suggest possibilities you may not have previously considered. Although all of these occupations offer the potential for career satisfaction, the future demand for some careers is anticipated to be greater than for others. Based upon our research, the occupations that are italicized in the list below are forecast to enjoy the fastest growth over the next several years.

COMPUTERS/TECHNOLOGY
- *Software developer: applications, systems*
- *Computer programmer*
- *Mobile application developer*
- Computer researcher and developer
- Network systems and data communications analyst
- Strategic planner
- New market or product conceptualizer
- Information services developer–computer programming

- Information services–new business developer
- *Networking specialist*
- Change management consultant
- Management consultant: computer/information services, marketing, reorganization
- Print designer
- Interaction designer
- *Network and computer systems administrator*
- Computer animator
- *Computer software engineer, systems software*
- Java programmer
- Software developer
- Cyber security specialist

Occupations falling into this category offer INTPs the opportunity to do what they do best—analyze problems and develop innovative solutions. Most INTPs enjoy working in technical areas, using their ability to understand complex systems and to find ways to eliminate errors or weaknesses.

They easily see how the product, service, or system fits within the context of the whole company, industry, or technology and enjoy creating new, more efficient ways of doing things.

HEALTH CARE/TECHNICAL
- Neurologist
- Physicist
- *Surgeon*
- *Physician*
- *Pharmacist*
- *Medical scientist*
- Scientist: chemistry/biology
- Pharmaceutical researcher
- *Biomedical engineer/researcher*
- *Veterinarian*
- Microbiologist
- Geneticist

These fields of medicine and other scientific technologies make good use of INTPs' excellent reasoning skills and facility with technical material. The rapidly growing areas of neurology, plastic surgery, and biomedical and pharmaceutical research are often interesting to INTPs because they are able to be on the cutting edge of innovative industries, some of which carry some amount of risk. Physics, chemistry, and biology offer opportunities to work with complex concepts, constantly learn new things, and repeatedly ask the question "What if?" These careers, especially when they involve a strong research component, allow the INTP to work independently. Because they are difficult and competitive fields, they tend to attract other intellectual and gifted people, whom INTPs find stimulating.

PROFESSIONAL/BUSINESS
- *Lawyer*
- Economist
- *Personal financial adviser*
- Psychologist/psychoanalyst
- *Market research analyst*
- Financial analyst
- Architect
- Investment banker
- Investigator
- Intellectual property attorney
- Legal mediator
- Corporate finance attorney
- Psychiatrist
- Entrepreneur
- Venture capitalist
- Business analyst
- Entertainment agent
- Physicist
- *Biophysicist*
- Anthropologist
- Intelligence specialist

These professional careers also offer INTPs plenty of opportunities to analyze and solve complex problems. Often extremely challenging, these careers require clear, logical thinking and innovative approaches to problems and challenges. The creative process is central to the work of both the architect and the psychologist. Seeing how one element or event fits into an overall pattern or system is a particular strength of INTPs and is a frequent aspect of the work of an investigator and financial analyst. From developing flawless legal strategies to forecasting subtle yet powerful economic trends, these professions offer the excitement and personal challenge INTPs thrive on.

ACADEMIC
- Mathematician
- Archaeologist
- Historian
- Philosopher
- *College professor*
- *Online educator*
- Researcher
- Logician
- College faculty administrator
- Economist
- *Interpreter/translator*
- Astronomer

The stimulating world of academia is one frequently enjoyed by INTPs. Because there is an emphasis on exploring and considering new and different approaches, INTPs often find career satisfaction in the role of college professor. They usually prefer teaching the more advanced and challenging students and courses. INTPs often enjoy the research element in any of the subject areas above and enjoy the opportunity to work alone and then share their insights and innovations with their intellectual peers. They work best when not restricted by excessive rules and bureaucracy, which many large universities and colleges are unable to avoid.

CREATIVE
- Photographer
- Creative writer
- Artist
- Graphic designer
- Entertainer/dancer
- Musician
- Agent
- Inventor
- Informational-graphics designer
- Columnist, critic, commentator
- Blogger
- Music arranger
- Producer
- Director: stage, motion pictures
- Film editor
- Art director

One of the strongest attractions of these careers for INTPs is the chance to create something entirely original. INTPs enjoy the creative process of working with different mediums and the variety of people and experiences they have access to. INTPs usually enjoy working alone or with small numbers of talented people who bring something different to the process. Depending upon their area and their interest in expressing their art, INTPs can enjoy performance. But they don't necessarily need to perform their works to find satisfaction in them. Many INTPs are inspired by the world of creative people and enjoy working as an agent. And their ability to create innovative and clever products or services often gives them success as inventors.

Remember, these are only some of the areas that provide satisfying expression for the unique natural talents of INTPs.

Customizing Your Job Search

Knowing the particular strengths and blind spots of your type can afford you a tremendous advantage in your job search campaign. In all aspects of the process, from conducting research into available positions, identifying and contacting prospective employers, developing personal marketing tools such as résumés, arranging and conducting job interviews, negotiating salaries, to finally accepting a position, people will act true to their type. Being able to capitalize on your assets and compensate for your liabilities can make the difference between a successful and an unsuccessful job search.

The differences between types are sometimes subtle and other times dramatic. It is the subtle variations in advice we offer that make the real difference between success or failure in a job search. The concept of "networking," or meeting with and talking to people to gather information about potential jobs, serves as a good example. Extraverts will naturally enjoy networking and are advised to do so on a large scale, while Introverts find more limited and targeted networking, especially with people they already know, easier. Sensors tend to network with people in a defined scope, while Intuitives will go far and wide to find people often seemingly unrelated to their field of interest. Further, Feelers take networking, like everything else, very personally and enjoy establishing warm rapport, while Thinkers will be more objective and detached in their style. Finally, Judgers tend to ask fewer and more structured questions during their networking, while Perceivers could ask questions of all sorts all day long! One valuable search technique, many ways to implement it.

Pathways to Success: Using Your Strengths

As we will detail in the following pages, your strengths and talents for the job search—creative problem solving and critical analysis of potential options—will go a long way toward helping you endure the less interesting or challenging detail-chasing phases. You may also need to make a conscious effort to establish rapport and communicate your vision in simple enough language for others to understand.

As an INTP, your most effective strategies will build on your abilities to:

See possibilities that don't exist at the present time.

- Look past what is known or represented to you as "the way things are." Use your imagination to generate possibilities that may arise within the near future and plan how you can best capitalize on them.
- Consider less obvious means of getting an interviewer's attention or setting yourself apart from other candidates.

Brian realized he needed a creative and attention-getting method of differentiating himself from the other people applying for a highly sought after job as marketing director of new products for a computer software company. So instead of creating a standard résumé, Brian designed one that looked like the screen of a super-high-definition color monitor. He sketched a logo of his name, which his girlfriend, a graphic designer, helped him reproduce with an appropriate typeface to match the look of the résumé/screen. He added color and used a plastic binder and patterned contact paper to create a cover that looked like the front of the monitor, with his résumé, as the software program, on the inside. He hired a delivery service to hand-deliver the package to the company's vice president with a cover letter that said he had a whole database of innovative ideas and was eager to meet and present them at the vice president's convenience.

Create your own job opportunities or an adaptation of existing but less attractive opportunities.

- Using your talents at anticipating future needs, develop a job description for a position that will solve current or future problems.
- Determine ways of altering and improving an existing opportunity into one that will use your strengths and still serve the needs of the employer.

Elaine's upcoming promotion would mean good news and bad news. The good news was an increase in her salary, a support staff she could delegate follow-through details to, and more autonomy. The bad news was the job would require almost daily meetings, and Elaine would be reporting to an individual she had had the displeasure of serving with on a committee, someone she did not respect. After a great deal of reflection, she admitted to herself that all the perks of the promotion would not make up for the negative aspects of the job. So she created a proposal for a special pilot program that would analyze the costs and benefits of several of the company's less profitable products, something her current supervisor had long been interested in. She outlined how the position would require the support services of only one full-time person and would free up an office by requiring the part-time use of one computer terminal. Elaine recommended that she conduct much of her work from her office at home and report, on a weekly basis, to her current

supervisor. Because the position would be at a higher ranking, the salary and benefits package would rival those of the other job. Her supervisor was impressed with her initiative and trusted Elaine enough to leave her alone to work on the pilot program for the following twelve months.

Anticipate the logical consequences of actions.

- Demonstrate your clear sense of cause and effect by offering examples of past experience where you were called upon to contribute the skill, and recount what the positive outcomes were.
- Use your critical thinking skills when considering any job offer to anticipate both the positive and potentially negative outcomes of any decision.

For her second interview for a teaching position in the mathematics department of a small private university, Sandra was glad to hear that she would be asked open-ended questions by the chairman of the department. The chairman presented several difficult challenges the department and university currently faced and asked her how she might handle them if she were a member of the staff. Sandra began by explaining how during her last job she had dealt with equally vexing problems. She spoke about the various possible outcomes of several solutions and what their future ramifications might be. Her interviewer was impressed with her long-range thinking skills and her ability to see many sides of an issue without becoming personally invested in any. It was obvious by the end of the interview that Sandra had considerable skills and could make important contributions to the team.

Create and implement an innovative job search.

- View problems that arise as challenges to be met and use your creativity to come up with ways of overcoming them.
- Set yourself apart from your competition by marketing yourself as a creative, alternative thinker and let all your materials and correspondence reflect that.

Everything was going well for Eric in his job search. He had had several excellent interviews with one of the partners of a prestigious architectural firm and was preparing for his final meeting with the firm's senior partner. The morning of the interview, he arrived to discover that the partner who had been interviewing him had left the firm unexpectedly. The senior partner did not have the interview with Eric on his calendar, nor did he know anything about him. Eric had to start from scratch.

Fortunately, he was able to get another appointment and left the firm determined not to let the setback get him down. He spent the next three weeks finding out everything he could about the senior partner's past projects and the history of the firm. He prepared himself for the type of interview he might expect from the person he was learning about. At the interview, he used that experience as an example when he was asked how he dealt with unexpected stumbling blocks. The senior partner was amused and impressed by his creativity, persistence, and candor.

Keep all your career options open to gather all relevant and important information.

- Stay cool and detached; never be pressured into making a decision that you haven't had adequate time to reflect on.

- Ask lots of questions during all interviews to be sure you have an accurate picture of the job, its responsibilities, and limitations before deciding whether to consider it further.

Possible Pitfalls

Although all people are unique, there are certain *potential* blind spots that many INTPs share. We specify "potential" because some of the following *may* be true of you, while others may clearly not apply. While considering them, you may notice that these tendencies do not relate just to the job search, but rather describe pitfalls that you may have experienced in other aspects of your life as well. It is therefore helpful to consider each one in terms of your past experiences by asking yourself, "Is this true for me?" And if so, "How did this tendency prevent me from getting something that I wanted?" You will probably notice that the key to overcoming your blind spots is the conscious and thoughtful development of your third and fourth functions (Sensing and Feeling). We recognize that many of the suggestions will be difficult to implement, but the more you use these functions, the fewer problems they will cause you in the future.

Make sure to eventually move your plans out of the conceptual stage and into practice.

- Once you have developed an innovative job search plan, ask yourself how realistic some of your ideas are. Is there time to get all you've imagined done? Is it possible to create what you have dreamed up? Decide on and hold yourself to a timetable to implement your ideas.
- Develop a step-by-step plan that includes all the facts (timetable, questions to ask,

reminder to send follow-up notes, etc.) so you will be more likely to attend to them.

Establish realistic objectives and goals based upon what is practical, not on what your confidence tells you is possible.

- Remember that, depending upon your level of experience and the field you are pursuing, a full career search can take from three to twelve months before you find the right job. Knowing that from the start and reminding yourself of it throughout the process will help keep you from becoming discouraged and disinterested.
- Ask for support from a close friend when you find your impatience mounting and/or confidence waning.

Make sure you don't appear condescending or arrogant to potential employers.

- Pay close attention to how others perceive you. Ask someone you trust to role-play with you and give you an honest appraisal of your perceived attitude. In an interview, blunt honesty can be perceived as rudeness.
- Take the time to listen fully to the interviewer's questions or comments before forming an opinion about him or her. Make it a goal to try to establish rapport early in the interview.

Remember to follow through on important details involved in the process.

- Social niceties, such as thank-you notes to people who have conducted informational interviews with you, may seem superfluous, but they are an important part of the process.

- Stay on top of follow-up calls and letters so you don't appear disinterested in a position you really do want.

Don't put off making a decision.

- After you have spent the necessary time considering your options and clarifying your needs and skills, take action! Discard less attractive options and decide to actively pursue good ones.
- Don't wait so long to decide that you inadvertently eliminate an opportunity by procrastinating.

The Final Piece: Changing or Keeping Your Job . . . the Key to Success for INTPs

Now that you have a solid understanding of your type, you can see how your natural preferences make you better suited for certain kinds of jobs. You can also see how knowledge of your type-related strengths and weaknesses can help you conduct a more successful job search. But as an INTP, you've already realized that you are not equally drawn to *every* career or field listed in the Popular Occupations section. The next and final step is to narrow down the field and find the work you were meant to do.

In addition to Type, several other factors—such as your values, interests, and skills—also contribute to your level of satisfaction on the job. The more compatible you are with your job, the happier you'll be. So prepare to use everything you've learned (in this book and in life) to create *your strategic career plan.* The exercises in Chapter 24, Putting It All Together, are designed to help you do just that.

However, you may have decided it makes more sense (if perhaps only for the moment) to stay in your present job or with your current employer. There may be many valid reasons—financial pressures, family considerations, a tough job market for your specialty, or just bad timing. But take heart! What you've learned in this book can also help you be more content and successful *in your current job*. And should the time come when you're ready to make a major career move, you'll have a much better idea of where you want to go, and how to get there.

"So, if you can't have the job you love (yet!)...love the one you've got."

The simple truth is, with the exception of work on a factory assembly line, the vast majority of jobs allow a good deal of flexibility in the way tasks are performed. Here are some ways you may be able to "massage" your current job into one that better fits your needs:

- If possible, delegate routine or mundane tasks to others.
- Make sure you have enough uninter-rupted time to develop your ideas and think things through.
- Find other creative people to bounce your ideas off.
- Work a different shift or arrange more flexible hours.
- Make sure you have influence over the hiring of your direct-reports.
- Try to find support people who are organized and good with details.
- Take courses and seminars to continue to expand your expertise and credentials.
- Change your focus if bored or not challenged.
- Develop a "critical friends" group to cri-tique each other's ideas and plans.
- Try to surround yourself with others whose talent and competence you respect.

One INTP turns lemons into lemonade:

An internal computer consultant, Lisa was candid about the most frustrating part of her job: "endless meetings with stupid people." Not only did she lack the patience to repeatedly explain basic concepts to novice end users, but the constant travel to meet with different groups ate up an enormous amount of her time. To solve her problem, she developed an interactive program that would address many of the common concerns of new users and placed it on the company website. By doing this, she was able to avoid answering the same questions over and over again and could spend more of her precious time dealing with the more complex, interesting problems of more experienced users.

Use what you've got to get what you need.

Simply put, the best advice on how to succeed is to *capitalize on your strengths and compensate for your weaknesses.* Learning how to do this can make the difference between succeeding or failing and loving or hating your work. To help you, we include the following inventory of your potential strengths and weaknesses. And while every individual is unique, as an INTP, many of the following should apply to you.

Your work-related strengths may include:

- Eagerness to "think outside the box" and consider new possibilities
- Ability to understand very complex and highly abstract ideas
- Great creative problem-solving skills
- Independence; courage to take risks, try new things, and overcome obstacles
- Ability to synthesize lots of information
- Intellectual curiosity and skills for get-ting information you need

- Ability to analyze things logically even under stress
- Great confidence and drive to continually increase your knowledge
- Objectivity; ability to address issues without taking them personally
- Confidence in your ideas and vision
- Ability to see the big picture; to see implications of actions and ideas
- Adaptability; you can shift gears and change directions quickly

Your work-related weaknesses may include:

- Tendency toward disorganization
- Overconfidence; you may misrepresent your abilities or experience

- Impatience with unimaginative and/or incompetent people
- Dislike of doing things in a traditional or established manner
- Tendency to lose interest in projects once problems are solved
- Difficulty communicating complex ideas simply
- Tendency to be so theoretical that you ignore or miss the realities
- Undisciplined about attending to and following through on important details
- Dislike of doing repetitive tasks
- Impatience with structures and people who are too rigid

Using your strengths is easy.
The secret to success for an
INTP
is learning to:

Be better organized, be patient with less intelligent people, and work at improving your social skills.

16 | ESTJ
Extraverted, Sensing, Thinking, Judging
"Taking Care of Business"

Profile 1: Steve

"I don't need other people to like me, but I want them to respect me as a professional."

Working hard isn't the only thing Steve does with conviction. He tracks his personal-best jogging times on a card on the dashboard of his car, he returns phone calls within twelve hours—no matter what—and he works toward a perfect "one wood" in his golf game, all with the same energy he puts into everything he does. Steve is a perfectionist, and the challenge of his work as a self-employed salesman of insurance and investment products keeps him "charged."

It's hard work. Steve admits that sometimes he's competing against others with less ethical motivations, so he needs to work harder. "Every day is like Game One of the World Series. Not the fifth game, when it's a total pressure cooker, or spring training,

when it's not critical to win. But Game One—the real thing."

Steve spends a large part of his day prospecting for new clients, who are almost entirely referral-based at this point. The cycle begins with a fact-gathering interview with a new client. Then Steve prepares formal recommendations, including the most appropriate life insurance, disability insurance, or other investment, and presents his recommendations. He usually closes the sale. He services ongoing accounts, meeting with clients once or twice a year to update their portfolios. He has six hundred to six hundred fifty clients, but only about two hundred are truly active on an ongoing basis. Steve is constantly updating his knowledge of the products he sells, spending fifteen to twenty business days a year in training. He is also pursuing the professional status of Chartered Life Underwriter accreditation.

The intellectual challenge is one of the aspects of the job that Steve likes best. "I also enjoy the fact gathering. I know more about the people I'm working with than their spouses do. But closing the sale is the best part. I've earned the financial part by the end of the process. I've worked for a block of time, used my creative energy to come up with the best approach, given the correct financial advice, and built trust. That's great!"

Occasionally the results aren't as positive, even when he's taken all the right steps along the way. "Putting time into recommendations which I know are right, and seeing the client decide to make an investment with someone else, based on incorrect information from a competitor, is hard. This industry is full of deadwood, the scum of the earth, really. People have phobias about insurance agents for good reasons." The other draining activity for Steve is knocking on doors and making cold calls. "I do some of it but not like I used to have to. Most of my contacts are referral-based but there are always going to be some cold calls. That's the nature of the business."

Steve has always been a salesman. When he was seven he sent away for hundreds of seed packets from a comic book and sold them all. He usually had a paper route, often several at one time. He went to college on a music scholarship to study trombone, with the aim of performing. He switched to the business school because he realized that, while he was talented, he was never able to visualize himself "performing with the big guys." He got an internship during college with a life insurance company, and the job became permanent after graduation. The position required Steve to manage the internship program, teaching him that he "didn't want to baby-sit college students." He took a break from work for a couple of months to bike across the country with a friend and returned to the same company to sell insurance. He made a conscious decision not to get into management for five years, allowing him to build his own business. That was six years ago and, at thirty-three, he isn't interested in a switch yet.

Steve is persistent, organized, and enthusiastic. He wants to be a big fish in a little pond. He strives to be in the "top quartile, recognized nationally among professional people in the field." He marks his own success by his membership in the 100 Lives Club, and the Million Dollar Round Table—national and international sales organizations. Achieving membership each year in both groups gives Steve the confidence to mingle with the top people in his industry. He competes in fierce sales competitions for trips and prizes, which sometimes is a source of stress as he becomes entirely focused on score sheets. But it motivates him, too. And the sheer amount of his activity helps him to eliminate the stress he experiences. That and running. "I can handle just about anything when I'm running. But it's work. I push myself to the edge when I run, just like in business."

Staying healthy is important to Steve. He's changed his eating and coffee-drinking habits lately to meet that goal. And his family life is becoming more important. Steve is married, with two stepchildren and a new baby. "The constant needs of kids have forced me to trade off business time for time to spend with them on their activities. And every Thursday night is family night. No appointments, no sleep-overs, just us. I keep my work and home lives very separate."

His convictions are also becoming stronger. "I have a clear set of ethics that I got from my parents. These used to be sort of unconscious. I just don't have the capacity to think outside of them and against my client's best interest. Sometimes I might lose a sale because of it, but that's OK. Rejection affects me like rain on wax."

Steve is also trying to set a good example for his children. He's finding that he is more involved in his church, partly to "set a good example" but also because "for ten or fifteen minutes I find I can really just *stop*."

Steve is also more efficient and more serious than he used to be. "I really get a kick out of working hard and being productive. And I like the fact that I'm a musician too, sort of an 'artsy' person, different from the norm. But I could never wear a bow tie, I don't think. That's just too weird for me.

"The most rewarding part of this job is that I'm directly compensated for the work I do. And I choose to work with clients who are that type of person. I wish the world were more that way. I believe that if you work consistently and do a good job, the financials will take care of themselves."

Why This Career Works for Steve

Steve has high ethical standards, as do many Traditionalists. Although he wants to be successful, it is important that he achieve his aim honestly, through hard work. He is comfortable working within an organization with many clear rules, goals, and requirements, and enjoys achieving the different status levels that indicate excellence. In his home life, his Traditionalist values predominate as well, as shown by his setting a good

example for his children and attending church. Also like many Traditionalists, Steve strives to keep his family and work lives separate.

Extraverting his Thinking (dominant) is something Steve does every time he lays out a logical, well-thought-out, and consequently convincing recommendation to a client. He focuses on cause and effect: what benefits his clients will accrue if they follow his advice. His (dominant) Thinking helps him persevere and not take rejection personally—an indispensable asset for a salesperson. Finally, his ability to organize and prioritize his time well enables him to be efficient and productive.

Steve relies on his introverted Sensing (auxiliary) to pay particular attention to the many facts and details in his business. He likes gathering information about his clients and broadening his knowledge base about the various products he offers. His strong Sensing comes in handy in other ways, such as prospecting for new clients and reviewing his tickler files to know when to contact existing clients for possible updates.

That Steve is developing his Intuition (third function) is demonstrated by his emphasis on building his business "with the long haul in mind." He clearly and consciously focuses on the future—tracking his clients' career progress so that he will be better able to meet their needs as they change and grow. Of course, this makes good business sense, since the more successful his clients become, the more life insurance and other financial services they will need. He is also working on his Feeling (fourth function), spending more time thinking about ethics, going to church, and making the choice to spend more time with his young and growing family.

Meet the Millennial

Name: Anne

Age: 23

Educational nonprofit: community and partner solutions team member

"Honoring the human right to education."

Backstory

Anne got her first lucky break in high school—a new charter school dedicated to theater arts opened in her town in New Hampshire, and she was one of a small batch of kids who got to attend. For Anne, an active participant in local theater productions since childhood, this was a dream come true. "It opened my eyes to the idea that there were other options for students besides the local public school. I became really passionate about other people being able to access those kinds of choices, even if they couldn't afford private school." Anne decided that she wanted to pursue education reform and give other kids the chance to experience the kinds of opportunities that she had.

In college, she worked at the New York State Education Department as a policy research intern, analyzing school and district data and preparing reports that dealt with proposed amendments to education law. In her senior year, with graduation looming, Anne began looking for jobs on Idealist.org and found a job posting for an education nonprofit start-up that was hiring. A "search engine for learning," the start-up is a website similar to Google that performs free and open searches for teachers and students, but comprises only the best education resources on the web. Anne was hired, and upon graduation she made the move from New York to Palo Alto and began work immediately.

Now Anne is part of a community and partner solutions team, working within the smaller subset of content partnerships. Her job is to communicate and coordinate with other organizations that have free and open educational resources and to curate their content into collections. The collections are basically streaming playlists of resources—videos, quizzes, articles—on a range of academic topics. Anne and her colleagues work to make this content available to teachers and students all over the world, and to ensure the resources are credited to their original creators.

A Good Fit

As a Traditionalist, Anne is service oriented, motivated by her company's mission to contribute to the world of education. Anne's job entails a combination of interacting with partners and keeping track of the site's extensive content across the web. She describes herself as "obsessed with organization," a necessity in a job that involves coordinating eight million resources and counting. Since her company is relatively new, the processes of organization are not as streamlined as those of other, more established companies. Anne has developed many of the systems to keep track of the enormous amount of content the website oversees. Her Thinking and Judging functions are constantly in use, and she derives a great deal of satisfaction from implementing the systems she has created. Anne is a detail-oriented Sensor, and a big part of her job involves quality assurance: double-checking content, entering data into spreadsheets, and generally making sure nothing slips through the cracks. An Extravert, Anne says that she loves her co-workers, who are motivated and good at multitasking, like her. "Everyone here is involved in too many projects, but that's how we thrive." The environment is fast paced and interactive, requiring extensive collaboration among departments. Best of all, everyone is working in service of the same mission and toward the same objective.

Looking Ahead

Anne's company is unique in that it positions itself as a training ground for future nonprofit start-ups. "The culture they've created is to have people spend two to three years developing and honing their skills and then move on to continue the mission to honor the human right to education. So even if they're not working here, we're all working toward the same goal." Anne can see herself spending a few years with her current employer before perhaps going back to school to study nonprofit management. "I'm so happy where I am now, and it's a new challenge every day. I'm learning new skills all the time." Someday she would love to start her own nonprofit focused on making arts education in schools accessible to all.

Profile 2: Marilyn

"I'm a person of great energy, so I accomplish what I set out to do."

Creating and sustaining a stellar reputation for her corporate meeting planning and special events production company is the goal that drives Marilyn. After three years, it seems to be working. "Everyone doesn't know about us yet, but those that we introduce ourselves and our services to always hire us!" Once Marilyn sells the client on the event idea, and the event is under way, "The client tells us it's better than they ever dreamed possible. The clients hug and kiss us because they're so thrilled. Imagine these gruff old businessmen hugging us!"

This is the fourth career for Marilyn, who just turned fifty. And after raising her two children, it's the one she has put the most of herself into. She and a partner plan and execute all aspects of a corporate meeting or special event, from developing schedules and arranging transportation and meals to creating themes, booking speakers or entertainers, and developing games. "We do everything ourselves but also hire the people necessary to carry our ideas off." They subcontract when necessary with vendors who do such specialty work as designing and producing invitations or props. Marilyn handles all phases of concept development, planning, budgeting, and setting up and taking down the event or meeting.

Marilyn and her partner also do all the sales for the company, one of the tasks she enjoys most. "Meeting new people, introducing ourselves, and getting hired is such a kick! It's actually better than doing the event itself! We become friends with our client, become extensions of the client's company, and that's great."

But maintaining total control has its downside, too. Sorting out bills, reconciling invoices, and all the "nitty-gritty" are the tasks Marilyn dislikes. "The hardest thing is trying to do more than one job at a time. Shifting gears is difficult because I become so totally focused on a project and then often get a phone call from another client or a potential client and have to immediately switch my thinking and focus on that other project. Sometimes if it's a potential client asking for ideas, I have to *sell* by coming up with something great—off the top of my head! By the end of the day, my eyes are rolling around in my head, I'm so tired."

Juggling several different and challenging projects at one time creates stress for Marilyn. So does worrying about cash flow and the unpredictable and undependable nature of being a self-employed small-business owner. "I told my partner when we first started that I would be willing to sit here for a year without any business and starve before I'd be willing to close up shop. That's how determined I am to make this work. I just know it's going to; it feels that right." To cope with the stress, Marilyn tries to get outside and walk each evening after work. "I walk for an hour. I try to really change modes and get into the trees and the air and the grass. The exercise really

helps. But I hate to take vacations because I really *want* to be at work!"

Marilyn's first career after college was as an elementary school special education teacher. She enjoyed the job for five years and stopped when she had her own children. "Being married and having children was so important to me. Teaching fit into a married life. I was totally satisfied." After the kids were in school, Marilyn helped her husband, a doctor, set up his medical office and then managed the office for a couple of years. But she was bored without a challenge so she became a real estate agent. She was top salesperson in the company for two years and loved it. The sudden, tragic death of her husband forced her to quit her job in order to settle the estate, close his practice, and relocate. She took some time to help resettle her kids and help them adjust to their new life.

Then she began volunteer fund-raising work for a national charity. She visited corporations and solicited funding. "I dreamed up events, and then ran them. It was great work, but after a while, 'thank you' wasn't enough anymore. I wanted to be compensated for my good work." Marilyn remarried and was encouraged by her businessman husband to find a job that would challenge and tap her many skills. Because she so enjoyed the volunteer fund-raising work, she decided to look for a job in a special events company. She met her future partner, who was also considering a new venture, and they developed a partnership.

Marilyn is proud of her accomplishments in her company. She hopes to add staff so that she and her partner can "stop killing ourselves doing everything." But the tenacity she demonstrates is one of her greatest skills. "Once I decide to do something, I'll do whatever it takes. I'm really devoted to my work, and the time just flies by until I realize it's seven o'clock at night!"

Marilyn's priority is her business but only because her husband is supportive and shares her goals and because her children are grown. "I couldn't do this if my kids were home. My kids have always come first and they always will. I used to need to keep track of them but they don't need me the same way anymore."

Over the past ten years, Marilyn has experienced major life changes with the death of her husband, her remarriage, and the maturity of her children. She is a more independent person and more goal-oriented than she ever was. "I find that I rely on my own inner resources, including my inner strength. I recognize my abilities better now, but then, I just never really thought about them either. I wanted to be a wonderful mother. I have fantastic kids and I believe that doesn't just happen. I put as much energy into my family as I now put into my career."

Career satisfaction for Marilyn is doing a good job and being recognized and rewarded for it. "We're becoming a real force in this city, developing a fine reputation. You know that you're doing well when your competitors stop talking to you because you've become a tremendous threat!"

Why This Career Works for Marilyn

For Marilyn, family is paramount. It is only since her two children have grown up that she has really immersed herself in her career. Like most Traditionalists, Marilyn takes her work very seriously (although she enjoys it tremendously). Her strong work ethic and philosophy of "do whatever it takes to get the job done" has helped her develop a reputation as the best in her field. And with it have come recognition and financial success, both of which are strong motivators for Marilyn.

What Marilyn loves best is making sales. Her dominant extraverted Thinking helps her present her ideas very logically and allows her to persist where a less assertive person might give up. It also assists her in planning and executing organized events, skillful budgeting, and tough negotiating. She even takes some pride in the fact that some of her competitors have given her the cold shoulder because they've felt threatened by her success.

Marilyn's introverted Sensing (auxiliary) helps her keep track of the hundreds of details that need attention in the planning and execution of an event. She also has a good sense of quality (using her Sensing to determine if an invitation, prop, or decoration is just the way it should be). Another indication of her preference for Sensing is that many of her events involve activities in which people actually *do* things; use *their* senses to become hands-on participants in games and activities relating to the theme of the event.

In recent years, Marilyn has clearly developed better access to her Intuition (third function). This is evident from her enjoyment in working with many creative people, such as entertainers and artists, and her desire to start her own new venture. Although she is not naturally an Intuitive, Marilyn's business is all about possibilities, and she is much more comfortable considering alternatives and untried approaches now than she was several years ago. Her Feeling side, while always engaged when it came to her family, has even begun to creep into her work life. She is amused, for example, when "gruff old businessmen," excited by the success of an event she produced for them, praise her great work and give her a hug.

Common Threads

Although Steve, Marilyn, and Anne have different backgrounds, experiences, and careers, there are certain common threads woven through their stories. Their specific interests, abilities, and values may differ, but owing to their similar temperament values, the *same hierarchy* of their psychological functions, and the world they use them in (inner or outer), there are certain observations we can make about the needs of many ESTJs.

What follows is a list of the most important elements—the formula, if you will—for ESTJ satisfaction. Given the uniqueness of all individuals—even those who share the same type—this list will not describe each ESTJ equally well. The important thing is that these ten elements, with varying degrees of intensity and in different orders of importance, identify what ESTJs need to be satisfied.

After you have reviewed this list, we recommend that you go back and prioritize the elements in order of *their importance to you.* When doing this, think of past work experiences as well as your present job, and what you found particularly satisfying or unsatisfying. Try to look for *themes* that run through several experiences, not just the events that might be true for one work situation but not for another.

As an ESTJ, career satisfaction means doing work that:

1. Lets me work systematically, organizing facts, policies, or people, and use time and resources efficiently toward a logical conclusion
2. Lets me use mastered skills while working on concrete and straightforward assignments with clear specifications, using my strong reasoning powers
3. Is measured and evaluated by fair, logical, explicit, and objective standards

4. Is done in a friendly environment with other hardworking and conscientious people who do not bring their personal problems to work or expect me to share my personal feelings on the job
5. Is realistic and tangible in nature and has practical applications and concrete results
6. Has clear expectations and reporting hierarchy
7. Lets me be productive, organizing the necessary steps and resources, following established procedures, and setting and meeting deadlines
8. Is done in a stable and predictable environment, but one that is also filled with action and a variety of people
9. Can be done with other people, enabling me to be in charge of myself and others
10. Lets me make decisions and have a great deal of control and responsibility; where my opinions, recommendations, and experience are considered important

Popular Occupations for ESTJs

In listing occupations that are popular among ESTJs, it is important to note that there are successful people of all types in all occupations. However, the following are careers ESTJs may find particularly satisfying and some of the reasons why. This is by no means a comprehensive listing but is included to suggest possibilities you may not have previously considered. Although all of these occupations offer the potential for career satisfaction, the future demand for some careers is anticipated to be greater than for others. Based upon our research, the occupations that are italicized in the lists below are forecast to enjoy the fastest rate of growth over the next several years.

SALES/SERVICE
- *Insurance sales agent*
- Salesperson (tangibles): computers, real estate
- Chef
- Military officer
- Teacher: trade/industrial/technical
- Government employee
- *Sales representative: wholesale and manufacturing*
- Security guard
- Sports merchandise/equipment sales
- Pharmaceutical salesperson
- Cyber security specialist
- Police/probation/corrections officer
- Funeral director
- Occupational health and safety specialist
- Ship and boat captain
- Regulatory compliance officer
- Purchasing agent
- Aviation inspector
- *Personal trainer*
- *Athletic coach*
- *Athletic trainer*
- Sales agent: securities and commodities
- Underwriter
- Credit analyst
- *Cost estimator*
- Budget analyst
- Police and detective supervisor
- Commercial airplane pilot
- Transportation coordinator
- Flight engineer
- *Construction and building inspector*
- *Real estate appraiser*
- *Paralegal*
- Legislative assistant
- Insurance adjuster
- Court clerk
- Hotel and motel manager
- Environmental compliance inspector
- *Recreational therapist*
- Sound technician

These occupations allow the ESTJ to work in the real world, on realistic and tangible projects. Most of these careers demand adherence to standard operating procedures and require a great deal of interaction with the public or groups of people. ESTJs enjoy being in positions of authority and enjoy giving orders. Sales of real things offers the opportunity to engage in work that achieves immediate and tangible results.

TECHNOLOGY/PHYSICAL
- Engineer: mechanical/applied fields
- *Auditor*
- General contractor
- *Construction worker*
- *Pharmacist*
- Clinical technician
- *Accounting internal auditor*
- *Technical trainer*
- *EEG technologist/technician*
- *Diagnostic medical sonographer*
- *Paralegal*
- *Network and computer systems administrator*
- Organic farmer
- *Database administrator*

These fields require the use of the ESTJ's technical and mechanical abilities. Each allows them to focus on gathering, organizing, and analyzing factual information, and engage in deductive reasoning. Each of these occupations requires a logical and organized work style, which is enjoyed by ESTJs who prefer a work environment that is orderly and neat. ESTJs are impatient with confusion and inefficiency.

MANAGEMENT
- Project manager
- Officer manager
- Administrator

- Factory supervisor
- *Database manager*
- Purchasing agent
- Regulatory compliance officer
- Budget analyst
- *Health services administrator*
- Chief information officer
- Management consultant: business operations
- Logistics and supply manager
- Bank manager/loan officer
- Credit analyst/counselor
- Property manager: commercial/ residential
- *Bill and account collector*
- Food service and lodging owner
- *Network and computer systems administrator*
- Nursing director
- *Construction manager*
- Association manager and adviser
- Treasurer, controller, and chief financial officer
- Private sector executive

The managerial fields are often satisfying for ESTJs because they like to be in positions of authority. They are good executives because they enjoy giving orders, making decisions, and supervising others. They are also very loyal to established institutions. Management requires constant interaction with other people and the ability to direct, monitor, and evaluate the work of others.

PROFESSIONAL
- Dentist
- *Physician: general medicine*
- Stockbroker
- Judge
- Executive
- Teacher: technical/trade
- Civil/mechanical/metallurgical engineer
- Corporate finance lawyer
- Electrical engineer
- *Primary care physician*
- *Food and drug scientist/technician*
- *Industrial engineer*
- *Paralegal*
- *Pharmacist*
- *Lawyer*
- School principal
- Chief information officer

The appeal of the professional fields is the ability to work in established, traditional institutions in positions of authority. Dentistry and medicine are technical occupations that generally include hands-on activities—working with real people and tangible objects such as teeth and gums (for dentists), and the human body (for general practitioners). These occupations make use of the ESTJ's powers of deductive reasoning and ability to understand cause and effect. They prefer to do things following a prescribed procedure proven effective by their own experience and others whom they respect.

Customizing Your Job Search

Knowing the particular strengths and blind spots of your type can afford you a tremendous advantage in your job search campaign. In all aspects of the process, from conducting research into available positions, identifying and contacting prospective employers, developing personal marketing tools such as résumés, arranging and conducting job interviews, negotiating salaries, to finally accepting a position, people will act true to their type. Being able to capitalize on your assets and compensate for your liabilities can make the difference between a successful and an unsuccessful job search.

The differences between types are sometimes subtle and other times dramatic. It is the subtle variations in advice we offer that make the real difference between success and failure in a job search. The concept of "networking," or meeting with and talking to people to gather information about potential jobs, serves as a good example. Extraverts will naturally enjoy networking and are advised to do so on a large scale, while Introverts find more limited and targeted networking, especially with people they already know, easier. Sensors tend to network with people in a defined scope, while Intuitives will go far and wide to find people often seemingly unrelated to their field of interest. Further, Feelers take networking, like everything else, very personally and enjoy establishing warm rapport, while Thinkers will be more objective and detached in their style. Finally, Judgers tend to ask fewer and more structured questions during their networking, while Perceivers could ask questions of all sorts all day long! One valuable search technique, many ways to implement it.

Pathways to Success: Using Your Strengths

Once you set your mind to finding the right job, no one will work harder searching for it than you. Your persistence and the seriousness with which you view the process will help you stay with the task until you find the work that is best for you. However, in your eagerness to accomplish your goal, you may be blinded to other possibilities, new information, or novel approaches.

As an ESTJ, your most effective strategies will build on your abilities to:

Organize and conduct an efficient job search.

- Use your organizational skills to stay on top of the project, make a plan, be on

time, remember to follow up with prospective employers, and so forth.
- Use your practical skills to plot out a realistic campaign, beginning with the most obvious opportunities within your own company and other companies or organizations with which you are familiar.

Make realistic decisions based upon known facts and objective data.

- Use your critical thinking skills to analyze the positive and negative aspects of each job option and eliminate those options in which you are not interested or qualified.
- Gather as much information about a potential employer's business and industry as possible, reading in local and regional business journals and newspapers in order to have a clear understanding of the company's history and objectives.

The following example of the process one ESTJ client went through illustrates how both of these recommendations can be put into practical use.

The first thing Jason did when he learned his company was downsizing and his job might be in jeopardy was to sit down and take stock of his situation. He prepared two "balance sheets"; the first was financial, reflecting his assets, liabilities, and monthly expenses to determine how long he could live without an income. His second balance sheet was his work-related strengths and weaknesses; what he had to sell in the marketplace.

Since he knew he wanted to stay in the same line of work, he next developed an impressive marketing plan, complete with potential employers, strategies, and projected timetables for accomplishing various tasks.

Jason contacted potential employers, conducted informational interviews to learn more about particular jobs, and researched specific companies to determine if they interested him. The point is, Jason approached this job search just as he had his job as a midlevel manager—with efficiency, skill, dispatch, and action.

Be direct and honest when giving a summary of how your skills and abilities will benefit the employer.

- Prepare before the interview by developing a list of questions the prospective employer might ask you. Practice answering these, focusing on your past experiences and accomplishments.
- Ask a friend to ask you potentially difficult questions so you can rehearse your answers.

When David was going through the "grueling interview process" for a CEO position, he was often asked difficult questions about what he might do in a hypothetical situation. Several times David wondered if the interviewer might be deliberately trying to make him angry, because he used a condescending tone. Instead of becoming insulted, David decided to be completely honest and told the interviewer exactly what he thought. He offered constructive criticism on how he thought the organization needed to be changed in order to succeed. Occasionally, during the five interviews, David wondered if he had done the right thing. He took a gamble because he wanted to demonstrate courage and the ability to make the necessary tough decisions. It paid off. Those were exactly the characteristics the company was looking for in a CEO.

Set and meet realistic job search goals.

- Develop a list of important characteristics in a new job, including salary, benefits, work schedule, location, room for advancement, and other important criteria. Use that checklist to evaluate each job opportunity.
- Realize that it can take as much as three to twelve months, and sometimes longer, to find the right job. Don't expect to find a job until you have gone through all the necessary steps.

After several years in the purchasing department of a small manufacturing company, Gina decided it was time to return to college to finish her business degree so she could get a job with more responsibility and a bigger salary. Because she couldn't afford to quit working completely and go to school full-time, she did a little homework and learned that a small private university offered the degree program she wanted, and something more. Because the school offered a tuition abatement program for employees, she applied for a job in the purchasing department, enabling her to take two courses a semester with no fee. She accepted the job with the full realization that it would take her two years to complete her degree, but she would be able to do so at no cost, while she was continuing to apply and sharpen her business skills in an area she was familiar with.

Present yourself as a capable, stable, and competent candidate.

- Express your skills in a clear and logical way on all written materials, including résumé and cover letter, and during all interviews. Be sure to include past experiences as examples to demonstrate your capabilities and accomplishments.

- Offer letters of recommendation from past employers attesting to your competency and quality of performance.
- Point out to prospective employers the ways in which you will be able to help the company accomplish its goals.

After working for one company for nearly twelve years, Tanya initiated a career change to find a more challenging position. Since she had always received excellent performance reviews from each of the three supervisors she had worked for during her tenure, she asked each one of them to write a letter of recommendation for her. She gave them guidelines for what she wanted them to focus on. She asked that they refer to her consistently excellent performance reviews, her skills, and her measurable contributions to the goals of their departments. During interviews, she volunteered photocopies of the letters and encouraged her interviewers to keep them in her file.

Network extensively.

- Enlist the help of people with whom you have worked over the years and who know you well to identify people to contact about career opportunities.

When Doug was looking for a new job, he contacted people on his softball team and in his church about opportunities within their own companies. After a series of informational interviews, one individual referred him to the director of the management training department at her company. Doug learned that a position was about to become available owing to the relocation of an employee. Doug applied for and got the job before it was ever publicized.

Possible Pitfalls

Although all people are unique, there are certain *potential* blind spots that many ESTJs share. We underscore "potential" because some of the following *may* be true of you, while others may clearly not apply. While considering them, you may notice that these tendencies do not relate just to the job search, but rather describe pitfalls that you may have experienced in other aspects of your life as well. It is therefore helpful to consider each one in terms of your past experiences by asking yourself: "Is this true for me?" And if so, "How did this tendency prevent me from getting something that I wanted?" You will probably notice that the key to overcoming your blind spots is the conscious and thoughtful development of your third and fourth functions (Intuition and Feeling). We recognize that many of the suggestions will be difficult to implement, but the more you use these functions, the fewer problems they will cause you in the future.

Avoid making decisions too quickly.

- Waiting even a few moments to ask yourself what you know and what you still do not know about a situation, and considering how you feel about the issue or choice at hand, will help you make a better decision.
- Try to ask more open-ended questions during all phases of the job search to get a better understanding of the possible implications of your choice.

Consider innovative or unconventional job search techniques as well as more customary practices.

- Enlist the help of friends or colleagues who may possess more Intuition (perception) to help you brainstorm alternative means of reaching a key decision maker within a company or a prospective employer.

Consider the long-range consequences in weighing job options.

- Attempt to look down the road and imagine how your goals or needs may change as you progress and age. Make a list of what your needs are now and try to predict how they may be different one year, five years, and ten years from today. Consider this information in making a decision with long-ranging implications.
- During the interview process, ask about growth potential within the company, relocation possibilities, and about the long-range goals of your prospective employer to be sure you are interested in going where the company may need to send you.

Try to establish rapport with interviewers and not be brusque and too businesslike.

- Try to relax before an interview and not allow the seriousness of the activity to affect your attitude negatively. Remember that you wish to be seen as someone with whom they could easily get along, one of the team.

Avoid being rigid and inflexible in job negotiations.

- Use your list of criteria as a guide in selecting a good job, rather than as rules cast in concrete. Be persistent about those elements without which you simply can't live, but be willing to be flexible about those that are less important.

- Try to give positive feedback before offering any negative criticism, knowing others can be offended and put off by a negative perspective.

The Final Piece: Changing or Keeping Your Job . . . the Key to Success for ESTJs

Now that you have a solid understanding of your type, you can see how your natural preferences make you better suited for certain kinds of jobs. You can also see how knowledge of your type-related strengths and weaknesses can help you conduct a more successful job search. But as an ESTJ, you've already realized that you are not equally drawn to *every* career or field listed in the Popular Occupations section. The next and final step is to narrow down the field and find the work you were meant to do.

In addition to Type, several other factors—such as your values, interests, and skills—also contribute to your level of satisfaction on the job. The more compatible you are with your job, the happier you'll be. So prepare to use everything you've learned (in this book and in life) to create *your strategic career plan*. The exercises in Chapter 24, Putting It All Together, are designed to help you do just that.

However, you may have decided it makes more sense (if perhaps only for the moment) to stay in your present job or with your current employer. There may be many valid reasons—financial pressures, family considerations, a tough job market for your specialty, or just bad timing. But take heart! What you've learned in this book can also help you be more content and successful *in your current job*. And should the time come when you're ready to make a major career move, you'll have a much better idea of where you want to go, and how to get there.

"So, if you can't have the job you love (yet!)...love the one you've got."

The simple truth is, with the exception of work on a factory assembly line, the vast majority of jobs allow a good deal of flexibility in the way tasks are performed. Here are some ways you may be able to "massage" your current job into one that better fits your needs:

- Find an efficient assistant.
- Implement efficiency systems and require direct-reports to use them.
- Provide agendas to help people prepare for meetings.
- Seek advice and opinions of colleagues who are different from you.
- Join professional organizations and create opportunities to network.
- Make sure to work around a lot of people to stay stimulated; delegate solitary tasks, if possible.
- If not in management, find a project that needs doing and volunteer to lead the effort.
- Ask your supervisors to be explicit about their expectations.
- Become part of a work team.

One ESTJ turns lemons into lemonade:

James, a life insurance salesman, was looking to replace his secretary. He knew he needed someone who would be both meticulous about the many details of his work and personable enough to handle considerable client contact. When traditional means of filling the position failed to attract the right person, he decided to try networking. He sent a letter to all the members of his local chamber of commerce,

put an ad in his church newsletter, and carried around copies of the job description and distributed them to select clients after sales calls. It was this last tactic that paid off. A client recommended an able administrative assistant who was returning to the workforce after a few years at home raising her children.

Use what you've got to get what you need.

Simply put, the best advice on how to succeed is to *capitalize on your strengths and compensate for your weaknesses.* Learning how to do this can make the difference between succeeding or failing and loving or hating your work. To help you, we include the following inventory of your potential strengths and weaknesses. And while every individual is unique, as an ESTJ, many of the following should apply to you.

Your work-related strengths may include:

- Practicality and focus on results
- Forcefulness in dealing with your commitments; you can be tough when necessary
- Ability to stay focused on the organization's goals
- Precision and accuracy and desire to get the job done right
- Desire to follow established routines and procedures
- Ability to recognize what is illogical, inconsistent, impractical, or inefficient
- Organizational skills; you're good at making objective decisions
- Belief in the value of a traditional structure and the ability to work within it
- Sense of responsibility; you can be counted on to do what you say
- Clear work ethic; need to be efficient and productive
- Common sense and realistic perspective

Your work-related weaknesses may include:

- Impatience with those who don't follow procedures or who ignore important details
- Reluctance to embrace new, untested ideas
- Discomfort with or resistance to change
- Little patience with inefficiency or processes that take too long
- Focus on present needs at the expense of future ones

- Tendency to overrun people in an effort to meet your goals
- Inability to see future possibilities
- Lack of sensitivity about how other people will be affected by policies and decisions
- Difficulty listening to opposing viewpoints; you may interrupt frequently

---

Using your strengths is easy.
The secret to success for an
ESTJ
is learning to:

Slow down, consider implications
for people, and be flexible.

17

ISTJ
Introverted, Sensing, Thinking, Judging

"Take Your Time and Do It Right"

Profile 1: Glenda

"Getting things done right—and achieving what I want for myself and for the institution."

Glenda likes being in charge. And she is in charge of a great deal as dean of the school of allied health professions at a large state university. She is an academic administrator; her main priority is facilitating the activities of the faculty and making sure they have the resources they need to do their jobs. She enjoys being able to decide on a course of action and then make it happen, whether the action is a small detail or a broad decision about the governing of the school.

Much of what Glenda does falls under the heading of either planning or decision making. She is responsible for all personnel decisions, including hiring and evaluating faculty, and making promotional and tenure recommendations to her supervisor, the university provost. She generates the regular reports and documentation for the school, makes decisions about the dismissal of students due to either academic or disciplinary reasons, oversees the acceptance of entering students, helps make plans for recruitment of students, supervises the staff liaison to the admissions department, and prepares and monitors the budget for the school. She also teaches one course each semester. Finally, she develops long- and short-range plans for the school and then evaluates whether those goals have been met. She represents the school on various committees and forums on and off campus. In her own words she "has a large capacity for work."

Having a real and documentable impact is something Glenda really enjoys about her career. She also finds teaching to be an energizing activity and looks forward to her class each week. "I am finding that public speaking of any kind is a fun thing to do. I also like chairing meetings because I like orchestrating the outcome of things." She's a person who doesn't mind rolling up her sleeves and getting to work. "If there's a major mailing that has to go out, I'll get in there and stuff envelopes just like everyone else. I don't differentiate. It's all work and it's all important."

Less enjoyable and more difficult for Glenda is being tactful. "I really hate having to bite my tongue and not be honest. It's not easy being honest, because people don't really want to hear bad things, like, you're not doing your job, or you made a mistake, or I can't get you what you want. I have to soften my words, and I don't like being unclear or indirect." Handling faculty evaluations and merit reviews is draining for Glenda because she has to be tactful but also listen to a bit of self-promoting from faculty. "There's money at the end of the process, you see. I sit and listen to each person tell me why they think they deserve a merit increase. Everyone is trying to put him- or herself in the best light. I must be positive and supportive in my feedback, even if I want to tell them something very different!" Glenda also dislikes the process of reprimanding or dismissing students. These are usually highly emotional sessions with students who are desperate and tearful when they hear that they may have to find a new course of study due to their unacceptable grades. Glenda has to try to cushion the blow and help redirect them to choose another career path. It's not a role she enjoys.

In addition to the stress of emotional confrontations, Glenda experiences stress from the uncertainty and lack of clear direction she sometimes receives from the central administration at the university. "I don't tolerate ambiguity well. I like clear answers to my questions. My supervisor often prefers to put off decisions and engage in a lot of talk about options. He's a 'maybe' person. So when it gets unbearable, I just make a decision myself. I've found it's easier to ask forgiveness than ask permission, and then wait indefinitely for an answer!"

At fifty-one, Glenda appears to have carefully planned and plotted her career path, although she never really had a grand scheme. She studied medical technology upon graduation and went to work in a major university hospital for eight years. "I loved it. And even today, I believe that if I wanted to leave academe, I could be happy to return to a hospital setting and be a full-time medical technologist." But she did leave to take on the added challenge of teaching students on a one-on-one basis. She soon became a faculty member, then decided she wanted to get some background in education, so she obtained her master's degree in education. Still on the teaching staff at the hospital, she received a Ph.D. in psychometrics. She was promoted to assistant dean of the allied health college at the university and continued in that job for another eight years. She was really happy at the hospital university and honestly thought she would retire there. But while serving on the board of an allied health association, she met the current dean of another university who was stepping down. She persuaded Glenda to apply for her job. "I tell people it was an offer I couldn't refuse: more money, more responsibility, and more control." She has been happy in her current position for five years but plans to become a college president someday.

Glenda considers her goal-directed nature to be one of her greatest assets. "I'm good at setting priorities and being very clear about what needs to be accomplished. I'm able to work with all kinds of people. I don't mind the full range of work, from the exciting to the mundane. I participate in all of it."

Glenda counts among her proudest achievements being elected president of a national professional association ten years ago, and receiving a leadership award for allied health professionals. She was chosen from a large pool of candidates and is pleased that her contributions to the field were recognized.

Lately, and as a result of what she has accomplished so far, Glenda finds she is more confident. She is more ambitious because she is able to perceive greater things for herself. "Growing up as a black female in the 1950s, there were three professions open to me: teaching, nursing, or social work. I was determined not to be any of those. Now I find it funny that I enjoy the teaching part of my career so much. But I have a greater feeling for my own capabilities, and I am less intrigued and impressed with the abilities of others!" She is more comfortable in the extraverted world and enjoys public speaking more than she has in the past. Money and possessions no longer hold the same appeal to her anymore. Today she values her family, longtime friends, and her frequent international travels. "I am terribly fascinated with other cultures and people and could probably have purchased a plane with all the tickets I've bought over the years!" Glenda feels that being healthy and working in a career that enables her to do good things are the most important things in her life.

She sees herself as a different person than she was ten years ago. "I never used to understand that the world is political. Now I understand and participate in the political process. I'm better at assessing what motivates other people and determining what they have to offer. My focus is so much broader, and I am becoming involved with both the larger university community and with broader issues of health care. I now see how the rest of the world impinges on my specific discipline."

Glenda hopes that other people remember her as the competent, intelligent, articulate person of integrity that she strives to be. "I learned some important lessons in a couple of big interviews during the last few years. Probably the most important is that an interview needs to be a two-way street. I think both sides need to ask some tough questions and give honest answers. It felt like I was taking a risk, because people don't always want to hear what I have to say. But I decided that the things I thought were really important, I would stick to and be clear about. My advice is to ask yourself how far you are willing to compromise on issues first. Only then can you position yourself best in the interview. Remember, the job is only going to be a good match if both sides are sure about what they're getting. I've learned it's OK for people to see me as I really am. I like to take charge, and if they aren't going to like that, they'd better know it from the start. And if it is a good match, I'll make it a better place through my hard work."

Why This Career Works for Glenda

Glenda's is a highly responsible position in a very traditional organization. Consistent with her Traditionalist values, Glenda works very hard in a structured environment and makes many important decisions during the course of her day. Like many Traditionalists, her career path has been a series of step-by-step progressions, starting as a medical technologist and ending up the chief educator of her field. One reason her work in both fields—medicine and education—has been so satisfying is that in both she has had the opportunity to serve others.

In her work, Glenda must keep track of lots of information. She is responsible for documenting all activities of the school, putting together reports, tracking personnel achievements, conducting performance appraisals, and so forth. She relies on her introverted Sensing (dominant) to assist her in all these tasks, as well as to engage in short-term planning, and in her own classroom teaching, which she does each semester.

Extraverting her Thinking (auxiliary) is how Glenda makes decisions—an activity which she clearly enjoys. She also enjoys establishing priorities in meetings, setting and meeting goals, and controlling the outcome of the projects for which she is responsible. Her Thinking helps her to be honest with people, and has given her a reputation for being direct and no-nonsense in her dealings with others.

In recent years, Glenda has begun to tune in to her Feeling side (third function). As a result, time with her family and friends has become more important. She has also become interested in learning about the cultures of different people and has begun to travel extensively. On the work side, her type development has resulted in helping her to be better at understanding and motivating others. There is also evidence that Glenda has begun to develop her Intuition (fourth function). She is now better able to see how the world impinges on her discipline, is more interested in the broad issues of health care, is more aware of, and has become a more effective participant in, the political process.

Meet the Millennial

Name: Jackie
Age: 25
Special assistant to the executive director of a nonprofit

"Always behind the scenes, making sure everything runs smoothly."

Backstory

Jackie's career path has been, as she puts it, "a long and winding road." When she graduated from college with a degree in psychology and East Asian studies, Jackie thought she wanted to be a school counselor. She transitioned immediately to a master's program in education, a precursor year to a second year getting licensed in school counseling. After the first year, Jackie did a summer teaching fellowship at an inner-city charter school, an experience that confirmed her passion for education and her desire to go back for year two to get her license in school counseling.

Upon obtaining her degree, Jackie worked as a guidance counselor at an inner-city public middle school for several months, but she kept meeting roadblocks to transferring her license from out of state. Additionally, the school environment was less than ideal, and Jackie considered the school principal inept and ineffectual. Jackie found that being a competent person in a disorganized and poorly run workplace meant that she had to do many people's jobs—without really getting to do her own.

After trying to improve the environment for several months, Jackie realized the problems were systemic, and so not within her power to fix. She found a job listing on Idealist.org and completed a rigorous set of six interviews before landing a position as special assistant to the executive director of an urban educational nonprofit. Now she functions as the grounding force for Tom, whom she describes as a visionary with "a lot of ideas; someone who wants to do everything, all the time. But because he moves so quickly from one project to another, he has a hard time getting anything done." Jackie is in charge of scheduling, logistics, and routine "realism check-ins"—playing a stabilizing role and helping to maintain clear communications across all teams.

A Good Fit

Jackie is a logistical mastermind. A dominant Sensing type, she is queen of the details, practical and down-to-earth, with a realist's sense of the world around her. She describes "finding the blank spaces for meetings"—that is, balancing multiple schedules and job sites, and making sure there is adequate time to get done everything that needs to get done. Whereas Tom is always focused on the long range, Jackie has a firm grasp on the present and helps fill in the gaps in his

abilities. For instance, before Jackie, Tom was chronically late to meetings because he never accounted for travel time. Jackie's auxiliary function of Thinking makes her a cool customer, rational and direct. As a Judger, she is prompt and planful: "I like being the person who organizes things, and I like following up with people." Like many Traditionalists, Jackie has a deep pull toward community service and helping others. She sees a common thread between her role as a counselor and her new role supporting Tom. "I just really enjoy being in the background and making sure that things are OK." In this job, Jackie the Introvert gets to play a supporting role to a cause that is important to her, serving the community in a real and meaningful way.

Looking Ahead

Since Jackie has been at her new job for only a couple of months, she's still focusing on adjusting to and learning the rhythm of the work. But she does see a future for herself within the organization and will soon be taking on more responsibilities, such as becoming the liaison for the school board, working with the director of finance, and playing a larger role in board governance. Jackie could see herself going back to business school and studying project management or possibly becoming a consultant. But for the time being, she thinks it will take a few more years to really get to know Tom and to understand how best to support him and the organization.

Profile 2: Dave

"Being responsible and working hard to accomplish my objectives."

As vice president and director of property management for a commercial real estate firm, Dave oversees the operations and maintenance of six different office buildings around the city. He acts as on-site property manager at some and supervises the on-site property manager at others. "It's soup to nuts—I'm responsible for taking care of everything that goes on in the buildings so the actual owner doesn't have to." Dave is extremely detail-oriented and thankfully so because the job requires constant maintenance and inspection. Dave makes sure the buildings are run in tip-top shape at all times, doing everything from picking up stray gum wrappers to having air conditioning systems repaired. It's all in a day's work.

Dave deals with a variety of situations and people throughout the day. He enjoys having a minimum of pure routine, because each day there are different problems that need to be fixed and different tenants' concerns to deal with. Dave contracts with cleaning, security, and trash-removal services and supervises the many mechanical personnel who keep the buildings operating. At any given moment, he might be handling a tenant complaint about the office temperature, trying to get a new electrical plug installed or a light bulb replaced. He usually carries around a checklist of things he notices need fixing and then assigns the staff member, or hires the contractor, to get the job done. Occasionally he spends time renewing existing tenants' leases or answering operational questions during a tour for a prospective tenant. It's all part of his objective and duty to keep things running smoothly.

What he enjoys and finds the most energizing is being able to make physical alterations in the buildings that will have real and positive results. "I was bothered by how dark an elevator area was, so I got new lighting columns installed. It was great to see how much improved the area was. And it was my idea!" He assesses and uses resources well, gathers plenty of important technical data, gets quotes from vendors, supervises the changes, and then sees the results of his labor and that of others. He gets a charge out of solving problems in effective and functional ways.

Less exciting are the more standard and routine tasks, such as the budgeting he has to do. "I end up having to redo my budgets several times because they go through so many revisions before they are approved by my bosses. And I really dislike extensive writing. I'm OK with brief letters and memos, but a full report that I have to start from scratch is really draining. But I love it when it's done!"

Getting things done is satisfying to Dave, so he has little patience with people around him who let interpersonal squabbles and "nitpicky politics" get in the way of doing their jobs. "I realize you can't like everyone you work with but you should find a way to get along so it doesn't interfere with your work." He finds the times he needs to mediate the personal problems of his staff wear him out, and he wishes others would adopt his matter-of-fact and easygoing style.

Trying to accomplish his objectives with inadequate or shrinking resources is a source of stress for Dave. "I need to keep my buildings looking like I had three times the budget that I have. And given the current condition of the real estate market, I sometimes am concerned about the financial solvency of some of these buildings. The real problem is I have absolutely no control, and that's stressful." But he doesn't experience enough stress to even feel the need for a coping strategy. He just turns it off, and gets a good night's sleep.

Dave's career path started a bit off track with a psychology degree he knew he would never use. But he discovered a graduate study program that would give him building operations and student activities experience while he worked toward a master's degree. He worked for two years in three different positions on a college campus—assisting in the operations of the campus center, developing student activities, and managing the campus pub. It was excellent hands-on experience that led to a full-time position as director of another university student center. He enjoyed the duties but found the more intellectual and politically active campus to be too serious an environment. After two years, he interviewed for an assistant property manager position at the real estate firm he works for now. He was hired and promoted to property manager within two years, and then to vice president and director of property management two years later. It's been a rapid rise, a bit too rapid for Dave. "I never said no to the offers. In fact, I always feel thankful for the opportunity to have more responsibility but I do feel I have a long way to go in this position. I'm content to stay where I am and continue to expand my duties by taking on more properties. Someday it might be nice to be a partner in a project and share some of the risk, but I have no desire to become a developer, which is often the path people in this job want to take."

Taking on difficult challenges and seeing them through is something Dave finds rewarding. He recently took over responsibility for a huge office complex that had been poorly managed for many years. With no experience with the property except one brief tour, he turned it around in three

months. "It was brutal, and I got very little sleep those three months, but I'm proud to say the place is running like a top today. I consider that to be a big accomplishment and one which led to the promotion to vice president." He believes his ability to put the job first, even over his personal feelings about it or the people he works with, as well as his responsive and realistic perspective help him succeed. "I try to be accommodating to all the people I deal with, from building owners to security guards. I'm no softie, but I get the job done and people think I'm a nice guy. That's important, too."

Lately, it's become more important to Dave to receive reinforcement and feedback for a job well done. "I like to be told positive things about my abilities and accomplishments. I know I do a good job, but it's good to hear that people I respect also notice it. I even prefer to hear about it secondhand because I tend to think the compliment is more truthful if I learn that someone was talking about me and said I did a great job." Dave is also striving to find a balance between his busy and productive work life and his home life, which includes his wife and two preschool children. "There's a natural shift when you have kids. I used to think my life was perfect when I had just one child. I couldn't imagine having a second. Now I do and it's perfect with two." But Dave feels the increased responsibility on his shoulders to provide for his family and keep his job in an uncertain market.

In addition to better focus and direction for his life, Dave continues to spend his free time involved in local-level politics and serving on his condominium association board. "I can see myself running for an elected position some day—town selectman or city council. I care about what happens to my community, and I plan to become more active in the process." In fact, at times, Dave surprises people with his humor and ability to perform. He did a stand-up comedy show at a Christmas party, confirming that "around people I know well, I'm the life of the party!"

"I think success is when people remember you after you've left a job as someone who did a great job and was good to work with. I'll never forget the surprise going-away party they threw for me at a job I held for only two months. It was a 'between jobs' job. It felt great to be appreciated enough that they would do that for me."

Dave's campaign to get the job with the real estate firm is a good example of what he's really all about. After the first interview, he later learned that the company executives weren't too impressed with him. But a second interview was held at his office at the campus center. "I think seeing me in my element, dealing effectively with everything I had to deal with (and still noticing to pick up a gum wrapper off the floor while I was walking with them) made them feel confident in my ability and impressed them with my conscientiousness."

Why This Career Works for Dave

Dave's work as a property manager suits his Traditionalist temperament well. He is in the business of maintaining real things, making sure operations run smoothly and equipment and facilities are kept up to standard and code. His job involves a good deal of responsibility—and both his tasks and the procedures required to accomplish them are clearly defined. Like many Traditionalists, Dave places a high value on his family life and is also involved in his community. And also like many Traditionalists, he has structured his schedule so there is little conflict between his home and work lives.

In his business, Dave must pay attention to everything. He is constantly "on alert" and uses his introverted Sensing (dominant) to notice how everything looks, sounds, feels, and even smells. As he inspects the properties he manages, he must pay attention to such things as lighting, temperature, and acoustics, down to the smallest details concerning the physical condition of the building. Additionally, he must keep track of the budget, making sure that maintenance schedules are carried out on time, necessary reports are filed, and established procedures are followed.

Another of Dave's responsibilities involves contracting with vendors, tradespeople, and maintenance and security staff. His extraverted Thinking (auxiliary) helps him to be fair and objective when evaluating the performance of the many people he supervises and tough when negotiating the most favorable terms of their contracts.

Evidence of Dave's development of his Feeling (third function) is that he seeks positive reinforcement and feedback and likes to hear that people think he is doing a good job. It is not only important to him that others appreciate his competence; he also wants people to like him. Also, it is only recently that Dave has decided he wants to, and has begun to, make a personal contribution to his community.

Common Threads

Although Glenda, Dave, and Jackie have different backgrounds, experiences, and careers, there are certain common threads woven through their stories. Their specific interests, abilities, and values may differ, but owing to their similar temperament values, the *same hierarchy* of their psychological functions, and the world they use them in (inner or outer), there are certain observations we can make about the needs of many ISTJs.

What follows is a list of the most important elements—the formula, if you will, for ISTJ satisfaction. Given the uniqueness of all individuals—even those who share the same type—this list will not describe each ISTJ equally well. The important thing is that these ten elements, with varying degrees of intensity and in different orders of importance, identify what ISTJs need to be satisfied.

After you have reviewed this list, we recommend that you go back and prioritize the elements in order of *their importance to you*. When doing this, think of past work experiences as well as your present job, and what you found particularly satisfying or unsatisfying. Try to look for *themes* that run through several experiences, not just the events that might be true for one work situation but not for another.

As an ISTJ, career satisfaction means doing work that:

1. Is technical in nature and lets me depend on my ability to use and remember important facts and details
2. Involves a real product or service done in a thoughtful, logical, and efficient way, preferably using standard operating procedures
3. Lets me be independent, with plenty of time to work alone and use my excellent powers of concentration to complete projects and/or tasks
4. Is done in a stable and traditional environment, where I will not be required to take unnecessary risks or use untested or experimental approaches
5. Has results that are tangible and measurable, where precision and exacting standards are used and respected
6. Has explicit objectives and a clearly defined organizational structure

7. Gives me adequate time to prepare before presenting or turning in my work, preferably in a one-on-one or small group setting
8. Gives me increasing levels of responsibility, with a minimum of social politics, where I am evaluated on how well I have achieved the requirements of the job description and am appreciated for my contributions
9. Is done in an environment where my practical judgment and experience are valued and rewarded
10. Allows me to set and reach stated goals by providing me with the necessary resources

Popular Occupations for ISTJs

In listing occupations that are popular among ISTJs, it is important to note that there are successful people of all types in all occupations. However, the following are careers ISTJs may find particularly satisfying and some of the reasons why. This is by no means a comprehensive listing but is included to suggest possibilities you may not have previously considered. Although all of these occupations offer the potential for career satisfaction, the future demand for some careers is anticipated to be greater than for others. Based upon our research, the occupations that are italicized in the lists below are forecast to enjoy the fastest rate of growth over the next several years.

BUSINESS
- *Auditor*
- Office manager
- *Accountant*
- Manager/supervisor
- *Executive assistant*
- Insurance underwriter

- *Bookkeeper*
- Logistics and supply manager
- Regulatory compliance officer
- Chief information officer
- Actuary
- Property manager: commercial/residential
- *Bill and account collector*
- *Construction and building inspector*
- Government inspector
- *Construction manager*
- Purchasing agent and contract specialist
- Insurance claims examiner
- Statistician
- *Information and records clerk*
- *Billing and posting clerk*
- *Technical writer*
- Association manager and adviser
- Project manager
- *Real estate appraiser*

ISTJs often enjoy careers in business and excel in the areas of managing systems and keeping things running smoothly. They usually prefer traditional, established organizations or businesses and by their presence provide a stabilizing effect on an operation. They are efficient and thorough in keeping track of costs and revenues and do not allow errors or omissions to go unchecked or uncorrected. As managers, they provide clear definition of roles and established ways of doing things for their employees. They often prefer businesses that produce tangible products or services.

SALES/SERVICE
- Police officer/detective
- IRS agent
- Government employee
- Military officer
- Real estate agent
- Sports equipment/merchandise sales
- Corrections officer
- Industrial safety and health engineer

- *Fire prevention and protection specialist*
- Ship and boat captain
- Commercial airplane pilot
- Probation officer
- Landscaping manager
- Flight engineer
- Postmaster and mail superintendent
- Environmental compliance inspector
- Immigration and customs inspector
- Architectural drafter
- Organic farmer
- Musical instrument maker
- Flight navigator

Careers in civil service often appeal to ISTJs' desire to serve their community. They enjoy maintaining systems that serve or protect all people. They work well within a structured environment, and can take and give direction and supervision well. ISTJs apply their knowledge and past experience to efficiently and decisively handle current problems. They have good memories for facts and details and use practical judgment in all they do. They tend to enjoy sales of real products with which they have personal experience.

FINANCE
- Bank examiner
- Investment securities officer
- Tax preparer and examiner
- Stockbroker
- Estate planner
- Credit analyst
- Budget analyst
- *Cost estimator*
- Treasurer, controller, and chief financial officer

ISTJs are often said to have a head for numbers. They use and remember facts and details and can cite evidence to support their views. They are not easily distracted and work painstakingly to complete tasks accurately and meticulously. Careers in finance often require the ability to work well alone, absorb great amounts of data, and follow through on the precise execution of the computation.

EDUCATION
- School principal
- Teacher: technical/industrial/math/physical education
- Librarian
- Administrator
- Archivist

Careers in education are often satisfying for ISTJs, especially those involving administration and/or technical subjects. They do well when overseeing the operation of a school or curriculum. They look for practical possibilities and ways to maintain systems. Administrative and library careers enable the ISTJ to work independently, using objective analysis in keeping order or monitoring data such as test scores and budgets. Teaching can be enjoyable for ISTJs when working with technical and practical subjects, where there are plenty of opportunities for hands-on teaching and learning.

LEGAL/TECHNOLOGY
- Law researcher
- Electrician
- Engineer
- *Paralegal*
- Mechanic
- *Computer programmer*
- *Software and web development engineer*
- *Construction and development engineer*
- *Technical writer*
- Legal secretary
- Pharmaceutical salesperson/researcher
- *EEG technologist/technician*
- Geologist
- Meteorologist

- Airline mechanic
- Mechanical/industrial/electrical engineer
- Agricultural scientist
- Reliability engineer
- *Database administrator*
- *Network systems and data communications analyst*
- Web editor
- Hardware engineer
- Hardware/software tester
- Judge/magistrate
- Criminalist and ballistics expert
- Court clerk

These careers offer ISTJs the chance to use their technical skills and work with products that demand exacting accuracy. Because they take nothing for granted, they catch slips and oversights, and follow necessary procedures and systems faithfully. Many of these occupations give ISTJs the chance to work alone, employing their tremendous powers of concentration and applying their excellent factual recall and mastery of skills.

HEALTH CARE
- *Veterinarian*
- *General surgeon*
- Dentist
- *Nursing administrator*
- *Health care administrator*
- *Pharmacist*
- *Lab technologist*
- Medical researcher
- *Primary care physician*
- *Biomedical technologist*
- Exercise physiologist
- *Veterinary technologist/technician*
- *Dental hygienist*
- *Pharmacist/pharmacy technician*
- *Surgical technologist*
- *Diagnostic medical sonographer*
- Orthodontist

- Coroner
- Optometrist
- *Public health officer*
- *Biology specimen technician*
- Environmental science technician
- *Medical records technician*
- *EEG technologist*

ISTJs are often drawn to medical careers, especially those that are within the traditional structure of a hospital. They pay close attention to the immediate and practical concerns of their patients. They listen carefully and offer thoughtful and conservative advice and treatment plans. ISTJs are also successful administrators within health care settings, working conscientiously and steadily to meet their responsibilities and honor their commitments. They enjoy an orderly environment and one that rewards task-orientation and jobs done on schedule. The more technical nature of dentistry and pharmacology is often enjoyable to ISTJs, who master factual information easily and retain it forever.

Customizing Your Job Search

Knowing the particular strengths and blind spots of your type can afford you a tremendous advantage in your job search campaign. In all aspects of the process, from conducting research into available positions, identifying and contacting prospective employers, developing personal marketing tools such as résumés, arranging and conducting job interviews, negotiating salaries, to finally accepting a position, people will act true to their type. Being able to capitalize on your assets and compensate for your liabilities can make the difference between a successful and an unsuccessful job search.

The differences between types are sometimes subtle and other times dramatic. It is the subtle variations in advice we offer that make the real difference between success or failure in a job search. The concept of "networking," or meeting with and talking to people to gather information about potential jobs, serves as a good example. Extraverts will naturally enjoy networking and are advised to do so on a large scale, while Introverts find more limited and targeted networking, especially with people they already know, easier. Sensors tend to network with people in a defined scope, while Intuitives will go far and wide to find people often seemingly unrelated to their field of interest. Further, Feelers take networking, like everything else, very personally and enjoy establishing warm rapport, while Thinkers will be more objective and detached in their style. Finally, Judgers tend to ask fewer and more structured questions during their networking, while Perceivers could ask questions of all sorts all day long! One valuable search technique, many ways to implement it.

Pathways to Success: Using Your Strengths

As we will detail in the following pages, your strengths and talents for the job search include your conscientiousness, desire to work hard, and ability to keep careful track of details and commitments. Beware of your tendency to stick only to the tried-and-true traditional methods of job hunting and miss clever or less obvious approaches.

As an ISTJ, your most effective strategies will build on your abilities to:

Research career options completely and conduct thorough data collection.

- Be patient in collecting information dur- ing the gathering stage of your job search. Remember that it often takes several months to find the right job.

- Network on a limited basis with people who know you well, especially those you have worked with in the past who are in different jobs, or people they recommend.

When Frank was looking for a position in the tax department of his state government, he asked a friend from the Rotary club to refer him to someone he knew in the tax commissioner's office. Frank talked at length with the person, who was able to show him the offices, give him a real sample of a typical week's work load, and even share some of the complaints people had about the job. As a result, Frank had a more realistic view of the job's advantages and disadvantages before actually applying for the position.

Carefully prepare your marketing materials.

- Look at your résumé and cover letters with an objective eye. Ask yourself what kind of message they send about you. Are they an accurate reflection of you?
- Be sure to include work accomplishments from your recent and more distant past and have letters of recommendation ready if needed.

Judy started work on her résumé by patterning it after a friend's in the same business. But she decided that what she needed was a finished product that would better sell her skills and experience. We helped her focus her résumé on accomplishments and the skills that each one utilized. In the work history section of the résumé, Judy showed how each position had given her increased levels of responsibility. When she mailed the résumé with personalized cover letters, she was confident that the person reviewing it would have a good picture of her experience and all she had to offer.

Patiently follow companies' recruitment and personnel procedures.

- Ask or read about company hiring procedures as part of your overall information gathering. Tailor your approach to the way the system works.
- Demonstrate the kind of employee you will be by going through appropriate channels, using the system, and respecting the chain of command.

When recruiters from a major manufacturing company came to Martha's university to interview graduate computer programming students, Martha decided to get some advance information before interviewing. She spoke to her career adviser and got the name of an alumnus who was currently employed by the company. She put what she learned into practice and was really prepared for the interview. Besides being ready for the standard questions, she was also ready to ask a few of her own to let the interviewer know that she had done her homework and knew something about the company. The interviewer was impressed with her initiative. More subtle, however, was a fact that Martha had learned from her contact—the company encouraged a conservative dress code. Martha even bought a traditional blue suit for the interview. It turned out the company representative conducting the interview was wearing an almost identical suit.

Follow through on all details.

- Focus your energy on completing large and small tasks relating to your job search. This includes mapping out a general plan, keeping track of your progress, writing thank-you letters, and making follow-up calls.

- Stay organized. Demonstrate your skills and don't be afraid to be persistent, showing your interest in a particular job.

Nancy had narrowed down her first choice in her career switch. She had decided she wanted to be the director of nursing at a nearby hospital. The position was still being posted internally, so, for the short term, Nancy would have to wait to find out if it would be opened to the public. She stayed in touch with each of her contacts at the facility and made regular calls to the vice president for personnel at the hospital to remind him of her interest. A couple of times during the wait, she had doubts about calling or sending a note. But she decided that she should continue to show that as hard as she would work to get the job, she would work just as hard once she got it. Her persistence paid off. When the position was open for outside application, she was the first, and last, applicant.

Make thoughtful, practical decisions.

- Ask for the time you need to carefully consider a job offer. Let your prospective employer know that you take your commitments seriously and want to give the offer the same attention you give to all of your responsibilities.
- Take a realistic look at the current job market and your skills. Employ your logical reasoning to help you make logical decisions.

After Gordon retired from the Navy, he began the process of making a career change by seeking career counseling. One of the ways he developed a list of realistic options was to review his skills and also research the job market in his home state. He considered using his training in physical education to work with a professional or collegiate sports team but determined that there were too few opportunities. So he pursued a career in high school physical education at a school with a need for a new varsity football and baseball coach. He was able to structure a job where he would be able to do both.

Possible Pitfalls

Although all people are unique, there are certain *potential* blind spots that many ISTJs share. We specify "potential" because some of the following *may* be true of you, while others may clearly not apply. While considering them, you may notice that these tendencies do not relate just to the job search but rather describe pitfalls that you may have experienced in other aspects of your life as well. It is therefore helpful to consider each one in terms of your past experiences by asking yourself, "Is this true for me?" And if so, "How did this tendency prevent me from getting something that I wanted?" You will probably notice that the key to overcoming your blind spots is the conscious and thoughtful development of your third and fourth functions (Feeling and Intuition). We recognize that many of the suggestions will be difficult to implement, but the more you use these functions, the fewer problems they will cause you in the future.

Consider career possibilities that are less obvious.

- Look for career possibilities that don't currently exist. Get help generating a long list of potential careers in which you are interested. Also look for careers that require the same skills you have, even if your skills are in a different field.
- Resist the urge to rule options out as unrealistic simply because you lack direct experience in the field.

Don't overlook the implications of your decisions.

- Try imagining yourself in any job you are considering. Imagine yourself five, ten, or twenty years from now. Is there growth potential? Opportunities to change areas or add responsibility?
- Develop a set of long-term and short-range goals to use as a measuring stick during your search. Compare potential jobs against both sets of goals to discover if you might be selling out a future goal for a short-range objective.

Avoid the tendency to be overcautious and rigid in your thinking.

- Try to keep yourself open to the possibility of doing something very different than you have in the past. Consider taking some reasonable and necessary risks to find career satisfaction.
- Continue to get help or counsel from friends or professionals if you think you might be slipping back into a routine in your thinking.

Remember to consider the human element in your search.

- Take the time to think about your true feelings and motivation as well as what makes logical sense, and what you are technically qualified for. Ask yourself what's really important to you in your life, as well as your work, and make sure you aren't compromising the former.
- Pay attention to the interpersonal subtleties during the interview process. Engage in what you may consider frivolous niceties simply because you now know that other people consider them important.

Express enthusiasm for the job and aggressively market yourself.

- Let people know if you really are interested in a particular job. Generate energy and enthusiasm for yourself and the position.
- Try not to underestimate your abilities and what you have to contribute to an organization. Demonstrate your confidence in yourself by talking about your accomplishments in the past and what you could offer the company.

The Final Piece: Changing or Keeping Your Job...the Key to Success for ISTJs

Now that you have a solid understanding of your type, you can see how your natural preferences make you better suited for certain kinds of jobs. You can also see how knowledge of your type-related strengths and weaknesses can help you conduct a more successful job search. But as an ISTJ, you've already realized that you are not equally drawn to *every* career or field listed in the Popular Occupations section. The next and final step is to narrow down the field and find the work you were meant to do.

In addition to Type, several other factors—such as your values, interests, and skills—also contribute to your level of satisfaction on the job. The more compatible you are with your job, the happier you'll be. So prepare to use everything you've learned (in this book and in life) to create *your strategic career plan*. The exercises in Chapter 24, Putting It All Together, are designed to help you do just that.

However, you may have decided it makes more sense (if perhaps only for the moment) to stay in your present job or with your current employer. There may be many valid reasons—financial pressures, family considerations, a tough job market for your specialty, or just bad timing. But take heart! What you've learned in this book can also help you be more content and successful *in your current job.* And should the time come when you're ready to make a major career move, you'll have a much better idea of where you want to go, and how to get there.

> *"So, if you can't have the job you love (yet!) . . . love the one you've got."*

The simple truth is, with the exception of work on a factory assembly line, the vast majority of jobs allow a good deal of flexibility in the way tasks are performed. Here are some ways you may be able to "massage" your current job into one that better fits your needs:

- Find an efficient assistant or secretary.
- Try to schedule work on one project at a time.
- Implement efficiency systems and require direct-reports to use them.
- Try to attend fewer meetings.
- Seek other points of view to balance your own.
- Ask people chairing meetings for a written agenda prior to meetings.
- Figure out how to avoid being interrupted (consider schedule changes, erecting physical barriers, forwarding your calls, moving your office, etc.).
- Ask your supervisors to be more explicit about their expectations.
- Set up short-term goals.

One ISTJ turns lemons into lemonade:

Though her boss knew she was a very hard worker, Julia could never finish her paperwork because of interruptions from people in her small, overcrowded office. Since there was no quiet office space available, Julia suggested she change her hours, so that by arriving one hour earlier than the other staff, she could do her work uninterrupted. As a bonus, Julia's leaving an hour early each day helped her avoid rush-hour traffic and made the trip to pick up her son at his day care center a much less anxious affair.

Use what you've got to get what you need.

Simply put, the best advice on how to succeed is to *capitalize on your strengths and compensate for your weaknesses.* Learning how to do this can make the difference between succeeding or failing and loving or hating your work. To help you, we include the following inventory of your potential strengths and weaknesses. And while every individual is unique, as an ISTJ, many of the following should apply to you.

Your work-related strengths may include:

- Precision and accuracy and desire to get the job done right the first time
- Readiness to follow established routines and policies
- Ability to focus and concentrate on one task at a time in great depth
- Ability to work alone
- Sharp organizational skills
- Thoroughness and close attention to the specifics: facts and details
- Belief in the value of a traditional structure and the ability to work within it
- Strong sense of responsibility; you can be counted on to do what you say
- Clear work ethic; you feel it is important to be efficient and productive
- Perseverance and determination to accomplish your goals
- Common sense and a realistic perspective

Your work-related weaknesses may include:

- Reluctance to embrace new, untested ideas
- Discomfort with or resistance to change
- Impatience with processes that take too long
- Unwillingness to focus on future needs at the same time as present ones

- Inflexibility; inability or unwillingness to adapt when necessary
- Inability to focus on "the big picture" and see the implications of actions
- Lack of sensitivity as to how people will be affected by policies and decisions
- Reluctance to change direction and shift gears when warranted
- Unwillingness to instigate or support needed change and calculated risks

---

Using your strengths is easy.
The secret to success for an
ISTJ
is learning to:

Be open to possibilities, consider
implications for people,
and embrace change.

18 ║ ESFJ
Extraverted, Sensing, Feeling, Judging
"What Can I Do for You?"

Profile 1: Robin

"Helping families get settled during a highly stressful time."

Robin's life is about families. Her children and husband are the most important things in her life, and her professional life has followed her personal values by helping other families. Her job as a real estate agent allows her to do what she needs to do, wants to do, and values, while still helping other people. She gets enormous satisfaction from her work but sees it as only a means to an end, not the end itself.

At forty-two, Robin describes herself as being "in the second stage of my life." She began her career with a degree in family relations and child development. She went to work for a social service agency as a social worker in the adoption department. During her first year, changes were taking place in the cultural climate of the times. "Adoption in the early seventies was changing quickly

from the traditional placement of white babies to the placement of more minority and handicapped children. Overall there were just fewer babies available to the couples who wanted them." To meet the new challenges of the field, Robin became part of a team of professionals who redesigned the program to meet the needs of "hard-to-place" babies. The program became a model for the rest of the state, and Robin became coordinator of adoption. "It was amazing that I got the job as coordinator because I don't have a master's degree in social work. My experience compensated for my lack of formal education. I really enjoyed the work and found it deeply rewarding to help people become a family."

After eleven years, Robin entered her "second stage" when she left the agency to have her first child. She enjoyed every minute of staying home and raising her daughter and then her son. Eventually, "I began to see all the things my kids wanted to do, like private music lessons, sports, and travel, and saw what they would cost. I decided that since they were both in school, I would find a job that would pay for all those special extras. But I was demanding; the job had to leave me totally flexible to be there whenever they needed or wanted me to be. My decision to go back to work was purely a realistic one motivated by how I would pay for what I wanted to give my kids."

Robin enlisted the help of a professional career counselor to help her identify options but followed the advice of her friends and her own real estate agent, who had all told her she would be great in real estate. She took the course and exam to obtain her license and was soon offered a job at an agency. She took the job on the condition that she would still have the flexibility and freedom she needed.

One of the greatest sources of satisfaction in Robin's work is best demonstrated through the example of her very first client. "These poor people had been through the wringer. They'd had a contract on their house and put a deposit on another house out of state when their agent let some important details slip and both deals fell apart. The people lost their deposit money and their buyer, too. They interviewed me and another agent with ten years' experience. When they chose me, I couldn't believe it. They told me it was my honesty and enthusiasm that persuaded them. Anyway, I sold their house in three days and four days after that had found them another great house to buy. When they had their first baby a few months after the move, I went to visit them in the hospital. It was so great to be able to really help these people during what was a terribly stressful time in their lives. I just loved the connection I made with these people. It was really rewarding."

Working with people and helping them find homes is the part of Robin's job she enjoys most. "Helping people solve their problems is great, especially when it involves a critical life decision. It feels good to find a home for someone, just like it felt good to find a permanent home for a baby!" Robin is also energized by the liaison role she fills during the negotiation process. "I help show each side that they are getting something and can help them understand when it's time to compromise their position a little in order to make the deal work."

But there are countless details between the making of a deal and the closing of a sale. Robin does it all herself, from developing strategies for selling the house, writing a sales brochure, staffing the open house, arranging work with appraisers, inspectors, and lawyers, writing newspaper ads, to communicating all the changes and progress to her clients. "The only part I really dislike is actually writing the brochure. I love taking the picture, but writing the words is awful. I don't feel I'm very good at it, so it takes me a long time and takes so much out of me. The end result is fine but I hate the process."

Robin rarely experiences job-related stress because she engineers situations to avoid the conflicts that would cause stress for her. "When I'm not able to meet someone's expectations, it's stressful, so I compensate by trying to explain early on in the process what they should expect. I'm very realistic and prepare them for the worst. The worst doesn't usually happen, but I avoid putting myself in the position of disappointing clients who expect a quick sale at a huge price if that's not realistic."

"Occasionally, it's stressful for me when I have an awful lot of people to deal with at once, because every situation requires at least twenty-nine phone calls. I want to take care of things the very best way I can, so I try never to overextend myself."

Robin also enjoys her work because it enables her to save her emotional energy for her family. "I never considered returning to social work and adoption when I began to look for a job. I knew it would be too emotionally demanding. It was fine before I had kids, but now I put them first and foremost in my life. They are, and will always be, my top priority."

Outside of work and her children, Robin enjoys sewing and her involvement in a Christmas craft group she has belonged to for nearly ten years. "We get together and work on all kinds of crafts, which we can use for holiday gifts. It's fun and useful, too." She is very involved in her children's activities such as her daughter's violin lessons and recitals, and in watching her son's Little League games. Robin has also recently become more involved in local politics, the children's elementary school Parent-Teacher Organization, and in environmental and world peace organizations. "I write to my congressional representatives and become informed about a whole range of world issues I don't have any background in."

In fact, these days Robin thinks more globally. "I would like to do something someday that has a bigger impact. But I know that's what I'm doing with my children, and the way I treat other people will ultimately have a bigger effect. It's the ripple effect, touching one person who touches others.

"I hope people think of me as fair, understanding, and caring. I've always loved children; my parents instilled that value in me. I'm working to have a good relationship with my kids, having fun together and understanding each other. My philosophy is 'be yourself.' When I looked for a job, I looked to see how it would fit into the rest of my life, not just what it would be like during the time I was actually at work. See, there is a time in life for each stage. While I'm in that stage, I'm going to really *be* in that time and place. Otherwise, I will have missed it all."

Why This Career Works for Robin

One reason why Robin's work is so satisfying is that it provides her the freedom to schedule plenty of time for her first priority—her family. But as an extension of this Traditionalist value, Robin also enjoys helping other people's families find and settle into a new home. Task-oriented and well organized, Robin likes the fact that her clients can rely on her to come through in a pinch. She enjoys working hard for her clients, just as hard as she works on her many other community projects.

Robin loves becoming a part of people's lives and establishing relationships with new people. She especially enjoys helping people by being able to "save the day" such as when the deal a client is counting on falls through and she puts it back together. When she is extraverting her Feeling (dominant), she is at her best, making connections and creating harmony between parties. She particularly enjoys negotiating to help each side win something and feel good about their interaction. Strongly extraverted, Robin enjoys the collegiality she shares with her associates and the many other people she interacts with on a daily basis.

Her introverted Sensing (auxiliary) helps Robin keep track in her head of an enormous amount of detail. On a typical day, she may be in contact with lawyers, mortgage brokers, appraisers, inspectors—not to mention buyers and sellers—all who have important information that requires her attention. And often, she must coordinate the schedules of many different people to get the job done. Her Sensing also comes in handy in assessing how a house will show to the public and in gauging the reactions of potential buyers to the properties they are looking at.

In recent years Robin has become interested in more global kinds of issues—one example of how she is developing her Intuition (third function). She wants to have an impact on a bigger scale and has become more philosophical about the kinds of contributions she wants to make to society—once her children are out of school and she is free to focus her energy on something else. She has chosen this job to fit into the bigger picture of her life, as opposed to only satisfying an immediate need, which also points to more comfort with long-range planning than she had in the past.

Meet the Millennial

Name: Kristin
Age: 31
Sales representative

"Building rapport with just about everybody!"

Backstory

Kristin has always been an outgoing and vivacious person. A musical theater major in college, Kristin worked throughout school as a bank teller, moving from senior teller to merchant teller, as well as performing customer service. "I liked it because I wasn't sitting behind a desk. I was talking to people all day long—it was fun!" After college, Kristin decided the stage wasn't for her, but she wasn't sure which path she was meant to take.

She spotted a posting online for a position in business-to-business outside sales with a competitive salary and benefits. The job was attractive to Kristin because it would entail selling business services to other businesses, and doing it face-to-face. "I presented well," remembers Kristin. "I didn't have a lot of experience, but I had a really nice résumé and cover letter, and was articulate and organized in the interview." She aced it and soon was selling an automated payroll service to small businesses looking for an alternative to hiring their own bookkeeper or accountant. Kristin continued in this job for two years, cutting her teeth learning sales and becoming the top representative in the region. Kristin felt as at home in sales as she had once felt on the stage, learning the "script" for a product and giving her pitch. "Everything else is shooting the breeze with the person you're with—chatting them up." She moved from that

(continued)

position to a job working as a premier client manager at a bank, a job she felt ill-suited for, but which ultimately got her to New York City. After two and a half years, Kristin was laid off when the bank merged and eliminated her division. "I was devastated at the time, but it turned out to be the best thing for me. I got to clear my mind and think, 'What do I really want to do? What is a job I would be proud to say I had, that I would want to wake up every morning and go do?'"

Kristin realized what she wanted to do was be back in an elite sales job. She met with recruiters and was interviewed and placed at a company selling dental equipment and products to dentists' offices. Her official title is senior territory manager, and she covers a territory that averages $1.3 million in gross sales annually. Kristin's job consists mainly of traveling around her territory of five counties, including upper Manhattan and Westchester, and either upgrading equipment or introducing new products that will help the practice become more efficient. Much of her job includes educating office staff on new products, but the lion's share of what she does is building relationships. "It's basically my job to befriend offices."

A Good Fit

Kristin's charisma makes her a natural at sales. "It's easy for me to build rapport. I can pretty quickly assess the energy someone is giving off to me, and I will match it." A dominant extraverted Feeling type, Kristin is warm and friendly, a self-described "open book," and genuinely enjoys meeting and building relationships with the many people she interacts with daily. "You have to be the kind of person who's willing to expose yourself a little in this job, especially when you're going into the same offices repeatedly. My offices know me. I'm a real person and they're real people, and we're not just robots having this mechanical dental conversation." With Sensing as her auxiliary function, Kristin is adept at memorizing and conveying detailed information about her wide assortment of dental products. Like many Judgers, she gets a competitive thrill from the hunt— seeking, and especially closing, a deal— and it is gratifying to see her efforts correspond with the concrete bump in commission.

Looking Ahead

Kristin enjoys her job and definitely wants to stick around for a while. "I consider myself a loyal person. This company has been good to me, and in return I want to be good to them." Farther down the line, in five to ten years, Kristin could see herself branching out into the medical industry. "I've always really wanted to be in surgical sales, in operating rooms doing orthopedic. Those are the really coveted and hard jobs to get. But I'd like to get to that level."

Profile 2: Dennis

"Helping other people to do their jobs better and more safely."

Thirty-eight-year-old Dennis is a patrolman for a suburban police department. He enjoys being a patrolman but has, for the past two years, been enjoying a new assignment: as an instructor in the training department. He enjoys the interaction, the variety, and the opportunity to give tangible and helpful information to his fellow officers, who are faced with the same dangers and challenges he knows firsthand. Dennis feels a great deal of satisfaction from doing a job well, doing it the way he feels it should be done, and being respected and appreciated by his peers.

Each week, Dennis works with a different group of police officers from his own department and other departments around the region, teaching a variety of courses that are mandated by the state governing board. The courses include everything from human relations and law updates pertaining to liability to ongoing recertification of firearms proficiency or defensive-driving courses. Dennis is given criteria for what is to be covered but can develop his own lessons for how he chooses to teach the material. He writes and submits lesson plans, researches his subject matter, presents the training sessions, and documents each class member's participation for their personnel records.

Dennis also works a patrol shift, but these days it's only on an overtime, occasional-need basis. While he enjoys those responsibilities, he enjoys the break from the constant "condition yellow" required of a police officer on duty, especially at night. "You're not on *full* alert but you're never relaxed, either. It's a situation where you're constantly scanning, staying ready for that radio call that may come at any time, and the uncertainty of what you may face. It's the anticipation that can be crazy."

Of all the courses Dennis teaches, he prefers the hands-on, more active and physical involvement. "I enjoy teaching about firearms or defensive driving because those just can't be taught in a classroom. The tasks I enjoy the most are the ones where I'm handed a ball and told to run with it, doing what I think is best." Dennis also volunteers as a counselor in the employee assistance program in the department. "I enjoy the interaction with other people in a more personal capacity. I like helping people with their problems, so I also help coordinate some of the training from that department. I guess it's the communication I find the most energizing. Listening to people, acting as a sounding board, giving information in a way that doesn't offend or hurt anyone, are what I do best."

The communication style that best suits Dennis is verbal. In fact, when he has to do paperwork or write reports to document the training department's accomplishments or justify changes in procedure, he finds himself completely drained. "I find it terribly difficult to express myself accurately in writing. So I avoid those tasks as long as possible." Dennis also finds that his open and accessible style sometimes results in being the sympathetic ear to things he'd rather not hear. "People tell me things to get them off their chests, but it can be awkward to be in the middle, between two co-workers. But I'd still rather have it this way than for people not to be able to talk to me."

The only real source of stress for Dennis, besides the occupational hazards of the job, are the times when he wants to get things done in the way he believes is best, that will have the most positive and practical benefit for other people, and runs up against obstacles and constraints that make this impossible. "I really like being in control of my own work and doing things right. It can be frustrating when I can only do something halfway." Dennis also wishes that there was some occasional downtime in his work. "During a shift, you're always on. I can be eating a sandwich at lunchtime, but if they need me, I'm theirs. There just isn't any personal time, like there is in a corporation." He relieves tension caused by work by exercising daily in the department gym. "First I work it off, then I talk it out with other people doing the same thing. It sure helps to just vent sometimes."

Dennis began his career as a police officer nearly thirteen years ago but not directly out of college, where he had been studying business administration. Instead he was drafted and served with an army medevac, missing a tour in Vietnam by a matter of days. He continued in the army reserves for eight years while working as a mechanic in his cousin's shop. He enjoyed it for several years, and raced cars on weekends. But he began to tire of the work and didn't see any growth or security in it. At the same time, he became friendly with several town police officers, and they encouraged him to study for and take the various eligibility tests required. He did and then applied to several departments, finally accepting a position with a governor's special security detail. Again he enjoyed it for about five years, but began to feel stagnant and eager for more responsibility and challenge. So Dennis began applying again to town police departments and was hired in the town where he still works. A patrol officer for ten years, he became an instructor two and a half years ago.

One of the accomplishments of which Dennis is particularly proud is helping to initiate and oversee a transition period from the use of revolvers to semiautomatic weapons for officers on the force. "I did all the research and then trained the force in the use of the new weapon. I felt strongly that it was an important change. It goes a long way toward attempting to even up the odds out there. Having semiautomatic guns not only allows the officers to protect the community better, it gives them added confidence when walking into a dangerous situation. It's a big step, and I'm proud of my involvement to make it a reality."

While Dennis is enjoying his current position, he is realistic enough to know there will be changes. He has decided to concentrate on preparing for the sergeant's exam next year and hopes to "make rank." "I think I'm a more analytical thinker when it comes to looking at work. I can see the cause and effect of decisions. I know, for example, that I don't want to be a detective, even though some people would say that's the direction I should be headed in. I've looked into it and can see that the disadvantages outweigh the advantages, for me. I have clearer and more focused goals than I ever had. I won't let my work interfere with my home life and the time I spend with my kids, now that they are getting older and are more able to do things with me." Dennis is also interested in making some less tangible contributions to his department. "I'd like to help change the philosophy of the department to be more appreciative of patrol officers. We need to recognize and use the untapped talent we have in the force. I think that change has started as younger people get into administration, but it's a contribution I think I might be able to facilitate. I'm interested in learning new things and helping other people to learn new things, too."

In fact, Dennis believes that in addition to his caring attitude, enthusiasm, and eagerness to work hard for what he believes, his willingness to ask for advice is part of the reason he has found career satisfaction. "When I was working as a mechanic, I used to ask those cop friends of mine what it was really like to be a cop and how I should go about becoming one. I wasn't afraid to ask for advice. And I listened, too. Usually, there is someone in the field that will help you learn about it if you ask. Find out what works for others. And maybe you can learn from other people's mistakes instead of having to make all your own!"

Why This Career Works for Dennis

As a police officer, Dennis is charged with protecting the public. As a Traditionalist, he is well suited philosophically to perform the responsibilities assigned to him, such as serving society's needs and enforcing its rules. Dennis works in a highly structured organization with a clear reporting hierarchy and well-defined objectives. Hard work and adherence to established policy and procedure are expected and rewarded. What is additionally satisfying to Dennis is the fact that he works for a small town with many people who share the same backgrounds and values, all of which add to the sense of community.

Dennis likes being respected and appreciated by his peers for doing a good job. An extraverted Feeler (dominant), he clearly follows his own values and ethics. People contact is important to him, whether teaching, counseling, or helping others with their personal problems; he likes to get involved and give advice. Similarly, the projects he most likes to take on are those that have real benefits for others, such as the program he initiated to assist the police force transition from revolvers to semiautomatic weapons. He believed it would better help protect both his fellow officers and the public.

Dennis's introverted Sensing (auxiliary) is critical since he must be alert to everything when he is on patrol at night and on weekends. He also uses his Sensing in his teaching and training of hands-on skills such as use of firearms and defensive driving. These are real-life skills learned and practiced in the field, not classroom courses involving theories. He also enjoys conducting research, gathering facts about new weapons and other equipment, testing them out to be sure they will work in the field or within the department.

Evidence that Dennis is developing greater access to his Intuition (third function) can be seen in his interest in helping the department to make changes, including philosophical changes. He likes looking for new approaches, learning and teaching new techniques and changes in the law. He has also begun to experience a pull in the direction of his Thinking (fourth function) as well, by deciding to prepare for the sergeant's exam—a promotion that would increase his stature and power. Additionally, he is more analytical, considering cause and effect in his thinking. Consequently, Dennis believes he makes better and more logical decisions.

Common Threads

Although Robin, Dennis, and Kristin have different backgrounds, experiences, and careers, there are certain common threads woven through their stories. Their specific interests, abilities, and values may differ, but owing to their similar temperament values, the *same hierarchy* of their psychological functions, and the "world" they use them in (inner or outer), there are certain observations we can make about the needs of many ESFJs.

What follows is a list of the most important elements—the formula, if you will—for ESFJ satisfaction. Given the uniqueness of all individuals—even those who share the same type—this list will not describe each ESFJ equally well. The important thing is that these ten elements, with varying degrees of intensity and in different orders of importance, identify what ESFJs need to be satisfied.

After you have reviewed this list, we recommend that you go back and prioritize the elements in order of *their importance to you*. When doing this, think of past work experiences as well as your present job, and what you found particularly satisfying or unsatisfying. Try to look for *themes* that run through several experiences, not just the events that might be true for one work situation but not for another.

As an ESFJ, career satisfaction means doing work that:

1. Lets me establish and maintain warm and genuine interpersonal relationships with other people working in real and tangible ways to improve their quality of life
2. Has practical benefits for people and gives me time to learn and master necessary skills before using them
3. Lets me exercise control, working with many people, and helping them work harmoniously toward a common goal
4. Has clear expectations, and where the evaluation of my performance is judged upon established and explicitly stated criteria
5. Is done in a cooperative environment, free from conflicts and tension between co-workers, supervisors, clients, patients, and others
6. Lets me make decisions and use efficient procedures to see that all the details of my projects are carried out to my specifications

7. Gives me plenty of opportunities to interact with other people throughout the day and to be an integral part of the decision-making process
8. Lets me organize my own work and that of those around me to ensure that things are run as smoothly and efficiently as possible
9. Is done within a friendly environment where people express their appreciation for my accomplishments, where I feel approval and support, and where I consider my co-workers to be my friends
10. Is done in a setting with existing structure, where the chain of command is known and understood, and where authority is respected

Popular Occupations for ESFJs

In listing occupations that are popular among ESFJs, it is important to note that there are successful people of all types in all occupations. However, the following are careers ESFJs may find particularly satisfying and some of the reasons why. This is by no means a comprehensive listing but it is included to suggest possibilities you may not have previously considered. Although all of these occupations offer the potential for career satisfaction, the future for some careers is anticipated to be greater than for others. Based upon our research, the occupations that are italicized in the lists below are forecast to enjoy the fastest rate of growth over the next several years.

HEALTH CARE
- *Registered nurse*
- *Medical/dental assistant*
- *Speech-language pathologist/audiologist*
- Exercise physiologist
- *Family physician*
- Dentist
- Medical secretary

- *Dietitian/nutritionist*
- Massage therapist
- Optometrist/optician
- *Pharmacist/pharmacy technician*
- Respiratory therapist
- *Veterinarian*
- *Veterinary technologist/technician*
- *Licensed practical nurse (LPN)*
- *Home health aide*
- *Primary care physician*
- *Physical therapist*
- *Home health social worker*
- *Personal fitness trainer*
- Hospice worker
- *Recreational therapist*
- *Radiation therapist*
- *Health care administrator*
- Chiropractor
- Corrective therapist
- *Dental hygienist*
- *Dialysis technician*
- *Fitness instructor*

The attraction of the health care field to ESFJs is the ability to work directly with other people in a helping capacity. Whether as a physician, nurse, or other practitioner, ESFJs enjoy using acquired skills to help make the lives of their patients easier, less painful, or less traumatic. They excel in careers that require hands-on application of practical skills and adherence to standard operating procedures. These careers in health care also enable ESFJs to establish and maintain strong personal relationships with their patients and co-workers.

EDUCATION
- *Elementary school teacher*
- Special education teacher
- *Child care provider*
- *Athletic coach*
- *Bilingual education teacher*
- *Nursing instructor*
- Director of religious education
- School principal

ESFJs teach by personal involvement and example. The younger student and those with special needs are especially appealing to ESFJs who find rewards in helping others by teaching them basic skills. Working directly with young children appeals to the ESFJ's natural energy and enthusiasm.

There is often a great deal of structure and order within a school setting, an environment which many ESFJs find comfortable. Many ESFJs also enjoy being physically active and teaching others physical skills and the importance of working on a team.

SOCIAL SERVICE/COUNSELING
- *Social worker*
- *Community welfare worker*
- Volunteer coordinator
- Religious educator
- *Counselor*
- Minister/priest/rabbi
- *Employee assistance counselor*
- *Child welfare counselor*
- *Substance abuse counselor*
- *Social worker (elderly and child day care issues)*
- Law clerk
- Legislative assistant
- Court clerk
- Court reporter
- Wilderness adventure leader
- *Paralegal and legal assistant*

ESFJs are strong supporters of their community and often volunteer their time to establish and maintain civic organizations. Therefore, they often experience career satisfaction in careers where they do the same type of work. The personal connection of social work—helping individuals and families overcome problems and become productive members of society—is rewarding for many ESFJs. Their ease and facility in meeting people and speaking to groups makes community action jobs satisfying for some ESFJs. Counseling, religious education, and the ministry attract ESFJs who enjoy the commitment of helping others in very specific and profound ways. ESFJs tend to be conservative and traditional by nature, and enjoy working within the context of existing and valuable organizations to make their contribution.

BUSINESS
- Public relations account executive
- Loan officer and counselor
- Sales representative (tangibles)
- Market research/focus group facilitator
- Office manager
- Retail owner/operator
- *Management consultant: human resources/training*
- Insurance agent (families)
- Credit counselor
- Merchandise planner
- *Customer service manager*
- Health club manager
- Lodging owner/innkeeper
- Property manager: commercial/residential
- Child care center director
- *Customer relations manager (technology)*
- Advocate (technology)
- Food service manager
- Nursery and greenhouse manager
- Hotel and motel manager
- *Real estate appraiser*

The world of business provides ESFJs the opportunity to meet a lot of people and to work hard to achieve their goals. They enjoy the active and busy pace of many businesses and enjoy the customer or client contact. When the business is of a personal nature, such as real estate or personal banking, many ESFJs find success because they are motivated to establish positive relationships with others and then work vigorously to maintain those relationships.

Public relations and marketing require the excellent interpersonal and communication skills most ESFJs possess. Both careers require careful attention to details and follow-through on all project coordination. The organizational skills of the ESFJ are used extensively in these careers.

Finally, sales is an area where ESFJs often experience a great deal of success using their interpersonal skills, their resourcefulness, and their sensitivity to the needs of others. ESFJs usually prefer the sales of tangible goods, rather than intangibles such as concepts, ideas, or complex systems. Retail is an area of interest because it involves public contact and the ability to become well versed in the features and benefits of special products.

SALES/SERVICE
- *Insurance sales agent*
- *Insurance and benefits representative*
- Flight attendant
- *Customer service representative*
- Funeral home director
- Hairdresser/cosmetologist
- Host/hostess
- *Personal care aide*
- Caterer
- Fund-raiser
- Travel consultant
- Eco-tourism specialist
- Real estate agent/broker
- Marketing executive: radio/TV/cable broadcast industry
- *Interpreter/translator*
- Genealogist
- Home health care sales
- Dental and medical sales
- Sports equipment/merchandise salesperson
- Insurance special agent

- Land leasing and development specialist
- Caterer

ESFJs often gravitate to the service industries primarily because of the ability to work directly with other people and provide services that help make an experience more enjoyable or less stressful. The job of customer service representative provides them an opportunity to do this. ESFJs are steadfast and dependable during difficult times, and often rise to the occasion to help take care of all details during a crisis. Funeral home directors must show an inordinate amount of sensitivity and concern for others in their work.

On the lighter side of life, ESFJs often enjoy the variety, travel, and interpersonal contact of being a flight attendant. Most ESFJs are warm and gracious and make excellent hosts/hostesses in the restaurant or catering business. ESFJs generally enjoy and often excel in sales, especially with real and tangible products and in instances where they can develop and cultivate long-term relationships with their customers.

CLERICAL
- Secretary
- Receptionist
- Bookkeeper
- *Administrative assistant*

Most ESFJs, in addition to having interpersonal skills required in many clerical positions, have good manual dexterity. Once a skill is learned by an ESFJ, it is never forgotten. ESFJs are able to perform routine tasks with unerring accuracy and usually have the facility with numbers required of bookkeeping. The critical elements in clerical careers for ESFJs are feeling appreciated as part of a team and the ability to socialize with co-workers on the job. Isolation is very draining to an ESFJ.

Customizing Your Job Search

Knowing the particular strengths and blind spots of your type can afford you a tremendous advantage in your job search campaign. In all aspects of the process, from conducting research into available positions, identifying and contacting prospective employers, developing personal marketing tools such as résumés, arranging and conducting job interviews, negotiating salaries, to finally accepting a position, people will act true to their type. Being able to capitalize on your assets and compensate for your liabilities can make the difference between a successful and an unsuccessful job search.

The differences between types are sometimes subtle and other times dramatic. It is the subtle variations in advice we offer that make the real difference between success or failure in a job search. The concept of "networking," or meeting with and talking to people to gather information about potential jobs, serves as a good example. Extraverts will naturally enjoy networking and are advised to do so on a large scale, while Introverts find more limited and targeted networking, especially with people they already know, easier. Sensors tend to network with people in a defined scope, while Intuitives will go far and wide to find people often seemingly unrelated to their field of interest. Further, Feelers take networking, like everything else, very personally and enjoy establishing warm rapport, while Thinkers will be more objective and detached in their style. Finally, Judgers tend to ask fewer and more structured questions during their networking, while Perceivers could ask questions of all sorts all day long! One valuable search technique, many ways to implement it.

Pathways to Success: Using Your Strengths

As we will detail in the following pages, your many interpersonal strengths and talents, as well as your great organizational skills, will enable you to implement an efficient job search. Beware of your tendency to be overwhelmed by the uncertainty of the process and become discouraged by rejection, even when it is not personal.

As an ESFJ, your most effective strategies will build on your abilities to:

Establish rapport with interviewers.

- Demonstrate to interviewers your ease at meeting new people and your ability to make others feel comfortable with you.
- Find a common interest, using your keen powers of observation and your ability to create a friendly atmosphere with others.

Neil was interviewing for a sales position at a health food distributor whose client base was small independently owned and operated health food stores. Neil was primarily interested in the job because, being a vegetarian himself, he wanted to use his sales experience selling something he believed in. While driving into the parking lot, Neil saw a woman get out of her car and enter the building. He noticed her car because of its "I Love Labrador Retrievers" bumper sticker. When he was escorted into the interviewer's office, he recognized her as the woman who owned the car with the bumper sticker. He immediately asked if she owned a dog. She seemed surprised that he knew until he mentioned the bumper sticker and offered the information that he and his wife also owned a Lab. They talked for several minutes about the joys and chaos of owning that breed of dog. The interview

went exceptionally well because Neil had made the effort to let his interviewer get to know him as a person.

Conduct informational interviews.

- Interview people in the careers that interest you to get a better understanding of what the job entails.
- Expand your existing network of friends and associates by asking people you meet to refer you to others who might know of positions you are qualified for.

During Abby's search for a career in social work, she called on everyone she knew. She started with her friends and family and expanded her list to include old college professors and even her childhood piano teacher. She rekindled relationships and obtained references from past employers and her minister to detail her involvement with community projects and to testify to her interpersonal skills. In all, she met, spoke on the telephone with, or wrote letters to nearly fifty people. All were eager to help her. When she was hired as a case manager for a health and nutrition program for pregnant inner-city teens, she traced her path to that specific job through eight people and over sixteen years of contacts.

Conduct an organized, well-planned job search.

- Develop a timetable and budget for your job search, including the cost of résumés, postage, and telephone calls, and how long you anticipate it will take. Set aside letter writing and follow-up telephone time each day, and keep a record of whom you have called and the status of each possibility.
- Demonstrate what type of employee you will be, using your job search as an

example. Use your excellent organizational skills by creating an easy-to-read, well-designed résumé and cover letter. Be on time for interviews and follow up with thank-you notes.

Jessica took on her job search the same way she took on every job she had ever had. She was enthusiastic, thorough, and precise in preparing her marketing materials and stayed on top of every detail. She impressed interviewers with her organization and communication skills and always followed up informational interviews with thank-you notes. The only problem she faced was the fact that she was offered two equally good opportunities on two successive days. She ultimately made her decision based upon which job would let her utilize the same skills she used in her job search, this time on a daily basis.

Sell yourself as a team player who will work hard to reach the goals of the organization.

- Emphasize your experience working with a diverse group of individuals in one organization or during your career, providing examples of situations that challenged and utilized those skills and abilities.
- Learn as much as you can about the organization's or company's "personality" by reading about principals and recent events within the company. Read newspapers and trade publications, and talk to people who know firsthand about the company before going into the interview.

Through Jim's career counseling, he had set his sights on working in property management. But he also learned from his research and informational interviews that some developers used approaches and tactics in business that went against his personal code of ethics. He was still sure that property management was what he wanted to do, so he set out to find a company he would feel comfortable being a part of. His search ultimately led him to a family-owned developer. He talked at length with the firm's president about the company's goals and philosophy until he felt sure that he would feel proud representing the firm. Interestingly, he was later told that it was his concern and refusal to sell out his principles that landed him the job because he was seen as someone the president could easily trust and depend upon.

Make decisions.

- Once you decide that you are interested in a position, act on it to minimize the risk of the opportunity slipping away.
- Eliminate unfeasible or less attractive options along the way so you can keep your focus on your goals. Remain realistic about your skills, interests, and needs so you aren't easily swayed by jobs that may tempt you with their excitement and glamour but won't provide the security or stability you seek.

Remember Dennis's love of car racing? While he always enjoyed the excitement of racing competitively, he ruled it out as a realistic career because it would not provide the long-term job security or consistent income he needed once he married and had a family. He still keeps his interest in cars by working on them in his spare time and occasionally races on the weekends. Even though the opportunity to race professionally presented itself, his decision to become a police officer has proved to be in his long-term best interest.

Possible Pitfalls

Although all people are unique, there are certain *potential* blind spots that many ESFJs share. We underscore "potential" because some of the following *may* be true of you, while others may clearly not apply. While considering them, you may notice that these tendencies do not relate just to the job search but rather describe pitfalls that you may have experienced in other aspects of your life as well. It is therefore helpful to consider each one in terms of your past experiences by asking yourself, "Is this true for me?" And if so, "How did this tendency prevent me from getting something that I wanted?" You will probably notice that the key to overcoming your blind spots is the conscious and thoughtful development of your third and fourth functions (Intuition and Thinking). We recognize that many of the suggestions will be difficult to implement, but the more you use these functions, the fewer problems they will cause you in the future.

Avoid the tendency to burn your bridges once you think you've crossed them.

- Try not to view situations or job options as either all good or all bad. Look for the gray area that exists in most things. Sometimes trade-offs must be made.
- Take time to reflect on your options. Don't run the risk of making decisions too hastily before you have had a chance to gather all the information you can.

Try not to become easily discouraged.

- Accept constructive criticism in the spirit in which it is intended and try not to take it personally.
- Seek out support and encouragement from friends during the sometimes trying job search process. Look for assis-

tance from other people who are also going through or have recently gone through their own job search.

Gather more objective criteria for decisions rather than relying exclusively on your personal feelings.

- Take a step back from the situation to enable yourself to look at it more objectively. Resist the urge to base your opinions of a job on your like or dislike for the person conducting the interview.
- Ask yourself what are the possible and logical consequences of taking a job or embarking on a course of action.

Adjust your focus to more long-range career planning.

- Create a set of goals for one, five, and ten years from now. When considering potential careers or jobs, check them against this list to see if they will help move you forward toward your goals.
- Resist the tendency to take stop-gap jobs because you are beginning to feel overwhelmed or uncertain about your security. Try not to compromise by taking jobs that will not provide satisfaction in the long run.

Look for career opportunities beyond what is already known.

- Ask yourself "what else?" when generating a list of possible jobs or careers. Consider less traditional approaches or settings if other important criteria exist. If needed, get help in brainstorming positions from friends (especially Intuitives) who know you well.
- Look for ways to demonstrate or explain how your skills are transferable from one work situation to another.

The Final Piece: Changing or Keeping Your Job...the Key to Success for ESFJs

Now that you have a solid understanding of your type, you can see how your natural preferences make you better suited for certain kinds of jobs. You can also see how knowledge of your type-related strengths and weaknesses can help you conduct a more successful job search. But as an ESFJ, you've already realized that you are not equally drawn to *every* career or field listed in the Popular Occupations section. The next and final step is to narrow down the field and find the work you were meant to do.

In addition to Type, several other factors—such as your values, interests, and skills—contribute to your level of satisfaction on the job. The more compatible you are with your job, the happier you'll be. So prepare to use everything you've learned (in this book and in life) to create *your strategic career plan*. The exercises in Chapter 24, Putting It All Together, are designed to help you do just that.

However, you may have decided it makes more sense (if perhaps only for the moment) to stay in your present job or with your current employer. There may be many valid reasons—financial pressures, family considerations, a tough job market for your specialty, or just bad timing. But take heart! What you've learned in this book can also help you be more content and successful *in your current job*. And should the time come when you're ready to make a major career move, you'll have a much better idea of where you want to go, and how to get there.

"So, if you can't have the job you love (yet!)...love the one you've got."

The simple truth is, with the exception of work on a factory assembly line, the vast majority of jobs allow a good deal of flexibility in the way tasks are performed. Here are some ways you may be able to "massage" your current job into one that better fits your needs:

- Work to resolve conflicts with co-workers, supervisors, direct-reports.
- Ask your boss to be clear about performance expectations.
- Leave environments where there is great interpersonal tension.
- Volunteer for a meaningful cause either inside or outside your organization.
- Make sure you have enough social stimulation during the day.
- Implement efficiency systems and require direct-reports to use them.
- If not a manager, identify a project you think needs doing and volunteer to take it on.
- Find people with complementary strengths to give you input and balance.
- Set up short-term goals that you can meet.

One ESFJ turns lemons into lemonade:

Jesse liked her job and company but felt somewhat unfulfilled. So, at a friend's urging, she volunteered to head up the annual United Way campaign. Because she was so organized and genuine, her hard work paid off and her company exceeded its contributions goal by 20 percent. Jesse got a great deal of gratification from doing something practical for a charity that would ultimately help thousands of people.

Use what you've got to get what you need.

Simply put, the best advice on how to succeed is to *capitalize on your strengths and compensate for your weaknesses.* Learning how to do this can make the difference between succeeding or failing and loving or hating your work. To help you, we

include the following inventory of your potential strengths and weaknesses.
And while every individual is unique, as an ESFJ, many of the following should apply to you.

Your work-related strengths may include:

- Great energy and drive to get things accomplished and be productive
- Ability to cooperate and create harmonious relationships with others
- Practical and realistic attitude and aptitude for working with facts and details
- Nurturing and helpful nature; you praise and reinforce good behavior in others
- Decisiveness and stabilizing factor
- Ability to maintain an organization's traditions
- Strong organizational skills and clear work ethic
- Loyalty and belief in the value of working within a traditional structure
- Sense of responsibility; you can be counted on to do what you say you will do
- Ability to follow established routines and procedures
- Common sense and realistic perspective

Your work-related weaknesses may include:

- Reluctance to embrace new and untested ideas
- Sensitivity to criticism; you feel stressed by tension-filled work situations
- Desire to focus on the present rather than the future
- Difficulty adapting to change and switching gears quickly
- Tendency to be oversensitive and avoid unpleasant situations
- Difficulty working alone for extended periods of time; strong need to socialize
- Tendency to show favoritism
- Tendency to become drained by taking on others' emotional burdens
- Inclination to make decisions prematurely before you have enough information
- Focus on specific details rather than implications and the "big picture"
- Tendency to be opinionated and rigid
- Difficulty hearing and accepting opposing viewpoints
- Tendency to become discouraged without praise or expression of appreciation
- Difficulty focusing on future needs as opposed to present ones

---

Using your strengths is easy.
The secret to success for an
ESFJ
is learning to:

Slow down, consider possibilities that don't already exist, and not take things quite so personally.

19 | ISFJ
Introverted, Sensing, Feeling, Judging

"On My Honor, to Do My Duty..."

Profile 1: Connie

"Making a dent in the world in a positive way."

Connie may have a slightly unusual job for an ISFJ. She is the supervisor of special education for a small suburban town, a position she really enjoys. What's unusual is that Connie spends huge amounts of time working with many other people, traveling around the town to attend meetings with some of the thirty-five professionals she supervises, and visiting the off-school sites where forty students are placed. It's a job that demands volumes of telephone work and perpetual meetings with parents, teachers, other educational professionals, and school administrators— none of which is usually enjoyed by ISFJs. But it's work that matters, and she's loved special education all her adult life.

At forty-three Connie is currently celebrating twenty-two years in the field of education. She's proud of the fact that she's not "burned out," like so many of the educators she has known over the years. She attributes that to the fact that special education is a sort of calling for her. She began as a special education teacher and couldn't imagine doing anything else. Now, instead of having a positive impact on a class of twelve or fifteen, she's able to have a greater impact on teachers, student teachers, parents, and the students themselves.

Connie spends about 70 percent of her time in the field, meeting with teachers and special education professionals, including school psychologists, speech pathologists, teachers of English as a second language, and—the bulk of her work—teachers of special education. Besides handling budgeting, hiring, and the other more routine administrative functions required of a supervisor, Connie's responsibility is to ensure that the school district complies with all state and federal mandates requiring that free and appropriate education be provided to all handicapped children. She appraises students by observing them in the classroom, meets with parents to help them accept the limitations of their child, and participates in formal diagnostic and placement conferences with teachers, parents, and other necessary professionals. She stays visible and accessible. Even when she's back in her office, she is barraged by telephone calls from parents and teachers looking for advice, direction, or resources.

What Connie enjoys most about her work is helping people. She likes being supportive and gets great satisfaction from "watching things happen—positive things, changes for the better." She is energized by the relationships she develops with parents, teachers, and administrators. "I just love seeing things through, making something that we knew would be a change for the better into a reality. For example, when one school really needed a staff psychologist, I did what it took to get the position filled. Today, it's so rewarding to see that person in place and really helping make the school work better." Connie also enjoys problem solving on complex cases involving a challenging child and very involved parents and teachers. "It takes a lot of thought and effort but is usually so worthwhile."

What Connie does not enjoy boils down to the lack of time she has in which to do everything with the same energy and meticulous care she wishes to bring to all parts of her job. When she returns to her office after several visits to different schools and other facilities, she is greeted by ten or twelve telephone messages. "Each one requires another call or two, minimum. There's just no easy closure on them! I'd so much rather be in the field than sitting at a desk, and it takes constant prioritizing, but I'm learning to accept the fact that I can't do everything."

The inefficiency of work left undone because there simply aren't enough hours in a day, and the fact that things take longer than she wishes they would, is a source of frustration for Connie. "It's stressful when I'm not able to do justice to everything—such as making a parent feel that I'm listening with my complete attention, when I see I have only minutes left to return several other calls before my next meeting.

"But the draining work is when we have totally unrealistic parents who refuse to accept, or just can't accept, the reality of their child's exceptionality and limitation. I'm very sensitive to their feelings and concerns, but we're then in a position where we can't change anything, because the parents won't accept the way their child is and will probably always be."

Connie copes with the frustrations and stress of her job by "sinking my teeth into it and getting more productive. That's what really works for me." She also tries to leave work at work but is finding that as her responsibilities expand, she needs to take work home or make phone calls from home in the evenings. "It's a balancing act because I need to be there for my daughter. I'm responsible for her. My husband laughs because I always have the weather channel on so I'll know whether or not my daughter needs to take her umbrella. But I'm responsible for that!" In fact, Connie's daughter helps her to relieve job-related stress because Connie finds that she can really lose herself in her daughter's activities.

Connie started her career in education and taught special education in the elementary schools for nine years, all ages and exceptionalities. She moved to a self-contained classroom after running a resource room, because it provided more control and independence. Looking for added responsibility, she started a diagnostic center within the school system. "It was a unique approach because we did testing and diagnostics and still taught in the same setting.

I enjoyed it more because it was professionally challenging, and I was part of a small team of really good people." After five years, she sought a more demanding job and became an administrator within the system. "One of the best parts of the job was training student teachers. That's where I realized I could have greater impact if I was helping teachers, because they would each be touching so many lives." After nine years, she began to hear from colleagues in smaller school districts that they had more responsibility and control in their jobs than she did in hers working for a large city. "I wanted more involvement in the big decisions affecting the children, so I began to apply for openings in the suburbs. It took four tries before I got this job. I had the practical experience but lacked the Ph.D. other candidates had. Then this opportunity came along in a small, very closely knit community. Parental support and involvement are tremendous here. It's a real community and I get to run the show!"

At this point Connie doesn't imagine changing jobs for some time. "I need to master all the skills I can before I feel ready to go after another challenge. Perhaps someday I'll apply for a principal's position in an elementary school. But for now, my goal is to be the best special education director in the whole state. When I do that to *my* satisfaction, I may go on to something else. And I may not."

Perhaps the only career regret Connie has is that she didn't get a broader base of experience when she was teaching. "I probably should have taught different levels of ability so I'd have a more well-rounded background. But it hasn't stood in my way yet. My ego doesn't need the Ph.D. anymore. But I'm certainly more ambitious than I used to be. I have a constant thirst for knowledge. It's my lifetime crusade to learn everything I can about the field of special education,

handicaps, genetic disorders, laws, funding sources—everything!"

Connie's greatest skills are her "people skills." She's sensitive, able to read people, and able to tell them how to become more effective. She's tactful and likes to help them become part of decisions. "I know when and how to push my supervisors to get what I know the people in the field really need. Usually it's because I'm able to give the support they need to make the changes happen and become a reality."

On the home front, Connie places her daughter and husband above everything else. "That's a lot easier to do now that my child is getting older and because my husband is so supportive. But my daughter has created a new meaning of home. Taking care of her and helping other people go hand-in-hand to give me the satisfaction I feel. I'm in a position to really help people and make a difference in their lives. That's so rewarding. And I've always felt that way. But I have changed too. I'm much more confident than I used to be. I'm more sensitive to the parents' concerns and issues because I'm a parent now. I can make the tough decisions a little more easily than I used to because I'm even more realistic and more efficient." But the big change is her increased ability to look long-range. "I have a supervisor who is truly visionary, a great long-range planner. I'm getting better at it by working with him. I used to not be able to see the forest for the trees, but now I can see the total picture better. But I'd still rather carry things out than try to look down the road and imagine what will be needed.

"I'd most like for people to think of me as an effective yet sensitive person. I hope to be remembered as someone who managed programs without losing sight of the needs of the individual parents and students. I want to keep giving instead of only taking."

Why This Career Works for Connie

Connie has spent twenty-two years working in education—an environment in which many Traditionalists (SJs) are found and find satisfying. She works in a highly structured, traditional organization with a clear mission—to oversee special education for a school system. She's in the business of helping both students and teachers get their needs met. Much of what she does involves complying with federal mandates and state regulations, and making sure that certain procedures are followed. Practically all activities Connie engages in are ones to which Traditionalists are particularly well suited.

Her introverted Sensing (dominant) helps Connie store the tremendous amount of information in her head required to help match students with the most appropriate services. Collecting and disseminating information is an important part of her job, and she draws on her own personal, real-life teaching experience to guide her. Attention to details such as budgeting, hiring, and completing administrative tasks makes good use of her Sensing, as do observing and appraising students in the classroom setting.

Another satisfying aspect of Connie's job is the opportunity it affords her to relate to many different people. She uses her extraverted Feeling (auxiliary) with the students, parents, teachers, and administrators with whom she interacts frequently. She also extraverts Feeling when promoting her strong values concerning how to improve the school, make it work better, and make people happier. And she enjoys the frequent collaboration she creates between parents, teachers, and herself in an effort to help a really challenging child.

Clearly, Connie's development of her Thinking (third function) has helped her make tough decisions more easily than she could in the past. Particularly challenging is learning how to stay sensitive to parents' concerns and still make the tough decisions. She believes that she is also developing better access to her Intuition (fourth function) as she becomes more comfortable with long-range planning and more able to "see the forest *and* the trees."

Meet the Millennial

Name: Erin
Age: 23
Labor and delivery nurse

"I love being passionate about what I'm doing. It just feels right, being here."

Backstory

If you had asked Erin in high school what she wanted to be, she would have told you without hesitation: an OB/GYN doctor. "I went to college thinking, 'This is it—I know what I want to do and I'm gonna do it!'" But during a summer program in New York City, everything changed. Shadowing OB/GYN doctors, Erin had "the first inkling that maybe it wasn't what I thought it was going to be. I had envisioned helping women through this rite of passage and being with them the whole time." But the doctors she shadowed seemed to spend more time diagnosing and less time one-on-one with patients.

Back at school, Erin learned about midwifery and found that it answered most of her concerns about traditional medicine, especially that it didn't spend nearly enough time attending to the emotional and social needs of the woman. She changed her path to get an accelerated degree in nursing and is now on track to become a midwife.

As a nursing student, Erin feels more at home. "What has drawn me to medicine in general is being there for and supporting people, and really what I've learned is, that's more the role of nursing. Doctors do a lot of diagnosing and problem solving and figuring things out. Nursing is definitely more holistic—you treat a person as a whole person and not just as the problem that's happening at the time."

A Good Fit

Like many Traditionalists, Erin is service oriented and driven to contribute meaningfully to society. Her dominant function is Sensing—a function that, in nursing, is constantly in use. In fact, noticing details can be a matter of life and death: a delivery "can go very quickly from being normal to being an emergency situation, and you have to be alert at all times and pay attention to so many details." Erin is adept at picking up and learning routines, and the set number of tasks is comforting to her. She

is able to face a new situation by visualizing a series of steps she needs to know, and once she learns them, she feels confident and capable. An organized Judger, Erin is well suited to the procedure-driven world of a hospital. Erin's auxiliary function of Feeling is very important in her job as a nurse, since she spends so much of her time in the "super emotionally charged situation" of labor and delivery. She is compassionate and empathetic, qualities that the best nurses utilize to put patients at ease. Erin's Feeling function also helps her to anticipate her patients' needs and allows her to be able to support them emotionally as well as physically.

Looking Ahead

In five years, Erin would like to be working as a nurse on an obstetrics floor. She's hoping this can happen in five years, since most hospitals now require one to two years of general nursing before specializing in labor and delivery, and sometimes it can take months to find a job as a new nurse. In ten years, Erin sees herself as a practicing midwife, although now she may be reconsidering. The more she enjoys OB nursing, the more Erin feels that it might be enough for her, especially since midwives often act like doctors in hospital births and are not present for the entire experience. Erin struggles with the stigma that being "just a nurse" in our society is somehow less important or respected than being a doctor or a midwife. Her continuing experiences, however, make it clear that her job is essential and allows her to make a daily difference in the lives of others.

Profile 2: Morty

"Accommodating other people and working around whatever problems arise to get the job done."

At forty-four, Morty has created a perfect career for himself. Since college, he knew he would become an accountant, but until recently, that career left him dangerously stressed, guilty about the lack of family time he had at the end of a crazy day, and completely overworked during the tax season. But he decided to change all that and now has found a truly satisfying career as a sole practitioner CPA, working exclusively for nonprofit organizations.

"The change came to me slowly. I was going nuts with the traditional individual and corporate tax practice. I searched my mind for a way to get out of the stressful hole I was in. I was making lots of money but the rest of my life suffered. My health was in jeopardy, and I never stopped thinking about work. I brought work home, and it interfered with my family and my personal interests. I had to make a change, so I sold the part of the practice that I didn't like and held on to and expanded the part I did like."

Today, Morty exclusively conducts audits of nonprofit organizations. His clients include a private school, a battered women's shelter, a family planning center, an adoption agency, a library system, and a host of other social service organizations. He reviews their financial statements before attaching his authorization that the statement is fairly presented. "Sometimes I need to do a certain amount of cleaning up, finding and correcting mistakes before I can prepare the final statement. The quality of the records depends wholly on the training and expertise of the bookkeeping staff. And that varies from client to client." Once an audit is completed, Morty presents the final financial statement to the organization's executive director or to its board of directors.

Being a part of human service organizations is one of the things Morty likes best about his career. "These are really good people, doing really good work trying to improve the community. Their goal isn't making a huge profit but satisfying their mission, which is helping others. I enjoy being associated with them." Morty also enjoys teaching the bookkeeping staff as he helps them improve their accounting practices and procedures. "I think I'm pretty good at explaining things to people. I like the teaching function of my job." But the energizing part comes when Morty presents the final product to the organization's leaders. "I like the show, standing up in front of a small group of smart people and being able to show them where they stand financially. It's very gratifying to be perceived as an expert, providing the answers they seek. It's a comfortable position for me because I'm the expert and I'm completely prepared. I'm not nervous because I deliver the goods."

The less enjoyable part of Morty's work is the "drudgery of the audit process." He spends days sifting through invoices, checking deposits, looking for authorized signatures on documents, and otherwise finding all the supporting paperwork to test all the assumptions made by the statement. "The ticking and tracing are important parts of the job, but I can't say I really enjoy them." And "messy situations," in which he must rely on the capabilities of the sometimes marginally trained staff to unravel an unclear or undocumented scenario, are the least satisfying. "Working with people who are really incompetent, even though they're very nice and they try very hard, is draining."

By redesigning his job, Morty has dramatically reduced the amount of work-related stress he experiences. "I used to be completely crazy from January to April fifteenth. Now, I still have a time crunch because most of my clients have deadlines imposed by their June thirtieth end-of-year, but I have until November to complete their audits. So I need to complete seventy-five percent of my clients' work in six months, but that's a whole lot easier than ninety percent of the work in four months!" The stress level has been so reduced that he doesn't really need to consciously cope with it anymore. "I believe the only way to deal with stress is to just work harder and faster to get the job done. So during these times, I work more seriously and conscientiously. I'm demanding with my clients, in my quiet way. And I guess I complain at home a little. But not like I used to!"

After serving in the Reserves, Morty began his accounting career in a series of firms, always moving from larger to smaller in size. His first job was as one of one hundred staff accountants at a large firm. After one year, he moved to a midsized firm with fifteen other accountants. Next he became one of four CPAs at a small firm. Each move allowed him to attain increased client contact and responsibility. But all of the jobs required primarily the "ticking and tracing" process and limited contact with the client. "Finally I decided to go out on my own. I wanted the control and freedom and the opportunity to deal directly with the clients. So I started out alone and built my practice over ten years to where I had two other CPAs working with me and a support staff. I'm really very proud of the fact I did it all on my own." But over ten years, Morty was experiencing too much of the stress and strain of the tax business. So two years ago, he located another person who was interested in buying an established accounting practice. "I was really lucky to find the right person who wanted to take over the tax end of my business. This person

moved in to share the office space, took over responsibility for the employees, bought the furniture, and handled the clients. I kept the part of the practice I enjoyed and built it up to where I have the volume I can handle and not have it run my life."

The greatest source of satisfaction in Morty's life is not at work. He enjoys spending time with his wife and daughter, his involvement with various committees in his community and synagogue, and his religious readings and studies. "I really look forward to my studies. I think my religion has been lying dormant until recently. I don't think I was ever mature enough to want to practice my religion. But reaching mid-life changed me a bit. Now my religious interest is self-motivated. I'm not doing it to please anyone but myself."

Morty is becoming less ambitious than he used to be. He used to think it was important to own a big practice with a lot of people working for him. "Now I understand that all equals stress for me. Instead I'm more concerned with maintaining my business so I can keep my family in focus. I used to never be able to say no, even to people who walked in my door on March fifteenth looking for preparation of their tax returns. I used to say yes to people I now will not and I won't deal with unscrupulous people. I'm just more selective."

These days Morty is focused on contributing to society on a daily basis by helping organizations meet their missions. Career satisfaction for Morty is working with decent people, attempting to give something back to society while keeping his priorities in order. "I hope I'm a nice guy. I sure try to be. I know I love my family and I'm devoted to them. I value the fact that I'm a humble person, that I'm considerate of others. I guess I'm a soft touch!"

In seeking the work that has proved to be satisfying for him, Morty claims the secret is in "being true to yourself. Never lie or mislead yourself or others into believing you can or want to do something that isn't right for you. In the end it won't make you happy. And you won't be able to make anyone else happy either."

Why This Career Works for Morty

Like most Traditionalists, Morty works hard, and takes his responsibilities very seriously. His job is particularly satisfying because it provides him the opportunity to use his well-developed and well-honed skills and abilities to help organizations in whose mission he believes maintain their financial stability. His work arrangement allows him to nourish an equally traditional part of him— the part that needs to have time to devote to his family and his religion.

Most accountants, like Morty, are (dominant) introverted Sensing types, and for good reason. Much of his time is spent alone or with a few people, reviewing financial statements, making sure that everything is accurate and complete. In accounting, attention to the smallest details is critical. The misplacement of a decimal point, for example, can result in serious consequences. Additionally, he must keep informed of constantly changing tax regulations and become familiar with new forms and procedures.

Morty uses his extraverted Feeling (auxiliary) often with clients. He enjoys teaching and explaining the rationale behind his recommendations to the staffs of the nonprofits he has as clients and when he makes presentations to a board of directors. His decision to work exclusively with service organizations is a testament to the powerful influence his own values have in shaping his career. He believes in doing good work and likes to be associated with others who do so as well.

Morty's Thinking (third function) played heavily into his decision to change the nature of his practice. Basically run by his Feelings (what he felt he *should* do) for the first half of his life, he recently made a decision that took into account what he *wanted* to do rather than what others wanted him to do. He has also become more assertive, and although he still doesn't like to say no, he can do it more easily now. Rather than just accepting things as they are, Morty has begun looking for the meaning behind them. This, and his recently renewed interest in his religion, may point to the emerging development of his Intuition (fourth function) as well.

Common Threads

Although Connie, Morty, and Erin have different backgrounds, experiences, and careers, there are certain common threads woven through their stories. Their specific interests and abilities may differ, but owing to their similar temperament values, the *same hierarchy* of their psychological functions, and the "world" they use them in (inner or outer), there are certain observations we can make about the needs of many ISFJs.

What follows is a list of the most important elements—the formula, if you will, for ISFJ satisfaction. Given the uniqueness of all individuals—even those who share the same type—this list will not describe each ISFJ equally well. The important thing is that these ten elements, with varying degrees of intensity and in different orders of importance, identify what ISFJs need to be satisfied.

After you have reviewed this list, we recommend that you go back and prioritize the elements in order of *their importance to you*. When doing this, think of past work experiences as well as your present job, and what you found particularly satisfying or unsatisfying. Try to look for *themes* that run through several experiences, not just the events that might be true for one work situation but not for another.

As an ISFJ, career satisfaction means doing work that:

1. Requires careful observation and meticulous accuracy, where I can use my ability to remember facts and details
2. Lets me work on tangible projects that help other people, often requiring great accuracy and attention to detail
3. Lets me express my compassion and devotion by working hard behind the scenes, but where my contributions are recognized and appreciated
4. Is done in a traditional, stable, orderly, and structured environment, where the results are practical and service-oriented
5. Requires that I adhere to standard procedures, use practical judgment, and follow through in a careful, organized way
6. Lets me focus all my energy on one project or one person at a time, working on products or services that have observable end results
7. Gives me a private work space so I can concentrate fully for extended periods of time and with a minimum of interruptions
8. Lets me work primarily one-on-one, helping others, or with other people who share my personal values and beliefs
9. Requires me to be organized and efficient in completing my assignments
10. Does not require too frequently that I present my work in front of groups of people without having adequate time to prepare well in advance

Popular Occupations for ISFJs

In listing occupations that are popular among ISFJs, it is important to note that there are successful people of all types in all occupations. However, the following are careers ISFJs may find particularly satisfying and some of the reasons why. This is by no means a comprehensive listing but is included to suggest possibilities you may not have previously considered. Although all of these occupations offer the potential for career satisfaction, the future demand for some careers is anticipated to be greater than for others. Based upon our research, the occupations that are italicized in the lists below are forecast to enjoy the fastest rate of growth over the next several years.

HEALTH CARE
- *Registered nurse*
- *Dental hygienist*
- *Family physician*
- *Medical technologist*
- *Physical therapist*
- Medical equipment sales representative
- *Health care administrator*
- *Dietitian/nutritionist*
- *Speech-language pathologist/audiologist*
- Optician
- *Medical records technician*
- *Pharmacist/pharmacy technician*
- *Radiological technician*
- Respiratory therapist
- *Veterinarian*
- *Veterinary technologist/technician*
- *Licensed practical nurse (LPN)*
- *Primary care physician*
- *Home health aide*
- *Medical/dental assistant*
- Pharmaceuticals salesperson
- Hospice worker

- Medical researcher
- Biologist
- Botanist
- Dentist
- Orthodontist
- *Occupational therapist*
- *Biochemist*
- Massage therapist
- *Surgical technologist and technician*
- *Dental laboratory technician*
- Corrective therapist
- *Dialysis technician*

These occupations allow ISFJs to work in a field where their contributions have a personal and direct impact on others. Many of these occupations require hands-on and one-on-one interaction with clients and patients. ISFJs like to be able to help others in real and practical ways. Many of these positions allow the ISFJ to work relatively independently within a traditional and organized culture. The field of medicine makes good use of ISFJs' ability to learn and practice technical skills and gives them the chance to establish personal connections with other people.

SOCIAL SERVICE/EDUCATION
- *Preschool teacher*
- Librarian/archivist
- *Social worker*
- *Personal counselor*
- Probation officer
- *Home health social worker*
- *Child welfare counselor*
- *Substance abuse counselor*
- *Social worker (elderly and child day care issues)*
- *Personal care aide*
- *Elementary school teacher*
- Special education teacher
- Genealogist
- Curator
- Educational administrator

- Guidance counselor
- Religious educator
- *Social worker*
- *Elder care specialist*
- Vocational rehabilitation counselor
- Historian
- *Athletic trainer*
- Fish and game warden
- Horticultural specialty grower
- Police identification and records specialist
- Stringed instrument repairer
- Residence counselor
- Organic farmer

Education is a field frequently of interest to ISFJs because it allows them to help other people and make a contribution to society. ISFJs often enjoy teaching elementary school because of the personal interaction with students and the ability to teach basic skills. Many ISFJs enjoy careers in educational administration, especially when they are responsible for a specific area of specialty (for example, special education) or a relatively small service area (one town rather than a large city school system). ISFJs enjoy working independently but within an organization where they are appreciated for their contribution and know what is expected of them.

The field of research offers satisfaction for ISFJs because it allows them to work independently and follow through on specific tasks of investigation. Curators are required to create and maintain complete and accurate records, which lets them use their organizational and factual recall skills.

While often personally challenging, the field of social work often provides great satisfaction for ISFJs. ISFJs find the contribution they make rewarding because they are able, through their involvement with their clients, to help them make practical and tangible improvements in their lives. These occupations offer the same opportunities for one-on-one interaction and independent working environments, all of interest to an ISFJ.

BUSINESS/SERVICE
- *Administrative assistant*
- Clerical supervisor
- *Customer service representative*
- Personnel administrator
- *Bookkeeper*
- Credit counselor
- *Paralegal*
- Home health care salesperson
- Lawn service manager
- *Tech support agent*
- Franchise owner (retail)
- Museum research worker
- Funeral director
- Grant coordinator
- *Preferred customer sales representative*
- Bed and breakfast proprietor
- Title examiner and abstractor

These careers require a great deal of interaction with people on a one-on-one basis and are often enjoyed by ISFJs. Many are support positions, which enable ISFJs to use skills in organization and follow-through of important details, especially when working in support of someone they respect and admire. These positions also require knowledge and use of both technical and communication skills to help others get the information or assistance they need.

CREATIVE/TECHNICAL
- Interior decorator
- Electrician
- Retail owner
- Artist
- Musician
- Merchandise planner
- Real estate agent/broker
- Jeweler

These careers are not necessarily related to one another but have some common characteristics and requirements. Each requires the person to work with real things that have to do with daily living. As an interior decorator, the ISFJ uses his or her aesthetic sense to find the right decor for the client. The job requires attention to detail and a strong ability to work with another toward satisfying that client's needs and wishes in his or her home. ISFJs usually place great importance on the way their own home is decorated and can easily understand and relate to the desires of their clients to create homes that are comfortable for them.

An electrician is responsible for technical accuracy and adherence to standard procedures and codes. ISFJs enjoy focusing their attention on tasks that require hands-on work and enjoy using skills they have mastered. If the ISFJ feels his or her contributions are valued and appreciated and if he or she has quality interaction with either the customer, partner, or co-workers, the job of an electrician can be satisfying.

Retail sales and merchandising are careers often enjoyed by ISFJs, especially when they are able to work in either a small specialty shop or one department of a larger store. ISFJs often make good owners of boutiques. Their attention to the details of how their shop looks and "feels" to customers often wins them longstanding repeat business. They enjoy spending time with one customer at a time, finding just the right item or accessory to work with what the customer already has. They enjoy following through and maintaining relationships with customers and treat staff with kindness and loyalty.

Customizing Your Job Search

Knowing the particular strengths and blind spots of your type can afford you a tremendous advantage in your job search campaign. In all aspects of the process, from conducting research into available positions, identifying and contacting prospective employers, developing personal marketing tools such as résumés, arranging and conducting job interviews, negotiating salaries, to finally accepting a position, people will act true to their type. Being able to capitalize on your assets and compensate for your liabilities can make the difference between a successful and an unsuccessful job search.

The differences between types are sometimes subtle and other times dramatic. It is the subtle variations in advice we offer that make the real difference between success or failure in a job search. The concept of "networking," or meeting with and talking to people to gather information about potential jobs, serves as a good example. Extraverts will naturally enjoy networking and are advised to do so on a large scale, while Introverts find more limited and targeted networking, especially with people they already know, easier. Sensors tend to network with people in a defined scope, while Intuitives will go far and wide to find people often seemingly unrelated to their field of interest. Further, Feelers take networking, like everything else, very personally and enjoy establishing warm rapport, while Thinkers will be more objective and detached in their style. Finally, Judgers tend to ask fewer and more structured questions during their networking, while Perceivers could ask questions of all sorts all day long! One valuable search technique, many ways to implement it.

Pathways to Success: Using Your Strengths

As we will detail in the following pages, your strengths and talents for the job search lie in your ability to demonstrate your efficiency, sincerity, and desire to work hard. However, your job search might become stalled if you fail to see workable alternatives or derailed when you take rejection too personally.

As an ISFJ, your most effective strategies will build on your abilities to:

Research opportunities thoroughly, collecting all relevant facts.

- Use all resources available to you, including the local library and trade publications, to find out as much as you can about the company, industry, or position you are considering.
- Spend the amount of time necessary until you are comfortable with your knowledge base before proceeding to the interview stage.

When Connie was beginning to consider a career change, she was counseled by several colleagues in other school districts to look at a smaller school system to get the added responsibility she was looking for. She fully researched the town she works in now to find out about the level of parental and town support for the special education program before even applying for the position. Because she knew those elements were critical to her satisfaction in the job and her ability to do her job well, she talked with parents, teachers, and other administrators to get a feeling for the emotional climate of the town.

Make thoughtful decisions based upon practical considerations.

- Establish a list of criteria and refer to it frequently during the job search process, comparing potential job opportunities against it.

- Try to be objective during the decision-making process so as to remain pragmatic and realistic about what a possible job will really be like, not just how you wish it might be.

Morty made a major career change to working with not-for-profits after determining that his personal and professional life were equally important to him. He wanted more time to spend with his family and on his religious studies. He weighed the pros and cons of the change and decided, after careful consideration, that the change would afford him the more relaxed and peaceful lifestyle he wanted, while still using his skills and experience in accounting.

Conduct an organized, well-planned job search.

- Prepare résumés with individualized cover letters to address your specific interests and qualifications for the job in question. Follow up with a telephone call to secure an appointment, rather than waiting for a potential employer to call you.
- Stay in contact with people who have given you time or an interview. Write them thank-you notes and send them notification when you find the right job.

While researching the personnel department of a large department store, Lisa decided she would apply for a customer service representative position. She called ahead to learn the manager's name and title and sent a personalized letter highlighting her experience and her interest in the company. After several phone calls, she secured an appointment and interviewed with the manager. There was no position

available at the time so Lisa continued to search while staying in contact with the manager. One day in the library, Lisa read an article about a new computerized preferred-customer tracking system being developed for use in retail. She sent the article with a brief note to the manager. A few days later, she was called for a second interview and later offered a job. The manager told her that her perseverance had won the job for her over candidates with more experience.

Capitalize on your solid, stable, dependable work experience.

- Provide prospective employers with several examples of past successes, including any citations, awards, or letters of recommendation.
- Demonstrate your consistency in meeting job requirements and reaching organizational goals.

Jeremy was a biology teacher at a college and an active faculty adviser to students. He had always been particularly interested in the problem of student attrition (students leaving the college before graduation). Over the many years of his tenure, he kept his own careful records of student attrition, which he collected from interviews with his own students, the college counseling center, and other faculty advisers.

When the associate dean of students position became available, Jeremy was interested. He might not ordinarily have been considered a likely candidate, but he took all the information he had collected over the years, and compiled it into a report. He met with the dean of students and shared his observations. His self-acquired but acknowledged expertise in the area of student trends, combined with his reputation as a caring and popular student adviser, helped move him into the front-runner's position for the job.

Possible Pitfalls

Although all people are unique, there are certain *potential* blind spots that many ISFJs share. We underscore "potential" because some of the following *may* be true of you, while others may clearly not apply. While considering them, you may notice that these tendencies do not relate just to the job search but rather describe pitfalls that you may have experienced in other aspects of your life as well. It is therefore helpful to consider each one in terms of your past experiences by asking yourself, "Is this true for me?" And if so, "How did this tendency prevent me from getting something that I wanted?" You will probably notice that the key to overcoming your blind spots is the conscious and thoughtful development of your third and fourth functions (Thinking and Intuition). We recognize that many of the suggestions will be difficult to implement, but the more you use these functions, the fewer problems they will cause you in the future.

Look for and stay open to considering possibilities that do not currently exist.

- Engage in the sometimes difficult exercise of brainstorming: generating lists of possibilities while resisting the urge to eliminate the seemingly impossible ones. Keep all ideas until you have generated a lengthy list. Consider each and ask yourself "Why not?" several times before discarding it as a viable option. You may want to call on the help of friends for whom brainstorming comes more naturally.
- Ask other people currently enjoying jobs you may wish to consider how they went about getting trained for the job or

obtaining an interview. Consider less traditional or unconventional approaches.

Be aggressive, or at least assertive, when planning and implementing your job search.

- Realize that the adage "the squeaky wheel gets the grease" is often true, especially in the competitive world of employment.
- Use all your excellent organizational and follow-through skills to stay on top of all opportunities. Follow up appointments with notes to remind the prospective employer of your continued interest in the position. Contact old friends and business associates and ask them to help you develop a list of potential people to add to your network. And most important, ask for interviews and tell interviewers of positions that you want!

Don't underrepresent your enthusiasm and interpersonal skills.

- Save the humility for another time and place. Speak up and tell prospective employers about your past accomplishments. Demonstrate your abilities by offering past reviews and letters of recommendation from supervisors.
- Work from the assumption that you are exactly what the prospective employer is looking for and that you have a lot to offer. You will project the confidence and energy most employers want in employees.

Try to be objective and do not allow your personal feelings to be the sole criterion of important decisions.

- Suspend making any decisions about a person or a position until you have left the interview and had some time to think back on it. Try to stay clear on the fact that it is easy to confuse rapport with friendship.

- Consider the cause and effect of your decisions. Make a list of possible outcomes and results of your choices, using your original list of criteria as a benchmark against which to measure potential jobs, rather than your personal feelings about the interviewer or the worksite.

Avoid being rigid and inflexible, seeing options as either all good or all bad.

- Again, refer to your list of criteria. Adhere to those elements that you simply can't live without, and be willing to be flexible about those that are less important.
- Try to imagine yourself in each job opportunity you consider. Ask a friend to help you generate a list of the pros and cons of each opportunity and look at both sides fairly before making any decisions.

Try not to take rejection personally and get discouraged.

- Remember that just because you look at the world from a personal perspective, that is not true for everyone else. Most rejections are not directed at you personally but at your qualifications for a job. It sometimes takes several weeks or months to find the right job. Patience will pay off if you keep going.
- Get support from friends or family members when you are starting to lose your energy and confidence. Ask for the encouragement you need. Let friends help *you* for a change.

The Final Piece: Changing or Keeping Your Job . . . the Key to Success for ISFJs

Now that you have a solid understanding of your type, you can see how your natural preferences make you better suited for certain kinds of jobs. You can also see how knowledge of your type-related strengths and weaknesses can help you conduct a more successful job search. But as an ISFJ, you've already realized that you are not equally drawn to *every* career or field listed in the Popular Occupations section. The next and final step is to narrow down the field and find the work you were meant to do.

In addition to Type, several other factors—such as your values, interests, and skills—also contribute to your level of satisfaction on the job. The more compatible you are with your job, the happier you'll be. So prepare to use everything you've learned (in this book and in life) to create *your strategic career plan*. The exercises in Chapter 24, Putting It All Together, are designed to help you do just that.

However, you may have decided it makes more sense (if perhaps only for the moment) to stay in your present job or with your current employer. There may be many valid reasons—financial pressures, family considerations, a tough job market for your specialty, or just bad timing. But take heart! What you've learned in this book can also help you be more content and successful *in your current job*. And should the time come when you're ready to make a major career move, you'll have a much better idea of where you want to go, and how to get there.

"So, if you can't have the job you love (yet!) . . . love the one you've got."

The simple truth is, with the exception of work on a factory assembly line, the vast majority of jobs allow a good deal of flexibility in the way tasks are performed. Here are some ways you may be able to "massage" your current job into one that better fits your needs:

- Work to resolve conflicts with co-workers, supervisors, and direct-reports.
- Find people with complementary strengths to give you input and balance.
- Ask your boss to be clear about performance expectations.
- Leave environments where there is great interpersonal tension.
- Implement efficiency systems and require direct-reports to use them.
- Volunteer for research projects in which you have a personal interest.
- Make sure you have plenty of uninterrupted time to do your work.
- Ask for meeting agendas in advance.
- Set goals that you can meet.
- Consider taking an assertiveness-training course.

One ISFJ turns lemons into lemonade:

Laura worked in the bookstore of a small college, but she had always been interested in research and was considered good with numbers. Knowing the college was experiencing some trouble retaining students, she volunteered to conduct a study that would interview students who were transferring to other schools. Not only did she enjoy the process immensely, but the information she collected helped administrators develop new programs that would reverse the trend. Helping her school in such a tangible way was very gratifying to Laura.

Use what you've got to get what you need.

Simply put, the best advice on how to succeed is to *capitalize on your strengths*

and compensate for your weaknesses. Learning how to do this can make the difference between succeeding or failing and loving or hating your work. To help you, we include the following inventory of your potential strengths and weaknesses. And while every individual is unique, as an ISFJ, many of the following should apply to you.

Your work-related strengths may include:

- Great depth of focus and concentration
- Strong work ethic; you're responsible and hardworking
- Good cooperation skills; you create harmonious relationships with others
- Very practical and realistic attitude
- Accuracy with facts and attention to details
- Love of being in service to others; you are supportive of co-workers and subordinates
- Strength at maintaining the organization's traditions and keeping track of its history
- Strong organizational skills
- Loyalty and comfort working within a traditional structure
- Excellence at managing sequential, repeated procedures or tasks
- Strong sense of responsibility; you can be counted on to do what you say
- Enjoyment using established ways of doing things; respect for status given by titles
- Common sense and realistic perspective

Your work-related weaknesses may include:

- Tendency to underestimate own value; you may not be assertive about your own needs

- Reluctance to embrace new and untested ideas
- Sensitivity to criticism; you feel stressed by tension-filled work situations
- Desire to focus on details and the present rather than implications and the future
- Tendency to take on too much
- Difficulty adapting or switching gears quickly

- Tendency to be overwhelmed by too many projects or tasks at the same time
- Propensity to become discouraged if you no longer feel needed or appreciated
- Difficulty changing your mind or position once a decision has been made

Using your strengths is easy.
The secret to success for an
ISFJ
is learning to:

Speak up, consider possibilities that don't already exist, and try to be more flexible and spontaneous.

20 | ESTP
Extraverted, Sensing,
Thinking, Perceiving

"Let's Get Busy!"

Profile 1: Lou

"I'm a naturally curious guy, and I can think on my feet."

Lou's work history can be described in one word: gumshoe. In fact, he remembers telling a high school girlfriend that he would someday be a private investigator. And he has been one, and more, for thirty-five years. The chief investigator for a state public defender's office, Lou has worked his way up through a variety of jobs to the one he enjoys now, each time taking what was to be learned and moving on when he became bored. Now, he finds the challenge and intrigue in the cases he handles very satisfying.

Lou is fifty-four years old and married, with three children. He supervises more than fifty investigators located around the state in more than thirty court sites and works on all phases of criminal defense investigation—searching for important, and often previously unknown, information to assist in the defense. His responsibility covers juvenile court through and including felony and capital felony court, which handles death penalty cases. Lou's job often involves traveling around the state to assist other investigators with complex cases by helping to gain access to special services such as forensic analysis. Lou also hires staff, conducts background checks of applicants, does training, and conducts any in-house personnel investigations of a sensitive nature.

"The job is really a problem-solving job with lots of personal contact. I find the most energizing parts to be the challenge to search for and solve problems. When I can get good defense material that an attorney might not even be aware of, that's the best!" Lou finds it rewarding to find out something about the "why" of a crime. "I don't excuse what a client did, but the hidden information often helps explain *why* they did it."

Lou dislikes all the "extraneous stuff in the job—the minute details like completing and filing my mileage reports and checking the mileage reports of my investigators. Then

294

I can't wait for the phone to ring to get me out of my office." And during a high-pressure trial, Lou often experiences the stress of providing services to a demanding attorney. "Trial time is all-consuming; there are no time-outs." Sometimes, with a major case and a conscientious attorney, Lou might be told to go to another state to find and return with a surprise witness to appear in court the next morning.

In order to cope, Lou spends as much time as he can on his powerboat with his wife and children. "Everyone knows that they'll find us on the boat every weekend. It's a family venture." Lou has pared down his many interests and hobbies. He used to be an avid hunter, fisherman, skier, and golfer. "I had to quit golf like I quit smoking: cold turkey. I was just too involved in it."

Having set his sights on investigation at an early age, Lou completed two years in college and two years' service in the Marine Corps before becoming an insurance investigator. For ten years he investigated casualty claims and managed an office of investigators. He decided he wanted to work for himself, so he led private investigations and insurance investigations for fifteen years. "I always enjoyed the private investigations most because I found them more challenging." His next job was as deputy sheriff and then investigator for the state's attorney. This gave him the opportunity to learn the prosecution side of investigation. But he was limited to the lower courts and didn't find the cases to be "intense enough." So after three years, he applied for an opening in a higher court in the public defender's division. He got the job and continued with it until an opportunity presented itself on a new unit devoted exclusively to death penalty cases. "I really enjoyed that job until the position here became available one year ago. Each job has

offered me more freedom and autonomy, and the intensity and seriousness of the crimes increased with each job as well."

Lou feels he has achieved his career goal in his present position. "I guess if there was a chief investigator job for the whole nation, I'd go for it. But there isn't. I've gone as far as I can go, so I'm satisfied. My job is really my life, but that doesn't mean my wife of twenty-seven years and my three kids aren't very important to me." Currently, Lou is looking ahead to retirement in the next three or four years and plans to remain near his children and aging parents, who need him more and more.

"I don't think I've changed much over time. I'm less aggressive than I used to be but, other than that, I'm pretty much the same guy I've always been. I really care about people and I can see the good in even the worst people. I've even developed friendships with people who have committed multiple homicides. I really just feel sorry for them."

Lou starts each day with enthusiasm. "I never look at work as drudgery." His secret is that he never takes setbacks personally. "I just stack 'em up behind me and keep going. I've applied for several jobs I didn't get. But if you keep trying, they'll remember you. Just put your neck out and people will remember you. Sometimes they'll give you a bone. Eventually, even if you were a loser for one job, you'll be the winner of another."

Why This Career Works for Lou

Among the strongest of Experiencer (SP) needs is freedom to act spontaneously. Lou has designed his job so he is often out in the field, where he can experience the more exciting aspects of his job while he satisfies his Experiencer curiosity. He also has a variety of tasks to perform, which ensures that he is seldom bored. Since his recreational life is also important to Lou, he has built in sufficient time to get away and relax on his boat.

The job of investigator requires the heavy use of extraverted Sensing—Lou's dominant function. In looking for clues, he has to be extremely observant—paying attention to the most minute and subtle details, seeking out and following up on tips, and carefully scrutinizing information provided by sources to determine if it is credible or accurate.

Once Lou has taken in all this information, he relies on his introverted Thinking (auxiliary) to make some sense of it. This he does quietly in his head, drawing logical conclusions, using deduction to solve problems. His introverted Thinking also

helps him to stay objective and not get personally involved in even the most grisly murder cases. In fact, this natural distancing allows him to develop friendships with multiple murderers—"nothing personal, they're just people, too."

Over the years, Lou has become less aggressive. And he has come to be able to see the good in even the worst people. This emerging sympathy, even for serious criminals, is probably related to the development of his third function—Feeling. He feels a growing commitment to his family, and the desire to care for his aging parents demonstrates his developing values and his interest in living according to those values.

Meet the Millennial

Name: Kristine
Age: 31
Air Force biomedical equipment craftsman

"Getting in on the action."

Backstory

Kristine has always been fascinated by how things work. "My dad is a computer-networking engineer, and I used to hover over his shoulder as he dismantled and rebuilt computers." By the age of ten, Kristine was reverse-engineering household appliances—taking apart VCRs, radios, and anything else her parents would let her get her hands on—just to figure out how they worked. A good student throughout middle and high school, Kristine hit a wall in college when the general education prerequisites

failed to interest and engage her. She began to skip class and ended up becoming academically disqualified. Kristine attended summer school, improved her grades, and was readmitted to the university. But her parents, upset with her deviation from the path, cut her off financially and she had no means to pay for tuition.

For the next three years, Kristine reports, she "had no direction." She attended community college, waited tables, and worked in a saddlery shop. Eventually, she started bartending, which marked an important turning point. "My customers would talk to me about their different family members joining the military and how much this had improved their lives. The military paid for their education and armed them with invaluable skill sets, which they were able to turn into lucrative civilian careers. With their stories of success rattling around in my head, I visited recruiters from every branch to decide which service was best for me."

Kristine settled on the Air Force. She earned high scores on the Armed Services Vocational Aptitude Battery, and her recruiter pushed her toward biomedical equipment repair, assuring her she would love the job. "He was absolutely correct!" After completing basic training in the top 7 percent of her class, Kristine started technical school. For the next year, she learned how to troubleshoot, maintain, and repair a wide variety of medical equipment. Upon graduation, she was stationed and has been an active-duty military member for the last six and a half years, winning an impressive array of honors, such as Outstanding Biomedical Equipment Repair Airman of the Year.

A Good Fit

Kristine's job is a perfect fit for her skills and personality. As an Experiencer, Kristine loves the aspects of her job that are hands-on. "The most energizing tasks are ones that require me to build and/or dismantle things." A dominant Sensor, Kristine is extremely practical and has a great eye for the details and mechanisms that make things work. She has acquired a vast amount of specific knowledge and skills, and puts these to good use daily. Kristine's auxiliary Thinking function makes her logical and objective, able to stay cool and calm in high-pressure situations. She is a natural and pragmatic problem solver and enjoys troubleshooting the equipment. The aspects of schooling that bored Kristine—all the theoretical, academic, and indoor activities—don't exist in this job. "I have the most fun in deployed environments. I've built tents, fixed plumbing, worked with generators, and many other things that require you to go outside and get dirty." She thrives on adrenaline and thrill, and can use this energy to go to extraordinary lengths: "If a piece of lifesaving equipment is down, I work twenty-five hours straight until the unit is up and running, and sit next to the patient for another six hours to ensure it doesn't fail again."

Looking Ahead

When asked what her dream job might be, Kristine answers without hesitation that she already has it. The ever-changing nature of the military makes it impossible to know where she might be in five to ten years. The career path for people in her position typically leads to running one's own maintenance shop. And although this would be an honor, Kristine feels it would take her away from the hands-on experiences she enjoys most. Luckily, her skills maintaining and repairing equipment translate easily to the civilian sector, where she could continue the same kind of work postservice if she wished.

Profile 2: John

"I define career satisfaction in two ways: my clients make money and I make money."

John's only regret about becoming a stockbroker is that he didn't get into it earlier—during the bull market of the early 1980s. Sometimes called a financial consultant, or investment broker, John spends 85 to 90 percent of his day talking on the phone, calling new prospects, servicing existing clients, monitoring hundreds of transactions, market indicators, and interest rates, researching companies, and trying "to figure out what the market is going to do." The frenetic pace, excitement, and unpredictability of his work, coupled with the constant possibility of "scoring big," keep John's adrenaline pumping all day—a sensation he thrives on.

What he likes best about his work is making money for his clients, turning a prospect into a client, and closing sales. He enjoys meeting and making contact with new people, and the competitive nature of the stock market. Once he closes a sale, it means money directly into his pocket, because he works exclusively on commission. Although he spends most of his day in an office looking at a computer screen and talking on the phone, his job is anything but dull. He is constantly absorbing and analyzing data, and making important, often split-second, decisions about what to do with what he has observed. A typical example of the way John must be ready to respond to a situation spontaneously happened recently when an asterisk appeared on his monitor indicating an announcement had just been made about an explosion at a major chemical plant. Since analysts speculated that 30 percent of the company's earnings would be affected, John had to analyze the situation and advise his clients who currently owned that stock if they should sell it immediately to prevent a bigger loss or hold on to it on the theory that the analysts were overreacting. Also he had to notify other clients that this stock might be a good one to buy in the next few days. John felt exhilarated when that day was over.

The only parts of his job that he doesn't like are attending to administrative details and doing paperwork. John realizes that chores such as tracking down lost dividend checks and mutual fund statements are important to his clients, but he still finds them frustrating. He dislikes being interrupted and forced to deal with small or routine matters, especially when he is right in the middle of tracking some exciting situation that requires his full attention and concentration or trying to land a new client. Finally, "I really don't enjoy dealing with clients who whine and moan and bitch and cry—usually over relatively small, and often temporary, losses."

A journalism/broadcast/film major in college, John was an outstanding varsity tennis player. Although as a kid he thought he'd always end up in business (even fantasizing about becoming a stockbroker someday), he instead became a tennis pro after college. He toured extensively and taught at a country club. After five years he left the club to work in the cable television industry. His first job was as a production assistant, where he shot, directed, and produced sports shows. Later, he became the manager of a small cable system. When his company was bought out by a larger rival, John lost his job. "I decided then that I wanted to be in a position to take advantage of such situations rather than be victimized by them. So I trained to become a stockbroker."

John's greatest strength is his ability to communicate well, in speech and writing, and to get along with all kinds of people. "I'm pretty good at making people feel comfortable, breaking the ice, cheering people up, and getting them to have a good time." He also values his ability to work hard, think fast, and analyze and interpret trends. John is most proud of accomplishing the production of several TV specials while he worked in cable TV, and his one-time number one ranking in a men's singles tennis competition ten years ago. A more recent milestone was the month he brought home a paycheck that would have annualized out to be more than $100,000. In addition to the financial benefits, John likes seeing other people succeed. "I love being a hero—recommending a stock to a client who ends up making a lot of money as a result of my hard work. That's great!"

Even for someone who seems to thrive on action, John finds the emotional highs and lows of the ever-volatile market stressful. "I marvel at the old brokers who seem to have icewater in their veins—nothing bothers them. For me a real source of stress is when something goes wrong, like when an order should have been placed, but wasn't, or if I don't get to the phone on time and I'm certain I've missed *the call*—the one from someone who just inherited ten million dollars and wants to know what to do with it!" Fortunately, John has several athletic outlets that he uses to alleviate job stress, such as jogging, biking, tennis, golf, and weight lifting. He also relaxes by spending time with his wife, family, friends, and pets, and having an occasional cocktail with friends.

John sees that he has become more work-oriented than he used to be. He is more practical, logical, and more career- and money-oriented. He places more importance on following through at work and finishing the projects he starts. "I'm also reprioritizing

the primary relationships in my life—my wife, parents, and my wife's family—they're all more important to me and I spend more time with them. Also my wife and I have been taking care of some older friends of ours. We take dinner to them pretty frequently and we really enjoy it." As he looks forward to the birth of his first child, religion is becoming more important to him. "I find that I make it to church more often than I used to. I believe that the church offers many of the values I believe are important, so I plan to raise my child by attending church together." Finally, John finds it easier and more interesting to look for the patterns and interconnections between business actions and their resulting effect on the stock market. As a result, he finds that he is more effective in his work, since it is easier for him to grasp the subtle influences of the market. But although his priorities have shifted, it's still very important that he enjoy and have fun in his work.

Since John has found a career that satisfies him, he has no desire to move on. "If I were forced to leave my present job, I'd still want to work in sales or marketing, although the idea of being a masseur at a Club Med sounds pretty good every now and then!" His immediate goal is to become more successful as a broker, earning a good income. "Longer-term, I'd like to achieve financial security—which to me means being wealthy but with the time to look out for my business interests, hobbies, and family."

Why This Career Works for John

John's is a high-energy, high-tension job. Responding to the moment, dealing with the unknown, and taking risks for which there may be enormous payoffs are situations that many Experiencers find extremely energizing. Like most people of his temperament, John thrives on the physical sensation of adrenaline rushing through his body. The most satisfying parts of his day occur when that is happening continually.

Extraverting his Sensing (dominant) is an important "job requirement" for John, since he must keep track of innumerable pieces of information, which he becomes aware of continuously throughout his day. He has to collect, absorb, and relay data to his clients, make recommendations, and place the transaction orders to buy or sell. He watches the monitor closely for changes so he can be ready to call a client to notify him or her of a move that should be made. All this is done with speed and accuracy.

John uses his introverted Thinking (auxiliary) to analyze the data he takes in. He is extremely logical—considering a particular stock's past, present, and likely future performance. Thus, deciding whether the situation he is analyzing is an isolated example or a possible trend is very important. He has to decide on the best course of action, with a cool head, even though he might be in the middle of a frenzy of trading activity. His decisions are made dispassionately, despite the potential for huge losses or profits.

John has developed much greater access to his Feeling side (third function) over the last few years. His relationships with both his own and his wife's family provide evidence of this. He has a renewed interest in participating in organized religion and is eagerly looking forward to the experience of parenting for the first time. He is also better able to draw on his Intuition (fourth function), probably because his job requires him to see patterns and connections, and he has the opportunity to use his Intuition successfully more in his current work than in previous jobs.

Common Threads

Although Lou, John, and Kristine have different backgrounds, experiences, and careers, there are certain common threads woven through their stories. Their specific interests and abilities may differ, but owing to their similar temperament values, the *same hierarchy* of their psychological functions, and the "world" they naturally use them in (inner or outer), there are certain observations we can make about the needs of many ESTPs.

What follows is a list of the most important elements—the formula, if you will—for ESTP satisfaction. Given the uniqueness of all individuals—even those who share the same type—this list will not describe each ESTP equally well. The important thing is that these ten elements, with varying degrees of intensity and in different orders of importance, identify what ESTPs need to be satisfied.

After you have reviewed this list, we recommend that you go back and prioritize the elements in order of *their importance to you*. When doing this, think of past work experiences as well as your present job, and what you found particularly satisfying or unsatisfying. Try to look for *themes* that run through several experiences, not just the events that might be true for one work situation but not for another.

As an ESTP, career satisfaction means doing work that:

1. Lets me meet and interact spontaneously with many people; offers something different every day, and is fun
2. Lets me use my keen powers of observation and my capacity for absorbing and remembering facts

3. Lets me use my ability to search for solutions to problems, using first-hand experience and then critically analyzing these solutions to find the best ones

4. Is active and full of adventure and fun, where things happen quickly, and where I am allowed to take risks and be alert to new opportunities

5. Lets me respond to unplanned situations, using unconventional approaches, where I can skillfully negotiate satisfactory solutions

6. Is done in an environment without a lot of rules or restrictions, where I work with other practical and lively people and am able to enjoy free time after completing my assignments

7. Lets me organize myself as I go along and as I deem necessary, rather than according to someone else's standards

8. Is practical and logical, where I can use my reasoning abilities to find discrepancies or flaws in the logic of a system and fix it on the spot

9. Leaves me free to respond to a crisis and work in an expedient manner dealing with pressing issues

10. Involves real people and things, not theories or ideas; where my efforts are directed to producing a tangible product or service

Popular Occupations for ESTPs

In listing occupations that are popular among ESTPs, it is important to note that there are successful people of all types in all occupations. However, the following are careers ESTPs may find particularly satisfying and some of the reasons why. This is by no means a comprehensive listing but is included to suggest possibilities you may not have previously considered. Although all of these occupations offer the potential for career satisfaction, the future demand for some careers is anticipated to be greater than for others. Based upon our research, the occupations that are italicized in the lists below are forecast to enjoy the fastest rate of growth over the next several years.

SALES/SERVICE/"ACTION"
- Police officer
- *Firefighter*
- *Paramedic*
- Detective
- Investigator
- Corrections officer
- Real estate agent
- Emergency medical technician (EMT)
- Exercise physiologist/sports medicine practitioner
- Respiratory therapist
- Flight attendant
- *Ambulance driver and attendant*
- Sports merchandise salesperson
- Insurance fraud investigator
- *Private investigator/detective*
- *Personal fitness trainer*
- Flight instructor
- Flight engineer
- Commercial helicopter pilot
- Ship and boat captain
- Military officer
- Intelligence specialist
- Probation officer
- Gaming facility manager
- *Pest control expert*
- Criminologist and ballistics expert
- Insurance adjuster/examiner

Many ESTPs find careers in the area of civil service to be satisfying because they offer a high degree of action, variety, and the opportunity to interact with many people from diverse backgrounds. Many of these positions require the ability to think and react quickly to rapidly changing situations and keep cool under stress. Naturally curious and observant, ESTPs often make excellent detectives and investigators.

FINANCE
- *Personal financial adviser*
- *Auditor*
- Stockbroker
- Banker
- Investor
- *Insurance salesperson*
- Budget analyst
- *Insurance agent/broker (sales)*

The world of finance is often interesting to ESTPs, especially when it involves rapidly changing situations and contains a certain amount of risk. A love of excitement and risk taking means they often do well gambling or "playing" in the stock market. They are realistic and pragmatic people, enjoying careers that require problem solving, even if it means using unconventional approaches. Most of these areas of finance include lots of interaction with the public, and ESTPs' friendly and easygoing style helps them meet people and acquire new clients.

ENTERTAINMENT/SPORTS
- Sportscaster
- News reporter
- Promoter
- Tour guide and agent
- Dancer
- Bartender
- Auctioneer
- *Professional athlete/coach/umpire*
- *Fitness instructor/trainer*
- Entertainment agent
- Radio and television talk show host
- Television camera operator
- Musician
- Studio, stage, and special effects technician
- Actor and performer

These "entertainment" careers offer plenty of opportunity to have fun, a critical element in career satisfaction for ESTPs. ESTPs live for the here and now and enjoy work that lets them be active and lively. They are natural promoters yet also enjoy the adventure and thrill of performance. Many ESTPs are sports fans and excel in jobs where sports are central, including competing with and training others. They prefer to work around other people as much as possible and can be charming and persuasive bartenders and auctioneers.

TRADES/"HANDS-ON"
- Carpenter
- Craftsperson/artisan
- Organic farmer
- General contractor
- *Construction worker*
- *Brickmason, blockmason, stonemason, tile and marble setter*
- *Robotics and manufacturing engineer*
- *Construction and development engineer*
- *Vehicle and mobile equipment mechanic*
- *Mechanic, installer, repairer: electrical and electronic equipment*
- *Team assembler*
- Chef/cook
- Electrical engineer
- *Technical trainer (classroom setting)*
- Logistics and supply manager (manufacturing)
- Network integration specialist
- *Civil engineer (repairs of transportation infrastructure)*
- *Biomedical engineering technician*
- Industrial/mechanical engineer
- *EEG technologist/technician*
- *Radiological technician*
- Aircraft mechanic
- Marine biologist
- Data processing equipment repairer

- Property manager: commercial/residential
- Systems support operator and installer
- *Video game developer*
- Lawn service manager
- Transportation coordinator
- Park naturalist
- Audiovisual specialist
- Landscape architect
- Forester
- Exercise physiologist
- Chiropractor
- Teacher: trade/industrial/technical
- Aviation inspector
- Soil conservationist
- Professional photographer
- Wilderness adventure leader
- Airplane dispatcher and air traffic controller
- Flight attendant
- Travel consultant
- *Construction and building inspector*
- Blacksmith
- Eco-tourism specialist
- Ship carpenter and joiner

The appeal of the trades to ESTPs is the opportunity to work with real things and use tools in efficient, economical, and skillful ways. They usually have good mechanical understanding and work well with their hands. ESTPs like working for themselves as long as they have the chance to be around other people. They enjoy the physical and active nature of these careers, including the sometimes high pressure of working within tight time frames (for example, in farming or cooking).

BUSINESS
- Real estate broker/agent
- Entrepreneur
- Land developer
- Wholesaler
- Retail salesperson

- Car salesperson
- *Management consultant (business operations)*
- Franchise owner
- Internet marketer
- Insurance claims examiner (property and casualty)
- Product safety engineer

In general, many ESTPs find the world of business too restrictive and slow-paced to be satisfying. However, these careers offer more flexibility in schedule, personal freedom, and variety, which may capture the ESTP's attention. ESTPs are excellent entrepreneurs, enjoying the element of risk found in starting a new business enterprise or being a developer. Because they are good at sensing subtle cues from other people, they make great salespeople. They enjoy the negotiation process and are fair arbitrators. They enjoy the competitive nature of insurance or car sales and do well within systems that offer incentives and prizes for sales goals.

Customizing Your Job Search

Knowing the particular strengths and blind spots of your type can afford you a tremendous advantage in your job search campaign. In all aspects of the process, from conducting research into available positions, identifying and contacting prospective employers, developing personal marketing tools such as résumés, arranging and conducting job interviews, negotiating salaries, to finally accepting a position, people will act true to their type. Being able to capitalize on your assets and compensate for your liabilities can make the difference between a successful and an unsuccessful job search.

The differences between types are sometimes subtle and other times dramatic. It is the subtle variations in advice we offer that make the real difference between success and failure in a job search. The concept of "networking," or meeting with and talking to people to gather information about potential jobs, serves as a good example. Extraverts will naturally enjoy networking and are advised to do so on a large scale, while Introverts find more limited and targeted networking, especially with people they already know, easier. Sensors tend to network with people in a defined scope, while Intuitives will go far and wide to find people often seemingly unrelated to their field of interest. Further, Feelers take networking, like everything else, very personally and enjoy establishing warm rapport, while Thinkers will be more objective and detached in their style. Finally, Judgers tend to ask fewer and more structured questions during their networking, while Perceivers could ask questions of all sorts all day long! One valuable search technique, many ways to implement it.

Pathways to Success: Using Your Strengths

As we will detail in the following pages, your strengths and talents for the job search include your energy, curiosity, realism, and ability to roll with the punches. Beware, however, of your tendency to be casual about the process, missing opportunities or communicating a lack of serious commitment.

As an ESTP, your most effective strategies will build on your abilities to:

Conduct an active, high-energy job search campaign.

- Use your large network of friends and associates to spread the word that you are looking for a job and to explore career options.

- Put all your focus on your job search campaign. Harness your tremendous energy; look at the process of finding the right career as an adventure.

Rich tackled his job search the way he tackled everything else in his life—with full force. While he was a bit nervous about approaching some of the decision makers, he decided to turn it into a game. He made a little bet with himself each day—how many people he could meet and how many jobs he could find out about in a day. He treated himself to a game of basketball at the gym when he reached or exceeded his bet. He found he looked forward to each day, and by the time he started his new job, he was in the best shape of his life!

Sell yourself.

- Establish rapport with interviewers quickly, demonstrating your ease and facility meeting new people and making them feel comfortable with you.
- Generate excitement about your abilities, talents, and energy that employers will find attractive and a valuable addition to their workforce.

Lisa was a bit intimidated when she arrived for her interview with the vice president of news at a local television station. She had the experience and good references from a station in her hometown. But this was a big step up. She took a deep breath and told herself she could do it and then walked into his office. After answering some standard questions, Lisa was asked why she wanted to work at that station. She began to talk about her love of investigative journalism and some stories done by reporters that she had admired. She found herself relaxing and becoming excited rather than nervous. The vice president was impressed with her ability to talk and her energy and enthusiasm for her work. She left his office a bit stunned because she was offered the job.

Use your powers of observation to discover important environmental factors.

- Tune in and pick up on subtle cues from other people to learn whether they really like working where they do—the amount of interaction, privacy, personal time, and flexibility they have on the job.
- Compare what you learn with what you realistically know about yourself and the things that are important to you. Find the flaws in the situation before making a commitment to invest a lot of your time there.

Cal was sure he wanted to sell real estate. He took the course, passed the exam, and got his real estate license. Now he just needed to find the right agency. He asked everyone he met for references to good agencies. He narrowed it down to several and finally got an appointment for an interview at his first choice. When he arrived at the office, however, he had second thoughts. Everyone seemed so serious and glum. He was ready for a competitive and active office, and he was disappointed to see that nobody seemed to be enjoying the work. He also noticed that everyone in the office was at least twenty years older than he—he had hoped to meet some new friends through work. Cal reconsidered his first choice and, following the interview, decided he needed to continue looking for a firm in which he would feel more comfortable and challenged.

Negotiate effectively and diplomatically.

- Decide ahead of time what is of critical importance to you and what you are willing to give in on. Then negotiate in a flexible and reasonable manner.

After retirement from professional football, Mac was recruited by a local television station to be the sports director. While several elements of the job appealed to him—the salary, celebrity status, and variety of sports he would report on—the job sounded a bit too restrictive to him. He wasn't looking forward to being responsible for supervising several other sports reporters, scheduling assignments, and being tied down to the studio for two on-air reports each day. So Mac made a deal.

Mac agreed to take the job and fulfill most of the requirements of the job, giving the station the benefit of having a high-profile, well-known sports figure with experience and contacts in the sports world. But for a slightly reduced salary, he negotiated a guarantee to cover ten special "on the road" assignments each year, which got him out of the studio and into the world of sports in a more active capacity. The weekend sports reporter filled in for him while he was on assignment and everybody was happy with the arrangement.

Assess and then capitalize on available resources.

- Begin to view your friends and associates (past and present) as resources to help you meet influential people within the organization you are pursuing. Use unconventional approaches if necessary to meet someone who may be difficult to reach through traditional methods.
- Use your natural spontaneity to take advantage of opportunities as soon as they present themselves by moving quickly, expressing your interest immediately, and responding to sudden deadlines.

Minutes after Jodie, a physical fitness specialist, learned about a corporate fitness center that was being built, she called the company to find out when they would begin to accept applications. She was one of the first to apply and the first to be hired. In fact, she was hired before the facility was even completed, which gave her the opportunity to be around when important decisions were being made about staffing, layout of staff offices, and the purchase of key exercise equipment.

Possible Pitfalls

Although all people are unique, there are certain *potential* blind spots that many ESTPs share. We specify "potential" because some of the following *may* be true of you, while others may clearly not apply. While considering them, you may notice that these tendencies do not relate just to the job search but rather describe pitfalls that you may have experienced in other aspects of your life as well. It is therefore helpful to consider each one in terms of your past experiences by asking yourself, "Is this true for me?" And if so, "How did this tendency prevent me from getting something that I wanted?" You will probably notice that the key to overcoming your blind spots is the conscious and thoughtful development of your third and fourth functions (Feeling and Intuition). We recognize that many of the suggestions will be difficult to implement, but the more you use these functions, the fewer problems they will cause you in the future.

Don't be limited to considering only career opportunities that are evident at the present time.

- Look beyond what you have already done to what you might like to do. Gen-

erate a list of ideas, even including those you think are impractical. Find out more about all of them before eliminating any.
- Focus on the future and try to imagine the possible implications of your actions down the road. Once you look past the material pleasures you may be aiming for, you may see how a job that looks good on the surface (or at the moment) may ultimately be unsatisfying in the long run.

Invest the time developing a long-range career plan.

- Curb your impulse to dive right into what may turn out to be the wrong direction for you. Spending the time carefully thinking about what is important to you and what your real motivations and wishes are will help you focus your energy and avoid dead-end jobs.
- Develop a list of criteria for career satisfaction (or use the one we have provided on page 305) and then set some long- and short-term goals. This will provide you with a yardstick against which to measure career options realistically.

Work on developing stick-to-itiveness and follow-through.

- Resist the urge to deal only with immediate problems instead of with the less exciting but still important follow-through necessary to conduct a thorough campaign.
- Prepare yourself for interviews by learning as much as you can about the job, its requirements, and the company so you can address yourself and your past

experience well to questions asked. This step will also give you the added advantage of knowing what you need to ask to get a clear picture of what the job will actually be like.

Avoid being perceived as unreliable or unpredictable.

- Go the extra mile in all cases, even if you don't think you'll pursue a particular option. Demonstrate your dependability by keeping all appointments, arriving on time or early, and calling back when you say you will.
- Remember that many people respect the standard way of doing things within organizations. Don't run the risk of offending someone because of your natural distaste for following rules.

Concentrate on communicating serious interest.

- Your easygoing and relaxed attitude can be charming and infectious. It can, however, also communicate a lack of seriousness to potential employers.
- Be careful not to be blunt or insensitive to the feelings of others. Tune in to the reactions of others and perhaps tone down your assertiveness so you won't offend others.

The Final Piece: Changing or Keeping Your Job . . . the Key to Success for ESTPs

Now that you have a solid understanding of your type, you can see how your natural preferences make you better suited for certain kinds of jobs. You can also see how knowledge of your type-related strengths and weaknesses can help you conduct a more successful job search. But as an ESTP, you've already realized that you are not

equally drawn to *every* career or field listed in the Popular Occupations section. The next and final step is to narrow down the field and find the work you were meant to do.

In addition to Type, several other factors—such as your values, interests, and skills—also contribute to your level of satisfaction on the job. The more compatible you are with your job, the happier you'll be. So prepare to use everything you've learned (in this book and in life) to create *your strategic career plan*. The exercises in Chapter 24, Putting It All Together, are designed to help you do just that.

However, you may have decided it makes more sense (if perhaps only for the moment) to stay in your present job or with your current employer. There may be many valid reasons—financial pressures, family considerations, a tough job market for your specialty, or just bad timing. But take heart! What you've learned in this book can also help you be more content and successful *in your current job*. And should the time come when you're ready to make a major career move, you'll have a much better idea of where you want to go, and how to get there.

"So, if you can't have the job you love (yet!) . . . love the one you've got."

The simple truth is, with the exception of work on a factory assembly line, the vast majority of jobs allow a good deal of flexibility in the way tasks are performed. Here are some ways you may be able to "massage" your current job into one that better fits your needs:

- Look around and find projects you would like working on and volunteer for them.

- Consider taking a time-management course.
- Ask supervisors to be clear about their expectations.
- Find time during the day to get outside and do something physical.
- Join the company's/organization's or outside recreational activity.
- Think about where you want to be five years from now.
- Get out from behind your desk or out of the office on a regular basis.
- Find others with complementary strengths to give your ideas balance.
- Suggest ways of making your work more enjoyable.
- Recruit and hire an efficient and organized assistant or support person.
- Delegate some of the follow-through of projects to others if possible.

One ESTP turns lemons into lemonade:

Cheryl enjoyed her job but wished her company wasn't quite so stuffy. When she learned her friend's firm had a policy of letting people dress more casually on Fridays, she immediately began lobbying her boss to implement the same practice. And after a few months the plan was adopted. Although this didn't drastically change the corporate culture, it created a little shift in thinking that allows Cheryl—and other employees like her—to feel a little less restrained and freer to be themselves at work.

Use what you've got to get what you need.

Simply put, the best advice on how to succeed is to *capitalize on your strengths and compensate for your weaknesses.* Learning how to do this can make the difference between succeeding or failing and loving or hating your work. To help you, we include the following inventory of your potential strengths and weaknesses. And while every individual is unique, as an ESTP, many of the following should apply to you.

Your work-related strengths may include:

- Keen powers of observation, with excellent memory for factual information
- Ability to see what needs doing and be realistic about what's necessary to complete a job
- Being charming and making friends easily
- Lots of energy; you enjoy being active on the job
- Ability to adapt well to change and shift gears quickly
- Ability to make work fun and exciting
- Enjoyment in being part of a team
- Practicality, realistic perceptions, and good common sense
- Process-oriented approach; you create a lively and fun atmosphere at work
- Flexibility and willingness to take risks and try new approaches
- Willingness to accept differences and ability to "go with the flow"

Your work-related weaknesses may include:

- Difficulty working alone, especially for long periods of time
- Dislike of preparing in advance; you have trouble organizing your time
- Tendency to be too casual with people's feelings and blunt and insensitive at times
- Inability to see opportunities and options that don't exist at the moment
- Impatience and/or intolerance with administrative details and procedures
- Difficulty making some decisions and/or prioritizing projects

- Tendency to be impulsive and easily tempted or distracted
- Difficulty seeing the long-term consequences of actions

- Dislike of excessive rules and structured bureaucracy
- Resistance to setting long-term goals and difficulty meeting deadlines

Using your strengths is easy.
The secret to success for an
ESTP
is learning to:

Think before you act, consider
people's feelings, and follow through
on your commitments.

21 | ISTP
Introverted, Sensing, Thinking, Perceiving
"Doing the Best I Can with What I've Got"

Profile 1: Art

"Fixing complicated problems quickly."

Like many businesspeople, Art travels by air to his business meetings. Unlike most people, Art pilots his own plane, a plane that he built in his basement. Art is like that, a man of many interests and talents. Art is the North American account manager for a Fortune 500 company in the high-tech industry. He represents an original equipment manufacturer, or OEM, that makes memory modules. He sells the modules to makers of larger electronic systems—Internet appliances such as routers, hubs, switchers, and servers. His varied customers include engineers and buyers for large corporations. Art describes his job as having two parts. The first is "consultative selling," in which Art listens to the needs of his clients and advises them on what to buy, sometimes arranging to customize products to meet the client's individual needs. When Art meets with

managers who focus on the business side of the deal, he talks about pricing, offshore materials, and saving on taxes. The second part of his job is working with engineers and offering them technical help with his products. Born into a family of engineers and having worked as an engineer himself, Art is able to speak the same language as the engineers he meets and to connect with them on a technical level, trading expertise.

Art began his career as an engineer, working in the field for ten years and following his natural curiosity about the way things work and how to improve them. Salespeople at his firm began taking Art along with them when they went to pitch engineers, and Art saw how the salespeople often mishandled the technical side of the pitch. Art understood that his fellow engineers needed to hold the hardware in their hands to truly appreciate it and to see it as Art did, as a thing of beauty. "I was the first to take the lid off the hardware and paint a picture of how it could work for them. A light went on, and people got it." When he started working as a salesperson, Art was put in charge of all the New England states, and he had to hustle to get his jobs. He worked with "tier one and tier two accounts—big money." One day a representative of the company Art now works for saw him making a presentation. The representative noticed how Art knew a lot about his customer. He approached Art and offered him the opportunity to be on a sales team that he was putting together. Art accepted, and three years later he remains with that company, thoroughly enjoying his job.

But Art's true passion is flying. A licensed pilot for twelve years, Art has figured out a way to marry his passion for flying with his occupation of selling, traveling in his own plane to and from business meetings around North America. Utterly independent yet compensated for supplying his own transportation, Art sees flying to work as his daily challenge. Combating weather delays and associated risks is the adventure that keeps Art going. Unlike commercial airline pilots, who "fly for five hours and then sit around for ten," Art answers only to himself. He is completely in charge of his travel time and relishes the thrills of piloting a small plane. Once on the ground, Art shifts gears to the salesperson role. Together, the two very different aspects of Art's work provide him with the versatility and variety that are the spice of life.

Art enjoys being an expert. He likes calling on his accounts and making PowerPoint presentations. He finds it fun to overcome his natural introversion and "get up on stage." Another aspect of the job that Art enjoys—and that most people would avoid—is meeting with angry or disgruntled customers. Art welcomes the chance to listen, in his customary cool and collected

way, to each complaint. He sees each problem as an opportunity. Art's motto is "doing the best with what you've got," and Art really does. He grasps the mechanics of things just as quickly as he picks up the language of an industry. Art loves being resourceful, and with his MacGyver-style ingenuity, he can see a solution to almost any engineering dilemma.

The aspects of the job that drain Art's energy are organizational tasks such as booking reservations for hotels and keeping track of his expenses. The thrill that Art finds in movement and action is matched by his dismay at sitting still. Fiercely independent, Art dislikes justifying his actions and having his authority or decisions second-guessed. Competence is paramount to Art, and as a hands-on guy he becomes impatient when things take too long or when change is slow in coming. He likens such delay to an "aircraft carrier that takes too long to turn." Making decisions is the bane of Art's existence, and having to make a decision twice is twice as bad. Once he makes a decision, he wants it to be done forever. Another challenge for Art is working out of his own house, as staying on task can fall victim to the hobbies and activities that surround him there. To the man for whom building an airplane in the basement is fun, paperwork can be a burden. Art becomes antsy and irritable when he is inactive. Art himself puts it this way: "In a crisis, on fire, in the weeds, upside down, I'm very cool and collected." Courage under fire is Art's MO. He is a good listener and doesn't feel the need to own the conversation. Adaptable, resourceful, and something of a chameleon, Art is a quick study. He can also explain complicated concepts on a layman's level without condescension, which earns him high marks across the board with clients.

Why This Career Works for Art

With his Experiencer (SP) temperament, Art is a born adventurer. He finds the excitement he desires by flying his plane, taking on high-end customers, and living in the moment. Nimble, flexible, and unencumbered by hierarchy or well-intentioned busybodies looking over his shoulder, Art is a free agent, master of his own time. His many outdoor pursuits and hands-on hobbies are never sidelined by his job. Most important, Art has found a way to incorporate his passion, flying, into his daily work, creating his own adventure within the sphere of the larger business world.

A dominant introverted Thinker, Art is endowed with a logical and competent mind perfect for the challenges of engineering. Cool and effective when confronted with emotional situations or crises, Art really is grace under fire. "Attuned to the drama of the sales call," Art has a head for negotiation and a shrewd business sense, and he projects an image of know-how and competence. Extraverted Sensing is Art's auxiliary function, and it shows up in his love of action and his affinity for the natural world. Comfortable in his body and able to keep track of many different factors at once, Art is an adept pilot who understands not only the mechanics of flying but also the mechanics of plane construction.

The development of Art's Feeling, his fourth function, is apparent in his twenty-five-year marriage to an ESFJ dominant Feeler. Whereas many ISTPs are not ready communicators, Art has built this skill through practice and is more in touch with his feelings and with relationships with clients than he might be by nature.

Meet the Millennial

Name: Alex
Age: 22
Energy systems engineer

"Doing something fun and real— not homework!"

Backstory

Alex considered two careers viable when he was seven years old: he could be either a garbageman or a construction worker. In high school, he became interested in astronomy and telescopes, excelling at AP physics and heading off to Cornell to major in astronomy. Alex realized in his senior year that a degree in astronomy was not as practical as a broader and more foundational degree in physics. He changed programs, planning to get a master's degree in engineering. "It was the most immediately practical way to switch to an engineering field."

Now in a master of engineering in energy systems program at the University of Michigan–Ann Arbor, Alex is learning about power systems in general, with a focus on renewable energy. For his thesis, he and a team of friends are entering the London Business School clean technology competition, a global contest for start-ups or other teams with ideas for green technologies. Alex's idea is to eliminate overnight idling of long-haul tractor-trailer trucks—a huge waste of fuel and major source of pollution—by creating a device in the exhaust smokestack to convert waste heat directly into electricity. The device would run in the smokestack during the day and charge a battery that, at night, would provide enough energy to accommodate the sleeper cab in the truck.

The competition itself acts as a workshop stage for the contestants, who are assigned two mentors who are academic or industry experts in the field. The teams have twenty-four hours to problem-solve what their mentors have deemed the biggest challenge specific to their project. The winners of the competition get a large cash prize with which to begin making their ideas a reality. Ever the pragmatist, Alex doesn't expect to actually win, but sees the contest as a great opportunity to refine his plans as well as network with some important industry professionals and venture capitalists.

A Good Fit

Like many Experiencers, Alex enjoys best the hands-on, physical world. A dominant Thinking type, Alex easily sees and understands mechanical systems. He is competent and quick at solving real-world problems with a pragmatic eye. "I enjoy identifying a problem and building up data for what it would be like under real conditions. You come up with sizing and controls, and then you basically start from scratch and make something." Alex's auxiliary Sensing function enables him to develop concrete and complex systems that depend on a wide array of quite specific knowledge and skills. Ownership and independence are important to Alex. Most rewarding is "when I get to begin with my own problem, end with my own solution, and focus on my own projects." He is less interested in "sitting in a library producing a graph from lab data" and more interested in getting hands-on and building things from the ground up. "I want to do something fun and real that doesn't feel like homework."

Looking Ahead

If things go well in London and the team receives positive feedback, they hope to find enough funding to develop several prototypes to give to truck fleets to try for free. If that works out, Alex would be interested in starting up a venture. Regardless, he will be developing the prototype this summer to fulfill his thesis requirements. "We're going to go to London and have fun and see what happens." A second-best-case scenario for Alex moving forward would be doing project-oriented work in the field of renewable energy, such as wind and solar farms. He'd never want to end up working at a desk job at some place like the Department of Energy. "It's more about adapting existing solutions as best as possible—optimizing whatever opportunity presents itself."

Profile 2: Jill

"Other people call them crises; I call them fun!"

After a series of unsatisfying jobs, Jill has finally found her niche. "I used to think I was just a misfit in the work world and that I'd never find anything more than just an adequate job, never a career." But today she is a successful and content product designer. Jill enjoys the variety, autonomy, individual and creative control, and the opportunity to create interesting and practical products for everyday living.

The company for which Jill works is a small design firm just outside of a large city where she is one of two product designers. There are two assistant designers and three mechanical artists who support Jill and the other designer. Each day is different, one of the things Jill enjoys most about the job. She makes sketches of her designs for products, such as packages for new food products, office supplies, and some technical equipment like lighting fixtures and the faces of telephone answering machines. She does much of her design work alone, after receiving the technical specifications from the client. After the designs are made, she creates models or "dummies" of the product for presentation to the client and for testing at the manufacturing plant. Once the design is accepted, Jill stands by to deal with any production problems that arise and to check the actual product while it is on the assembly line.

"The really fun part of my job, after getting to draw and play at my desk, is the troubleshooting. I might get a call that the design needs a size or proportional change in the testing phase or that there's some problem with folding and assembly during the actual production. I run over to the plant and tinker around with it right there on the lines. It's a kick!" She also enjoys helping the other designer with his technical challenges. She takes a particularly vexing problem and quickly finds a way to fix it, usually by making a few quick sketches and making a rough dummy. "My co-workers think I'm pretty handy. It's almost like a magic trick to fool around with some paper and come up with a new container that stacks properly, or solves whatever the problem was. I get excited about responding to those situations. Other people call them crises. I don't, because I think they're fun."

What isn't fun for Jill are some of the client meetings she is required to attend. "I'm not cut out for meetings anyway. But sometimes they run so long and it seems as if everybody just wants to hear the sound of their own voice. I hate having to be polite and act like I really care about what a person is saying when I know they're just spouting off." She also tends to dislike long phone calls or clients who are afraid to take a risk with a design or approach.

The really draining projects are those that require dozens of revisions in the design for what doesn't seem to be logical or functional reasons, but purely because of one person's taste. "The jobs that stick around the design room too long are draining. I'm usually eager to start something else and am not interested in just making changes for the sake of showing the client something different." She also finds the intra-office bickering and squabbles draining. "I get a real headache when the assistants come to me to complain about who stayed out for lunch ten minutes longer than everyone else. I can't stand arbitrating that kind of stuff, but luckily the people I work with are pretty self-sufficient."

Jill came to her career after some very unsatisfying work experiences. After high school she had no interest in attending college, so she spent the next two years working in several different restaurants as a waitress and bartender. She also helped out at a horse stable so she would be able to ride for free. Her parents persuaded her to try returning to school, but instead of college, she enrolled in a professional art and design school because she had always enjoyed drawing. She discovered graphic design and graduated with a degree in graphic and commercial design. Her first job out of school was at a large advertising agency in the city where she worked as a mechanical artist doing layouts and paste-up for magazine ads. At first it was challenging, but she began to get bored with the repetition and the fact that the office was so busy she never had time even to leave the studio for lunch. "I wanted to do some of the design work, but the structure of the agency was so rigid that if you were hired as a mech artist, you were never permitted to try anything else. The only way to move up was to move on. So I did." Her next job was at a smaller design firm as an assistant designer. She enjoyed the work and respected her immediate supervisor, the art director. But the office politics were intense. "I was shocked by the number of inadequately prepared jobs that were forced on clients and then rushed through production simply to make the owner a fast dollar. The owner was a complete fake and totally dishonest to both his clients and his staff." When Jill finally spoke up to him about her disagreement with his selection of a graphic approach, she was fired for insubordination.

Her next job was at a printing company, where she learned about production. She worked as a traffic manager, supervising projects through the production process, scheduling printing, ordering paper, and preparing cost estimates. The job required enormous organizational abilities and more

follow-through than Jill naturally possessed. Jill was also working sixty hours a week and had no time for any of her friends or hobbies. She lasted less than one year. But, capitalizing on her production experience, she accepted a position as an assistant product designer and learned firsthand about product design by carrying out the ideas of the designers. They would hand her a rough sketch and she would execute it with accuracy. The job also enabled her to occasionally go with the designer to see the job on the presses. She enjoyed that part best. After four years, one of the designers left, and she was promoted to designer. That was two years ago, and Jill thinks this job will last for a long time.

Among her best skills, Jill ranks her eye-hand coordination and ability to visualize how things work at the top. "I think I'm also a very straightforward and honest person. I don't judge other people, and I take people at their word." She gets satisfaction from doing her job well and creating products that are attractive but also practical and workable.

Outside of work, Jill gets great satisfaction from being outdoors and working with animals. She now owns her own horse and often rides him after work as a way of "really getting far away from any little stress created at work. I generally am able to leave work at work. In fact, I have arranged things so that sometimes, I can take time off during a beautiful day to go ride and make up the design time at night. Having the time to enjoy myself and do the things I like to do is really important to me."

Recently Jill has made some changes in her life. She got married two years ago and is thinking about starting a family. Her work used to be just a job, but now she views it as a career she wants to continue even after she has a baby. "I'm sure that I'll be able to work at home for a while and then go back once the baby is bigger. I'm really curious about being a mother and am looking forward to that experience."

Jill sees herself changing at work as well. She now finds that she enjoys the creative process, including brainstorming with other designers. "I like considering new ways of working out a problem after we've tried the old stand-bys. I think that, while the product has to be useful and functional, the best projects I've worked on are also things that are unique." Jill is also finding more success at reading some of the nonverbal behavior cues of her clients and thinks she has a better sense of what might be going on behind the scenes. In the past, those mixed messages used to just confuse and frustrate her.

Jill doesn't have a lot of career goals. She hopes to combine work and family and occasionally thinks about having her own agency some day. "I would have to be with really great people whose work I respected and who would deal with the clients and the business stuff so I could be free to design and take vacations! Anyway, I have all the elements of career satisfaction now—fun, freedom, good money, challenging projects, and quality people to work with."

Why This Career Works for Jill

As a product designer, Jill may work on dozens of different products a year. Since each project has its own unique challenges and problems to solve, Jill's job necessarily involves a great deal of variety. And she gets to work with her hands—drafting and making models and dummies. Like most Experiencers, Jill enjoys her relative autonomy and the lack of structure in her day-to-day activities. She also enjoys the money she makes, which allows her to buy the things that she likes (like her horse). Although she has to deal spontaneously with production and other problems, she doesn't find these stressful—in fact, they are kind of fun.

It is Jill's introverted Thinking (dominant) which helps her to think through, in her head, how something will work best. Hers is largely a technical job requiring close attention to details such as size, proportion, color, and spatial relations. Her dominant Thinking helps her stay objective—she is dealing with things, not people or their feelings. She is most satisfied when she feels she's done her best work, and met her own very demanding internal standards.

Jill uses her extraverted Sensing (auxiliary) to get a realistic sense of which materials work best and how the product will realistically be used, and to make drawings, models, and dummies. Also the products she designs involve mostly practical products, such as food packaging and technical equipment, so she must focus on how the product will *actually* be used and under what conditions. She prefers to get her data by talking with production people and, in some cases, clients and end users.

In recent years Jill has started to use her Intuition (third function) to do some long-range planning—concerning both her professional and her personal life. She has begun thinking about where she wants to end up and is considering starting a family. She finds brainstorming more enjoyable than she has in the past and is more interested in trying out new ways instead of relying so much on standard methods. She has also increased her ability to understand the nonverbal behavior cues of her clients and has more interest in reading between the lines or figuring out what is happening behind the scenes.

Common Threads

Although Art, Jill, and Alex have different backgrounds, experiences, and careers, there are certain common threads woven through their stories. Their specific interests and abilities may differ, but owing to their similar temperament values, the *same hierarchy* of their psychological functions, and the "world" they naturally use them in (inner or outer), there are certain observations we can make about the needs of many ISTPs.

What follows is a list of the most important elements—the formula, if you will—for ISTP satisfaction. Given the uniqueness of all individuals—even those who share the same type—this list will not describe each ISTP equally well. The important thing is that these ten elements, with varying degrees of intensity and in different orders of importance, identify what ISTPs need to be satisfied.

After you have reviewed this list, we recommend that you go back and prioritize the elements in order of *their importance to you*. When doing this, think of past work experiences as well as your present job, and what you found particularly satisfying or unsatisfying. Try to look for *themes* that run through several experiences, not just the events that might be true for one work situation but not for another.

As an ISTP, career satisfaction means doing work that:

1. Lets me identify and use resources that are available to me in the most efficient manner possible
2. Lets me practice, master, and then use skills I have acquired, especially mechanical skills or those requiring the use of tools
3. Lets me apply my understanding and technical knowledge of the world around me and see the logical principles underlying my work; lets me engage in troubleshooting and problem solving
4. Has clear directions; where I can work expediently and deal with real and practical products
5. Is fun and active and lets me work independently with frequent opportunities to get out of my work space and be outdoors
6. Is done in an environment without excessive rules or operating standards imposed by others; where I can enjoy spontaneous adventures and step in to manage any crisis
7. Lets me work independently, with a minimum of supervision, and where I am not required to closely supervise others
8. Gives me plenty of time to pursue my interests and hobbies
9. Gives me a substantial amount of enjoyment and is continually challenging
10. Lets me use an economy of motion and energy and does not require needless routine or procedures

Popular Occupations for ISTPs

In listing occupations that are popular among ISTPs, it is important to note that there are successful people of all types in all occupations. However, the following are careers ISTPs may find particularly satisfying and some of the reasons why. This is by no means a comprehensive listing but is included to suggest possibilities you may not have previously considered. Although all of these occupations offer the potential for career satisfaction, the future demand for some careers is anticipated to be greater than for others. Based upon our research, the occupations that are italicized in the lists below are forecast to enjoy the fastest rate of growth over the next several years.

SALES/SERVICE/"ACTION"
- Police/corrections officer
- Race car driver
- Pilot
- Weaponry specialist

- Intelligence agent
- Marshal
- *Firefighter*
- Sports equipment/merchandise salesperson
- Pharmaceutical salesperson
- *Private investigator/detective*
- Child support, missing persons investigator
- High school and college athletic coach
- Photographer
- Criminalist and ballistics expert

The appeal of action careers for ISTPs derives from their desire not to feel confined by a lot of structure and regimentation. They work well on impulse and enjoy situations that are spontaneous and call on their ability to quickly assess their resources and then take appropriate actions. They work well alone but will pull together as part of a team when necessary. ISTPs often enjoy mastery of tools or machinery of a specialized style and enjoy being outdoors and physically active.

TECHNOLOGY
- *Electrical/mechanical engineer*
- *Civil engineer*
- *Technical trainer (one-to-one setting)*
- Information services developer
- *Software developer: applications, systems*
- Alternative energy systems engineer
- Logistics and supply manager (manufacturing)
- *Networking specialist*
- *Computer programmer*
- Marine biologist
- Quality assurance technician
- Reliability engineer
- Systems support operator/installer
- Network systems and data communications analyst
- Home network installer/troubleshooter

- Product tester
- Software engineer
- Geologist
- Product safety engineer

ISTPs often find satisfaction in technical careers because they are interested in how and why things work. They tend to be good in mechanical areas because they possess great observational powers and a capacity to remember and use important facts and details. They usually enjoy working with their hands and like work that provides them with a constant source of sensory information. Their logical analysis is best used when based upon solid facts that they themselves gather through their five senses.

HEALTH CARE
- *EEG technologist/technician*
- *Radiological technician*
- Emergency medical technician (EMT)
- Exercise physiologist
- *Dental assistant/hygienist*
- *Surgical technician*
- *Emergency room physician*
- Medical evacuation coordinator
- Transportation coordinator

These health care fields are particularly satisfying to ISTPs owing to their highly technical nature. Each requires the use of exacting precision, a well-developed practical and mechanical sense, and the patience and concentration necessary to operate and maintain sensitive diagnostic equipment.

BUSINESS/FINANCE
- Securities analyst
- Purchasing agent and buyer
- Banker
- Economist
- Legal secretary
- Management consultant (business operations)

- *Paralegal*
- *Cost estimator*
- Insurance adjuster/examiner

Pragmatic and accurate with numbers, ISTPs can find enjoyment in business and financial careers. The working environment is extremely important, however, and needs to allow for personal freedom and flexibility for ISTPs to be satisfied. Opportunities that allow the ISTP to work autonomously, without excessive meetings or office politics, are best.

ISTPs are often able to bring order to confused data and unrecognizable facts. They easily see the realities of an economic situation and are ready and able to respond to immediate changes.

TRADES/"HANDS ON"
- *Computer repairer*
- Airline mechanic
- *Robotics and manufacturing engineer*
- *Ambulance driver and attendant*
- *Coach/trainer*
- *Carpenter*
- *Bicycle repairer*
- *Mechanic, installer, repairer: electrical and electronic equipment*
- *Mechanic, installer, repairer: security and fire alarm systems*
- Automotive products retailer
- Commercial artist
- Lawn service manager
- Landscape architect
- Forester
- Park naturalist/ranger
- Audiovisual specialist
- Television camera operator
- Insurance appraiser: auto damage
- Criminal investigator
- Ship and boat captain
- Commercial airplane pilot
- Flight instructor
- Flight engineer

- Commercial helicopter pilot
- Locomotive engineer
- Military officer
- *Organic farmer*
- Airplane dispatcher and air traffic controller
- Studio, stage, and special effects specialist
- *Brickmason, blockmason, stonemason, tile and marble setter*
- *Vehicle and mobile equipment mechanic*
- *Construction worker*
- *Heavy and tractor-trailer truck driver*
- Silversmith
- Taxidermist
- Gunsmith
- Cabinetmaker and finish carpenter
- Musical instrument maker
- Sketch artist
- Model and mold maker

The independence and hands-on practicality of the trades often appeal to ISTPs. ISTPs prefer tasks that are real and concrete and provide the opportunity to use their hands. They work the most diligently on projects that fully absorb their interest, so if theirs is a love of sports, they will enjoy coaching and training much more than another seemingly similar trade career. Making a career out of a hobby is an excellent strategy for the ISTP.

Customizing Your Job Search

Knowing the particular strengths and blind spots of your type can afford you a tremendous advantage in your job search campaign. In all aspects of the process, from conducting research into available positions, identifying and contacting prospective employers, developing personal marketing tools such as résumés, arranging and conducting job interviews, negotiating salaries, to finally accepting a position, people will act true to their type. Being able to capitalize on your assets and compensate for your liabilities can make the difference between a successful and an unsuccessful job search.

The differences between types are sometimes subtle and other times dramatic. It is the subtle variations in advice we offer that make the real difference between success or failure in a job search. The concept of "networking," or meeting with and talking to people to gather information about potential jobs, serves as a good example. Extraverts will naturally enjoy networking and are advised to do so on a large scale, while Introverts find more limited and targeted networking, especially with people they already know, easier. Sensors tend to network with people in a defined scope, while Intuitives will go far and wide to find people often seemingly unrelated to their field of interest. Further, Feelers take networking, like everything else, very personally and enjoy establishing warm rapport, while Thinkers will be more objective and detached in their style. Finally, Judgers tend to ask fewer and more structured questions during their networking, while Perceivers could ask questions of all sorts all day long! One valuable search technique, many ways to implement it.

Pathways to Success: Using Your Strengths

As we will detail in the following pages, your strengths and talents for the job search include your careful attention to detail, logical analysis of current problems, and unpretentious communication style. However, your need for honesty may sometimes prevent you from seeing the importance of establishing rapport with potential employers.

As an ISTP, your most effective strategies will build on your abilities to:

Gather and remember all relevant data.

- Use your tremendous powers of observation to notice the people and surroundings of a potential workplace. Compare your recollections later as you think about whether the setting is right for you.
- Explain your ability to serve as a walking storehouse of information. Provide examples of how that capability has proved useful to past employers.

When Susan interviewed for a new job, she did her homework. She found people who were knowledgeable, people she respected, and sought their advice. She tried to think through the possible interview questions before the interview. Once she was prepared and ready, she felt comfortable winging it on some less important issues.

Adapt and take advantage of available resources.

- Persevere in your job search even when faced with obstacles.
- Demonstrate your skills at developing instant solutions to immediate problems when they pop up during your job search or during an interview.

From her research talking to friends, Margie knew the attorney who interviewed legal secretaries liked to ask hypothetical questions. Rather than be thrown by it, Margie decided to act as though the situation were a real one that currently existed, since she knew that she was good at on-the-spot problem solving. So when presented with the scenario, she was able to come up with a good solution to a "real" problem and impress the attorney in the process.

Demonstrate to potential employers your ability to think things through carefully and logically.

- Take time to apply your ability to figure out how things work to assess the organization and the people in it. Ask yourself how your prospective role will fit within it as it currently exists.
- Be straightforward and honest in your responses to all questions.

During a performance review, Rich was asked what he thought of a newly adopted reporting system. He knew that giving a completely honest answer might hurt his chances of being promoted because he did not think that the system was an improvement. Rather than speaking with his usual naked honesty and blunt style, Rich took a minute and answered that while the system apparently provided more important information, he didn't think it really affected him because he continued to work according to his own high standards.

Analyze opportunities objectively.

- Use your well-developed logic to see the natural consequences of actions and choices.
- Let prospective employers know you can remain calm, even during unexpected changes in plan or during a real crisis. Include in your listing to prospective employers the ability to keep your head about you when others are upset.

Stan found himself in an interesting spot while interviewing for a position as surveyor for a town building department. About ten minutes into the interview, the town manager got an emergency call from the field. One of the surveyors had been hurt in a fall. Seeing that his interviewer was flustered about what to do, Stan suggested that he call 911 while the town manager drove out to the site. Stan made the call and then followed in his own car, arriving before the emergency team. He pulled a blanket from his car and was able to help comfort the injured man until the professionals arrived. Stan's interview continued over a beer with the rest of the crew once they learned their co-worker was going to be all right.

Take reasonable risks.

- Look for opportunities when it is appropriate to be impulsive and spontaneous. Show your true colors—a person who enjoys working hard and also having a good time. People are more likely to view you as a member of the team if they can imagine having a cup of coffee with you.
- Demonstrate your ability to troubleshoot by researching some of the potential problems being faced by a prospective employer and offering your suggestions for ways to solve them.

Peg was beginning to get bored in her job in the corporate finance department of a large insurance company. She had been in many jobs during her long career there and usually got "antsy" after a couple of years. She was about to put out the word that she was interested in a new assignment when she was asked to serve on a panel to look into a way to restructure the entire company. During her evaluation of the company, she determined that her current position would no longer be needed under the new structure. She reported the findings, with the knowledge that she might be out of a job. She was. But she was offered a new and challenging position once the reorganization was begun. The risk proved to be a win for her.

Possible Pitfalls

Although all people are unique, there are certain *potential* blind spots that many ISTPs share. We specify "potential" because some of the following *may* be true of you, while others may clearly not apply. While considering them, you may notice that these tendencies do not relate just to the job search but rather describe pitfalls that you may have experienced in other aspects of your life as well. It is therefore helpful to consider each one in terms of your past experiences by asking yourself, "Is this true for me?" And if so, "How did this tendency prevent me from getting something that I wanted?" You will probably notice that the key to overcoming your blind spots is the conscious and thoughtful development of your third and fourth functions (Intuition and Feeling). We recognize that many of the suggestions will be difficult to implement, but the more you use these functions, the fewer problems they will cause you in the future.

Try to plan ahead and follow an organized job search.

- Don't move on to a more exciting challenge before waiting to see if your previous efforts have paid off.
- Make a conscious effort to develop your perseverance, remembering that hard work and sticking to your plan of action will give you the results you really want.

Look for possibilities beyond those that exist at the moment.

- Try not to take stopgap jobs. Resist the temptation to prematurely end the process by accepting an adequate but not truly satisfying option.
- Set long-range goals for yourself and your career. Ask yourself what you hope to accomplish five and ten years from now.

Assess whether the job you are considering will help you reach those goals.

Beware of the propensity not to exert any more effort than is absolutely necessary.

- Avoid taking tempting shortcuts even though you readily see them. Pay close attention to all phases of your job search and conduct each with the same energy and diligence.
- Remember that employers look for conscientiousness in employees. Demonstrate your willingness to go the extra mile to get the job done right.

Don't postpone a decision too long.

- Make decisions and then move on. Eliminate poor options and keep yourself in the running for job options you really want.
- Don't let yourself appear undependable and lacking direction by procrastinating too long.

The Final Piece: Changing or Keeping Your Job . . . the Key to Success for ISTPs

Now that you have a solid understanding of your type, you can see how your natural preferences make you better suited for certain kinds of jobs. You can also see how knowledge of your type-related strengths and weaknesses can help you conduct a more successful job search. But as an ISTP, you've already realized that you are not equally drawn to *every* career or field listed in the Popular Occupations section. The next and final step is to narrow down the field and find the work you were meant to do.

In addition to Type, several other factors—such as your values, interests, and skills—also contribute to your level of satisfaction on the job. The more compatible you are with your job, the happier you'll be. So prepare to use everything you've learned (in this book and in life) to create *your strategic career plan*. The exercises in Chapter 24, Putting It All Together, are designed to help you do just that.

However, you may have decided it makes more sense (if perhaps only for the moment) to stay in your present job or with your current employer. There may be many valid reasons—financial pressures, family considerations, a tough job market for your specialty, or just bad timing. But take heart! What you've learned in this book can also help you be more content and successful *in your current job*. And should the time come when you're ready to make a major career move, you'll have a much better idea of where you want to go, and how to get there.

> *"So, if you can't have the job you love (yet!) . . . love the one you've got."*

The simple truth is, with the exception of work on a factory assembly line, the vast majority of jobs allow a good deal of flexibility in the way tasks are performed. Here are some ways you may be able to "massage" your current job into one that better fits your needs:

- Ask supervisors to be clear about their expectations.
- Seek an opportunity to use your negotiation skills.
- Try to get as much independence as you can.
- Find time during the day to get outside and do something physical.
- Think about where you want to be five years from now.
- Make sure you have enough uninterrupted time to concentrate on your work.

- Consider taking a time-management course.
- Seek others with complementary skills to help you evaluate ideas.

One ISTP turns lemons into lemonade:

Ted was a whiz with computers, and frustrated co-workers were constantly asking him for help when they had problems. Although he enjoyed helping out, it took him away from his regular work and left him swamped when deadlines loomed. Recognizing the need for his talent, he suggested to his boss that he be relieved of some of his duties (the ones he really didn't enjoy anyway!) so he could be a part-time consultant within his department. This worked well for both Ted and his co-workers, and for the company as a whole. Employees could get their problems fixed more quickly, which made them more productive; Ted gained independence and the opportunity to spend more time solving technical problems—something that he really liked and at which he was naturally adept.

Use what you've got to get what you need.

Simply put, the best advice on how to succeed is to *capitalize on your strengths and compensate for your weaknesses*. Learning how to do this can make the difference between succeeding or failing and loving or hating your work. To help you, we include the following inventory of your potential strengths and weaknesses. And while every individual is unique, as an ISTP, many of the following should apply to you.

Your work-related strengths may include:

- Ability to work well with defined tasks and tangible products
- Keen powers of observation and an excellent memory for factual information

- Ability to bring order to confusing data and to recognizable facts
- Aptitude for working alone or alongside others you respect
- Ability to stay calm and cool in a crisis or under pressure
- Ability to recognize what needs doing and what is necessary to complete the job
- Aptitude for working with your hands and with tools
- Ability to adapt well to sudden change and shift gears quickly
- Practicality and good common sense
- Ability to identify and make good use of available resources
- Flexibility and willingness to take risks and try new approaches

Your work-related weaknesses may include:

- Difficulty seeing the long-term consequences of actions
- Lack of interest in verbal communication, especially superficial conversations

- Dislike of advance preparation; you have trouble organizing your time
- Little patience for abstract and complex theories
- Tendency to be blunt and insensitive to the feelings of others
- Tendency to get bored and restless easily
- Difficulty seeing opportunities and options that don't exist at the moment
- Impatience with administrative details and procedures
- Unwillingness to repeat yourself
- Difficulty making some decisions
- Strong independent streak and dislike of excessive rules and structured bureaucracy
- Resistance to setting long-term goals and difficulty meeting deadlines

Using your strengths is easy.
The secret to success for an
ISTP
is learning to:

Communicate, consider people's feelings, and follow through on your commitments.

22 | ESFP
Extraverted, Sensing, Feeling, Perceiving

"Don't Worry—Be Happy!"

Profile 1: Larry

"If the sky were the limit and I could do anything, I'd do just what I'm doing now."

Larry is a forty-one-year-old pediatrician specializing in childhood arthritis. He keeps the thank-you notes and letters he has received from patients and their families. It's one of the ways he knows that he's doing a good job. But the living testimonial he uses is the story of the child who was referred to him by a stumped therapist. The two-year-old was experiencing fevers, aches, and pains. Larry wasn't satisfied with the blood test results and ordered more. From those tests, Larry diagnosed leukemia. The child immediately started on a treatment program and today is in remission. "When I come up with a diagnosis that hasn't been found before and I can help a child, that's really satisfying."

Larry is a staff physician at a children's hospital and is assistant professor of pediatrics at a university. He is married and

has two sons, aged thirteen and two. Larry spends about 60 percent of his time seeing children aged one through eighteen from all around the state and the region. Most are referred by the child's pediatrician for evaluation of joint problems. Larry reviews previous X rays, examines the child, talks with the child and parents, and makes a diagnosis. Larry uses his well-developed skills of establishing rapport and communicating with both the child and parents. Next, he maps out a treatment plan, which usually involves medication, some form of physical therapy, and, occasionally, surgery. "There are some eighty to one hundred disorders but, practically speaking, we see about twenty on a regular basis."

Larry also teaches. "Most of it is bedside teaching of residents with the patient. We go over a diagnosis and examine the patient together." Larry also gives formal lectures once or twice a month to the residents and physician's assistants, does community

326 | *Part Three: Getting to Work*

teaching at hospitals, and occasionally teaches nationally. He participates in formal scientific studies on medications and writes reports for publications in medical journals. Finally, Larry is required to spend a portion of his time doing administrative tasks. He completes insurance forms, serves on several hospital committees, including one that he chairs, and spends about two hours a day on the telephone talking with patients' parents and physicians.

It's the patient care that Larry enjoys the most. "Seeing patients, working with families, helping kids to minimize their pain and improve their functions—just giving the best possible care—that's what I like." He's particularly energized by "diagnostic puzzles." "I'm good at determining the real source of pain. And diagnosing an illness like Lyme disease is energizing because it is *curable.* I can tell a family that everything will be fine. It's not too often I can say that."

The diagnostic situations that are less clear are those involving psychosomatic disorders. "Those drain me because there are so many issues to deal with. Usually, it's teens who have other social problems as well." Larry also is drained by situations where a patient doesn't respond to treatment. "The family is still angry about the child's condition, and angry at me, rather than just feeling the natural sadness and grief at the loss of the perfect child." He also finds his energy being sapped when dealing with a patient the same age as one of his sons, because he identifies too closely with them and their parents.

While it's less intense, Larry finds the paperwork of his job to be a drain. He completes numerous insurance and disability forms and school reports. "I'm frustrated by the politics of the hospital structure in my community. In order to meet with other specialists, I have to run around to different

hospitals because of the lack of consolidated services." It's a coordination headache.

Larry doesn't remember deciding to become a doctor and jokes that when he was a child, perhaps his mother whispered into his ear while he slept each night: "You will become a doctor." He went to a high school geared toward science and math and then took premed in college. During his rotations in his third year of medical school, he worked in pediatrics. "I love kids, and I looked forward to going to work each day, so I knew that would be my choice." During his studies, he had a teacher, a rheumatologist, who became a major influence. "I loved his manner and could talk with him for hours. I picked up some real pearls of wisdom from him." Larry's mentor influenced him to choose a specialization in pediatric rheumatology. In fact, Larry agreed to take a job at a hospital where his mentor worked before meeting his actual boss, "a big mistake because he was a tyrant!" After two years, Larry relocated and started a clinic at the university and a general pediatric practice "to feed myself." He gradually cut back on the amount of general pediatrics as the rheumatology part of the practice got busier. He was hired as a staff physician at the children's hospital nine years ago, part-time at first, and then full-time three years later. When he was hired, the program served fifty-five children a year, and Larry increased it to three hundred in the first year. He currently sees about twelve hundred patients a year, three hundred and fifty of whom are new patients.

While Larry originally expected that he would ultimately become a partner in a private pediatric practice, he is much happier at the children's hospital because he has found a specialty that allows him to combine his love of kids and his interest in rheumatology, as he was encouraged to do by his mentor.

Outside of work, Larry enjoys tennis, skiing, fishing, camping, and spending time with his wife and sons—a top priority for him. "It's really important that I spend quality time with them and that I have physically and emotionally healthy children." He's placing a greater emphasis on improving his communication with his wife and being a more attentive son to his aging parents. "It's becoming more important to me to be on good terms with them and to get closer with my brother. It's a struggle to find and balance the time, however. When Josh, who's thirteen, was little, I wasn't as busy as I am now while Michael is little. I have more time commitments, and I'm trying to do quality things in less time. It's the structure of my life that has changed."

Also increasing in importance is doing the best job he can do at work. Larry has, in effect, reached one goal of creating and running an excellent program at the hospital. Now his goals are more academic. He is making arrangements to conduct more research, which will lead to additional publications that will bring him more national recognition. He also hopes to enlarge the program by adding another physician, which will reduce some of the dreaded administrative time.

Larry is seeing a change in his professional attitude about his patients. "I'm becoming more secure in my own skills and abilities and less tolerant of mistakes and inappropriate treatments. By the time most of these kids get to me, they've been through the mill. I'm an advocate of early, appropriate treatment, *fast*."

Larry is also gaining a better perspective on his patients. "I've developed a better sense of the kids, particularly the psychiatric cases where lots of information is unknown and needs to be discovered."

Career satisfaction for Larry is as simple as the eagerness to "get up in the morning and get to work." But it is also the recognition and thanks he receives from patients and families, and the feedback and support he receives from his peers. "I hope people think of me as a caring and competent physician, and I hope my family and friends think of me as someone who cares, is a good listener, and is available to them when they need me."

Why This Career Works for Larry

Larry's Experiencer (SP) temperament draws him to be an active participant in life, and it is no accident he has chosen work in which he is constantly moving from one challenge to another. His natural curiosity and love for children combine to drive him to discover important facts about their condition that help him treat them. And interacting with children on their level allows him to "play" a lot, another important criterion for Experiencers.

One of the reasons he finds his work so satisfying is that it requires and allows him to use his (dominant) extraverted Sensing continuously. He is constantly gathering data about his patients, using his keenly developed senses to observe, listen, touch, and even hear the subtle symptoms and signs that will help him correctly diagnose a patient's illness. Larry keeps careful track of changes in his patients' progress or changes in their symptoms or condition.

Larry's (auxiliary) introverted Feeling moves him to care deeply for his patients. Being a feeling type, he is naturally empathetic. Because he *introverts* his feelings, he feels things passionately and is driven to act on his own personal values; chief among them is a drive to help others.

Larry is demanding about the quality and consistency of care his patients receive, feels great compassion for their parents, and is upset when the children have been shipped around to several doctors before finding the real cause of their pain or disability.

Finally, Larry is at an age where he is probably developing his third function—

Thinking. Evidence of this can be found in his emerging emphasis on competency—setting increasingly high standards for himself and others, a recent focus on accomplishing goals, such as expanding his department and conducting and publishing more research, and a desire to gain national recognition for his work from his peers.

Meet the Millennial

Name: Joanna
Age: 27
Marine mammal trainer

"Forming relationships with animals and people."

Backstory

Most kids love animals. But Joanna wasn't most kids. She brought home stray dogs and cats, and volunteered on Saturdays at the local animal shelter. It was a trip to the aquarium in ninth grade, however, that really changed her world. "I remember watching the penguins and pressing my nose against the dolphin tank, trying to get a better look. When it was time for my class to go back to school, I felt like I was *leaving* home instead of going home."

Although Joanna was never that interested in school in general, she did enjoy the sciences, and decided to pursue marine biology in college. During her sophomore year, she had an opportunity to attend the Career Camp program at an aquatic theme park. "It was the best summer of my life. Every morning we would dig through huge cases of fish,

sorting for the different animals. It was kind of gross, but really cool because in the afternoon we got to help the trainers feed the animals. We would shovel snow for the penguins and then feed them by hand. They loved to get up close to us."

After that summer, Joanna was determined to find a way to end up back at the park and eventually become a marine mammal trainer. Always a strong athlete and swimmer, she spent the summer after graduation teaching swimming and becoming certified in CPR and as a scuba instructor. In the fall, Joanna started waitressing at a theme restaurant in the park. Although Joanna enjoyed interacting with guests—especially the little kids, so excited to be there—she saw it only as a means to an end. She quickly made friends with the other staff, and when a position opened up as an apprentice trainer, Joanna was the first to hear about it. And naturally, she went for it.

Joanna spent two years as an apprentice trainer, learning how to train, feed, and care for the animals, and in the process getting to know their personalities as well. She spent another year as an associate trainer and is now qualified as a marine mammal trainer, specializing in dolphins.

A Good Fit

Like all Experiencers, Joanna loves to have fun—and her job is a blast! She gets to work hands-on with animals every day, being physically engaged and working outside. A dominant Sensing type, Joanna is purely in the moment and especially enjoys the very physical and tangible parts of her job—swimming with the dolphins and holding them during veterinarian visits. Her auxiliary Feeling function is also constantly in play. "My favorite part is really getting to know the animals, forming relationships with them. They light up when they see you. Each trainer works mostly with one animal, because the trainers and animals have to know each other, trust each other, especially if you're performing together." An Extravert, Joanna loves the performances and is great in front of a crowd. She's comfortable talking to and answering questions from the audience, and is warm and sociable with both animals and people. "What's not to love about my job? We're in wet suits, playing with animals all day!"

Looking Ahead

Joanna's goal in the next five years is to become a senior trainer, because she wants to work with orcas—a job that requires at least four years as a trainer, due to the inherent safety risks. Senior trainers also perform in the majority of park shows, an aspect of the job Joanna enjoys. And as a senior trainer, Joanna would help to train new apprentices, which she feels she would be especially good at.

Profile 2: Eve

"I found my calling in early childhood education purely by happenstance."

Eve describes her job as director of a private, not-for-profit child care center as "early childhood advocate." She plays that role whenever she can, whether it's directly with the children or the teachers or with parents visiting the center who are considering enrolling their children. "I like to give people something they can walk away with, like the fact that sharing is really an adult concept, although we tend to expect that three-year-olds will grasp it."

Eve spends most of her time "meeting the pressing needs of the day." And each day can be very different. During the course of the day she fills in for a teacher on a break, answers requests for information over the telephone, meets with prospective parents and their child, sits in on planning sessions with her staff, plans staff development programs and parent activities, and prepares to make formal, monthly reports to the board of directors. She also serves on the quality committee of a child care collaborative in the area, working to define quality and assess the needs of centers. Her aim is improving and enriching the level of quality in all child care.

Eve has been at the center for twenty-seven years, first as a teacher and now as director. She started her career with a degree in secondary physical education. "I was always a jock and thought I would change the world by helping young people develop a wonderful attitude toward physical education. But after one year, I'd had enough of public education!" After her first child was born, Eve was offered a job at a child care center on the campus of a nearby university. She taught three- and four-year-olds for two years. "I loved it. I realized I had found a better direction for myself." After a move, the birth of her second child, and a divorce, Eve looked for a job. She learned about the position because she was friends with the current director. She was hired as a part-time teacher. For twenty-one years, she taught four-year-olds, obtaining a master's degree in early childhood education during her tenure. Six years ago, she decided that it might be time for a change. "There began to be lots of turnover. I kept spending my time training the new director! I moved again and needed a bit more time to commute, and I wanted more flexibility in my hours. I was tired of punching a clock because students and parents were waiting for me." She applied for the directorship and was hired.

"Seeing the kids respond and develop in creative ways, seeing things I believe in—in action—is the best part of this job. When I hear the children problem solving or see them jump from something high for the first time or express their feelings in words, it's so satisfying!" Eve also is energized by watching the staff handle situations in positive and creative ways. "Then I know I've reached them."

The difficult times involve confronting problems and handling people's negative experiences. "When I see a teacher doing something I feel is just not right, I get very stressed. I can't say anything right then, usually, because the child is present. And I don't like having to tell the teacher I don't like what she's doing or how she's performing. But I have to. It's part of the job." Eve dislikes having to fire someone or tell parents they owe the school money. She also is unhappy when she can't pay teachers what she wishes she could and what she believes they are worth.

Unresolved conflicts among her staff are also draining for Eve. "I see a certain increase in the amount of selfishness these days among all kinds of people. That's disturbing, but I consider it a challenge, too." And she puts off anything having to do with money, as well as the endless scheduling required to keep the school running and properly staffed. She avoids written evaluations of her staff, preferring to "talk it rather than write it." She prefers to talk out her stress by seeking the confidence of someone close to her—her husband, her assistant, or a close friend.

Eve's most significant work-related accomplishment is "keeping this school going—riding the tide." But she is rewarded by meeting a new parent who has heard about the center from another pleased parent. "And I love reading in the paper or hearing about 'graduates' of this school going on and becoming successful." Her own career goal is being met each day. "I'm scared to retire because I won't be challenged, and I won't have much of a mission anymore."

Why This Career Works for Eve

Eve most enjoys responding spontaneously to the pressing needs of the day. She loves the variety of activities she engages in, as well as the people (students, teachers, and parents) she interacts with. Something is always happening, and most of it is unplanned. The playfulness of Experiencers is a particularly important part of Eve.

A virtual "radar machine," Eve monitors everything with her (dominant) extraverted Sensing. She is constantly scanning all that is going on: using her eyes to watch a kid make it to the top of the climber without falling, her ears to hear them talk out problems with their peers, her arms to hold an unhappy child, even her nose to decide whose diaper needs changing! All the while she is also monitoring her staff to see how she can help them with their jobs.

Her strong feelings and convictions about what child care should be like come from Eve's introverted Feeling (auxiliary). She tries to instill her ideas—her "calling," really—into everyone and everything that happens at the school. As do other people who introvert their feelings, Eve develops long-lasting personal one-on-one relationships with students, staff, and parents, and takes great pride that many of the parents of her current students were once students at the school themselves.

Thinking is Eve's third function and although she doesn't particularly like it, she can be tough when she has to in dealing with money or issues of discipline. Since she is over fifty, she is also developing better access to her Intuition (fourth function), which she has had to use in the planning of the school's future and anticipating what the community's child care needs will be in the years to come. Although she could retire soon, she fears she would lose her "mission" and is still energized by new challenges.

Common Threads

Although Larry, Eve, and Joanna have different backgrounds, experiences, and careers, there are certain common threads woven through their stories. Their specific interests, abilities, and values may differ, but owing to their similar temperament values, the *same hierarchy* of their psychological functions, and the "world" they use them in (inner or outer), there are certain observations we can make about the needs of many ESFPs.

What follows is a list of the most important elements—the formula, if you will, for ESFP satisfaction. Given the uniqueness of all individuals—even those who share the same type—this list will not describe all ESFPs equally well. The important thing is that these ten elements, with varying degrees of intensity and in different orders of importance, identify what ESFPs need to be satisfied.

After you have reviewed this list, we recommend that you go back and prioritize the elements in order of *their importance to you*. When doing this, think of past work experiences as well as your present job, and what you found particularly satisfying or unsatisfying. Try to look for *themes* that run through several experiences, not just the events that might be true for one work situation but not for another.

As an ESFP, career satisfaction means doing work that:

1. Lets me learn from hands-on experience, where I look for solutions to problems from gathering all the facts at my disposal and by using common sense
2. Lets me get personally involved in the tasks at hand, working directly with clients or customers, out in the field rather than away from the action
3. Lets me work with lots of other people in an active and social environment, with variety, fun, and spontaneity

4. Requires skillful handling of people and conflicts, the ability to ease tensions to help groups work more cooperatively, and the ability to motivate others

5. Lets me juggle multiple projects or activities, especially those that utilize my aesthetic taste and sense of design

6. Lets me interact throughout the workday with other easygoing and social people who share my enthusiasm, energy, and realistic point of view

7. Lets me work on projects that are of immediate utility and take into account the needs of people around me

8. Is done in a friendly and relaxed environment, without hidden political agendas

9. Rewards my hard work and good intentions, and where I feel appreciated for my contributions

10. Lets me have fun, enjoy everyday surprises, and where there is a minimum of bureaucracy, rules, or restrictions

Popular Occupations for ESFPs

In listing occupations that are popular among ESFPs, it is important to note that there are successful people of all types in all occupations. However, the following are careers ESFPs may find particularly satisfying and some of the reasons why. This is by no means a comprehensive listing but is included to suggest possibilities you may not have previously considered. Although all of these occupations offer the potential for career satisfaction, the future demand for some careers is anticipated to be greater than for others. Based upon our research, occupations that are italicized in the lists below are forecast to enjoy the fastest rate of growth over the next several years.

EDUCATION/SOCIAL SERVICE
- *Early childhood education teacher*
- *Elementary school teacher*
- Child care provider
- *Teacher: art/drama/music*
- Teacher: physically or visually impaired
- *Athletic coach*
- *Home health social worker*
- *Elder care specialist*
- *Personal care aide*
- *Substance abuse counselor*
- *Child welfare counselor*
- Developer of educational software
- Special education teacher

ESFPs often find careers in education satisfying, especially when working with young children. Elementary and pre-elementary grades sometimes are less formal and structured and offer plenty of opportunities for spontaneous learning experiences. ESFPs enjoy teaching basic skills and helping children get along with one another, a major emphasis in the early grades. They enjoy the activity, energy level, and variety of learning found in elementary school settings. ESFPs, usually active and physically skillful themselves, often enjoy athletics and athletic coaching. Playing sports, learning teamwork, and being active outdoors are enjoyable activities for ESFPs. They are enthusiastic, encouraging, and supportive coaches and teachers.

HEALTH CARE
- *Emergency room nurse*
- *Social worker*
- *Dog trainer/groomer*
- *Medical assistant*
- *Dental assistant/hygienist*
- *Licensed practical nurse (LPN)*
- *Physical therapist*
- *Primary care physician*
- *Home health aide*

- Massage therapist
- *Dietitian/nutritionist*
- Optician/optometrist
- Emergency medical technician (EMT)
- Exercise physiologist
- *Pharmacy technician*
- *Radiological technician*
- Respiratory therapist
- *Veterinarian*
- *Veterinary technologist/technician*
- *Diagnostic medical sonographer*
- *Occupational therapist*
- *Personal fitness trainer*
- *Home care worker for the elderly*
- Hospice worker
- *Emergency room physician*
- Podiatrist
- *Speech-language pathologist/audiologist*
- Pediatrician
- Vocational rehabilitation counselor
- Art therapist
- Chiropractor
- *Registered nurse*
- *Nursing instructor*
- *Cardiology technologist*
- *Transplant coordinator*

Health care and social work provide ESFPs with the opportunity to help others. These careers require the acquisition and then repeated use of skills. Most ESFPs enjoy working directly with other people and thrive on a varied and fast-paced workday. Emergency room nursing requires quick thinking and the ability to calm frightened people during a crisis. Many ESFPs love animals and enjoy working with them either in a medical setting or as trainers. The field of social work allows ESFPs to meet and work with many different people, helping them identify resources available to them. They establish rapport easily and find satisfaction from helping make life easier for someone else.

ENTERTAINMENT/"ACTION"
- Travel consultant/tour operator
- Photographer
- Film producer
- Musician
- Dancer
- Comedian
- Promoter
- *Special events coordinator*
- Painter/illustrator/sculptor
- *Costume/wardrobe specialist*
- News anchor
- Character actor
- Park naturalist/ranger
- Marine mammal trainer
- Flight instructor
- Commercial helicopter pilot
- Entertainment and sports agent
- Forester
- Television camera operator
- Cartoonist/animator
- Insurance fraud investigator
- *Fire investigator*
- Police officer
- Wilderness adventure leader
- Radio/television announcer
- Sketch artist
- Organic farmer
- *Carpenter*

ESFPs enjoy entertaining others, in a formal capacity or informally with friends. They often have a strong sense of aesthetics and a good eye for the fresh and beautiful. Some ESFPs enjoy performance of their art; others simply want to be among other artists in the exciting and ever-changing world of entertainment. ESFPs enjoy travel and make good travel agents because they listen well to what their customers want in a vacation and work hard to find the right match. They are adept at juggling several projects or elements of a project at once, and often find career satisfaction in special event coordination.

BUSINESS/SALES
- Retail merchandiser/planner
- *Public relations specialist*
- Fund-raiser
- Labor relations mediator
- *Receptionist*
- Merchandise planner
- *Diversity manager: human resources*
- Team trainer
- Travel salesperson/broker
- *Insurance agent/broker: health or life*
- *Customer service representative*
- *Insurance and benefits representative*
- Real estate agent
- Sports equipment salesperson/marketer
- Retail salesperson/manager
- Home health care salesperson
- Manufacturer's service representative

ESFPs do not generally enjoy the world of business, especially the corporate world. But those jobs that involve a high degree of interaction with others, and where there is a less structured schedule, can be enjoyable to ESFPs. They often enjoy real estate sales because they spend much of their time out of the office, working directly with a variety of people, showing all kinds of homes. They often enjoy public relations, fund-raising, and mediation, where they are able to use their naturally persuasive nature. These careers let them use their interpersonal skills and their ability to gather information. Many ESFPs are drawn to retail careers, especially when they are able to use their eye for fashion and flair for the dramatic.

SERVICE
- Flight attendant
- *Administrative assistant*
- *Receptionist*
- *Waiter/waitress*
- Host/hostess
- Floral designer

- Police/corrections officer (specialty: remedial training, rehabilitation, counseling)
- Landscape architect
- Chef/head cook
- Interior designer
- Recreational therapist
- *Fitness instructor*
- Gamekeeper
- Landscaper and grounds manager
- Exhibit builder
- Eco-tourism specialist
- Professional photographer
- Merchandise displayer

SCIENCE
- Environmental scientist
- Social conservationist
- Zoologist
- Marine biologist
- Geologist

The service industry attracts ESFPs primarily because of the interpersonal contact and the ability to use acquired skills. ESFPs are often warm and friendly and have the ability to make others feel relaxed and at home. They enjoy the atmosphere present in many restaurants and clubs and are sociable and generous hosts. Their present-moment orientation makes them fun to be around, and it is said that the party often follows the ESFP.

Customizing Your Job Search

Knowing the particular strengths and blind spots of your type can afford you a tremendous advantage in your job search campaign. In all aspects of the process, from conducting research into available positions, identifying and contacting prospective employers, developing personal marketing tools such as résumés, arranging and conducting job interviews, negotiating salaries, to finally accepting a position, people will act true to their type. Being able to capitalize on your assets and compensate for your liabilities can make the difference between a successful or unsuccessful job search.

The differences between types are sometimes subtle and other times dramatic. It is the subtle variations in advice we offer that make the real difference between success and failure in a job search. The concept of "networking," or meeting with and talking to people to gather information about potential jobs, serves as a good example. Extraverts will naturally enjoy networking and are advised to do so on a large scale, while Introverts find more limited and targeted networking, especially with people they already know, easier. Sensors tend to network with people in a defined scope, while Intuitives will go far and wide to find people often seemingly unrelated to their field of interest. Further, Feelers take networking, like everything else, very personally and enjoy establishing warm rapport, while Thinkers will be more objective and detached in their style. Finally, Judgers tend to ask fewer and more structured questions during their networking, while Perceivers could ask questions of all sorts all day long! One valuable search technique, many ways to implement it.

Pathways to Success: Using Your Strengths

As we will detail in the following pages, your strengths and talents for the job search lie in your easygoing and friendly nature and your ability to easily establish rapport. Beware, however, of your tendency to put play before work so that your job search suffers from a lack of results. If this happens, you may become discouraged and settle for a less than ideal job rather than sticking with it and holding out for a career that's really right for you.

As an ESFP, your most effective strategies will build on your abilities to:

Establish rapport and sell yourself.

- Present yourself as a member of a work team, eager to take on new challenges and get along well with others.
- Demonstrate your ability to adapt to new situations and remain cool in a crisis.

When Jake arrived for his interview with the school principal to discuss a job as a social studies teacher, the principal met him at the door to explain that they had had an emergency and the interview would have to be postponed. During a routine fire drill, the office sprinkler system had been activated and several offices were flooded. Water was still pouring out of the ceiling, and the fire department had been summoned but hadn't yet arrived. Jake offered to help. He took off his jacket, grabbed a wrench, and climbed onto the desk. In minutes, the water stopped, and Jake helped the principal carry a table and two chairs into a dry classroom where they conducted the interview. Jake was offered the job then and there, not only for his experience and good references, but because the principal already saw him as a member of the team.

Use your common sense and ability to adapt to turn unexpected problems into opportunities.

- Demonstrate your ability to troubleshoot by recalling for interviewers how you have successfully managed problems in past jobs.
- Look for ways of explaining how your skills can be used in different work situations.

Darcy was ready for a change. She had enjoyed being a travel agent, but now that her children were grown, she wanted to work in some of the exciting places she had sent her clients to over the years. She applied for a position as a tour guide at a Caribbean resort and was worried because one of the requirements for the job was on-site experience. She expected she might be asked about her experience handling some of the unexpected problems that often came up when visitors were touring some of the more rugged areas of the resort. Her career had consisted mostly of sitting behind a desk. So when the question came up during the interview, she was ready. She described how she often handled what her agency called "high-maintenance customers." One couple changed their itinerary so many times that the morning of their flight to Europe, their reservations were accidentally canceled. Darcy noticed this on her computer. Quickly, she checked with several other carriers and booked new reservations on the last available seats for a flight leaving only fifteen minutes after the original one. She printed out new tickets and took them to the airport to meet her customers as they were getting out of their cab. The couple were a bit confused but rapidly became aware of how narrowly Darcy had averted a disaster for them. They made the flight, and Darcy saved the agency a client. The interviewer could see how Darcy's skills would be easily transferred to the "real world" of touring.

Demonstrate a willingness to compromise. Be flexible in negotiations.

- Decide ahead of time what criteria are of critical importance to you in a job and which ones are not. Demonstrate your flexibility by giving in on less important points.

Upon graduation from veterinary school, Rob was interviewing for a staff job at a prestigious emergency animal clinic. While he was similar in standing to many other candidates, Rob got the job because he was willing to accept a rather unusual schedule. For a year, he committed to work three twenty-four-hour weekends a month. The rest of the month was his own, except for being on call for emergencies two other days a month. The other candidates had families or just weren't interested in that kind of schedule. Rob didn't mind because it gave him the free time he wanted to spend with his friends and also pursue his new interest in hang gliding—a sport that is often very crowded at the times when most people are off from work.

Gather a great deal of information, using your keen powers of observation and your ability to get others to talk.

- Talk directly with people working for the company you are considering to learn about some of the less obvious but very important elements worth considering.
- Notice what people wear, what staff offices and lounge areas are like, to be sure that the position you are considering is in a place that you wish to spend your days.

When Tammy and her husband relocated, she began looking for another job in retail merchandising. She started by going to many of the large department stores to see firsthand what they were like. She talked with several sales representatives about how they liked their jobs, what the management was like, and how flexible working conditions were. After she had narrowed her choices down to four stores, she used her personal references from past jobs to gain interviews. She was able to make selections using realistic information, not just what the store management wanted her to know about them.

Conduct lots of informational interviews, using your large network of friends and associates.

- Most people are happy to help you, so ask them to refer you to others who may know of available jobs. Call on the assistance of past employers who know personally your abilities and skills.
- Ask informational interviewers to look at your list of skills and help you brainstorm other kinds of jobs or careers you might be well suited or qualified for.

Even though Jason had been out of college for several years, when he was making a career change, he called on his old college career counselor. They got together over lunch one day and generated a list of possible career options based upon Jason's type, skills, and interests, and the experience he had gained from four years in the real world of work. Jason's career counselor was able to help him see beyond his present career to other, less obvious, possibilities.

Possible Pitfalls

Although all people are unique, there are certain *potential* blind spots that many ESFPs share. We underscore "potential" because some of the following *may* be true of you, while others may clearly not apply. While considering them, you may notice that these tendencies do not relate just to the job search but rather describe pitfalls that you may have experienced in other aspects of your life as well. It is therefore helpful to consider each one in terms of your past experiences by asking yourself, "Is this true for me?" And if so, "How did this tendency prevent me from getting something that I wanted?" You will probably notice that the key to overcoming your blind spots is the conscious and thoughtful development of your third and fourth functions (Thinking and Intuition). We recognize that many of the suggestions will be difficult to implement, but the more you use these functions, the fewer problems they will cause you in the future.

Invest the time in preparing a job search plan before jumping in.

- Spend some time reflecting on where you have been and where you wish to see yourself in the near and distant future to add a long-range perspective to your thinking.
- Examine your real needs in a career and your true motivations before rushing into action.

Consider possibilities in addition to those that currently exist.

- Generate a list of possibilities without prejudging any of them during the process. Include even those that seem outlandish or those for which you may not consider yourself qualified.
- Ask a creative friend to help you imagine what you might do outside of your current career area and list how your skills might transfer to another area.

Develop and follow through on your job search plan.

- Even the tedious parts of the job search—follow-up phone calls, sending thank-you notes after informational interviews, and calling back to check on a possible availability—are important to finding the right job.

- Resist the urge to drop what you've started when a more interesting situation arises or when friends invite you to socialize. It sometimes helps to look at a job search as a job in itself.

Try not to take rejection personally.

- If it happens, remember that you are being turned down for a job only. Many employers make very impersonal decisions, and it is not a personal rejection of you.
- Try not to let yourself get discouraged when things don't happen as quickly as you would like them to. Finding the right job can take several months, but career satisfaction is worth the wait and the hard work.

Don't put off making decisions.

- Waiting to gather enough information before making a decision can be wise. However, if you wait too long, your opportunities may be eliminated and choices made for you.
- Use some critical thinking to see the cause and effect of options you are considering. Ruling out options can help you focus on the best choices for you.

The Final Piece: Changing or Keeping Your Job...the Key to Success for ESFPs

Now that you have a solid understanding of your type, you can see how your natural preferences make you better suited for certain kinds of jobs. You can also see how knowledge of your type-related strengths and weaknesses can help you conduct a more successful job search. But as an ESFP, you've already realized that you are not

equally drawn to *every* career or field listed in the Popular Occupations section. The next and final step is to narrow down the field and find the work you were meant to do.

In addition to Type, several other factors—such as your values, interests, and skills—also contribute to your level of satisfaction on the job. The more compatible you are with your job, the happier you'll be. So prepare to use everything you've learned (in this book and in life) to create *your strategic career plan.* The exercises in Chapter 24, Putting It All Together, are designed to help you do just that.

However, you may have decided it makes more sense (if perhaps only for the moment) to stay in your present job or with your current employer. There may be many valid reasons—financial pressures, family considerations, a tough job market for your specialty, or just bad timing. But take heart! What you've learned in this book can also help you be more content and successful *in your current job.* And should the time come when you're ready to make a major career move, you'll have a much better idea of where you want to go, and how to get there.

"So, if you can't have the job you love (yet!)...love the one you've got."

The simple truth is, with the exception of work on a factory assembly line, the vast majority of jobs allow a good deal of flexibility in the way tasks are performed. Here are some ways you may be able to "massage" your current job into one that better fits your needs:

- Make sure you get enough time to interact with co-workers and colleagues.
- Consider taking a time-management course.

- Ask supervisors to be clear about their expectations.
- Find time during the day to get outside and do something physical.
- Try to find people with opposite strengths to consult with.
- Volunteer to help run and/or participate in recreational or socially responsible activities.
- Think about where you want to be five years from now.
- Set some short-term, achievable goals.
- Make sure you have a variety of tasks to perform; try to avoid routine jobs.
- Avoid working alone for extended periods of time.

One ESFP turns lemons into lemonade:

Because of added responsibilities at work, Sandy found she could no longer make it to the gym to work out on a regular basis. As a former fitness instructor, exercising was something she really liked and missed. After taking an informal survey of people at her company, Sandy discovered several people would be interested in a lunchtime aerobics class—if she ran it. She was able to convince the progressive-minded human resources manager that employees who worked out regularly were happier, healthier (fewer paid sick days!), and therefore more productive. He provided her with a room, bought twenty mats, and agreed to pilot the program for six months to see how it went.

Use what you've got to get what you need.

Simply put, the best advice on how to succeed is to *capitalize on your strengths and compensate for your weaknesses.* Learning how to do this can make the difference between succeeding or failing and loving or hating your work. To help you, we include the following inventory of your potential strengths and weaknesses. And while every individual is unique, as an ESFP, many of the following should apply to you.

Your work-related strengths may include:

- Lots of energy and enjoyment of being active on the job
- Ability to adapt well to change and shift gears quickly
- Sensitivity to people's needs and desire to help them in real ways
- Caring nature; you're a cooperative team player
- Ability to make work fun and exciting
- Practicality and great common sense
- Loyalty to the people and organizations you care about
- Process-oriented approach; you create a lively and fun atmosphere at work
- Flexibility and willingness to take calculated risks and try new approaches
- Desire to cooperate, pitch in, and help people in real and concrete ways
- Ability to clearly assess current resources and conditions and immediately see what needs to be done

Your work-related weaknesses may include:

- Difficulty working alone, especially for extended periods of time
- Tendency to accept things at face value and miss deeper implications
- Dislike of advance preparation; you have trouble organizing your time
- Difficulty seeing opportunities and options that don't exist at the moment
- Tendency to take criticism and negative feedback very personally

- Trouble making decisions
- Impulsiveness and tendency to be easily tempted or distracted
- Dislike of excessive rules and structured bureaucracy

- Difficulty making logical decisions if they conflict with personal feelings
- Resistance to setting long-term goals and difficulty meeting deadlines
- Difficulty disciplining self or others

Using your strengths is easy.
The secret to success for an
ESFP
is learning to:

Think about the future implications,
not take things too personally, and
follow through on commitments.

23

ISFP
Introverted, Sensing, Feeling, Perceiving

"It's the Thought That Counts"

Profile 1: Carol

"Helping the patients and contributing to a smooth-running day."

Carol's newly found career satisfaction is only three years old. For most of her adult life, she held jobs in the insurance industry, doing work she didn't enjoy or look forward to. "I was biding my time all through my children's early years, when I needed to put them first. And I always hoped I would be able to find work I enjoyed someday." Today, Carol looks forward to getting to work, where she feels needed, valued, and appreciated. Carol is a medical assistant in a busy internal-medicine physicians group. She spends her day performing medical diagnostic tests on patients as they wait to see one of the five staff doctors.

Carol's job is about 90 percent patient contact. She performs a variety of medical tests, from blood pressure, weight, and pulse, to more complicated X rays, EKG tests,

and urinalysis. She assists the physicians during examinations and helps the patients before and after the procedures. "I take care of a lot of older patients who need help getting on or off the examination table or getting dressed after the exam. And I see lots of children, too, and enjoy performing the eye tests and other requirements of school physicals." Between patients, Carol files charts, prepares the schedule of patients for the next day, and handles a minimum of billing and insurance, the tasks she never looks forward to. When the office is particularly busy, Carol answers phones, calls in prescriptions for patients, and makes appointments.

"I really love this job because of the patient contact. I'm fascinated with the whole field of medicine, and I'm curious about disease and what makes people get better. I get to perform interesting procedures all day long, and I get to keep learning! The inner workings of the human body are amazing to me. I like the fact that I'm always investigating something new. And I ask the doctors a lot of questions and stay involved in a patient's progress long after my duties with him or her are finished."

Carol's enthusiasm for her work is dampened only when she returns to the task of processing insurance forms (or even looking up an answer to an insurance question), or when she is interrupted from the one-on-one patient contact to answer the busy office phones. The only real source of stress for Carol is when the doctors get behind in their schedule because of their own disorganization. "When that happens, and I know there are lots of people waiting in the reception area and in each exam room, I start to feel stress. There's nothing I can do to help, so I have to return to the tasks I don't enjoy—like answering phones or filing—simply to pass the time until I can get back to working with a patient again. And of course, the patients are upset by the delay, which I don't like to see happen. But I'm pretty easygoing and I know how to take a deep breath and let the stress pass. I even calm the rest of the staff. And at the end of the day, I leave the work at the office and turn my attention to my family."

Carol's family has always been a focus for her. She began working when she left a liberal arts college after two years to get married. She considered continuing her education toward working in occupational therapy or nursing but after a divorce went to work in an insurance company because, "that was the place to meet a lot of men!" It worked because she met and married her husband of eighteen years and continued to work in a variety of claims positions for the next twelve years (interrupted twice for the birth of her son, now fifteen, and her daughter, fourteen). Carol worked at either part-time or temporary positions during those years so she could have time off in the summers and during school vacations to be with her children. "Every job was pretty much the same—all figure work. I sat at a desk with a calculator, completing forms and figuring out rates and commissions." When the jobs became computerized, Carol learned the computer operations. But she was never satisfied. In fact, she wasn't even very conscientious about her job, occasionally calling in sick or leaving work early.

About three years ago, Carol again became a temporary employee at one of the insurance companies so she would have the flexibility to begin looking around for more interesting work. She read a newspaper ad for a temporary medical assistant position. "They offered on-the-job training, which was perfect for me because I had the interest but not the skills. I loved it right away and quit my other job, even before the doctors offered me a permanent one. Eventually a permanent job opened up, and I've been there ever since."

Carol's strengths are dealing with the always varied, often irritable, and sometimes difficult, public. "I'm able to soothe demanding patients and tolerate the interpersonal squabbles in the office. I love to have fun and laugh and so I guess I'm a peacemaker. I just figure if you're nice to others, they'll be nice to you. I use that ability to keep from getting flustered when the office goes crazy so I can help keep things moving smoothly." In fact, Carol credits her contributions to the office as one of her greatest work accomplishments. That, and the courage it took to leave the tried-and-true, safe world of insurance for a totally different career.

But her work is not her life. Her children, husband, and friends are still central to her happiness. She enjoys getting together with a group of close friends to play games and is always reading at least one book. "I panic if I finish one book and don't have another ready immediately!" These days, Carol finds she is more confident and conscientious about her work. "Because I enjoy it so much, I'm more careful about not making mistakes."

As Carol has gotten older, she realizes that she always wanted to be a nurse but spent the early years paying attention only to the present moment rather than doing a lot of planning for the future. "I've never been terribly career-oriented and kept things on the back burner while my kids and husband came first. I think I'd really like to go ahead and get my degree in nursing at some point. I think I would enjoy a hospital setting, but I'd probably be happy at a lot of jobs within the medical field. It'll happen when I'm ready."

Carol is much more self-confident than she used to be, with strong self-esteem and a clearer sense of direction for her life. While she still considers herself easygoing and tolerant, she has a better idea of what she wants and is ready to make that a priority. "For me, the realization came that my life was about half over and I wanted to do something good with what was left. I didn't want to find that I was stuck in a rut, trapped, and unable to make any changes because I was too old. I actually make *less* money today than I did in insurance, but that doesn't really matter to me because I feel I'm doing something worthwhile that benefits other people. It's so rewarding to hear the patients say how much I helped them. But if I wasn't appreciated, they couldn't pay me enough money to stay!"

Why This Career Works for Carol

Carol loves the fact that her job keeps her so busy. Her work combines two factors that many Experiencers (SPs) find gratifying: the opportunity to use specific physical skills they have mastered and the chance to use them with a variety of different people. Like many Experiencers, Carol is also a very curious person, and she is most curious about how the human body works. Her job involves investigating and constantly learning more about it, which she finds fascinating. Another reason Carol loves her work is that she only works regular hours, which leaves plenty of time to enjoy her free time with her family and friends.

As an introverted Feeler (dominant), Carol is motivated by what she believes is right and what feels good to her. Because she is naturally a sympathetic and caring person, she receives tremendous gratification from helping patients get well. Carol is also a harmonizer. Her gentle nature helps keep the office running smoothly, and she gets additional rewards from working with doctors who appreciate her. In fact, experiencing supportive relationships is so important to her, she took a pay cut to accept this job. Carol deals in data. Taking patient histories, performing examinations, recording test results, explaining and conducting procedures on patients, and assisting the doctors with certain procedures and treatments are some of the ways Carol extraverts her Sensing (auxiliary).

The emergence of Carol's Intuition (third function) probably played an important role in helping her leave the insurance field in which she had worked for most of her adult life. It was only when she started soul-searching and asking herself what work would really be meaningful to her that she made the change. Her Intuition has also helped her to take a longer-range view and consider pursuing a nursing degree, for, although she loves what she does now, she realizes that she might need other challenges in the future.

Meet the Millennial

Name: Matt
Age: 32
Musician and record producer

"Music is really all about people."

Backstory

Music has been the main love of Matt's life ever since he picked up a saxophone in the fourth grade. He played saxophone in his high school jazz program, traveling for competitions and gigs, and played guitar in three different bands outside of school. However, there weren't a lot of career musicians around for Matt to emulate: "Nobody ever really suggested that you could write or play music for a living." So Matt went off to college and spent a few years with an undeclared major, finally settling on a double major in music and American maritime studies.

In college, Matt got into a cappella and other vocal arrangements, and began to think he could build a career arranging and recording music. In his senior year, he met with some alumni who worked in the music industry. Choosing to attend an arts and technology school in Florida called Full Sail University, Matt matriculated into the recording arts program. There he became familiar with the technical side of recording, studying signal flow and electricity and learning how recording equipment works. "I learned how to take things apart and put them back together, how to use all the gear and about acoustics—all that practical techie stuff." He became

proficient in Pro Tools, and after graduation he moved to Los Angeles and started applying for internships at all the major recording studios.

After a few starting gigs interning and working at recording studios, Matt landed a job as an assistant recording engineer at a major studio. Though the work was grueling—fourteen-hour workdays, seven days a week—Matt was happy to be moving up. "I was just stoked to be involved; to get to contribute in any way with these major bands was just a really big deal." He quickly progressed to editing, and when they found out he could play horns, he started adding his parts to the recordings. "That was amazing—getting not only to edit but to contribute musically to these records." After a year, Matt began handling more of the recording side of things, working with artists and garnering greater experience and independence.

After four years, Matt had learned enough to strike out on his own, and he started working freelance with singer/songwriters, alternately writing, engineering, and recording music in Los Angeles and New York. "I definitely took a big pay cut, and I wasn't working on the prestigious Billboard top-ten stuff I was used to. But I didn't have anybody hovering over me, and I was my own boss, which felt really good." He also joined the band Reel Big Fish and now tours six to seven months of the year as a saxophone player and backup vocalist.

A Good Fit

As an ISFP, Matt is a dominant Feeling type. He is soft spoken, even keeled, and patient, and his specialty is what he calls "studio manner"—like bedside manner in medicine. "I'm good at making other artists feel comfortable, so I tend to get good performances out of them. People have fun and feel comfortable in the studio, and they like recording with me because I make it easy for them." Relationships with people are also what Matt loves about touring and performing, although in a totally different way. He enjoys the camaraderie with his bandmates and gets a buzz off of the audience. "Doing something onstage and getting that instant feedback, like somebody cheering for that particular part you just played, looking right at you and screaming because they think what you did was awesome, is a really good feeling." Matt likes to sense that his work has an impact on people, and seeing people enjoying the product of his labors is very gratifying. With Sensing as his auxiliary function, Matt is good at staying in the present and has a great capacity to understand the complex and technical aspects of sound engineering and recording. Being an Introvert makes the intimate studio setting ideal, and Matt forms real one-on-one relationships with artists. As an Experiencer, Matt finds freelance much more appealing because he is able to be his own boss, managing his own time and working outside of the constraints of a typical nine-to-five job. "I can't think of any other job in the entire world that I'd want to spend time doing."

Looking Ahead

Matt already feels like he has his dream job. However, he would make a few adjustments if he could, including touring less with his band. Spending four months of the year on the road and eight months at home making music would be ideal. In five to ten years, he would like to be doing what he is doing now with more time at home, and can see wanting to stay put and have a family.

Profile 2: Thomas

"For me there's really no line between work and play."

Thomas is an elite craftsperson—building something most people will never own. He designs and builds made-to-order lightweight, premium bicycle frames and assembled bicycles. Thomas is a racing cyclist and an uncompromising perfectionist in both the design and construction of flawless frames. He's been in business by himself for nearly twenty years doing something that sometimes gets awfully close to being a hobby for him. "It's my business, but it's also who I am."

Thomas's clients place orders from all over the country for the highest-quality bicycle frames available. The frames are the most crucial part of the bike, especially for a racer, because a less than perfectly aligned bicycle can create problems and injuries for the racer. Although many of his customers never race the bikes he makes, all of them can afford the top-quality product. Thomas compares his bikes to custom-made performance cars or, at the very least, a tailor-made outfit. The frames are made to the size, riding, and handling style of the person who will ride it. After the extensive measurements are made, Thomas cuts the finest-quality tubing to size and then uses complicated and very precise joining processes. He has specially created paints and ornamental finish work done on the frames so they are as handsome as they are functional. He works alone in his studio, producing eighty to one hundred frames a year. "It's an extremely precise operation. It's time-consuming, and there's no faking it here. But it doesn't take any longer to do a good job than to do a mediocre job."

Thomas enjoys everything about his work. He loves making something all by himself. He handles everything that happens in his business, even answering the telephone and shipping orders. He enjoys the direct involvement he has with his customers and the emotional attachment he feels to each piece he makes. And because he is a user first and a maker second, there exists a natural and close tie between his thriving interest—bicycle making—and his lifestyle—bike racing.

Thomas is energized by attaining near-perfection. "You have to bear in mind that they are handmade, so flawlessness is impossible. But I have very exacting standards and only sell those frames that meet or exceed my standards. So when I occasionally exceed even my standards, I find that thrilling."

There's very little about the business that Thomas doesn't enjoy. However, some of the purely business activities and tasks create some stress for him. "I don't really know anything about business, but I've been winging it since 1974 and it's worked fairly well. It's sometimes difficult not knowing when the next order will come in, or if overseas suppliers will continue to provide critical supplies so I will always be ready for the next order. It can be chaos in my head planning the business things." In fact, he usually does a year's worth of taxes and accounting the last weeks of the calendar year while everyone else is out holiday shopping. "I realize I probably pay more in taxes than I would have to if I did them quarterly and all that. But I just can't get up for it more often. I'm not in this business for the reason most people are in business. I'm doing this because I enjoy it."

The only sources of stress are the occasional customers who want to "make a project out of me. They feel compelled to call all the time to check on the status of their bike. For them, it's a big purchase, and they're spending their leisure time on the phone finding out about their newest leisure product. I won't have any unhappy customers, so I won't turn any away. And I'm not real assertive about telling them I haven't got the time to talk on the phone. My customers spend a good deal of money, so I guess they think that talking to me about their biking experiences, and whatever else, is part of the package. That can be wearing."

Thomas used to dwell on that stress and think about it at home and on his daily rides. But he's learned to detach himself a bit and not be bothered by the decreased number of bikes he's producing, because he maintains the superior quality of his products.

His career in bicycle making began quite by accident. Waiting six months for a delayed admission to college, he traveled to Europe to "kill some time and do something interesting." Already an avid cyclist, he took a job learning to make bikes in a family-operated bike-making business, simply for the experience. He returned to the United States, and again, quite by coincidence, got a job with an importer of bicycles made by the same family he had worked with in Europe. For two and a half years, he helped the company expand their bike line, working at trade shows, doing some repairs, and acting as a technical expert. "I still didn't know very much, and I was really just enjoying myself using someone else's money to make bikes. Eventually the owner began to pressure me to increase my productivity and began making my work into a chore. I simply didn't have the skill to make bikes any faster. It took me a while, but I finally just left." With a small investment from his family, and no business or long-range plans, he started his own business. "I was only motivated to keep doing what I liked."

These days Thomas is proud of the longevity he has in his business but with characteristic modesty attributes that only to the fact that he just never stopped doing what he's doing. He receives a great deal of publicity in biking magazines and other press and is often described as being uncompromising. "My experience as a racer helps me always remember that I'm making a quality bike that has to work perfectly. But I'm also pleased that I am good at making something real, something that gives people joy." The tangible evidence of his customers' pleasure is the huge box of thank-you letters and notes he keeps in his shop.

Outside of his work and his riding, Thomas's mother, sisters, and aunt are the most important element in his life. He is unmarried and without children, so his small and very close group of friends means a lot to him, too.

He continues always to strive to learn from his mistakes and *never* be rushed into anything. "I just won't do something I'm not really sure about, so some things take me a long time to do. Like advertising. It's a necessity, but it took me a while to decide to commit to it."

"I've really gotten pretty good at dealing with all kinds of people. I think socially I'm better prepared, or savvy as they say, dealing with the really high-society people who are my customers. See, I'm just the same with everyone." He's also better able to separate himself from his work. "I used to have a real emotional reaction when things didn't go right, or people didn't understand the difference in quality between what some magazine said was the best new thing and what I make, which is tried and true. But I don't take things as personally anymore." He also sees himself and his business within the large context of expert craftspeople and artisans of all kinds. "I find myself looking around more and having a clearer perspective on myself within the world. I can see trends in this business and am less surprised by the ebb and flow of business.

"I guess the part that feels like success and satisfaction to me is that I'm not trying to sell anything, I'm just doing what I enjoy, being honest and true to my convictions. I have an enthusiasm for life and work. But it all turns on whether my customers like what I do. I am totally satisfied when I create something that meets my high standards and people try it out and tell me that the bike is as good as they thought it would be. Other people can assign accolades to my work. I just like what I do and love it when other people do, too."

Why This Career Works for Thomas

As with many Experiencers, one of the reasons Thomas's work is so satisfying is that it is also fun. He loves everything about bikes—building, riding, and racing them.

Therefore, it is both the process—the building—and the product—the bikes themselves—that Thomas enjoys. Another satisfying aspect of his work for Thomas is the freedom that it provides him. He is totally autonomous and free to close his shop—for an hour to go for a ride or a week to go on a tour—whenever the spirit moves him. Thomas also enjoys the physical activity involved in building bikes—a component that is also important to many Experiencers.

For Thomas, building bikes is a labor of love. He puts all of himself into each bike he makes. In fact, he feels as if he is giving away a part of himself when he sells a bike. This depth of feeling, and his belief that a bike must be made by hand to each person's unique specifications and be of absolute top quality, come from his introverted Feeling (dominant). But Thomas also builds relationships—lasting relationships—with his clients, whom he gets to know and often stays in touch with for many years.

Thomas extraverts his Sensing (auxiliary) in many ways. First he finds out all the pertinent facts about the person he is building the bike for, including such detailed information as size, weight, and build, exactly how the person pedals, and what he or she wants the bike to do. Then he takes meticulous measurements. He does all the physical work by hand, including bending metal, filing, finishing. His Sensing also helps him handle the ordering, buying, and billing for his company.

Evidence that Thomas is developing his Intuition (third function) can be found in the fact that recently he has begun looking at the biking industry from a larger perspective. Rather than focusing only on his part, he is now more interested in trends—where the industry is going, and how it is changing. He has also developed a curiosity about other custom craftsmen who work with different

products but in a style similar to his. He even shows signs of developing his Thinking (fourth function) in his growing objectivity about others' reactions—he doesn't take them so personally, and he can let them go rather than dwelling on them.

Common Threads

Although Carol, Thomas, and Matt have different backgrounds, experiences, and careers, there are certain common threads woven through their stories. Their specific interests and abilities may differ, but owing to their similar temperament values, the *same hierarchy* of their psychological functions, and the "world" they use them in (inner or outer), there are certain observations we can make about the needs of many ISFPs.

What follows is a list of the most important elements—the formula, if you will—for ISFP satisfaction. Given the uniqueness of all individuals—even those who share the same type—this list will not describe each ISFP equally well.

The important thing is that these ten elements, with varying degrees of intensity and in different orders of importance, identify what ISFPs need to be satisfied.

After you have reviewed this list, we recommend that you go back and prioritize the elements in order of *their importance to you*. When doing this, think of past work experiences as well as your present job, and what you found particularly satisfying or unsatisfying. Try to look for *themes* that run through several experiences, not just the events that might be true for one work situation but not for another.

As an ISFP, career satisfaction means doing work that:

1. Is consistent with my strong, inner values, and is something I care deeply

about and want to contribute my energy and talents to

2. If done with others is in a supportive and affirming climate where I am a loyal and cooperative member of a team

3. Requires attention to detail, where I work with real things that benefit other people and have practical applications

4. Gives me freedom to work independently but nearby other compatible and courteous people, and where I don't feel restricted by excessive rules, structure, or inflexible operating procedures

5. Lets me be adaptable yet committed; where I have a sense of purpose and am able to see and experience the actual results of my accomplishments

6. Lets me use my sense of taste and aesthetics to enhance my physical work space, personalize it, and make others feel more comfortable

7. Is done in a quietly cheerful and cooperative setting and where interpersonal conflicts are kept to a minimum

8. Gives me an opportunity to experience inner growth and development within a context of work that I feel is important

9. Lets me handle problems promptly and simply, offering practical help

10. Does not require me to perform regular public speaking, lead a large group of people I don't know well, or give people negative feedback

Popular Occupations for ISFPs

In listing occupations that are popular among ISFPs, it is important to note that there are successful people of all types in all occupations. However, the following are careers ISFPs may find particularly satisfying and some of the reasons why. This is by no means a comprehensive listing but is included to suggest possibilities you may not have previously considered. Although all of these occupations offer the potential for career satisfaction, the future demand for some careers is anticipated to be greater than for others. Based upon our research, the occupations that are italicized in the lists below are forecasted to enjoy the fastest rate of growth over the next several years.

CRAFTS/ARTISAN
- Fashion designer
- *Carpenter*
- Jeweler
- Sound designer
- Musician
- Recording engineer
- Gardener
- Potter
- Painter
- Dancer
- Designer: interior/landscape
- Chef
- Artist
- Cartoonist/animator
- Sketch artist
- Tailor
- Musical instrument maker

The chief appeal of these careers for ISFPs is the opportunity to work with their hands in the creation of something attractive and, oftentimes, useful. They enjoy using their five senses in a practical way as well as working with real things in the real world. Many of these careers offer ISFPs the chance to work flexible hours and the freedom to schedule their own work. Most ISFPs prefer to be autonomous, without having to conform to administrative guidelines.

HEALTH CARE
- *Visiting nurse*
- *Physical therapist*

- Massage therapist
- *Radiology technologist*
- *Medical assistant*
- *Dental assistant/hygienist*
- *Veterinary assistant*
- *Home health aide*
- *Primary care physician*
- *Dietitian/nutritionist*
- Optician/optometrist
- Exercise physiologist
- *Occupational therapist*
- Art therapist
- Respiratory therapist
- *Licensed practical nurse (LPN)*
- *Surgical technologist*
- *Personal fitness trainer*
- *Surgeon*
- *Veterinarian*
- *Speech-language pathologist/audiologist*
- *Pharmacist*
- *Emergency room physician*
- Pediatrician
- *Cardiology technologist*
- Audiometrist
- Pharmaceutical researcher
- *Registered nurse*
- *Physician's assistant*
- Hospice worker/director
- *Substance abuse counselor*
- *Pheresis technician*
- Recreational therapist

ISFPs often find satisfaction in health care careers, especially those where they are able to work directly with clients and patients. They enjoy the hands-on element of many of the therapy occupations, helping others either physically or emotionally, during or after a crisis. They are generally very observant and able to respond well to subtle changes and like short-term problem solving. An essential ingredient in satisfaction within these careers and any other career for ISFPs is to be able to see and experience feedback

for their contributions and to believe in the importance of the work they are doing.

SCIENCE/TECHNICAL
- Forester
- Botanist
- Geologist
- Mechanic
- Marine biologist
- Zoologist
- Television camera operator
- Soil conservationist
- Archaeologist
- Systems analyst
- Aviation inspector
- Electrical home appliance repairer

ISFPs often enjoy work that deals with facts rather than with theory. They tend to prefer using practical and active skills. The opportunity to be out-of-doors is particularly appealing to ISFPs, and they welcome change and variety in their work.

SALES/SERVICE
- *Elementary school teacher: science/art*
- Police/corrections officer
- Crisis hotline operator
- Storekeeper
- Beautician
- Travel salesperson
- *Preferred customer sales representative*
- Merchandise planner
- Sports equipment salesperson
- Home health care salesperson
- *Home health social worker*
- *Child welfare counselor*
- *Social worker (elderly and child day care issues)*
- *Personal care aide*
- Animal groomer/trainer
- *Preschool teacher*
- Teacher: emotionally impaired
- Teacher: physically challenged
- *Teacher's aide, paraprofessional*

- Landscape architect
- *Child care worker*
- *Elder care specialist*
- Art therapist
- Fish and game warden
- *Bicycle designer/repairer*
- Insurance fraud investigator
- *Interpreter/translator*
- Locomotive engineer
- Airplane dispatcher and air traffic controller
- Commercial airplane and helicopter pilot
- High school and college athletic coach
- Genealogist
- Residence counselor
- *Recreation worker*
- Horticultural specialty grower
- Florist
- Organic farmer
- *Firefighter*
- Wilderness adventure leader

Many ISFPs find fulfilling work in service careers. Careers that let them help meet the needs of people or animals in specific and tangible ways are most rewarding. They tend to prefer work environments that share their values and foster and encourage interpersonal harmony, cooperation, and appreciation for the work of all. Many ISFPs enjoy teaching a specific subject area, usually with young children, where they have the opportunity to include lots of spontaneity and fun.

BUSINESS
- Bookkeeper
- Legal secretary
- Clerical supervisor
- Administrator
- *Paralegal*
- Insurance appraiser
- Insurance examiner: property and casualty

Clerical careers, if in the right kind of environment, can provide satisfaction for ISFPs. The critical factor is the ability to use their excellent practical skills but in a supportive and affirming climate. ISFPs work best when working as part of a team, in a stable work group that respects the individual need for privacy and growth. They prefer work settings that allow them to create and maintain a pleasant and personalized work environment.

Customizing Your Job Search

Knowing the particular strengths and blind spots of your type can afford you a tremendous advantage in your job search campaign. In all aspects of the process, from conducting research into available positions, identifying and contacting prospective employers, developing personal marketing tools such as résumés, arranging and conducting job interviews, negotiating salaries, to finally accepting a position, people will act true to their type. Being able to capitalize on your assets and compensate for your liabilities can make the difference between a successful and an unsuccessful job search.

The differences between types are sometimes subtle and other times dramatic. It is the subtle variations in advice we offer that make the real difference between success or failure in a job search. The concept of "networking," or meeting with and talking to people to gather information about potential jobs, serves as a good example. Extraverts will naturally enjoy networking and are advised to do so on a large scale, while Introverts find more limited and targeted networking, especially with people they already know, easier. Sensors tend to network with people in a defined scope, while Intuitives will go far and wide to find people often seemingly unrelated to their field of interest. Further, Feelers take networking, like everything else, very personally and enjoy establishing warm rapport, while Thinkers will be more objective and detached in their style. Finally, Judgers tend to ask fewer and more structured questions during their networking, while Perceivers could ask questions of all sorts all day long! One valuable search technique, many ways to implement it.

Pathways to Success: Using Your Strengths

As we will detail in the following pages, your strengths and talents for the job search lie in your personal warmth, desire to please others, and commonsense approach to problems. However, in order to find a satisfying career, you will need to work hard at developing your assertiveness and objectivity so you don't take rejection personally and become discouraged.

As an ISFP, your most effective strategies will build on your abilities to:

Conduct research and collect a lot of data.

- Read as much as you can about the field, position, or organization you are consid- ering. Gather information about a spe- cific company by reading past articles that discuss the company or the industry as well as company annual reports.
- Go check out the company or business as part of your preparation for inter- viewing. Look at the way people dress, act, and seem to feel about working where they do. Can you imagine your- self there?

Marc was preparing for an interview for an assistant curator position at a science museum. He decided to get as familiar with the museum and its current exhibits as he could before the interview. He spent hours in the museum getting a feel for the layout and organization. He read as much as possible about the new curator to learn about her career path and her goals for the museum. By the time the interview came, Marc had plenty of questions and was able to offer specific thoughts about what was needed when he was asked what he might contribute to the organization.

Conduct limited, targeted networking.

- Start with your close friends, family, and co-workers (past and present). Ask them to help you generate a list of people who might know of jobs for which you would be qualified.
- Conduct informational interviews with people who actually hold the position you are looking for. Ask them questions to learn what the job, its responsibilities, and limitations really are.

Roger began his networking at one of many summer backyard cookouts he and his friends had each summer. He began telling his friends of his boredom with his current job and how he wanted to do something different. His friends began brainstorming ideas and then came up with people they knew for Roger to talk to. It was more of a game than a task, and Roger was surprised how much help he got from just one evening of talking.

Build and use a support system.

- Remember that searching for a job often takes more time and energy than per- forming a job. Ask friends for advice and support during this difficult period.
- Take people up on their offers to help. Many of the best contacts are made through purely social connections. Don't rule out anyone as a source of information.

Learn by doing.

- Look for opportunities to be trained on the job, or where employers offer a training program, giving preference to trainees after completing the program.
- Offer your services on a volunteer basis to learn the skills needed to perform the job you seek. You will have both the skills and some real experience to demonstrate to prospective employers.

Remember how Carol found the job she enjoys? The physicians' office offered on-the-job training, which she took while working temporarily at her previous job. She got the chance to learn on the job and quickly understood what the job would really be like. Luckily for Carol, she didn't need to try more than one program.

Follow your impulses and natural curiosity.

- Use your short-term problem-solving capabilities by organizing the sometimes long and overwhelming job search into manageable pieces. Reward yourself when you meet each goal of people contacted or phone calls made.
- If an obstacle arises, meet the challenge with a willingness to adapt. Demonstrate to prospective employers your ability to accept and respond to changing situations.

After careful consideration, Colleen decided that she would enjoy being a dog trainer—it matched her interests, her love of animals, and the opportunity to work hands-on with dogs and with their owners. She researched the best grooming and training center and went on an interview. To her disappointment, she learned that there were no openings for a trainer, but she was offered a job in the grooming department

and told there was the possibility that a training position would open up "down the road." Her desire to work with animals and the chance to be associated with the high-quality operation she saw during her interview persuaded her to take the job. She decided it was worth the gamble and that it would also give her a chance to demonstrate to the owner her ability to learn quickly and become a valuable member of the staff. After four months, Colleen's patience was rewarded when a trainer position became available and she was offered the job.

Possible Pitfalls

Although all people are unique, there are certain *potential* blind spots which many ISFPs share. We specify "potential" because some of the following *may* be true of you, while others may clearly not apply. While considering them, you may notice that these tendencies do not relate just to the job search but rather describe pitfalls that you may have experienced in other aspects of your life as well. It is therefore helpful to consider each one in terms of your past experiences by asking yourself, "Is this true for me?" And if so, "How did this tendency prevent me from getting something that I wanted?" You will probably notice that the key to overcoming your blind spots is the conscious and thoughtful development of your third and fourth functions (Intuition and Thinking). We recognize that many of the suggestions will be difficult to implement, but the more you use these functions, the fewer problems they will cause you in the future.

Consider all data available to you, even those that may contradict your personal feelings.

- Look at the "hard consequences" of your actions and decisions. List the pros and cons of a job so you are sure to consider both the positive and the potential negative as well.

- Develop a method of analyzing information before accepting it at face value.

Look for options besides those readily available at the moment.

- Generate a list of possible job options without limiting yourself to what you have done in the past or what you are immediately qualified for.
- Use your ideas of a fantasy job as a springboard to thinking more creatively. Ask a friend who knows you well to help you, and make it a game.

Work hard to prioritize your activities and keep yourself organized.

- Use your skills at short-term planning to get things done and to keep from becoming overwhelmed with the size of the task.
- Develop a complete outline for your career search. Include all the perceivable steps that will be necessary along the way.

Try to make more objective decisions.

- Don't overemphasize the importance of rapport developed with an interviewer. Try to develop some healthy skepticism about others to avoid being too trusting.
- Pay attention to the less tangible but critically important factors, such as the corporate culture and employer's philosophy, which will help keep you from becoming disillusioned after taking the job.

Focus your attention on the future so you will see beyond the present reality and understand choices in their larger context.

- Try imagining a job one, five, and ten years from now. Will this opportunity be one that allows you to grow, or will you be limited in the company or organization?
- Look at the business within the market and decide if the way it is growing or changing will still be acceptable to you in the future. Be sure it isn't just the people you will be working with *now* that make the job appealing.

The Final Piece: Changing or Keeping Your Job . . . the Key to Success for ISFPs

Now that you have a solid understanding of your type, you can see how your natural preferences make you better suited for certain kinds of jobs. You can also see how knowledge of your type-related strengths and weaknesses can help you conduct a more successful job search. But as an ISFP, you've already realized that you are not equally drawn to *every* career or field listed in the Popular Occupations section. The next and final step is to narrow down the field and find the work you were meant to do.

In addition to Type, several other factors—such as your values, interests, and skills—also contribute to your level of satisfaction on the job. The more compatible you are with your job, the happier you'll be. So prepare to use everything you've learned (in this book and in life) to create *your strategic career plan*. The exercises in Chapter 24, Putting It All Together, are designed to help you do just that.

However, you may have decided it makes more sense (if perhaps only for the moment) to stay in your present job or with your current employer. There may be many valid reasons—financial pressures, family considerations, a tough job market for your specialty, or just bad timing. But take heart! What you've learned in this book can also help you be more content and successful *in your current job*. And should the time come when you're ready to make a major career move, you'll have a much better idea of where you want to go, and how to get there.

"So, if you can't have the job you love (yet!)...love the one you've got."

The simple truth is, with the exception of work on a factory assembly line, the vast majority of jobs allow a good deal of flexibility in the way tasks are performed. Here are some ways you may be able to "massage" your current job into one that better fits your needs:

- Seek help to resolve any interpersonal conflicts.
- Consider taking an assertiveness-training class.
- Ask supervisors to be clear about their expectations.
- Find time during the day to "recharge" by yourself.
- Do things that will allow you to help, support, and connect with co-workers.
- Try to make sure there is some variety in your daily activities.
- Participate in recreational activities.
- Seek others with complementary skills to help evaluate your ideas.
- Think about where you want to be five years from now.
- Set short-term, achievable goals.
- Try to find others at work who share similar interests and values.

One ISFP turns lemons into lemonade:

Dana worked for a large pharmaceutical company. When she recently became widowed, she became aware of how many other women in the company were also facing the challenge of working and raising children alone. Although hardly a natural organizer, Dana put an ad in the company newsletter to see if there was any interest in forming a group to help each other with everyday challenges, like carpooling kids to activities, baby-sitting, etc. To her surprise and delight, more than a dozen people responded. The group ended up meeting more than her immediate, practical needs. It became a source of emotional support as well, and she developed several close and sustaining friendships.

Use what you've got to get what you need.

Simply put, the best advice on how to succeed is to *capitalize on your strengths and compensate for your weaknesses.* Learning how to do this can make the difference between succeeding or failing and loving or hating your work. To help you, we include the following inventory of your potential strengths and weaknesses. And while every individual is unique, as an ISFP, many of the following should apply to you.

Your work-related strengths may include:

- Ability to welcome change and adapt well to new situations
- Sensitivity to people's needs and desire to help them in real ways
- Practicality and realistic perceptions
- Good common sense
- Warmth and generosity
- Loyalty to people and organizations you care deeply about
- Attention to important details, especially those that concern people
- Thoughtfulness and ability to focus on current needs
- Willingness to support the organization's goals
- Ability to clearly assess current conditions and see what needs fixing
- Flexibility and willingness to take calculated risks and try new approaches

Your work-related weaknesses may include:

- Tendency to accept things at face value and miss deeper implications
- Inability to see opportunities and options that don't exist at the moment
- Tendency to take criticism and negative feedback very personally
- Dislike of preparing in advance; you have trouble organizing your time
- Trouble making decisions

- Dislike of excessive rules and overly structured bureaucracy
- Difficulty making logical decisions if they conflict with personal feelings
- Unwillingness to risk disharmony to fight for your idea or position
- Tendency to become overwhelmed by large or highly complicated tasks
- Resistance to setting long-term goals and difficulty meeting deadlines
- Difficulty disciplining direct-reports or criticizing others

*Using your strengths is easy.
The secret to success for an*
ISFP
is learning to:

Assert yourself, step back and consider the "big picture," and not take things too personally.

24 PUTTING IT ALL TOGETHER

Creating Your Personal
Career Plan

The unique individuals we have met in the previous pages show the infinite variety of satisfying job options available for people of all types. Indeed, there are probably several careers you would find satisfying. But it's not enough to select a job from a list of careers other people of your type have found satisfying. It's not even enough to know your type. Real success lies in taking your awareness of your type-related strengths and weaknesses and combining it with an honest appraisal of your personal interests and values. The goal is to find the right match—the career that will let you do what you do best and enjoy most, one that corresponds to your personal interests and is consistent with your basic personality functions and values. And that combination will be unique to you.

To begin to help you visualize the process for yourself, here are examples of how several clients of different types successfully blended their skills and experiences with their individual interests to find the career of their dreams.

Ernie had a career that many ENFPs would have enjoyed. As an organizational development consultant, Ernie worked with teams in businesses to help them understand one another and work more effectively

together. While he enjoyed being self-employed, he was growing bored with teaching virtually the same program year after year and was also thirsty for the intellectual challenge of learning something new. When we asked him to develop a list of interests, Ernie placed the law near the top. His father had been a lawyer, and Ernie had always been fascinated with the legal system and enjoyed watching television shows and seeing movies about lawyers. But he didn't have enough interest in the technical side of law to go through law school and become a lawyer himself. Instead, he decided to use his consulting skills and understanding of psychology to become a trial consultant. Today, Ernie works directly with attorneys, helping them increase their own communication and presentation effectiveness. He also helps attorneys select jurors who are more naturally predisposed to view their side of the case favorably.

Paula, an ENTJ, had been a journalist for nearly twenty years, working her way up to the position of editorial writer at a major daily newspaper. She enjoyed the opportunity to "shine a light on the injustices in society" and spur government to make important changes. She enjoyed the challenge of her job and the daily opportunities to see her articles published in the newspaper.

As a child of the sixties, Paula had been an active and vocal member of the women's and civil rights movements, and led the charge to clean up the environment. She maintained those interests long after the sixties were over. In her job as an editorial writer, she began to believe she could do more to further those long-held goals and interests. She decided that she wanted to be a shaper of policy rather than a commentator of change.

So Paula made a list of all the people she knew in her area whose opinions she respected and whose values were similar to her own. She called on these individuals, taking many of them to breakfast or lunch to inquire about potential job opportunities. At one breakfast, she met with a politician she admired. He told her that a position as his executive assistant would become available soon. One of the things he was asking all candidates to do was write a speech on a highly technical financial strategy. Paula researched the information over the next two days and wrote and submitted an excellent speech by the deadline. She was offered the job and is enjoying her newfound opportunity to make a real difference and be a part of important policymaking decisions.

After graduating from high school, Janice, an ISFJ, got a good job as an executive secretary for a busy real estate developer. While she made a few friends with the other support personnel, was well paid, and didn't even mind the long hours she put in, she just didn't feel she was making a significant contribution. She was a natural "helper" and the only person she was helping was her boss—to get richer. Back in high school, Janice had considered becoming a nurse or doctor, but her parents had been unable to afford to send her to either nursing or medical school. While she had managed to

save some money, she couldn't afford to quit her job and go to medical school. Finally, Janice decided to follow her original ambition but realized she needed to consider a less expensive alternative to becoming a nurse or doctor. She enrolled in a night program to become a dental hygienist. She kept her job with the developer and gave up her lunch hour a couple of times a week to work for one of the other secretaries, who in turn stayed late when necessary on the nights Janice had class. After two years, Janice was able to leave the developer's firm and start working for a small group dental practice that emphasized education with its patients. Janice was able to work using her new skills, helping other people learn about taking care of their teeth and health. Through working closely with her patients and helping them become healthier and happier, Janice found the satisfaction she had been missing.

Matching Your Personality to a Career You Can Love

Evaluating opportunities to determine if they are really right for you is sometimes a difficult task. Guided by the criteria for career satisfaction and the job search strategies in your type chapter, you've most likely been considering specific career options already, perhaps psychologically trying on the various possibilities. To develop those options into concrete opportunities, you'll need to examine them closely and measure their suitability for you. A job that's great for one person may not be quite right for another—even if they share the same type.

Ten Steps to Creating a Personal Career Plan

While it's helpful and even fun to learn from other people like you as you did in your type chapter, you are a unique individual and need to now take the time to put on paper a true and honest assessment of yourself. The following exercises have been created for you to complete right here in the book, to get the most out of your type chapter. We strongly suggest you take your time with this important process because answering the questions as thoughtfully and honestly as you can will help you to zero in on satisfying career options and then to design a job search campaign that gets results. Good luck!

Step 1: Your Unique Personality Strengths and Weaknesses

This exercise can help determine whether you have identified your "true" type and highlight some of your most important personality characteristics. How well does this brief description fit you?

Using your type profiles from Chapter 3 (Mirror, Mirror), list the key words or phrases which are MOST true of you and provide examples that demonstrate these qualities.

1. _____

_____

Example:

_____

_____

2. _____

Example:

_____

_____

3. _____

Example:

_____

_____

Which phrases (if any) are NOT true about you?

1. _____

Example:

_____

_____

2. _____

Example:

_____

_____

3. _____

Example:

_____

_____

Again, using your type profile from Chapter 3, Mirror, Mirror, list the two blind spots which are MOST true for you. Then provide one or two examples showing how that blind spot prevented you from accomplishing or achieving something you wanted.

1. _____

Example:

_____

_____

Example:

_____

_____

2. _____

Example:

_____

_____

Example:

_____

_____

Step 2: Work-Related Strengths and Weaknesses

Our greatest satisfaction comes from doing what we do best. That's why it's so important to identify our work-related strengths so we can make sure our job will be enjoyable.

Using the list of work-related strengths from your type chapter, rank your three greatest strengths and provide one or two examples from your work life that demonstrate how you've used each strength successfully.

STRENGTHS:

1. ————————————————

Example:

————————————————————
————————————————————

2. ————————————————

Example:

————————————————————
————————————————————

3. ————————————————

Example:

————————————————————
————————————————————

Using the list of work-related weaknesses from your type chapter, rank your three greatest weaknesses and provide one or two examples from your work that illustrate how they prevented you from accomplishing or achieving something you wanted.

WEAKNESSES:

1. ————————————————

Example:

————————————————————
————————————————————

2. ————————————————

Example:

————————————————————
————————————————————

3. ————————————————

Example:

————————————————————
————————————————————

Step 3: Criteria for Career Satisfaction

Review the list of important criteria for career satisfaction for your type in the Common Threads section of your type chapter. Prioritize the list, determining the most- to least-important elements for you. This will take some serious consideration, since it may be difficult to give more weight to some elements than to others. But your efforts will be rewarded, because the results will be a clearer picture than you ever had before of what it takes to satisfy you.

• Record the top five criteria below:

1. ————————————————
2. ————————————————
3. ————————————————
4. ————————————————
5. ————————————————

Step 4: Career Satisfiers at Work

Using your current job (if it's satisfying) or a past job that was satisfying, describe one or more situations in which each of the top *three* satisfiers were present.

• Record your observations below:

————————————————————
————————————————————

_____

_____

_____

Step 5: What Interests You?

Think about your strongest interests. They may be specific activities like hiking or writing, or general areas such as music or business. In either case, try to identify those things you enjoy so much you would do them for *free* (if you could afford to!).

• Record your observations below:

_____

_____

_____

_____

_____

Step 6: Identifying Your Skills

To identify what you do well, review the Skills and Abilities list below. Decide which of these (as well as any others not listed) describe you best. Select your top five skills and generate an example of how you have used each in the past. (Don't limit your observations only to past work experiences. Consider recreational uses of these skills as well.)

SKILLS AND ABILITIES
Writing
Talking
Public speaking
Persuading
Selling
Negotiating
Working on a team
Working with others
Supervising others
Teaching
Coaching
Counseling
Coordinating projects/tasks
Managing
Meeting people easily
Working with numbers
Collecting information
Interpreting data
Solving quantitative problems
Concentration/focus
Research
Attention to detail
Manual dexterity
Understanding how tools/machinery work
Physical stamina
Meeting deadlines
Precision
Aesthetic sensitivity
Imagination with things
Imagination with ideas
Disciplining others
Making decisions
Seeing possibilities
Mentoring
Facilitating
Resolving conflicts
Developing prototypes
Observing accurately
Establishing procedures/rules
Managing crises
Synthesizing information
Analyzing problems
Strategizing
Maintaining systems
Critiquing
Assessing priorities
Learning new skills
Understanding complicated ideas
Working with theories
Adapting to changing situations
Flexibility

• Record your top five skills below:

_____

_____

_____

_____

_____

_____

- Record your examples of how you have
  used each in the past below:

_____

_____

_____

_____

_____

_____

Step 7: Careers to Consider

Generate a list of possible careers or jobs
that are of interest to you at this point. Refer
to the Popular Occupations section of your
type chapter to help you, and add any other
occupations not listed which interest you.
Briefly note what appeals to you about each.

- Record your observations below:

_____

_____

_____

_____

_____

Step 8: Evaluating Your Career Options

Analyze each position individually, asking
yourself:

1. How well does it make use of my best
   skills and abilities?
2. How well does it make use of my
   work-related strengths? (Refer back to
   Step 2 for your work-related strengths.)

3. How well does it meet my top five
   criteria for career satisfaction? (Refer
   back to Step 3 for your top five
   selections.)

- Record your observations below:

_____

_____

_____

_____

_____

_____

Step 9: Researching Your Potential Career

To learn as much as you can about the
specific fields or occupations you have
identified above as a good match for you,
you'll need to research them thoroughly.
Here are some tips for evaluating good
career options:

1. Conduct informational interviews with
   people already in the job or field to
   find out what it is really like and how
   that person found the job. Ask your
   interviewers how they see your
   interests, skills, and qualifications
   fitting with the specific job in question.
2. If additional or specialized training or
   education is required, contact local
   colleges, universities, or training
   facilities to learn the cost and length of
   time such training would require.
3. Conduct research into areas of interest
   and specific companies by using the
   Internet. (See the next section, which
   outlines how to take advantage of this
   great research tool.)
4. Research any geographical
   considerations such as where the jobs
   are, whether a move will be required,

and whether that's a possibility for you.

Step 10: How to Get There from Here

Developing a customized job search plan which capitalizes on your natural strengths and compensates for any possible type-related weaknesses is the critical next step.

Consider each Pathway to Success, and think of several instances in the past when you've demonstrated these abilities. (Remember, don't limit your observations to work activities.)

- Record your observations below:

_____

_____

_____

_____

_____

_____

Strength: _____
Example: _____
Strength: _____
Example: _____
Strength: _____
Example: _____
Strength: _____
Example: _____

Now consider each Possible Pitfall and again try to remember instances in the past when NOT paying attention to these blind spots prevented you from achieving something or got you into trouble.

- Record your observations below:

Blind spot: _____
Example: _____
Blind spot: _____
Example: _____
Blind spot: _____

Example: _____
Blind spot: _____
Example: _____

The World at Your Fingertips: Taking the Job Search Online

With such an enormous market, it makes sense that entrepreneurs have rushed to take advantage of the opportunities the Internet has to offer. There are dozens of popular career sites to choose from, but their sheer number and the redundancy of their content can make using them a little overwhelming. Essentially, the steps of a job search are still pretty much the same ones we've always taken. But it's the *way* we go about taking them that is so radically different. If this is your first technology-driven career search (or job change), here are some of the advantages of the Internet. Online, you can:

- Research career options. There are hundreds of websites that allow you to browse a variety of descriptions and research salary levels, educational and experience requirements, forecasts for future growth, and typical career paths.
- Learn about specific companies and organizations. All major companies have websites that can help you learn more about the company and its corporate climate, which can be a great help when you're preparing for a job interview. A wealth of information can be gathered from a company's site with relative ease. Most companies also post specific job openings and career opportunities.
- Locate specific job opportunities. This is the most obvious—and productive—use of the Internet when you're looking for a job. There are literally millions of job postings on thousands of websites at any given time. You can use the site's search function to target the type of job,

salary range, and geographic area you are looking for. In addition to sites that carry general listings, there are numerous sites that cater to specific industries, such as pharmaceuticals, computer technology, and medicine. Some are run by professional associations, others by recruiters. Sites like Indeed, Simply Hired, CareerBuilder, Idealist.org, and Craigslist are some of the most popular options now, and new sites are coming on the scene every day.

- Identify educational and training facilities. The Internet makes it easy to find educational and training opportunities in almost any field. All schools, colleges, and other educational organizations in the United States and around the world now maintain websites. Online applications are common, and the recent explosion of accredited online universities lends a greater flexibility to people wishing to fit higher education into a busy lifestyle.
- Network, network, network! Another huge boon to the online job search is the proliferation of social networking. Sites like LinkedIn, Plaxo, and Jobster allow users to design professional profiles, post skills and experience, and network with colleagues and other professionals. To a lesser degree, sites like Facebook and Twitter can aid in the job hunt, but make sure your online presence is professional and well curated.

A few things to keep in mind about using the Internet to find a job…

Websites are a great tool in the job search, but using them is not unlike shopping at a consignment shop—you have to check in often because the inventory changes constantly and moves erratically. For days you may see nothing, and then one day you see ten career options that might be right for you. Patience and persistence are key.

Also, remember that your chance of finding a terrific job online increases greatly if you are willing to relocate. The more specific your requirements, especially in regard to geographic area, the less likely you are to find a good match. And if you post your résumé and don't receive a job offer, don't be discouraged! This is not a reflection of your worth as a candidate. Like the old-fashioned method of mailing résumés in response to newspaper ads, posting is not always the most efficient or the savviest way to go. Posting a résumé is only one of many, many strategies available to you.

On Your Mark…Get Set…GO!

Now that you've had a chance to identify at least one—and perhaps several—potentially satisfying jobs and have learned how to take advantage of the Internet, we suggest you keep your type chapter well marked and return to the Customizing Your Job Search section whenever you need to as you begin to implement your plan of action.

One final message of inspiration. Writing this book has taught us many things, most of which we learned directly from the many wonderful, career-satisfied people we interviewed. And perhaps the most important message we have to share is that if your belief in something is strong enough, if it's really right for you, or you feel you were meant to do it, then you will find the inner resources to make it happen. Work can be exciting, fulfilling, rewarding, and fun; it can be what you need and want it to be and you can even be well paid! There is at least one great career out there with your name on it—a career that really rewards you for using your natural gifts and lets you do what you enjoy most and do best. It's possible, you deserve it, and you don't have to settle for anything less.

25 ENCORE! ENCORE!

Success Stories of Baby Boomers Finding Satisfying Second Careers

"'Do not go gentle into that good night'!"

When Welsh poet Dylan Thomas wrote these words, he was referring to not giving in to death without a fight. But we'd like to repurpose his quote to mean: "Don't give up on finding satisfying work after retirement." In fact, many baby boomers will experience *greater* fulfillment in their "encore careers" than they found in jobs they worked at for most of their lives. This chapter is designed to help you do just that.

The seventy-six million boomers (born between 1946 and 1964) continue to exert a dominant influence over practically every facet of American life. Two aspects that affect our society the most are wealth and politics. Representing 44 percent of the U.S. population, boomers hold 70 percent of disposable income and buy almost 50 percent of total consumer-packaged goods.

How do boomers spend their money? Not surprisingly, the three largest buckets are education, mortgage debt, and health care.

Today's outstanding student loan debt is more than $1 trillion, and one-third of that is held by people over the age of forty. Fifty-nine percent of parents provide financial support to children who are no longer in school, helping them with college expenses or loan payments.

And the days of inviting your friends over for a mortgage-note-burning party are long gone: 75 percent of middle-aged and older workers still have mortgages.

In recent years, health-care-related costs have risen 30 percent for forty-five- to fifty-four-year-olds and 21 percent for fifty-five- to sixty-four-year-olds, with insurance premiums nearly doubling as a share of health care expenditures for both age groups.

Boomers also have an inordinate amount of clout, because politics drive public policy and boomers make their voices heard: in the 2008 Obama/McCain election, 75 percent of boomers were registered to vote and 69 percent did. Today, the generation many consider responsible for ending the Vietnam War has perhaps the most powerful lobby in Washington—AARP—with an estimated forty million members. The implications of so much influence by baby boomers are profound, as boomers and members of other generational cohorts compete for very scarce government resources—especially with regard to health care.

You'll Be Doing Something…But What?

Boomers are leaving the workforce in huge numbers: ten thousand boomers reach the age of sixty-five daily, and while the average retirement age is sixty-seven, many are forced to leave their jobs at much earlier ages—often in their mid to late fifties.

In reality, a relatively small percentage of retirement-age boomers either are financially *able* or *want* to completely retire. It's estimated that 70 percent will work in some capacity during retirement; of these, about 30 percent will continue because they have to. And according to an AARP survey, 40 percent plan to work "until they drop."

At the same time, the average life expectancy in the United States has increased to 78.5 years (76 for men, 81 for women). As a result, a significant percentage of boomers leaving the workforce will have between *ten and twenty years* to do… something! This chapter will help you discover the "something" that will be intrinsically satisfying, because it makes use of your natural gifts and is in sync with your values. In other words, because it enables you to "do what you are."

Some Good News…Some Bad News… Some Even Better News!

First the good: you are probably going to live longer that your parents did. However, you

are also likely to be forced to retire before you want to or feel you can comfortably afford to. But the best news is, you now have an opportunity to find work—either paid or volunteer—that will result in the greatest career satisfaction you've ever had.

A 2012 *Parade* magazine survey asked readers: "If you could do it all over again, would you choose the same career?" It might surprise you to learn that 59 percent said they would *not* select the same career. There are many reasons why this is the case, but here's the shorthand version: Most people make their most important career decisions at a time when they're least prepared to do so. At sixteen or seventeen, students who will soon be graduating high school need to think seriously about their future. Will they go to college (for those lucky enough to have that option), and if they do, what will they study? Most colleges require students to declare a major by the end of their sophomore year—when they're nineteen or twenty years old. Decisions made then start students down a path that will influence their entire life.

Take a moment to think back to how well you knew *yourself* at that age. If you're like most people, the answer may be "Yikes! Not very well." Still, this is when we are all pressured to make our most important life-altering decisions.

Consider this pretty common scenario: Brendon is a smart kid without any particular passion in high school. But because he likes to argue, his parents have been telling him from a very early age that he'd make a great lawyer. So Brendon enrolls in a liberal arts college and at nineteen decides to major in policy and government—often recommended for prelaw students. While he likes his courses all right, they neither uncover nor ignite in Brendon a passion for the law.

Brendon's parents invest close to $200,000 in his undergraduate education. And upon graduation, they pressure Brendon to make sure their investment pays off by enrolling in law school. Three years later, after passing the state licensing exam, Brendon becomes an esteemed member of the bar. To pay for law school, Brendon took out a loan, so on graduation day he is $150,000 in debt.

Now the pressure begins in earnest. Fortunately, Brendon manages to land a job pretty quickly as an associate at a midsized firm. Although he is making decent money, he has a grueling schedule, often working fifty to sixty hours per week. Still, he is one of the lucky ones, as a year later many of his classmates are still desperately seeking their first job.

Fast-forward three years. Brendon, now twenty-seven, has a new fiancée and—between his student loans, car and mortgage payments, and condo fees—hefty monthly living expenses. Still working a ridiculous number of hours, Brendon is hoping to grab the brass ring and someday make partner.

The only problem is, Brendon doesn't really *like* being a lawyer. The other, more exotic and lucrative specialties within his field don't appeal to him, either.

Unfortunately, Brendon's story is not terribly unique: almost half of the lawyers surveyed by the American Bar Association reported dissatisfaction with their careers, and only 40 percent said they would recommend a legal career to others. And Brendon is one of the *lucky* ones! For seventeen- to eighteen-year-old students who *don't* have a college option, the challenges of finding satisfying and fulfilling work are even greater.

As strange as it may sound, most people put more time and energy into researching which new car to buy than which career would bring them the greatest satisfaction

and success. The real point of this story is that many—perhaps most—of us end up in careers that are not intrinsically satisfying. And even though we might recognize this pretty early on, we put off making a major career change, "at least for now." But time moves quickly: days turn into weeks, weeks into months, and months into years. And there comes a point for many of us when we simply feel like we're unable to make the change.

But Now, Things Are Different!

You know yourself so much better. With age and experience comes a certain amount of wisdom. You understand your strengths and your blind spots. You know the kinds of activities that energize and drain you. You've learned what kinds of people drive you crazy and, hopefully, how to avoid them.

As you've matured, so has your value system. Time has given you the ability to better see the big picture and know what's *truly* important in your life. Clearly, many things have changed for, and in, you over the last twenty, thirty, or forty years. But what hasn't changed is your personality type and your temperament—the keys to finding a more satisfying, fulfilling encore career.

Why Temperament Is the Key to Career Satisfaction

In Chapter 4, What a Character!, we introduced the theory of temperament, which we think of as four different human natures.

For those of you who like more depth, this might be a good time to take a few minutes to reacquaint yourself with Chapter 4. But the majority of you will find the summary we provide here all you need to know to understand the important role your temperament plays in helping you find a satisfying encore career.

You may remember there are four temperaments, which we've labeled Traditionalists, Experiencers, Idealists, and Conceptualizers. And there are four personality types that fall under each temperament.

Traditionalists (SJs): ESTJ ISTJ ESFJ ISFJ
Experiencers (SPs): ESTP ISTP ESFP ISFP
Idealists (NFs): ENFJ INFJ ENFP INFP
Conceptualizers (NTs): ENTJ INTJ ENTP INTP

Why is temperament so critical to career satisfaction and success? Because it reflects our core values and key motivations. Below is a thumbnail sketch of each of the four temperaments:

‖ Traditionalists
Approximately 46 percent of the American population

Traditionalists are driven to be of service. They are super responsible and extremely hardworking. When they say they will do something, they will—their word is their bond. Traditionalists take a conventional approach to life and place great value on the importance of family and institutions. They trust and respect authority, follow rules, and expect others to as well.

Career Satisfiers:

- Being of service
- Having a high level of responsibility and control
- A stable, predictable work environment
- Clear expectations and directions
- Being able to see the results of their efforts

‖ Experiencers
Approximately 27 percent of the American population

Experiencers enjoy living life to its fullest, experiencing as much as they possibly can. Having the freedom to be spontaneous and able to respond to opportunities and experiences as they arise makes them feel alive. Experiencers tend to take a more laid-back, casual approach to life and often enjoy being physically engaged.

Career Satisfiers:

- Having fun; enjoying their work and co-workers
- Freedom to act; not being micromanaged
- A casual work setting without too many rules
- Being physically engaged
- Using established skills to perform real, concrete tasks

‖ Idealists
Approximately 16 percent of the American population

Idealists seek and thrive on having meaningful personal relationships. Perceptive about people and extremely empathetic, they derive great satisfaction from helping others. To Idealists, authenticity—in themselves and in others—is nonnegotiable. Sensitive and collaborative, Idealists often feel compelled to take on causes that improve people's lives.

Career Satisfiers:

- Work that is personally meaningful
- Work that helps others
- A tension-free, supportive work environment

- Close personal relationships with colleagues, clients, etc.
- Being able to provide creative input

Conceptualizers
Approximately 10 percent of the American population

Conceptualizers are on a lifelong quest for knowledge. They are quick studies who enjoy intellectual challenges and being able to solve problems creatively. Global and strategic, Conceptualizers set high standards for themselves and others, and place a very high value on competence. Independence is also a hallmark in these people, who have a strong drive to be successful.

Career Satisfiers:

- Work that continually challenges them
- Applying their creativity to solve problems
- Continuing to learn and develop new competencies
- Having a great deal of independence
- The opportunity for career advancement

How This Chapter Can Help You

In this chapter, you will find two examples of people of each temperament who have found satisfying encore careers. It's most important for you to read the profiles of people who share *your* temperament, which should resonate strongly with you. Each profile describes the person's first and encore careers. This is followed by our analysis of *why* this second career choice is a good one for each person profiled.

In our analysis, we discuss the importance of temperament as well as each person's dominant function. As you may remember from Chapter 5, Who's on First?, each personality type has one aspect that represents that type's greatest natural strengths. We call this the dominant function. Why is it important to know what your dominant is? Because when we are engaging our dominant function, we are more satisfied and successful. Using our dominant actually energizes us. For example, suppose your dominant is Intuition (seeing possibilities and making connections). After a long day at work, you may be bone tired. But if a friend were to ask you to help brainstorm some possible solutions to a problem he or she was having, you might suddenly come to life and find new energy. This is because you would get the chance to use your dominant Intuition. It's easy to see how much more satisfied people are whose job allows them to use their dominant function a lot. And how dissatisfied people are whose job does not allow them to use theirs very much.

Our analysis also touches on the role that each person's type development plays in making that particular encore career a good choice. Why is this important to know?

Carl Jung, upon whose theories Personality Type is based, believed that we are all born with our personality type, which we have for our entire lives. However, as we reach mid-life and come to accept that our journey will eventually end, we seek "wholeness." This comes from using the parts of our personality type that do not come naturally to us. Other Type experts have even laid out a timeline by which each of the sixteen types works (unconsciously) to develop various aspects of that type. So although we might say "Once an ISTJ, *always* an ISTJ" (which is true for all types), a fifty-year-old ISTJ may find herself drawn to use different parts of her personality than a twenty-year-old ISTJ.

An example: if a person who is naturally a Thinking type (logical and objective) is now developing her Feeling function (sensitive and value driven), she might exhibit more interest in others and have greater access to her own emotional life. A job that involves helping people work out their problems—which might not have appealed to her early in her career—might be very appealing now. (For a more in-depth discussion of type development, see Chapter 7, Aged to Perfection.)

Now it's time to read the two profiles that reflect your temperament.

|| Traditionalists

Profile 1: Jay

"From running a company to managing a classroom."

Jay was a government major in college, and his first career was as a newspaper reporter, writing four or five articles a week. "It was great being able to go out and talk to people making news in a small town like Albany." Although Jay enjoyed the job, he left after two years to work as the publicity manager for a PR firm. A few years later, he moved back to Connecticut for family reasons. He worked as a financial analyst and got his MBA at the same time. Jay enjoyed accounting and found financial analysis fun, but he left after five years to take an opportunity to work in his family's manufacturing business.

Jay started as a salesperson at the family-owned company, which had been manufacturing industrial sewing machine parts for the garment industry for 160 years. After only two years, Jay became the president. "I loved being able to apply everything I had learned in schooling to a real-life small business. But being a manager in a union shop also presented some real challenges." Because the garment industry

had moved to Mexico, Central America, India, and China, competition was fierce. Realizing that if he stayed with the company, he would spend most of his time traveling, Jay decided it was time to leave. As it turned out, the economic handwriting was on the wall: a year later, the family sold the company's assets.

While he was running the business, Jay had been coaching sports on the side. And with four boys within six years of each other, he got lots of practice. So he decided "it was time to follow my heart," and became a teacher. He spent the next four years substitute teaching as he earned a second master's degree in curriculum and instruction.

Encore! Encore!

After working for twenty-five years in various businesses, Jay began his encore career at the age of forty-six, teaching history and social studies in a suburban high school in New England. What Jay loves best about teaching is being able to put together plans to reach all kids. He enjoys seeing his plans implemented and watching each student grow. Jay chose to teach high school students because the students are old enough to relate the lessons to their life experiences and make higher-level contributions. But as with any job, Jay experiences frustrations: "It's hard to accept that even with seven days [in a week], I can't do everything that I think I should be doing for these kids. There just aren't enough hours in the day."

Another challenge for Jay is that teachers are required to teach new courses each year. "While this makes me more versatile, it's hard to reinvent the wheel. Frankly, I'd prefer to be able to dive deep and really get to know the content—that would make teaching easier for me." Also draining for Jay is the sheer amount of time required: "The first few years were brutal—I learned that if you're not careful, you can easily find yourself working seven days a week."

As for his decision to leave business for teaching, Jay says: "Although it was an economic sacrifice for a few years, I'm really glad I made the change—and wish I'd done it sooner."

Why This Encore Career Works for Jay

After four years teaching, Jay received tenure. While job security is desired by all types, it is particularly valued by Traditionalists, as is being of service: "My role for the rest of my working career is to help as many people as I can." He appreciates the structure and clear expectations endemic to public schools, like the requirements tied to teaching core competencies. Jay enjoys having a lot of responsibility and control: "I have guidelines for what I have to teach every semester, but I like to create my own lesson plans." Finally, it's important for Jay to be able to see the results of his efforts: "I love to see that light go on for kids who struggle. With hard work and extra help, they're able to really get it."

As an ISTJ (Introverted, Sensing, Thinking, Judging), Jay is a dominant Sensor, so it's not difficult to understand why he would be drawn to teaching history—the chronicling of real events, experienced by real people, over a very long time. But evidence is abundant that Jay is in the process of developing his third function, Feeling. In the last few years, "it's become more important than ever to make sure I'm a really good role model to my boys, in everything I do." And as he and his wife have traveled around the world, he has become much more sensitive to the plight of others in less affluent cultures. He describes his "enormous admiration" for his wife, Ashley, who started

Asante Sana for Education, a nonprofit organization that builds schools in Tanzania. In addition to supporting her efforts, Jay has developed new empathy for the needs of local people as well, often spending vacation days working in soup kitchens.

Profile 2: Rob

"From insurance claims to adult college advising."

After graduating with a BS in communications, Rob applied to a large insurance company where he hoped to land a job in public relations. Unfortunately, a hiring freeze made it impossible for him to get into the company for two years. When the freeze thawed, Rob found it much easier to get into claims, and planned to move to public relations eventually. But eighteen months later, Rob was promoted to supervisor, and now firmly ensconced in claims, he spent the next twelve years as a supervisor and team leader.

What Rob loved best was coaching employees and helping them do their jobs better. "Many were new college grads, and I enjoyed providing them with their first introduction into business and helping them understand organizational behavior." What Rob liked least was collecting data and having to fill out reports—things that didn't involve the people and relationship side of the business. Although he was technically a field employee, he actively participated in facilitating training at the company's nationally recognized education-focused institute. "My company kept developing me and I kept developing others, which was mutually beneficial. This gave me a chance not just to keep my knowledge to myself, but to share it with others." He also loved meeting people from all over the country who came to the institute, and took pride in his ability to make insurance fun.

In 1996, Rob moved to another insurance company and became a supervisor and account manager in charge of commercial accounts. "Although I got to learn about something completely different—commercial insurance and contracts—I still yearned to do more training and coaching." While he continued to work, Rob went back to graduate school in 2000 for a master's in organizational behavior.

Rob's next job was also in insurance, but this time it was as the director of training and development. The company was growing very rapidly, and when they lost their major account, they were forced to go out of business. So Rob moved on to another insurer—this one specialized in providing medical malpractice insurance. "I always had great respect for doctors. I took it to heart. I didn't want medical errors to happen, and in this job I got to point out where docs made mistakes and helped them to be better."

Rob's tenure at this company lasted ten years. But when the economy turned, Rob was laid off once again. Through luck or providence, he discovered a program run by Leadership Greater Hartford called Encore!-Hartford—a program that helps managers and professionals find work in the nonprofit sector. The program provided him with training, contacts, and confidence that led to his next assignment, as an organizational development consultant at a local hospital, where he was primarily in charge of facilitating groups. While Rob enjoyed the exciting pace, the job as a whole did not turn out to be a great fit.

Encore! Encore!

In 2011, Rob secured his dream position at a local university. "Everybody has a path, and my path has taken me in lots of directions,

but this is the greatest job I've had yet." It allows him to use many of his greatest skills in service of a mission he deeply believes in. As assistant director of the Center for Adult Academic Services, Rob recruits and consults with adults who want to secure undergraduate or graduate degrees. And ironically, a fair amount of the job involves public relations—the field that Rob sought to begin his career in so many years earlier.

In addition to recruiting and advising, Rob does a lot of outreach, speaking at community colleges, corporations, and professional associations. There are about 150 adults in the program at various stages of pursuing degrees. "It's especially moving on graduation day when I get to meet their families and celebrate the payoff for the incredible sacrifices they made to get an education. I've been given the privilege of helping these people develop their skills and the confidence to move ahead in their lives."

Why This Encore Career Works for Rob

As an ESFJ (Extraverted, Sensing, Feeling, Judging), Rob is not only a Traditionalist but also a dominant Feeler. An important reason why Rob likes this position so much is that it is in sync with many of his Traditionalist values: Rob believes wholeheartedly in the program's mission, and he gets to help people in real and concrete ways every day. Rob knows exactly what is expected of him and is given the responsibility and resources to do his job well. Traditionalists such as Rob have a very strong work ethic and a desire to see concrete proof that their hard work is paying off. Rob's need for a personal connection with students is also frequently reinforced when he receives feedback that his efforts helped them succeed.

This is the time in his life when people of Rob's type develop their third function—

Intuition. A few years ago, at age forty-one, Rob started asking why more, seeking answers to questions that he hadn't thought much about in the past. This manifested itself in more curiosity and an eagerness to learn new things. Not coincidentally, this was about the time he decided to go back and get his master's degree. Rob also reports that he's become more open-minded and "a little more accepting of the changes that life invariably throws at us."

Experiencers
Profile 1: Cindy

"Definitely not your typical banker..."

After graduating from Skidmore College in 1983, Cindy spent the next twelve years holding a variety of positions in banking: retail bank manager, private banking officer, regional sales manager in brokerage services with supervisory responsibility, and ultimately training and development manager. Although she enjoyed certain aspects of banking—especially helping customers and building relationships with co-workers—there was much that rubbed this natural free spirit the wrong way. She found the repetitive nature of several of her day-to-day responsibilities tedious and boring. And there were way too many rules! "I wanted to do the job the way I thought it should be done best, but that just wasn't the way that banks worked. My attitude was: 'Tell me what you want me to do, give me a deadline, then leave me alone and let me do it.' But the way you had to do things was so scripted."

Itching for the chance for more real interaction with people, Cindy enrolled in a graduate program that would give her a master's degree in training—and even got

the bank to pay for it. Cindy wisely chose a program that fit her well: "Their focus was not theoretical. I don't do theory, it's not real. I'm not conceptual; I'm pragmatic and like to focus on practical applications." Looking for some hands-on experience, Cindy approached her manager and offered to train all of their new reps. And with previous managerial experience already under her belt, she was in a great place to apply—and be hired—when a training manager position became available in the Financial Services division. Cindy loved working with her team to create all the training programs, but once the programs were in place, it felt repetitive and boring. When her bank was acquired, she transitioned into a senior training manager role, where she worked for another two years.

After that, Cindy got married and moved to New Hampshire, where her husband worked. Her career in banking was about to undergo a big change. While her old bank had 18,000 domestic employees, her new community bank had only 135. Cindy loved the change because she could actually see the application of what she was teaching, observing her students using skills that she had taught them the day before. Although she had started working part-time, Cindy was quickly promoted to VP of employee education and development. She stayed at this job for ten years and "pretty much loved every minute of it. I can count on two hands the number of times they said no to something I wanted to do."

In 2008, Cindy and her family moved to Virginia. After twenty-five years of waking up and going to a bank every day, she took a little more than a year off and set up her own consulting practice. Unfortunately, the economy didn't cooperate, and everything fell apart. So in 2010, she went back into banking.

Encore! Encore!

While Cindy's first career was as a banker, her new career is as an educator of bankers. "I found a way to be a free spirit and independent inside a bank." Now the director of training at a community bank in Virginia, Cindy plays a variety of roles, designing, developing, and delivering educational initiatives. "I love the delivery, enjoy the design. The development is doable but drains my energy big time." She also does organizational development work—helping people and teams communicate more successfully, and building leadership curricula, which help people develop trusting relationships. "I help people understand how they learn best, so that they can absorb the knowledge they need to be effective at work. I am a great believer in leveraging people's strengths and helping them truly know their natural capabilities."

Why This Encore Career Works for Cindy

There are many reasons this new career works for Cindy the Experiencer, whose full type is ESTP (Extraverted, Sensing, Thinking, Perceiving). Cindy naturally craves action and loves to work on a variety of tasks, both of which she experiences daily in this position. As the leader of education in the bank, she has a lot of control over what she does and how she does it. Cindy is in her comfort zone, getting to apply her established skills in an industry she already knows well.

Like all Experiencers, Cindy enjoys being in the moment and acting spontaneously. For example, she might be training one module but realize the group needs to go in a totally different direction. "I love having the freedom to turn on a dime." Because she's a dominant Sensor, she "sees things that others just don't see," and her auxiliary Thinking almost compels her to point these things out. However, Cindy's type development plays a role in her success as well. This is the stage in life where ESTPs naturally develop Feeling (their third function). Cindy has become a much more patient and sensitive listener, great at paraphrasing what people are saying and helping them see new perspectives.

Profile 2: Sergio

"From court officer to tax preparer."

Born in Argentina, Sergio was eight when he moved to the United States. He spent the first six years in Philadelphia, before moving to Long Island, and eventually Connecticut. When he entered community college, Sergio had no clue what he wanted to do. So he dropped out and explored various options. One job he took was as an assistant teacher of math in a high school equivalency program. "It was great. They let me do whatever I wanted to. I wore shorts and had long hair." What he liked best was using real-life examples that his students related to and could understand. "With drug dealers, I might say something like: 'OK, you have fifty pounds of coke, and you sell twenty-three pounds. How much coke do you have left?'"

Eventually, Sergio went back and graduated college with a BS in grant writing. In need of a job, he wrote and received a grant to create a public access television show produced by underprovided kids. "They did everything, from writing the scripts and making the props to designing the sets and filming the show." The show ran for twelve episodes and was highly successful. Afterward, Sergio applied for and was offered three different jobs. He chose to work for the state of Connecticut in the judicial department.

In 1980, Sergio began working as a court officer in child support. His job involved combing through data to find people who were delinquent in payments, trying to make a deal to get them to comply, and then presenting their cases to various judges. What he liked was the flexibility he was afforded managing his own caseload. "I got to set my own priorities and organize my time to make it all work." Sergio was energized when he was put in charge of creating an education program. He traveled around the state teaching workers how to do things like use the computer system and present a case in court, and he got to create a regular newsletter. He was disappointed when the project was turned into a permanent job but given to someone else.

As for his regular duties, there was much that Sergio did not find satisfying. "All the judges were different, so there was practically no consistency. There was a ton of politics and no team approach. Promotions were heavily influenced by who you knew." His promotion to supervisor made the situation worse: "I lost all freedom. Now I had to supervise a lot of ... crazies"—some who would file petty grievances against him for reasons he considered frivolous. "Every day when I walked in the door, I thought: 'Let the games begin!'"

However, the state did provide a large degree of security, which allowed Sergio to meet his family obligations, so he continued to work in this field until he retired in 2009 at the age of fifty-six.

Encore! Encore!

Unfortunately, Sergio's wife got sick soon after he retired, and their plans to travel were curtailed as her illness progressed. Sergio didn't know anything about taxes but was good at math, and on a whim he took a course with a national tax preparation company. One of the draws for him was the promise of a job if he passed the exam, which of course he did.

Since 2010, Sergio has been helping people prepare their taxes. "I really enjoy the variety. One of my clients was an elephant trainer, another teaches etiquette. People come in with all sorts of problems, and I get to help them." Sergio also enjoys the flexibility a seasonal job affords him. He's very busy for about four and a half months, and for the rest of the year gets to take classes that increase both his knowledge and his compensation. "I hate the winter but love the summer, and this job gives me lots of time to do the things I love, like biking, kayaking, and playing tennis." Requiring a solid skill that's in demand, at a company with offices all over the world, this position affords Sergio a lot of options. It's a job he could see himself doing for a while.

Why This Encore Career Works for Sergio

While at first blush, preparing taxes might seem too sedate a job for a normally action-seeking Experiencer, it does provide much that Experiencers thrive on: variety, flexibility, and freedom. One of the most dissatisfying parts of Sergio's first career as a court officer—and especially as a supervisor—was the lack of freedom and autonomy. After so many years, he had basically seen it all—been there, done that. But in his encore career, every person that walks through his door has a different story.

As an ESFP (Extraverted, Sensing, Feeling, Perceiving), Sergio has a dominant function of Sensing, which serves him well in a job that requires very close attention to detail. And he is dealing with real people facing real challenges, something that more literal-minded Sensing types relish. But it is his auxiliary function—Feeling—that compels him to want to help others, and Sergio's Feeling function is nourished by being able to do this every day.

As for Sergio's type development, he now has much greater access to his third function, Thinking. Criticism from a tough supervisor, for example, "just rolls off my back, which wasn't always the case." Sergio credits his type development with helping him in other aspects of his life as well.

‖ Idealists

Profile 1: Guthrie

"From college professor to spiritual life coach."

Guthrie graduated from Princeton in 1971 and spent the next four years "bouncing around the United States and Europe, traveling and doing a bunch of odd jobs and all the crazy stuff of the era." After moving to New York City in 1975, he got a job working in book publishing as an administrative assistant but quickly rose to director of promotion. His position provided some amazing opportunities for this former English major. One day, he asked an editor colleague if he could read the next book that the editor thought would become a best seller. That book turned out to be *The World According to Garp,* by John Irving. Guthrie remembers, "This was the reason I went into publishing. It was amazing! I couldn't put the book down and spent every spare moment trying to develop a following and get it into bookstores." When he got to meet author John Irving, he told him, "I feel like Holden Caulfield [from *The Catcher in the Rye*]! Sometimes you want to call up an author and talk to him, and here you are in my office."

A casualty of massive publishing layoffs in the late '70s, Guthrie freelanced various publishing assignments for a while before moving back to Connecticut and trying his hand at journalism. What he liked best about being a reporter was the autonomy and opportunity to write stories he was interested in, but he was frustrated by being "restricted to using a sixth-grade vocabulary." He left the paper and became a freelance journalist. One day, he got an assignment that required a historical context that he didn't have. "I started reading and didn't stop until I had a Ph.D."

Upon entering graduate school, Guthrie's goal was to become a college professor. "What I immediately liked about academia was that I could use my entire vocabulary! The whole endeavor seemed to be about exchanging ideas and finding truth—looking for meaning in the past so that people could understand the present more deeply and completely."

While he enjoyed mastering the material, presenting it clearly, and watching students become engaged and make progress, eventually the appeal of the teaching game began to fade. "I lost faith in the whole enterprise of using an academic discipline like history as a way of finding truth. I had proved my competence to myself but needed more meaning."

Encore! Encore!

After seven years of being firmly ensconced in the ivory tower, Guthrie began his second career as a spiritual life coach. There are probably as many approaches to life coaching as there are coaches, but Guthrie's is clearly spiritual: "I introduce people to themselves at their deepest level." Guthrie's work is profoundly personal and intensive. "I create enough safety for people to share their deepest pain and vulnerability. Often people think this pain is proof of their weakness and failure. But I help them to understand how precious the pain is, because it helps them appreciate not only their own humanity, but everybody else's." Guthrie has truly found his calling: "It's the thing I do best and it serves other people, and that is deeply, deeply gratifying."

Guthrie is also on the faculty of a coaching school. He leads online classes, runs small groups, and mentors other coaches. "Working one-on-one is amazing and provides a maximum impact. In a short time, I'm able to understand my mentees on a deep level and make a difference in their journey—especially their belief in themselves as people who can make a difference with their clients."

While being a life coach is clearly fulfilling, there are occasional frustrations. Being a solo practitioner and having to attend to the mundane details of business can be draining. And "after a particularly energizing session, it's hard to go back and do the more routine parts of the business." But Guthrie is very aware of this natural blind spot and uses it to help himself and his clients grow as a result. "I try to practice what I preach. I'm rigorous about always being fully ready for a session and clear about financial arrangements. Although these can be uncomfortable conversations to have, my clients grow from my modeling this positive practice."

Why This Encore Career Works for Guthrie

Of the four Idealist types, INFPs (Introverted, Intuitive, Feeling, Perceiving), like Guthrie, find it most important to have work that is personally meaningful and that resonates with their deepest values. Not only is it a core value of Guthrie's to be genuine, but one of his missions is "to help others discover and become their authentic selves." Through coaching individuals, mentoring

other coaches, and giving workshops, Guthrie has developed many deep and cherished relationships. His extraordinary empathy allows him to experience others' pain and joy, a quality driven by his well-developed, dominant Feeling function.

Over the last five to ten years, Guthrie has become more conscious of the importance of being completely present for others and fully inhabiting his body. He does this by walking in the woods, working out, and practicing yoga—consciously engaging his third function, Sensing. In helping others to become their full, most authentic selves every day, Guthrie finds himself developing his own truest self, and nothing could be more satisfying.

Profile 2: Deb

"From corporate salesperson and manager to therapist and career counselor."

Deb's plan to save the world took an unexpected detour when she went to buy a new phone and ended up spending the next twenty-four years working for the phone company.

Graduating with a BS in child development, with a minor in human sexuality, Deb had originally planned to be a sex therapist. "I fantasized about being the next Masters and Johnson." It was while job-hunting that Deb happened to walk into the phone store and discover job openings that were paying $11,000, plus tuition reimbursement. Deb compared this with the $6,000 salary she would have received working for a child care center, and figured she'd take the job, get her master's paid for, and then go on to save the world.

Deb began her career at AT&T selling long-distance services to small business and went on to sell international services to global companies for most of her career. Deb loved creating relationships, selling, mentoring, and coaching. "I truly believed that I was helping people by providing a service." As she climbed higher and higher up the corporate ladder, she got to work with very powerful people and travel to exotic places. "I could pretend that I was one of them, and that made me feel important. They accepted my input and respected me, which made me feel affirmed."

What she didn't like was having to pay so much attention to details, or forecasting and delivering bad news to clients or employees. Also, there was little tolerance in her work environment for expressing one's emotions, which made being a Feeling type challenging at times. Deb grew frustrated at the reality that the bottom line—not customers' needs or feelings—drove most business decisions. And although she enjoyed much that came with having such an important job, it could be especially stressful when a customer had a crisis that she had to respond to immediately. "Whenever I had to travel and leave my family, I left with a suitcase full of guilt."

Deb had been at AT&T for twenty-four years when she got sick and landed in the hospital. Feeling compelled to work, even in the midst of an illness, was an awakening. "I realized that I was always taking care of others and not myself." Coincidentally, her job was about to get much more technical, requiring additional education—but not in a field that interested her. Deb decided to take an early retirement package. As part of the deal, she could get a master's degree of her choice. She spent the next two years studying and three in internships before opening a practice as a licensed marriage and family therapist and career counselor.

Encore! Encore!

Deb has an eclectic practice, though she spends the majority of her time working with couples in transition: "What's especially gratifying is that since I know the business world so well, many of the male clients are able to relate to me. Because I know their stresses and frustrations and speak their language, they feel safe enough with me to be able to access their emotions." She also helps people changing careers, kids moving from college to the corporate world, and retirees trying to figure out what's next.

Because she was so different from most of her colleagues at the phone company (an Intuitive Feeling type in a very Sensing Thinking culture), Deb often felt like "the odd man out." While her career path may seem an unorthodox training for a therapist, Deb says, "If I could have a do-over, I wouldn't change a thing. My long corporate experience separates me from other therapists. I feel like I'm able to bring a different and very useful perspective that few others have." Deb is thrilled with the way her career path played out. "I'm happier than I've ever been. It's taken a while, but I feel like I've finally found my authentic self."

Why This Encore Career Works for Deb

There's a good reason why more therapists are Idealists than any of the other temperaments. Deb's combination of Intuition and Feeling gives her both extraordinary perceptiveness and empathy. Sitting with clients, Deb not only feels how much pain they're in, but also sees a path to how they can heal. "I'm an optimist by nature, and I'm able to reassure people that there is a light at the end of the tunnel: they will feel better." Of course, Deb also has superb communication skills, a quality shared by many Idealists.

One of the most fulfilling parts of Deb's first career involved building close relationships with her customers and colleagues, which was driven by her dominant Feeling function. Deb sought every opportunity to be helpful and supportive in that role. But as a therapist and counselor, this ENFJ (Extraverted, Intuitive, Feeling, Judging) has natural gifts that are used and nourished, every single day.

With the development of Deb's third function, Sensing, and fourth function, Thinking, has come a more pragmatic approach to life. In the past, she used to be the enabler, who would help everyone at the expense of herself. "Today, I'm able to put the oxygen mask on first: to take a breath and ask, 'Who am I doing this for, the other person or myself?' I feel great that the answer is me."

‖ Conceptualizers
Profile 1: Adam

"From journalist to international child welfare advocate."

Adam discovered his first passion — journalism — while writing for his college newspaper, an activity that ultimately led to a twenty-two-year career working at the *Boston Globe.* Adam started as a copy editor, but over the span of his tenure, he had about twenty different jobs, including foreign editor, Washington news editor, diplomatic correspondent, national political correspondent, and family and children's issues reporter.

In addition to the actual writing, what Adam liked best was "chronicling history: the genuinely important mission of

journalism to shape people's understanding, leading to change of policies and practices that have real impact on people's lives." He found it exhilarating and exciting to cover the biggest stories of the day, which included the fall of the Berlin Wall, the Philippine revolution, the Gulf War, the Middle East peace process, the O. J. Simpson trials, and several presidential elections. "These were vital and important stories about people's lives — some were history changing, others were small and touching."

What Adam liked least were the "bureaucratic aspects and detail stuff — like sitting in on editorial meetings to decide what stories to cover and who would write them," and of course, dealing with internal politics, budgets, and other minutiae.

Encore! Encore!

The seeds of Adam's second career were sown while he was still at the *Globe,* when he and his wife adopted their son. At the first informational meeting he attended, Adam got excited about the adoption process. "I saw a world I didn't know much about and that few people understood, yet affected so many." He pitched a three-part series on adoption to his editors. Although they were initially resistant, Adam persisted, and ultimately the series was not only published, but nominated for a Pulitzer Prize. Adam explains, "Every journalist wants to write a book, and I had found my topic." He took a leave to write *Adoption Nation* — which he wrote with the intent to educate the world and have a lasting impact. *Adoption Nation* changed the conversation and is now considered a seminal book.

As a result of his research, Adam realized that writing *Adoption Nation* was more than a mere journalistic exercise. "It was about my kids as well as other people's kids, and about policies that were unfair to so many people."

He rewrote the book to make it more personal, which helped him clarify his new mission and ignite his second career as a child welfare advocate.

With a growing reputation as a national expert, Adam decided to strike out as a consultant and was soon offered the position of executive director of the Evan B. Donaldson Adoption Institute, a national nonprofit that is the preeminent research, policy, and education organization in its field.

Adam's primary responsibility as executive director is to carry out his agency's mission: to improve the lives of everyone touched by adoption. When he first arrived, the agency was in trouble and quickly running out of funds. Adam takes pride in having turned it around, helping to expand the operation from two to nine employees and secure its financial footing. Adam's daily activities involve a variety of important yet disparate tasks. He develops programs, provides testimony, writes and edits publications, raises money, and manages the board and a staff. Adam also spends a significant amount of time utilizing the media to reach out to the professional and lay communities to further his mission and its impact. Under his leadership, the organization "has become an activist think tank that develops, synthesizes, and disseminates knowledge and works to implement best practices."

Adam's greatest satisfaction comes from "seeing the difference we make in real people's lives." He loves the personal interactions when he gives speeches and conducts training. And he's energized when he's able to change laws "so that gay and lesbian people can have their families" or when he receives a call from an agency to say they use his best practices to train other people. "This is the stuff that really makes me feel like I'm doing something right."

Why This Encore Career Works for Adam

As Conceptualizers, people like Adam are driven by a strong need for competence. And because they set high standards for themselves and others, they often excel at whatever they choose to do. People who share Adam's temperament are often also lifelong learners, continually seeking to increase their knowledge and expertise, as Adam did in becoming an international thought leader in the field of adoption. And Conceptualizers are quintessential visionaries who often have the confidence necessary to inspire others to embrace their ideas and causes.

Adam, like most dominant Thinkers, is almost obsessed with fairness. He sees inequities in how people are treated and feels compelled to try to right those wrongs. Logical and objective, Adam is assertive in airing his views. Rather than help people individually, he is energized by creating policy changes that affect the masses.

It's no surprise that people who share Adam's personality type—ENTJ (Extraverted, Intuitive, Thinking, Judging)— are found at the top of most organizations. Their Extraversion draws them into the world, their temperament provides them with a clear vision, and their Judging function practically compels them to make an impact. But as Adam has grown older and developed his third function, Sensing, he has also become more realistic about just how long it takes to effect real change.

Profile 2: Ronnie

"From inside corporate HR to outside consulting."

"You'd be good in personnel." That observation, offered by a job interviewer for a large retail department store, started

Ronnie on a path that led to a thirty-plus-year career in corporate human resources and a second career as a coach, consultant, teacher, and community volunteer.

Although she was not completely sure what the term "personnel" meant, Ronnie was hired as a management trainee and got her first store placement working in personnel. The best part was that "they treated us like we were part of the management team—personnel was strategically integrated into the business." After four years, she got a promotion when she moved to another department store to work in HR. Four years later, and ready for some new challenges, Ronnie was hired as the first HR director at Barnes & Noble, a job that lasted only eighteen months. "Let's just say we didn't see eye to eye. In truth, I went way too far out on a limb and tried to do too much. For example, I tried to change the payroll system—when I didn't know enough about payroll to take on that large a project."

But Ronnie quickly landed on her feet and was hired as the director of HR at a large and prestigious Wall Street law firm. "These were some of the smartest people in the entire world. And they were driven. They drove you—they drove everybody." What did she like best? "Anything I saw as a problem, I got to touch and fix." But time passed, and soon Ronnie was pregnant with her second child, tired of a grueling daily commute, and eager to spend more time with her family. Plus, "I realized that I'd done everything I could do there." As a result of a job search in North Carolina, nearer to her family, Ronnie was hired at the innovative and highly respected Center for Creative Leadership.

She loved CCL's mission but after a time realized she'd fit better in a more business-driven, less process-oriented organization. "How many retreats can you sit through? I went from Wall Street, where no one ever hugged me in ten years, to CCL, where my first large staff meeting ended with a group hug." So after three years, Ronnie moved back into retailing, but not before getting CCL to train her to be a coach.

Her next assignment was as vice president for HR at Carlyle and Company jewelers. The best aspect of the job was being part of a management team that dealt with business strategy. At Carlyle, she began to understand that "just finding the right answer and implementing it and moving on is not a strategy for success—you have to build relationships, too." And because she had negotiated a four-day workweek, Ronnie was able to continue coaching for CCL. "One of the driving threads through all the changes was that I learned how to use vision to set achievable goals." When the company went bankrupt, Ronnie shepherded it through the liquidation and bankruptcy process, while creating a home office, networking, and building her consulting practice.

Encore! Encore!

Since 2010, Ronnie has been an executive coach and HR consultant. She also teaches a leadership and career course in the MBA program at the University of North Carolina. Additionally, Ronnie is an active volunteer, working with organizations that support families and children. "People think of me as the consummate networker—I know everyone in town." As if that's not enough, she is the president of the board of "a very funky artists collective."

She considers consulting with nonprofits to be her sweet spot: "I bring in the hard stuff—business strategy and finance—and marry it with organizational development, the softer sciences." For Ronnie, juggling several balls at once is energizing, and each activity satisfies a different need: "With coaching, I get to hear people's stories, connect what's happened in the past, look at all the factors, and help them achieve their goals." And as a volunteer working to help organizations become more effective, she gets to apply all of her business and strategic skills.

Why This Encore Career Works for Ronnie

Conceptualizers like Ronnie need to continue to learn and grow. Never content to rest on past achievements, they continually seek new challenges, a tendency that is evident in Ronnie's career path. They are also gifted problem solvers and strategists; Ronnie gets to draw on these strengths in helping individuals and organizations meet their objectives.

Ronnie is an ENTP (Extraverted, Intuitive, Thinking, Perceiving), and as a dominant Intuitive type, she sees possibilities everywhere, easily makes connections, and thrives on problem solving. Throughout her entire work history, Ronnie has chosen time and again to take on a variety of endeavors simultaneously—a theme consistent with many Conceptualizers, but especially true of ENTPs.

In mid-life, people who share Ronnie's type often gain access to their less developed Feeling side. As she prepares to send her youngest child off to college, she's surprised at how much it is affecting her. Further evidence of her emerging Feeling side is Ronnie's more recent desire to create and connect with a community.

26 | FOR CAREER PROFESSIONALS ONLY

If this has been your first introduction to Personality Type, you are no doubt impressed with how powerful a tool it can be for helping clients in every aspect of the career development process. Reading this book is a good start, but it is *only* a start. If you are one of the thousands of career professionals who already use Type in your work, this book has confirmed much of what you know, but it may also have reminded you of how much there is yet to learn.

Since Type provides such a rich model for understanding people and their career-related needs, it is not something that someone can read one, two, even ten books about and become an expert. To use it effectively and ethically takes extensive experiences working with many different types of clients and requires some in-depth professional training.

We'd like to urge you to continue to increase your understanding and competence using Type by attending training programs specifically designed for career professionals. Since 1982, we have trained thousands of career counselors, outplacement advisers, and human resource and personnel specialists. Through experientially based introductory-, intermediate-, and advanced-level workshops, we have taught counselors how understanding Type can not only help their clients but can also help counselors become more effective working with all types of clients.

Using Type Ethically

We often remind workshop participants that Type is a powerful tool—not unlike a hammer. In the hands of a Michelangelo, it can be used to sculpt a wondrous masterpiece such as the *Pietà*. But in the hands of a maniac, it can be used to smash someone's skull.

The difference lies in the skill and motivation of its wielder. The point we wish to drive home is: people take their type results very seriously, sometimes much more so than we counselors fully appreciate. Therefore, we have an especially strong obligation to make sure we are both skilled and well-intentioned in our use of Type. The ethics concerning the use of Type is a subject of some debate. This is true for many reasons, among them the fact that there are so many applications and people from so many different disciplines and backgrounds using Type.

Access to the Type model is, of course, available to the public through dozens of books published on the subject. But access to the MBTI® and various related materials is restricted to people who meet the publisher of the MBTI®'s qualifications. If you are interested in learning about becoming qualified to purchase, administer, and interpret the Myers-Briggs Type Indicator®, we suggest you contact its publisher, Consulting Psychologists Press, for complete details about their qualification requirements (see the Organizations listing in the Resources section), which may include taking a course on the MBTI® offered by a number of training organizations.

In an effort to promote the ethical use of Type, the Association for Psychological Type (APT) has developed a set of Ethical Principles, which appears in their 1994–1995 Membership Directory. Since not all users of this book are members of APT, and therefore may not see these guidelines, with the permission of APT we have paraphrased them below. We encourage all career professionals to become familiar with, and use them when working with clients.

Association for Psychological Type, "Ethical Principles"*

1. **People taking the MBTI® should be informed of the purpose and intended use of results before taking the instrument. As with other psychological instruments, taking the MBTI® should be voluntary.**

2. **Individual type results should not be shared with others without the permission of the respondent.**

   In other words, a person's type is confidential information. However, group data which doesn't identify individuals may be shared. For example, if you have administered the MBTI® to a freshman English class, it is permissible to present a type table showing the distribution of types, as long as no individuals are identified by name.

3. **Type information should be used to enhance individual or group satisfaction, not to restrict or limit individual or group functioning in any way.**

   The MBTI® should enhance the workplace. It is unethical to use the MBTI® for screening people out in the hiring process. Also, it is unethical to restrict work assignments based solely on a person's type. Type is helpful in team building and understanding the behavioral preferences of workers.

4. **Adequate information about Type theory and the individual's results should be given in a face-to-face setting.**

   This often presents a dilemma when someone wants to take the MBTI® and receive their results by mail or e-mail. The main reason for offering face-to-face feedback is to increase the chances

*Excerpted and paraphrased, with permission, from the "Ethical Principles" of the *Association for Psychological Type Directory 1994–1995.*

of helping the person verify his or her type, and to ensure that enough time is provided to assure that the client has an adequate understanding of his or her MBTI® results. Although face-to-face feedback is preferable, e-mail can be used effectively if clients have ample opportunity to ask questions and discuss in depth any concerns they have about their results.

5. **Respondents should always have an opportunity to "verify" their types as accurate for them.**

   In our view, this is probably the single most important guideline, and one which is unfortunately not always adhered to. We believe that any practitioner who uses the MBTI® or Type should have enough skill and time to help all takers of a type instrument verify his or her type, which includes offering to the client a full written description of the type(s) to be explored for verification.

6. **Type characteristics should be described in positive and nonjudgmental terms, using words like "preference," "tendency," and "inclination."**

7. **Respondents should be told that Type reflects an individual's preferences, not abilities or intelligence, nor is it a predictor of success. People should not be counseled toward or away from certain jobs *solely* (our emphasis) on the basis of their type.**

   In reality, type preferences often are related to certain abilities. For example, extraverted Feeling types— ESFJ and ENFJ— often have very good "people skills." However, because this is a tendency, rather than an absolute reality, it is dangerous to attribute specific skills to specific types. A danger is that people of a certain type might feel uncomfortable if they don't possess that skill or that people might not believe that someone of another type also possesses that skill.

   As to counseling people toward or away from certain jobs, the key phrase here is "solely on the basis of their type." While type is an important factor in predicting career satisfaction, it is certainly not the only factor that must be considered.

8. **The individual is considered the best judge of whether the type description "fits" or not.**

   This often presents a conflict for experienced users of Type, for it is not uncommon for a client to score as one type, and the counselor to believe quite strongly that the client is really another type.

   It is suggested that you gently explore your tentative hypothesis about the client's type with her or him, but ultimately it is the client who must decide which type he or she is most comfortable with, and you must respect that decision.

9. **Counselors should not state or imply that Type explains everything, but rather it is one important component of our very complex human personalities.**

   The "Type explains everything" syndrome is one experienced by many people who become enamored with Type. There are so many applications for this model that it is easy to get carried away. Therefore, counselors are cautioned to be aware of the tendency so as to avoid falling into this trap.

10. Interpreters should be sensitive to their own type biases and try not to communicate them to clients.

This is far easier said than done, because all people have biases based upon their own types. It is especially important for people who are new to Type to pay close attention to how they present Type concepts and describe preferences to make sure they are doing so in as positive, or at least as neutral, a way as possible.

One way to hone this skill is to practice explaining Type to people with different preferences, and to ask them to critique the objectivity of your presentation.

11. Practitioners should not use Psychological Type indicators whose reliability and validity have not been demonstrated.

Although the MBTI® is the most widely used Type assessment, in recent years other instruments have been developed, some better than others. Counselors should be aware of this and, as with any other testing instrument they use, make sure they have confidence in an instrument's reliability and validity.

12. Practitioners should accurately represent their competence and experience to respondents receiving Type information.

We believe this is true for all counselors, not just those who use Type.

Finally, APT stresses that one of the responsibilities of Type users is to become familiar with the research data available about Type. Inferences about Type or scores on any type indicator should not go beyond the data. The *Journal of Psychological Type* and the Type Resources Library at the Center for Applications of Psychological Type are excellent resources for Type research.

With Whom Should Type Be Used?

Personality Type is a useful and powerful tool for people of all ages and stages of development. Clearly, the age of the person will affect greatly the level of self-understanding he or she may gain, but with nonjudgmental and accurate explanations, most clients will be able to harness the new insights to make much better career decisions for themselves. In career counseling, we have found Type to be particularly useful with people from the following groups:

1. High school juniors and seniors
2. College students
3. Graduate students
4. People who have been outplaced
5. Mid-life career changers
6. Retirees, or "encore career" seekers

Some general guidelines for using Type with clients include:

1. **Discuss the purpose of learning about one's type and get their reactions to participating in the process:** prepare them for receiving results by assuring them there are no better or worse, healthier or sicker, smarter or dumber types— that whatever type they come out is fine—and that the information can be very useful in helping them in the career development process. Explain that they will receive their confidential results during the sessions.

2. **Explain that there are four dimensions to the Type model and describe the most important characteristics of the eight preferences.** There are many different materials available which describe the preference differences in list form, including Chapter 2.

3. **After you have explained each dimension, give clients the opportunity to estimate their preferences on each dimension.** Make a note of their guess.

4. The next step is for the clients to **read the appropriate profiles for their type in Chapter 3 of this book or by using another verifying profile such as the Brief Personality Description section of The Career and Life Planning Profiles** of the type or types they may be, and to see which one fits best. Some clients need to read several profiles until they have found the right fit.

5. Once you have identified the type your clients feel comfortable with, you may **begin to address the issues that brought them to you in the first place:** career choice, help with the job search, etc.

Using the MBTI®

To learn about the qualifications for purchasing and administering and about the materials needed for interpreting and using the MBTI®, we suggest you contact the publisher, Consulting Psychologists Press.

Providing Type Feedback to Clients

Giving Type feedback to clients is an important part of the process, and therefore we have paraphrased, with permission, some essential recommendations from *Guidelines for Explaining the MBTI®* by Gordon Lawrence, respected educator and author of *People Types and Tiger Stripes,* and have added some suggestions based upon our experience.

1. Explain that the MBTI® is not a "test," but an "indicator" which has no right or wrong answers, good or bad, sick or well types. All are equally valuable with different natural strengths and weaknesses.

2. Point out that scores do not indicate the quality of any particular preference, just the relative strength of one element over another.

3. Try to explain the concepts of Type as simply and clearly as possible. Point out that words associated with Type (Thinking and Feeling, for example) often have different connotations from the way we use them in our everyday language.

4. Be aware of your own possible type bias and present the information in as neutral and positive a light as you can.

5. Use words like "tendency" and "patterns" to describe Type

preferences. When providing results, you should avoid asserting: "This is the way you are," but rather ask: "Is this true for you?"

6. Expect some confusion, and be prepared to reassure the client that this is a normal reaction. Explaining Type concepts requires skill and patience.

Using Type to Be a More Effective Counselor

In addition to assisting your clients, an understanding of Type can be enormously helpful to you as a counselor. Basically, we are in the business of communicating—understanding others, and trying to convey ideas that will be helpful. But as any enlightened educator knows: "You've got to reach 'em to teach 'em."

Although this is not a workshop on communication, we think it would be helpful to pass along some of what we've learned about Type and communication:

1. People of the same or similar types usually understand each other fairly easily. *(This does not mean they always agree with each other.)*

2. The converse is also true: in general, the more different your type is from your client's, the greater the likelihood of miscommunication. The result is often a mutually frustrating experience.

3. We tend to follow the golden rule when it comes to communicating: we do unto others as we would have done unto us.

   To communicate effectively, however, we should rather: Do unto others as they would like done unto them. In

other words, we need to speak *their* language.

4. Type provides a powerful tool for helping communicate more effectively with clients of all types.

As career counselors, you often work with clients whose types are very different from your own. To help you meet this challenge, we offer a look at what you can expect from people with different preferences, and some specific suggestions for communicating most effectively with them.

It is important to remember that people are not just Es or Is, Ss or Ns, etc., but a combination of different preferences. Therefore this should be taken into account when reviewing the following suggestions, which for simplicity's sake are presented by individual preference.

|| EXTRAVERTS

- They are likely to give information freely and act quickly, sometimes without enough forethought.
- Their orientation is one of breadth, and they need to be encouraged to explore issues in depth.
- They often need help sticking to exercises or activities which are long and slow, and they should be encouraged to write things down that they want to remember.

A challenge to counselors is to get Extraverts to slow down enough to really think things through before taking action. Some suggestions:

- Let them talk (usually, this won't be a problem!).
- Include a variety of topics.
- Communicate verbally.
- Expect a high energy level.
- Ask them to listen.

‖ INTROVERTS

- Are less likely to let you know what they are thinking and feeling.
- May have a hard time translating ideas into active steps. *When presenting ideas, give them enough time to think about their response (this may range from seconds to days, depending on the importance of the issue).*
- Introverts, especially introverted sensors, are less comfortable brainstorming and fantasizing about future possibilities and are better at concrete exercises.

A challenge to counselors is to help Introverts move from the thinking stage to the action stage. Some suggestions:

- Ask, then listen.
- Talk about one thing at a time.
- Give them adequate time to reflect and prepare.
- Provide material to read.
- Let them set the pace.

‖ SENSORS

- Are less likely to want or be able to see options or brainstorm possibilities.
- Are more likely to be influenced by past experiences and known ways of doing things. *Counselors can capitalize on their ability to focus on the details in helping to get an accurate picture of their strengths, skills, etc.*
- Are better at and get more out of concrete tasks than fantasy exercises.

A challenge to counselors is to help Sensors see possibilities that don't exist at the present and focus on the big picture and long-range implications. Some suggestions:

- Present facts accurately.
- Use real and concrete examples; be explicit.

- Present information step by step.
- Stress practical application.
- Make specific recommendations and suggestions.

‖ INTUITIVES

- Are less able and willing to deal with specifics, and prefer to focus on the big picture.
- Think in global terms. *Counselors can appeal to their problem-solving abilities (especially NTs) to get them involved in the process. Avoid exercises which are tedious and require patience with details, and watch facts closely.*
- They may have trouble keeping on task or following directions (especially ENPs).

A challenge for counselors is to help Intuitives realistically evaluate career options and plans. Some suggestions:

- Talk about the "big picture" and implications.
- Talk about possibilities.
- Use analogies and metaphors.
- Engage their imagination.
- Don't overwhelm them with details.

‖ THINKERS

- Evaluate ideas and decisions logically and impersonally.
- Need to be convinced that a specific exercise or activity "makes sense" before they will put energy into it. It may be difficult to find out their true feelings about issues, and they may not think their feelings are particularly relevant to the matter at hand. Because they are naturally critical, they are not likely to show their appreciation for the counselor's abilities or concern. *Knowing this may help counselors (mostly Fs) not to take it personally.*

- Are impressed by competence and the end result.

A challenge for counselors is to remind Thinkers of the human consequences of their decisions, both for themselves and others. Some suggestions:

- Be organized and logical.
- Focus on consequences.
- Emphasize results and outcomes.
- Ask what they think, rather than how they feel.
- Don't repeat yourself.

|| FEELERS

- Make decisions based upon their own values, are more people-oriented and aware of others' feelings.
- Like to please others and may need to be encouraged to be assertive in getting their own needs met.
- Are happiest in friendly, supportive, cooperative environments, and any potential work situation should be looked at to see if it will meet this important criterion.

A challenge for counselors is to help Feelers evaluate options more objectively and not to take rejection or setbacks personally. Some suggestions:

- Mention points of agreement before any criticism.
- Appreciate efforts and contributions.
- Recognize the legitimacy of their feelings.
- Talk about "people" concerns.
- Respect their values.

|| JUDGERS

- Like to take in just enough information to make a decision, and prefer to make plans and follow them.

- Are usually well organized, so structured exercises appeal to them (especially STJs). *They will work toward goals, but may become frustrated when they experience too many delays.*
- May need assistance in reforming plans into more manageable steps.

A challenge for counselors is to help Judgers delay making decisions prematurely, and to stay open to new information. Some suggestions:

- Be organized, on time, and prepared.
- Come to conclusions—try to resolve issues.
- Be decisive and definite.
- Be efficient and don't waste their time.
- Point out the benefits of being flexible.

|| PERCEIVERS

- Prefer not to decide but to continue collecting information, to keep their options open.
- Enjoy those exercises and activities which allow them to learn something new, and have fun doing it.
- Are flexible, adaptable, and change gears quickly so they may be amenable to many different approaches and techniques. *Their natural curiosity makes them open to explore options.*

A challenge for counselors is to help keep Perceivers on task and to nudge them into making decisions when it is appropriate. Some suggestions:

- Expect many questions.
- Don't force decisions (unless you have to).
- Provide opportunity to discuss options.
- Allow time to process.
- Point out that decisions are not irrevocable.

…That's All, Folks!

Everything we see and hear confirms our belief that our society is moving toward increased self-direction, increased self-management of our careers. Some statistics claim we will have as many as five to seven different careers and as many as ten or twelve different jobs within those careers during work lives that will last nearly fifty years! The more we know about ourselves, and the more we can help our clients know about *themselves,* the better able we will be to respond to the many changes we will all face and make sounder decisions for our lives. Type is a powerful way to begin and further that discovery process. And you, as the career professional, are poised to ride the wave of this exciting technology.

We encourage you to continue the learning process and invite you to help us continue with ours. If you have ideas or suggestions for future editions of this book, or experiences using Type with clients you'd like to share, we'd love to hear from you. Until then, we wish you great luck and success in your most important mission—helping people find true career satisfaction.

Paul D. Tieger, Barbara Barron,
and Kelly Tieger
www.PersonalityType.com

Some Final Thoughts and Resources

For those of you eager to learn more about Personality Type, we've compiled a bibliography listing several excellent books written about Type. Although of necessity this is only a partial listing, you can obtain more comprehensive information about available resources from many of the organizations we describe.

Need More Help?

For some of you, this has been your very first look at yourself as it pertains to your career development. For others, you've felt stuck for a while and may now finally see some light at the end of the tunnel. For still others, doing the work in this book has helped you identify some good options and has propelled you along the road to career satisfaction. Whatever your current status, perhaps the time is right to enlist the help of a qualified career professional to help you take the next important steps. In fact, at many points in the process, nothing can replace the one-to-one attention, support, advice, and *real contacts* that a career counselor can provide. Here are three resources that will help you locate professionals near you. Write or fax them with your request and they will send a list of qualified professionals in your area.

National Career Development Association (NCDA)
    305 N. Beech Circle
    Broken Arrow, OK 74012
    (866) FOR-NCDA
    (918) 663-7060
    Fax: (918) 663-7058
    Website: www.ncda.org

National Board for Certified Counselors, Inc. (NBCC)
    3 Terrace Way
    Suite D
    Greensboro, NC 27403
    (336) 547-0607
    Website: www.nbcc.org
e-mail: nbcc@nbcc.org

The Association for Psychological Type (APT)
    9650 Rockville Pike
    Bethesda, MD 20814-3998
    (800) 847-9943
    (301) 634-7450
    Fax: (301) 634-7455
    Website: www.aptinternational.org
    e-mail: info@aptinternational.org

Also, try contacting your local community college or YWCA, or check the local listings in the yellow pages for career centers and independent career counselors/consultants. No matter whom you contact or how you get to them, be sure to ask if they use

Personality Type in their practice, or if they are familiar with this book. It's also smart to ask in advance what their rates are and if they see clients on an hourly or project basis.

If you're interested in taking the Myers-Briggs Type Indicator®, we recommend you contact a college or university career-planning office or private career-counseling firm and inquire if they administer and interpret the MBTI® test instrument.

Bibliography

General Introduction to Psychological Type

Berens, Linda V. *Understanding Yourself and Others: An Introduction to Temperament*. Huntington Beach, Calif.: Telos Publications, 2000.

Berens, Linda V., and Nardi, Dario. *The 16 Personality Types: Descriptions for Self-Discovery*. Huntington Beach, Calif.: Telos Publications, 1999.

Brownsword, Alan. *It Takes All Types*. Herndon, Va.: Baytree Publication Company, 1987.

Duniho, Terrence. *Wholeness Lies Within*. Gladwyne, Pa.: Type & Temperament, Inc., 1991.

———. *Patterns of Preference*. Gladwyne, Pa.: Type & Temperament, Inc., 1996.

Giovannoni, Louise C., Berens, Linda V., and Cooper, Sue A. *Introduction to Temperament*. Huntington Beach, Calif.: Cooper, Berens, 1986.

Hirsh, Sandra, and Kummerow, Jean. *Lifetypes*. New York: Warner Books, 1989.

Keirsey, David, and Bates, Marilyn. *Please Understand Me*, 3rd ed. Del Mar, Calif.: Prometheus Nemesis, 1984.

Kroeger, Otto, and Thuesen, Janet M. *Type Talk*. New York: Delacorte Press, 1988.

Kroeger, Otto, and Thuesen, Janet M. *Type Talk at Work: How the 16 Personality Types Determine Your Success on the Job*. New York: Dell, 2002.

Kroeger, Otto, and Thuesen, Janet M. *16 Ways to Love Your Lover: Understanding the 16 Personality Types So You Can Create a Love That Lasts Forever*. New York: Delacorte Press, 1994.

Lawrence, Gordon D. *Finding the Zone: A Whole New Way to Maximize Mental Potential*. Amherst, N.Y.: Prometheus Books, 2010.

Myers, Isabel Briggs, with Myers, Peter. *Gifts Differing*. Palo Alto, Calif.: Consulting Psychologists Press, 1980.

Myers, Isabel Briggs. *Introduction to Type: A Guide to Understanding Your Results on the Myers-Briggs Type Indicator*, 6th ed. Palo Alto, Calif.: Consulting Psychologists Press, 1998.

Myers, Isabel Briggs, and McCaulley, Mary H. *Manual: A Guide to the Development and Use of the Myers-Briggs Type Indicator*. Palo Alto, Calif.: Consulting Psychologists Press, 1985.

Myers, Isabel B., with revisions by K. Myers & L. Kirby. *Introduction to Type*. Palo Alto, Calif.: Consulting Psychologists Press, 1993.

Myers, Katharine D., and Kirby, Linda K. *Introduction to Type Dynamics and Development*. Palo Alto, Calif.: Consulting Psychologists Press, 1994.

Pearman, Roger R., and Albritton, Sarah C. *I'm Not Crazy, I'm Just Not You: The Real Meaning of the 16 Personality Types*. Palo Alto, Calif.: Davies-Black, 1997.

Quenk, Naomi L. *Beside Ourselves: Our Hidden Personality in Everyday Life*. Palo Alto, Calif.: Consulting Psychologists Press, 1993.

Saunders, Frances W. *Katharine and Isabel: Mother's Light, Daughter's Journey*. Palo Alto, Calif.: Consulting Psychologists Press, 1991.

The Type Reporter. Published five times a year. Contains articles and information on various topics of interest concerning psychological Type. Susan Scanlon, Editor, 11314 Chapel Road, Fairfax Station, VA 22039. (703) 764-5370. Website: www. typereporter.com

Yabroff, William. *The Inner Image: A Resource for Type Development*. Palo Alto, Calif.: Consulting Psychologists Press, 1990.

Careers

Bolles, Richard Nelson. *What Color Is Your Parachute 2006: A Practical Manual for Job Hunters and Career Changers*. Berkeley, Calif.: Ten Speed Press, 2005.

Dunning, Donna. *What's Your Type of Career? Unlock the Secrets of Your Personality to Find Your Perfect Career Path*. Palo Alto, Calif.: Davies-Black, 2001.

Edwards, Paul, and Edwards, Sarah. *Finding Your Perfect Work: The New Career Guide to Making a Living, Creating a Life*. New York: J. P. Tarcher, 2003.

Martin, C. R. *Looking at Type and Careers*. Gainesville, Fla.: Center for Applications of Psychological Type, 2009.

Children/Education

Allen, Mollie, Claire Hayman, and Kay Abella. *Discovering Type with Teens: A Comprehensive Leader's Guide with Materials for Presenting*

Psychological Type to Young People. Gainesville, Fla.: Center for Applications of Psychological Type, 2009.

Barger, June R., Barger, Robert R., and Cano, Jamie M. *Discovering Learning Preferences and Learning Differences in the Classroom.* Columbus, Ohio: Ohio Agricultural Education Curriculum Materials Service, Ohio State University, 1994.

Fairhurst, Alice M., and Fairhurst, Lisa. *Effective Teaching, Effective Learning: Making the Personality Connection in Your Classroom.* Palo Alto, Calif.: Davies-Black, 1995.

Ginn, Charles W. *Families: Using Type to Enhance Mutual Understanding.* Gainesville, Fla.: Center for Applications of Psychological Type, 1995.

Golay, Keith. *Learning Patterns and Temperament Styles.* Newport Beach, Calif.: Manas-Systems, 1982.

Lawrence, Gordon. *People Types and Tiger Stripes: A Practical Guide to Learning Styles,* 3rd ed. 1993. Gainesville, Fla.: Center for Applications of Psychological Type, 1993.

Meisgeier, Charles, and Murphy, Elizabeth. *A Teacher's Guide to Type: A New Perspective on Individual Differences in the Classroom.* Palo Alto, Calif.: Consulting Psychologists Press, 1989.

Murphy, Elizabeth. *The Developing Child.* Palo Alto, Calif.: Consulting Psychologists Press, 1992.

———. *Exploring Personality Type: Discovering My Best and Your Best.* Gainesville, Fla.: Center for Applications of Psychological Type, 2008.

Neff, LaVonne. *One of a Kind: Making the Most of Your Child's Uniqueness.* Gainesville, Fla.: Center for Applications of Psychological Type, 1995.

Payne, Diane, and VanSant, Sondra. *Great Minds Don't Think Alike! Success for Students Through the Application of Psychological Type in Schools.* Gainesville, Fla.: Center for Applications of Psychological Type, 2009.

Peters, Martha M., and Peters, Don C. *Juris Types: Learning Law Through Self-Understanding.* Gainesville, Fla.: Center for Applications of Psychological Type, 2007.

Provost, Judith A., and Anchors, Scott. *Applications of the Myers-Briggs Type Indicator in Higher Education.* Palo Alto, Calif.: Consulting Psychologists Press, 1987.

Schaubhut, Nancy A., and Thompson, Richard C. *MBTI® Type Tables for College Majors.* Gainesville, Fla.: Center for Applications of Psychological Type, 2009.

Tieger, Paul D., and Barron-Tieger, Barbara. *Nurture by Nature.* New York: Little, Brown, 1997.

Wirths, Claudine G., and Bowman-Kruhm, Mary. *Are You My Type? Or, Why Aren't You More Like Me?* Palo Alto, Calif.: Consulting Psychologists Press, 1992.

Counseling/Management

Brock, Susan A. *Using Type in Selling: Building Customer Relationships with the Myers-Briggs Type Indicator.* Palo Alto, Calif.: Consulting Psychologists Press, 1994.

Duniho, Terrence. *Personalities at Risk: Addiction, Codependency and Psychological Type.* Gladwyne, Pa.: Type & Temperament, Inc., 1992.

Grant, Richard D., *Symbols of Recovery: The 12 Steps at Work in the Unconscious.* Gladwyne, Pa.: Type & Temperament, Inc., 1990.

Hartzler, Margaret. *Making Type Work for You: A Collection of Exercises and Worksheets.* Gaithersburg, Md.: Type Resources, Inc., 1992.

Hartzler, Margaret. *Management Uses of the Myers-Briggs Type Indicator.* Gaithersburg, Md.: Type Resources, Inc., 1992.

Hartzler, Margaret. *Using Type in Career Counseling.* Gaithersburg, Md.: Type Resources, Inc., 1985.

Hartzler, Margaret. *Using Type with Couples,* 2nd ed. Gaithersburg, Md.: Type Resources, Inc., 1998.

Hirsh, Sandra K. *Using the Myers-Briggs Type Indicator in Organizations: A Resource Book,* 3rd ed. Palo Alto, Calif.: Consulting Psychologists Press, 1998.

Hirsh, Sandra K., and Kise, Jane A. G. *Work It Out: Clues for Solving People Problems at Work.* Palo Alto, Calif.: Davies-Black, 1996.

Hirsh, Sandra K., and Kummerow, Jean M. *Introduction to Type in Organizational Settings: A Resource Book.* Palo Alto, Calif.: Consulting Psychologists Press, 1987.

Hirsh, Sandra Krebs, and Kummerow, Jean M. *Introduction to Type in Organizations,* 3rd ed. Palo Alto, Calif.: Consulting Psychologists Press, 1998.

Isachsen, Olaf, and Berens, Linda V. *Working Together: A Personality-Centered Approach to Management,* 3rd ed. San Juan Capistrano, Calif.: Institute for Management Development, 1995.

Jones, Jane Hardy, and Sherman, Ruth G. *Intimacy and Type: Building Enduring Relationships by Embracing Personality Differences.* Gainesville, Fla.: Center for Applications of Psychological Type, 2011.

Kummerow, Jean M. *New Directions for Career Planning and the Workplace: Practical Strategies for Career Management Professionals,* 2nd ed. Palo Alto, Calif.: Davies-Black, 2000.

Kummerow, Jean M., Barger, Nancy J., and Kirby, Linda K. *WorkTypes: Understand Your Work Personality— How It Helps You and Holds You Back, and What You Can Do to Understand It.* New York: Warner Books, 1997.

Pearman, Roger R. *Hardwired Leadership: Unleashing the Power of Personality to Become a New Millennium Leader.* Palo Alto, Calif.: Davies-Black, 1998.

Provost, Judith A. *A Casebook: Applications of the Myers-Briggs Type Indicator in Counseling.* Gainesville, Fla.: Center for Applications of Psychological Type, 1984.

Stein, Murray, and Hollwitz, John, eds. *Psyche at Work: Workplace Applications of Jungian Analytical Psychology.* Wilmette, Ill.: Chiron Publications, 1992.

Religion/Spirituality

Grant, Richard D. *The Way of the Cross: Christian Individuation and Psychological Temperament.* Gladwyne, Pa.: Type & Temperament, Inc., 1990.

Grant, W. Harold, Thompson, Magdala, and Clarke, Thomas E. *From Image to Likeness: A Jungian Path in the Gospel Journey.* Mahwah, N.J.: Paulist Press, 1983.

Harbaugh, Gary L. *God's Gifted People,* expanded ed. Minneapolis, Minn.: Augsburg Fortress Publishers, 1990.

Hirsh, Sandra K., and Kise, Jane A. G. *Looking at Type and Spirituality.* Gainesville, Fla.: Center for Applications of Psychological Type, 1997.

Hirsh, Sandra K., and Kise, Jane A. G. *Soul Types: Finding the Spiritual Path That Is Right for You.* New York: Hyperion, 1998.

Keating, Charles. *Who We Are Is How We Pray: Matching Personality and Spirituality.* Mystic, Conn.: Twenty-Third Publications, 1987.

Kise, Jane A. G., Stark, David, and Hirsh, Sandra K. *LifeKeys: Discovering Who You Are, Why You're Here, What You Do Best.* Minneapolis, Minn.: Bethany House, 1998.

Michael, Chester P., and Morrissey, Marie C. *Prayer and Temperament: Different Prayer Forms for Different Personality Types,* rev. ed. Charlottesville, Va.: Open Door Press, 1991.

Moore, Anthony T., *Father, Son, and Healing Ghosts.* Gainesville, Fla.: Center for Applications of Psychological Type, 2000.

Oswold, Roy, and Kroeger, Otto. *Personality Type and Religious Leadership.* Washington, D.C.: Alban Institute, 1988.

Richardson, Peter Tufts. *Archetype of the Spirit: Origins of Spirituality—Individual and Collective.* Rockland, Maine: Red Barn Publishing, 2007.

Type and Research

CAPT Bibliography. Gainesville, Fla.: Center for Applications of Psychological Type. Contains nearly 9,000 entries.

Macdaid, Gerald P., McCaulley, Mary H., and Kainz, Richard. *Atlas of Type Tables.* Gainesville, Fla.: Center for the Application of Psychological Type, 1986. A compendium of hundreds of tables reflecting the type distribution of people in a variety of occupations.

The Type Reporter. Published five times a year. Contains articles and information on various topics of interest concerning psychological type. Susan Scanlon, Editor, 11314 Chapel Road, Fairfax Station, VA 22039. (703) 764-5370.

Zeisset, Ray M. *Statistics and Measurement: An Introduction.* Gainesville, Fla.: Center for Applications of Psychological Type, 2009.

Other Resources/Organizations

SpeedReading People, LLC (SRP)
100 Allyn Street
Hartford, CT 06103
(860) 249-2000
Fax: (860) 249-2001
Website: www.speedreadingpeople.com
e-mail: info@speedreadingpeople.com
SRP is a communication company that specializes in harnessing the power of Personality Type to create innovative yet practical software solutions that help managers, teams, and salespeople communicate most successfully.

The Association for Psychological Type (APT)
9650 Rockville Pike
Bethesda, MD 20814-3998
(800) 847-9943
(301) 634-7450
Fax: (301) 634-7455
Website: www.aptinternational.org
e-mail: info@aptinternational.org
APT is a an international membership organization open to all people interested in Personality Type. APT conducts workshops and publishes materials, including the *Bulletin of Psychological Type,* and conducts the APT MBTI® Qualifying workshop. APT sponsors a biannual international conference, and local chapters throughout the country and around the world meet regularly to share information about Type.

Center for Applications of Psychological Type (CAPT)

2815 NW 13th Street
Suite 401
Gainesville, FL 32609
(800) 777-CAPT
Fax: (352) 378-0503
Website: www.capt.org

CAPT provides training in Type for professionals and the public, offers consulting services for training and research, publishes Type-related materials, compiles research to advance the understanding of Type, does computer scoring of the MBTI®, and maintains the Isabel Briggs Myers Memorial Library.

American Management Association (AMA)

1601 Broadway
New York, NY 10019
(877) 566-9441
(212) 903-8060
Fax: (518) 891-0368
Website: www.amanet.org
e-mail: customerservice@amanet.org

AMA offers Myers-Briggs Type Indicator (MBTI®) certification training.

Linda Berens Institute

(714) 625-9475
Website: www.lindaberens.com
e-mail: info@lindaberens.com

Based on the work of Linda Berens, this organization offers training in the Interaction Style Approach as well as consulting in the areas of leadership development, team building, and communication enhancement.

Consulting Psychologists Press (CPP, Inc.) and Davies-Black® Publishing

1055 Joaquin Road, 2nd Floor
Mountain View, CA 94043
(800) 624-1765
(650) 969-8901
Fax: (650) 969-8608
Website: www.cpp-db.com

The publisher and distributor of the Myers-Briggs Type Indicator instrument and related materials, CPP also provides training and consulting services for organizations. Davies-Black® Publishing, a division of CPP, Inc., publishes business and career management titles.

Type Resources

36 Pauline Road
Louisville, KY 40206
(800) 456-6284
(502) 893-3677
Fax: (502) 893-3673
Website: www.type-resources.com

e-mail: info@type-resources.com

An organization that specializes in training and consulting with organizations that use the MBTI® and FIRO-B™ for leadership coaching and team development. They also offer MBTI® qualifying workshops and distribute a variety of Type-related books and materials.

Qualifying.org, Inc.

250 Executive Park Boulevard, Suite 106
Winston-Salem, NC 27103
(336) 774-0330
Fax: (336) 774-0104
Website: www.qualifying.org

Qualifying.org offers a variety of consulting and training opportunities in the Myers-Briggs Type Indicator (MBTI®) and other instruments, including the Emotional Quotient Inventory (EQ-i®).

Psychometrics Canada Ltd.

7125 77 Avenue
Edmonton, Alberta
Canada
T6B 0B5
(780) 469-2268
Fax: (780) 469-2283
Website: www.psychometrics.com
e-mail: info@psychometrics.com

A leading Canadian publisher of tests and assessments relating to personality, abilities, and interests for business, education, and government, Psychometrics Canada Ltd. offers training programs, expert advice, scoring services, and ongoing research, as well as consulting in the areas of test development, personnel selection, and organizational development.

Career/LifeSkills Resources Inc.

116 Viceroy Road
Unit B-1
Concord, Ontario
Canada
L4K 2M2
(905) 760-0111
Fax: (905) 760-0113
Website: www.career-lifeskills.com

Career/LifeSkills Resources Inc. specializes in resources for personal, professional, and organizational development and provides a variety of assessment tools, including the Myers-Briggs Type Indicator, Strong Interest Inventory, and True Colors. They also offer a wide range of career and life skills books and quality certification and professional training programs.

Institute for Type Development (ITD)

29-31 Joseph Street
Lidcombe, NSW 2141

Australia
(+61) (2) 9749-1369
Fax: (+61) (2) 9749-1359
Website: www.itd.net.au/
e-mail: type@itd.net.au
ITD provides training and resources for
Psychological Type, Personality Type, Myers-Briggs
Type Indicator (MBTI®), and Temperament Theory;
offers accreditation programs; and runs seminars
and training programs. ITD also distributes a wide
range of Type-related books, tapes, and workshop
materials.

OKA (formerly Otto Kroeger Associates)
3605 Chain Bridge Road
Fairfax, VA 22030
(703) 591-6284
Fax: (703) 591-8338
Website: www.oka-online.com
OKA provides training and resources for
Psychological Type, Personality Type, Myers-Briggs
Type Indicator (MBTI®), and Temperament Theory;
offers accreditation programs; and runs seminars
and training programs. OKA also distributes a wide
range of Type-related books, tapes, and workshop
materials.

Oxford Psychologists Press Ltd. (OPP®)
Elsfield Hall
15–17 Elsfield Way

Oxford, OX2 8EP
United Kingdom
+44 (0)1865 404500
Fax: +44 (0)1865 310368
Website: www.opp.co.uk
e-mail: enquiry@opp.eu.com
Oxford Psychologists Press Ltd. provides HR
professionals and consultants with tools to help
them enhance decision making in the areas of
selection and assessment, individual and leadership
development, team building, organizational change
and consulting, and career counseling. They
distribute the Myers-Briggs Type Indicator as
well as provide training and product-specific
workshops.

Career Planning and Adult Development Network
543 Vista Mar Avenue
Pacifica, CA 94044
(650) 359-6911
Fax: (650) 359-3089
Website: www.careernetwork.org
e-mail: admin@careernetwork.org
This organization publishes a bimonthly newsletter
and quarterly journal for career practitioners,
produces the annual International Career
Development Conference, and certifies Job and
Career Transition Coaches (JCTC).

Acknowledgments

There are literally thousands of people we could thank for contributing to our understanding of Personality Type. We begin with the hundreds of clients we have worked with over the years and the thousands of career professionals and other workshop participants who, through sharing their stories and experiences, have taught us so much.

We also wish to thank our friends and associates for referring so many of the fascinating and talented people we interviewed. To each of the people profiled in this book and the many others whose input added to each of the five editions of this book, we are indebted for their generous gift of time, experience, and insights. We went to the sources and were taught by the masters—the real experts—about their own career needs and criteria for true satisfaction. It was a pleasure and a privilege to get to know them and to tell their stories.

Although we have studied with and learned from many highly respected teachers, we are particularly grateful to Mary McCaulley and Gordon Lawrence, who first taught us about Type. Their contributions to the world's understanding of psychological type have been enormous, and their passing leaves a huge void. We also wish to express our gratitude to the late Terry Duniho for greatly increasing our understanding.

We thank Nellie Sabin for her immeasurable contribution to the overall quality of this book. Her infusion of creative energy, as well as her many great ideas, thought-provoking questions, and careful organizational assistance have made this a much better, and more helpful, book.

We are grateful for the excellent skills of research assistant Rachel Esch and editorial assistant Alexandra Scully in the updating of this fifth edition. Thanks are due to Matt Brown for his tech wisdom and Chris Littler for his discerning eye. We thank the many editors we've worked with at Little, Brown, including Tracy Behar, our editor for this edition, and our agent Colleen Mohyde. We are especially indebted to the late Christina Ward, our first editor, later our agent, and always our good friend, for her unfaltering and enthusiastic support since the very beginning of our journey as writers. You are greatly missed, Kit. Thanks also to the hundreds of readers who have taken time to contact us with their stories of how the book has helped them improve the quality of their lives. You cannot imagine the gift that feedback is to us. Thank you.

We owe a special debt of gratitude to our family and friends, who have allowed us to learn what Type is really about by experimenting on them over these many years.

Index

About the Authors

Paul D. Tieger is the founder and CEO of SpeedReading People, LLC, a company that harnesses the power of Personality Type to create innovative yet practical online solutions. SRP products help managers motivate, engage, and retain employees; help teams collaborate more productively; and increase salespeople's effectiveness with prospects and clients. An avid researcher, Paul has developed an entirely new paradigm he calls Macro-Typology, which explains how Personality Type shapes the values and behavior of groups and cultures. He works and lives in Hartford, Connecticut.

Following her own good advice, **Barbara Barron** made a career shift and now works as an advancement consultant. She coaches independent schools and other nonprofits to help them raise money to meet their strategic goals, and create high-functioning development programs. Barbara continues to use her knowledge of Type in her daily interactions, both personal and professional. She lives in Marin County, California.

The daughter of two Personality Type experts and authors, **Kelly Tieger** has been studying and applying Type her entire life. Kelly was an editorial assistant on the previous edition of *Do What You Are,* and her role in this edition expanded considerably to researching major job forecasts over the next decade, conducting in-depth interviews with millennials, and providing incisive analysis on what makes their career choice a good fit. A millennial herself, Kelly lives in Brooklyn, New York.

The only parenting book written specifically about *your* child!

Every parent knows that children, even babies, have distinct personalities. So it's only natural that parenting strategies that work with one child may be less effective with another child. With this one-of-a-kind parenting guide, you can use Personality Type analysis—a powerful and well-respected psychological tool—to understand your child as never before and become a more loving and effective parent.

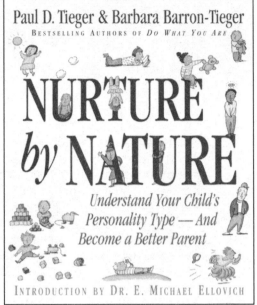

In *Nurture by Nature* you'll learn:

- Which of the 16 different types best matches your child's personality

- How this personality type affects your child in each of three stages of development—preschool, school age, and adolescence

- How other parents deal with a wide array of parenting joys and challenges you may encounter with your child

- Strategies for adapting your parenting style to your child's type

Whether your child is a tantrum-prone toddler, a shy third-grader, a rebellious teen, or somewhere in between, *Nurture by Nature* will give you the power to raise healthy, happy, and responsible children.

To learn more about *your* child, visit us at
www.nurturebynature.com

ISBN 978-0-316-84513-7
Available in paperback at bookstores everywhere
Little, Brown and Company

There are dozens of books about relationships…
but only one about *yours!*

Create the relationship you've always wanted using the secrets of Personality Type. Hundreds of books have been written about relationships, but *Just Your Type* is the only one written about yours! Based on groundbreaking scientific research and interviews with hundreds of satisfied couples, *Just Your Type* describes the joys and challenges of your and your partner's type combination and shares the wisdom of couples a lot like you who have used Type to understand, accept, and truly appreciate their partners.

From the authors of *Do What You Are*, the 500,000-copy bestseller

Just Your Type
Create the Relationship You've Always Wanted Using the Secrets of Personality Type

Paul D. Tieger & Barbara Barron-Tieger

What readers say about *Just Your Type:*

"It's taken my husband and me thirty years to figure each other out. If we'd had *Just Your Type*, we could have done it in the first hour!"

"This book made us talk about issues we hadn't talked about since we were dating—like what really mattered to each of us and what we really wanted. It helped reconnect us in a very profound way."

"I was always frustrated trying to tell my husband what I needed. But with *Just Your Type* I could actually show him a list! It's amazing, but that's what it took for him to finally get it!"

To learn more about *your* relationship, visit us at
www.PersonalityType.com

ISBN 978-0-316-84569-4
Available in paperback at bookstores everywhere
Little, Brown and Company

Also by Paul D. Tieger & Barbara Barron

Maximize your success in the job search *and* on the job!

Wouldn't it be great to have X-ray vision into other people's personalities—to know what they are thinking, what they care deeply about, their likes and dislikes? During an interview or in everyday life, you'd know best how to pique their interest, how to strike a bargain, or how to simply put them at ease.

The Art of SpeedReading People shows how simple it is to identify and understand key personality characteristics and gives you a powerful advantage in communicating with all kinds of people.

In *The Art of SpeedReading People* you'll learn how to:

- Instantly "read" and connect with job interviewers

- Negotiate with everyone more effectively

- Manage all types of employees better

- Sell your ideas, products, or services like never before

To learn more about SpeedReading People, and for the most comprehensive information available on Personality Type, please visit us at
www.PersonalityType.com

ISBN 978-0-316-84518-2
Available at bookstores everywhere
Little, Brown and Company